Sources
and
Studies
in World
History

Kevin Reilly, Series Editor

THE ALCHEMY OF HAPPINESS
Abu Hamid Muhammad al-Ghazzali
Translated by Claud Field, revised and annotated by Elton L. Daniel

LIFELINES FROM OUR PAST
A New World History
L. S. Stavrianos

NATIVE AMERICANS BEFORE 1492
The Moundbuilding Centers of the Eastern Woodlands
Lynda Norene Shaffer

GERMS, SEEDS, AND ANIMALS
Studies in Ecological History
Alfred W. Crosby

BALKAN WORLDS
The First and Last Europe
Traian Stoianovich

AN ATLAS AND SURVEY OF SOUTH ASIAN HISTORY
Karl J. Schmidt

THE GOGO: HISTORY, CUSTOMS, AND TRADITIONS
Mathias E. Mnyampala
Translated, introduced, and edited by Gregory H. Maddox

WOMEN IN WORLD HISTORY:
Volume 1—Readings from Prehistory to 1500
Volume 2—Readings from 1500 to the Present
Sarah Shaver Hughes and Brady Hughes

MARITIME SOUTHEAST ASIA TO 1500
Lynda Norene Shaffer

THE COURSE OF HUMAN HISTORY
Economic Growth, Social Process, and Civilization
Johan Goudsblom, Eric Jones, and Stephen Mennell

ON WORLD HISTORY
Johann Gottfried Herder
An Anthology
Edited by Hans Adler and Ernest A. Menze
Translated by Ernest A. Menze with Michael Palma

On World History

Johann Gottfried Herder

An Anthology

Edited by
Hans Adler and Ernest A. Menze

Translated by Ernest A. Menze
with Michael Palma

Routledge
Taylor & Francis Group

LONDON AND NEW YORK

First published 1997 by M.E. Sharpe

Published 2015 by Routledge
2 Park Square, Milton Park, Abingdon, Oxon OX14 4RN
711 Third Avenue, New York, NY 10017, USA

Routledge is an imprint of the Taylor & Francis Group, an informa business

Library of Congress Cataloging-in-Publication Data

On world history : an anthology / Johann Gottfried Herder / Hans Adler and
Ernest A. Menze, editors; translated by Ernest A. Menze with Michael Palma.
      p.   cm.—(Sources and studies in world history)
Includes bibliographical references and index.
ISBN 1-56324-540-X (alk. paper).—ISBN 1-56324-541-8 (pbk. : alk. paper)
1. Herder, Johann Gottfried, 1744–1803—Contributions in philosophy of history.
2. History—Philosophy.
I. Adler, Hans.
II. Menze, Ernest A.
III. Series.
D16.8.J625   1996
901—dc20
96-19973
CIP

ISBN 13: 9781563245411 (pbk)
ISBN 13: 9781563245404 (hbk)

Contents

List of Sources

The translations appearing in this anthology are based in the main on the following two sources (exceptions are noted in the detailed list of chapters, below):

Johann Gottfried Herder, *Sämmtliche Werke,* ed. Bernhard Suphan, 33 vols. (Berlin: Weidmannsche Buchhandlung, 1877 ff.). (Abbr. SWS [vol.], pp.)

Johann Gottfried v. Herder, *Outlines of a Philosophy of the History of Man,* translated from the German *Ideen zur Philosophie der Geschichte der Menschheit* by T. Churchill (London: 1800). (Abbr. Churchill.)

Chapter 1: Johann Gottfried Herder, *Schriften zur Ästhetik und Literatur 1767–1781,* ed. Gunter Grimm (Johann Gottfried Herder, *Werke in zehn Bänden,* eds. Günter Arnold et al., vol. 2.), (Frankfurt am Main: Deutscher Klassiker Verlag, 1993), pp. 11–23.

Chapter 2: SWS 4, pp. 351–53.

Chapter 3: SWS 5, pp. 501–13.

Chapter 4: SWS 18, pp. 286–91.

Chapter 5: SWS 24, pp. 326–29, 332–33.

Chapter 6: SWS 23, pp. 72–73.

Chapter 7: SWS 23, pp. 213–17.

Chapter 8: SWS 23, pp. 485–91.

Chapter 9: SWS 16, pp. 51–83.

Chapter 10: Johann Gottfried Herder, *Schriften zum Alten Testament,* ed. Rudolf Smend (Johann Gottfried Herder, *Werke in zehn Bänden,* eds. Günter Arnold et al., vol. 5.), (Frankfurt am Main: Deutscher Klassiker Verlag, 1993), pp. 11–30.

Chapter 11: SWS 17, pp. 115–22.

Chapter 12: SWS 17, pp. 137–43.

Chapter 13: SWS 13, pp. 4–11; Churchill, pp. vi–x.

Foreword

Johann Gottfried Herder (1744–1803) is often recognized as a founder of German Romanticism, nationalism, and anthropology but less often celebrated as a father of world history. In this volume of Herder's writings, Hans Adler and Ernest Menze demonstrate the important steps Herder took "on the way to world history."

Before Herder, Christian theology taught a vision of time in which God's Providence was revealed in human action. Herder showed that while human actions reveal the will of God, they also reveal a rich tapestry of human motivations, societal causation, and cultural conditioning. For Herder, even the synoptic gospels could be understood in terms of the very human history of first-century Judaism. History could exist separately from theology.

But just as Providence could have no meaning without God, history could have no meaning without a philosophy. Herder was one of the first "moderns" in his recognition of the variety of historical subject matter. His avid cultivation of folk tales and folk songs vastly expanded the realm of historical sources. His study of the history of language convinced him (as it had Vico earlier) of the overriding importance of change. The past was too rich, and too inconstant, to be neatly catalogued without some philosophy of history to serve as a principle of organization and selection.

Herder made his organizing principle humanity itself. Nothing less than the entire history of humanity would give coherence to his study of the past. Indian, Chinese, and Native American art and mythology would stand by the Greek classics, the Hebrew Bible, and European literature. He would study world history in order to appreciate the variety of God's creation and its process of change.

In this regard, we are all children of Herder. As modern historical writing embraces ever more aspects of popular culture and social life, as historical "facts" are produced at an ever increasing rate, we world historians also make Herder's leap of faith. We choose to focus on an even larger canvas—indeed, the largest canvas of all—in order to sharpen our focus and give meaning to our work.

Kevin Reilly
Series Editor

Acknowledgments

The editors wish to thank the Deutscher Klassiker Verlag for kind permission to translate parts of their editions of Herder's *Critical Groves* (Chapter 1) and *On the Earliest Documents of Humankind* (Chapter 10). Also, thanks are due to Stiftung Weimarer Klassik, Weimar, for kind permission to reproduce the Herder portrait on the cover. Hans Adler thanks Monica Macauley (Madison, Wisconsin) for her assistance in making information available. He also warmly appreciates the hospitality extended by Hartmut Reiners, of Berlin, during the winter of 1995, where in the appropriate location of the Herderstrasse a major part of the commentary was completed.

Ernest A. Menze wishes to thank Iona College, Br. John G. Driscoll (New Rochelle, New York), Jack Rudin (New York), and the Roberta C. Rudin Foundation for making possible a year's leave to Jerusalem and Weimar, where major parts of the translation were completed. A warm note of thanks goes also to Rev. Thomas Stransky (Institute for Ecumenical Studies, Jerusalem), Regine Otto (Stiftung Weimarer Klassik, Weimar), and their staffs, for hospitality extended. Both of us are gratefully aware of the work of generations of Herder scholars whose toil has informed our efforts, beginning with T. Churchill's translation of Herder's *Ideen* of the year 1800, which was thoroughly revised to form the basis of much of Part III and all of Part IV of this volume.

On World History

On the Way to World History: Johann Gottfried Herder

Hans Adler and Ernest A. Menze

This volume brings together in thirty-eight chapters a translation of texts on world history by Johann Gottfried Herder. About a third of the texts have been translated into English for the first time. The other two-thirds are a line-by-line revision of the relevant chapters of the T. Churchill translation of Herder's *Ideen zu einer Philosophie der Geschichte der Menschheit (Reflections on the Philosophy of the History of Humankind)* of the year 1800, amounting to a new translation that retains the tone and some of the phrasing of that work.

The introduction that follows provides information concerning the author (Part I), his position in the context of the historiography, philosophy of history, and theoretical assumptions of his day (Part II), and, based on a few samples from the *Ideen* of his treatment of selected areas of the world, his worldview and objectives (Part III).

I.

The man whose pen produced the contributions to this collection, Johann Gottfried Herder, is not the most widely known representative of German intellectual history of the eighteenth century, but he is one of the most influential.[1] He is considered the "father" of Storm and Stress (Sturm und Drang), the epoch in German thought and letters from the late 1760s to the early 1780s that, notwithstanding its brief duration, revolutionized German literature by freeing it from the compulsion of petrified form and the burden of rules. Herder is considered the father of German romanticism. Many see

3

him as the founder of anthropology, and some even feel that, as expressed in 1940 by the prominent German anthropologist Arnold Gehlen, "Philosophical anthropology has not made the slightest progress since Herder. . . ."[2] Herder is considered one of the originators of the modern philosophy of history and one of the first to study and collect folk songs and folklore in general. Given the attribution to him of so many spiritual paternities, foundations, and inventions, the question arises as to why Herder is not more widely known, as familiar as, for example, Kant or Lessing. Furthermore, to be more precise, even when Herder is known, it is often only his name, and not his work, that is known. Even his contemporaries were fond of retaining his ideas while forgetting or repressing the memory of the man by not giving him proper credit.

Johann Gottfried Herder was born on August 25, 1744, in Mohrungen (now Morąg), East Prussia, as the third child of Anna Elisabeth and Johann Herder; his father was sexton and schoolmaster in a girls' school. The young Frederick II, on his way to earning the appellation "Great," was Herder's sovereign. While the young Herder was being raised and was receiving his early education in Mohrungen, David Hume's *Philosophical Essay Concerning Human Understanding* appeared (1748–53), Johann Wolfgang Goethe was born (1749), and Johann Sebastian Bach's *Kunst der Fuge* (*The Art of the Fugue*) was composed (1748–50). The French *Encyclopédie* began to appear (1751–72), and the Seven Years' War turned Prussia—which barely survived it—into one of the major European powers. Jean-Jacques Rousseau published his *Discours sur l'origine et les fondements de l'inégalité parmi les hommes* (1755), and in the same year, the disastrous Lisbon earthquake occurred—the earthquake that, with its 30,000 dead, shook Europe's faith in God's benevolence. Johann Joachim Winckelmann opened a new perspective on Greek antiquity with his *Gedanken über die Nachahmung der griechischen Werke* (*Reflections on the Imitation of Greek Works of Art*) (1755); and nine years later, with his *Geschichte der Kunst des Altertums* (*History of the Art of Antiquity*) (1764), he laid the foundation for modern art history.

In 1762, the year in which Rousseau's *Social Contract* appeared, Herder, at the age of eighteen, enrolled as a student of theology at the University of Königsberg. Since he was of limited means—a fate shared by many bourgeois intellectuals of his day—he made do with occasional jobs and work as a temporary teacher.

It was not so much theology as it was the person of Immanuel Kant that attracted Herder in Königsberg. It must be stressed that Kant at this time was not yet the famous founder of transcendental philosophy; the first of his critiques appeared in 1781. Just as Herder recognized and valued Kant's qualities, Kant also appears to have appreciated Herder, since he not only excused him from paying lecture fees but also entrusted to him the critical reading of some of his texts prior to their publication.

Along with Kant, who also, before 1781, demanded thoroughly rigorous systematic standards of philosophy, Herder came to know the intellectual outsider and critic of all rationalist systems, Johann Georg Hamann, with whom he formed a lasting and fruitful friendship. Hamann introduced Herder to English philosophy, and strengthened him in his high esteem for that which cannot be systematized and quantified. Thus Herder grew to be one of those German representatives of the Enlightenment who helped to advance the manifold process of enlightenment and simultaneously subjected it to critical examination. Herder was among the men of the Enlightenment who were critical in their search for self-understanding; in short, he was part of the self-enlightening Enlightenment. While Hamann critically ground into the dust the orthodox rationalism of the Enlightenment as hubris in the face of the Christian God, Herder took a different tack, the historical one. That is to say, the world, as it was and as it is, is neither only what it appears to be to human reason and common sense, nor is it only as God created it according to the account of creation in the Bible. Rather, Herder says, everything that is, has come to be. The present owes its existence to the past, as the future will be beholden to the present. Herder calls this perspective "genetical."

In 1764, Herder accepted a position offered at the Cathedral School in Riga; here he was successful as a teacher, and even more so as a preacher. He remained in Riga until 1769, producing during this time his first (immediately and widely noted) publication, *Über die neuere deutsche Literatur: Fragmente (On Recent German Literature: Fragments)* (1766–67) and his *Kritische Wälder (Critical Groves)* (three parts, 1769). But now he was gripped by the urge to depart. Notwithstanding his successful activity in Riga, he left, dissatisfied with his life up to this point, and dissatisfied above all with his existence as a man of book learning, whom life was passing by without his leaving any traces upon it. In May 1769, Herder sailed for France, arriving in July and remaining until the end of the year. We owe to this journey a programmatic document, composed after the fact, Herder's *Journal meiner Reise im Jahr 1769 (Journal of my Travels in the Year 1769)*. Although published for the first time posthumously, in the year 1846, the work documents in outstanding fashion the effort to strike a blow for intellectual liberation from the confinement of absolutist petty states, and from a world in which intellectuals are allowed a voice but no influence. With enormous élan, past and future are surveyed so broadly that new fields of learning are envisioned by the dozen, and the old disciplines, including the discipline of history, are confronted with the obsolescence of their erudition. Herder wants nothing less than "universal history of the foundation of the world."

A brief episode as private tutor ended in Strasbourg, where he began a friendship with Goethe, five years his junior. From 1771 until 1776, Herder held the position of Counselor of the Consistory and Superintendent at Bückeburg, Central Germany, in the service of the Count of Schaumburg-Lippe. It was for Herder a very productive time, and also a time in which his writings significantly broadened his renown. In 1773, he found in Caroline Flachsland a devoted wife with whom he would raise their eight children. In 1771, Herder received the prize of the Prussian Academy of Sciences for his widely known essay *Über den Ursprung der Sprache* (*On the Origin of Language*), a prize he was to receive twice more, in 1775 and 1780. In Bückeburg he composed his sketch of a philosophy of history, *Auch eine Philosophie zur Geschichte der Bildung der Menschheit* (*This, too, a Philosophy on the History of the Formation of Humankind*) (1774), a programmatic essay which is comparable in its élan to the *Journal of my Travels in the Year 1769*, and which presents pregnant outlines of much that will be worked out later, especially in the Weimar Philosophy of History.

Along with a second-prize essay, *Über den gesunkenen Geschmack bei den Völkern da er geblühet* (*On the Lowered Taste of Peoples among Whom It Once Flourished*), major theological writings were produced, of which the *Älteste Urkunde des Menschengeschlechts* (*The Most Ancient Document of Humankind*) in particular makes clear Herder's genetic-historical approach. Genesis is not divine rhetoric but the presentation of creation as perceived by a particular culture of the past. Rather than offering a transcendent exegesis of the text, Herder contextualizes not only the content but also its form.

With the support of Goethe, Herder received the call to become general superintendent in Weimar, to assume responsibility for all the schools and the religious life of the Duchy. Weimar, then a minor princely residence with 6,000 inhabitants—although on its way to becoming, with Goethe, Schiller, Wieland, Herder, and others, the famed "Court of the Muses"— was then also an oppressively confining location, rife with intrigues and backstabbing. This was not a good environment for Herder who, as head of ecclesiastical and educational affairs, moreover reacted to any form of oppositon, intrigue, or correction, even and particularly when it came from above, with intense irritation.

This is not the place to account for Herder's astounding productivity as a writer, despite the many duties of his office, which often seemed to overwhelm him. We limit ourselves to the works pertaining to history and the philosophy of history. However, given the large role ecclesiastical affairs played in his life, a brief sketch of Herder's approach to the historical interpretation of scripture is appropriate here.

In the second of his three *Collections of Christian Writings* (*Zweite Sammlung der Christlichen Schriften*), entitled "On the Savior of Humankind. In Accordance with Our First Three Evangelists" ("Vom Erlöser der Menschen. Nach Unseren Drei Ersten Evangelisten"), Herder discusses the historicity of the synoptic gospels.[3] As pointed out by Thomas Zippert, one of the coeditors of the volume, Herder develops his thoughts in this piece by engaging Lessing's hypothesis of the evangelists as merely human historians.[4] Throughout the essay, Herder struggles with the need to reconcile the unquestionable historical reality of the gospel stories with the leap of faith that is required to link known effects to unknown causes. Untroubled by apparent discrepancies in the stories related by the synoptics, and by the contradictions between them and the fourth gospel, Herder views the evangels as the "genuine writings of some Christians who had sprung from Judaism; fruits of the second half of the first Christian century."[5] Acutely conscious both of the delicacy of the transition from the oral tradition to the written historical record and of the questions raised by some of his own contemporaries regarding the historical authenticity of the gospels, Herder struggled valiantly to establish the synoptic evangelists as historians of a special kind, transcending Greek and Roman historiography. For Herder, the historical style of the evangelists is rooted in that of the ancient Hebrews, belonging, like their poetry, "to the childhood of the human race." He asks us to place ourselves inside the character of a nation that did not know other literatures and that dwelt in the sacredness of its ancient books as in the sacred shrine of all wisdom.[6] The evangelists sprang from this nation and recorded their gospels in the spirit of their fathers. Calling the essay "part of the business of my life,"[7] to which he has repeatedly and for the most varied reasons devoted "impartial examinations," Herder links his theological interests closely to his all-encompassing historical imagination and method. For him, the evangelists are the successors of Moses and the prophets, historians rooted in the unique experience of the Jewish people. Writing in 1796, and elaborating thoughts that had occupied him for a dozen years before they found their final expression in this essay, Herder reiterates what he had already asserted as a twenty-three-year-old in the "Early Leaves" of the *Critical Groves,* which form the first selection of the present collection; he said then that the reader, even in reference to a history of art, "has the twofold obligation to believe and to examine."[8] In his own historical approach to scripture, Herder consistently abides by this "twofold obligation." By likening the "historical genius" that informs the record of the past and transcends its sophistry to the dramatic genius that transcends the rules of the theater, Herder establishes the study of history as an art as well as a science. The selections of this volume bear out the visionary qualities that underlie his meticulous examination of tantalizing philosophical questions and historical problems. Much of what Herder wrote and taught with respect to history lends itself readily to very modern and entirely secular interpretations, but a false image of Herder would be conveyed if these interpretations were not informed by an awareness of "the business of his life," which was and remained always that of a Christian minister and teacher of his countrymen.

In addition to Herder's significant writings on aesthetics, epistemology, and theology, we should also note his magnum opus, the *Ideen zur Philosophie einer Geschichte der Menschheit* (1784–91). In the *Ideen,* he endeavored to tie together his insight into and his encompassing knowledge of many fields. Aesthetics, physics, geography, anthropology, theology, mythology, psychology, and many other aspects of human cognition and knowledge were brought together, with the intent to demonstrate that the actions of all humankind do have, if not a goal, nevertheless a general direction. Moreover, when viewed in a long-range perspective, this globally focused activity of humankind conforms to the fixed laws of nature without itself being subject to such fixation. The huge undertaking of the *Ideen* had of necessity to remain a monumental fragment, and it was no more than consistent that Herder, in the *Briefe zu Beförderung der Humanität* (*Letters on the Advancement of Humanity*) (1793–97), turned more in the direction of the examples provided by fortunate moments of history, and by the hypothetical organization of an international intellectual public. Herder wanted this public to be understood not only as a public of living persons, but as a concept transcending all borders and ages. Thus, justice would be done to a present pregnant with the past. It is a peculiarity of German history that this urgently desired public had to dwell between the covers of books rather than asserting itself in parliamentary assemblies. During the last years of his life, from 1799 to 1803, Herder concentrated with dogged persistence on an unyielding confrontation with Kantian philosophy. At the same time, he was ceaselessly engaged in the composition of essays, which were brought together in collections under the title *Adrastea,* the name of the goddess who rigorously meted out that truth and justice which the old Herder saw as pervading all history.

The man who was one of the most important figures of the German Enlightenment, German Classicism, and early Romanticism, and who, with Kant, Goethe, Schiller, Wieland, Moritz, Novalis, and Friedrich Schlegel, to name only a few, shaped the age in which he lived, died embittered and isolated on December 18, 1803, in Weimar, where he is buried in "his" Church of St. Peter and Paul, the "Herder–Kirche."

II.

In Herder's time, historiography was in the process of transformation. With regard to the history of the German language, a peculiarity pertaining to the term *Geschichte* should be noted. In the modern sense of the word, as a "collective singular,"[9] the term *Geschichte* appears around the middle of the seventeenth century, and by the beginning of the eighteenth century it starts to take the place of the loanword *Historie,* which had preeminently denoted the narrative of past events.[10] With that, the German term *Geschichte* became increasingly ambivalent, as it could convey both the process of history and the narrative of what happened.[11] The unfolding of the collective singular *Geschichte,* which may be applied to different dimensions of history, from the *History of Osnabrück* to *World History,* according to the thesis of Reinhart Koselleck, "unchains philosophy of history."[12]

Philosophy of history is a term new to the eighteenth century, coined by Voltaire,[13] who wanted to draw principles and regularities from the contingencies of successive and simultaneous historical events, in order to render history more comprehensible on the basis of its immanent rationality. As early as 1742, Voltaire had written, "Ce qui manque d'ordinaire à ceux qui compilent l'histoire, c'est l'esprit philosophique."[14] With that, Voltaire subordinated history to philosophical reflection, and he freed history from the primacy of theology, which, as in the case of Bossuet, had conveyed the course of history as determined by divine intervention, thereby placing the principle of history outside itself.[15] In the context of the German *Aufklärung,* which is set apart from the European Enlightenment, or *Lumières,* by its particular relation to theology, the unfolding of philosophy of history is decisively shaped by the epistemological context—for, in the constituent process of philosophy of history, fused together in one discipline are two stages of cognition, which in the rationalist discourse of cognition actually follow one another. On the one hand, there is the level of the facts of experience, made accessible by the "cogniton of that which is or happens."[16] In the terminology of the time, this stage of cognition was called *cognitio historica,* or historical cognition. On the other hand, there is the level of the truths of reason, which become accessible through the "cognition of the causation of that which is or comes to be."[17] Thus, since theology no longer offers a vantage point beyond history that would make the unity of history as a collective singular at least credible, it is philosophy of history that establishes the immanent foundation of history as conceivable totality and order.

As indicated by the organization of the contents of this volume, our reflections on philosophy of history are essential for making clear, on the one hand, what could come to be "world history" in the context of the eighteenth century, and, on the other hand, how our author, Herder, approached this global perspective. For, in order to assume a "world historical" point of view, one must attain a not-at-all-self-evident conceptualization that not only fuses some events into a particular context, but synthesizes *all* events *all* over the world into *one* context: world history. This may be done in two ways. In one mode, the global context is striven for successively, by means of regionally or nationally confined histories presented in narratives and tied to one another on the level of events by means of points of contact. Bryce comments on this approach: "Most of the books of this class have been narratives, pursuing the course of events in one country and then in another, without setting forth any more connexion between them than their political relations at some moments involved."[18] This is the cumulative approach to the writing of history, signifying that world history represents itself as the sum of particular histories.

Rather than tracing events in narrative form, another mode of world history approaches them by emphasis on their effects, causation, and driving forces. Here enters the philosophical-hermeneutic assumption, that what appears as fact has not only its function, but its meaning in the whole. The hermeneutic achievement consists in "making the facts speak," that is, in transforming mute objects into telling symbols by means of the restoration of the relations of cause and effect. In this manner, the world of isolated data and factuality becomes a seamless web, a text (the Latin term *textura*). This text, like any text expressed in words, has its rules, which the text does not express explicitly but whose effects are shown in its form. The uncovering of the rules governing the text of history, however, is the task of philosophy of history. World history as a whole is not unlocked by the endless narrative approximation of a totality that is located ever further into the future. Rather, the uncovering of the laws that "rule" the integration into one totality promises human comprehension of world history. Beginning with Ibn Khaldun (1332–1406), including Vico, Montesquieu, and Voltaire, and continuing to Hegel, Bryce names such philosophers of history, but he leaves out Herder, as, later, Karl Löwith also did in his grand settling of accounts with philosophy of history.[19]

This somewhat extensive review was called for in order to make clear that world history in the eighteenth century is not something given that could be grasped by mere narrative presentation. Then as today, world history, like any other kind of history, must be created. No history is transcribed from reality, however that reality is perceived. History is written: that is to say, it constitutes itself as text.

In the Germany of the eighteenth century, professors of the then-progressive Göttingen University were preeminent in giving a decisive impulse to history as an academic discipline. Theologians separated the truths and the spirit of the Christian religion from its manifestations, thereby historicizing theology[20] in such a way that pre-Christian cultures could be taken account of in the same context. Just as Johann Lorenz von Mosheim, the "father of modern Church history,"[21] freed Church history from dogma to reveal its genuine historical dimension, and Ludwig Timotheus Spittler secularized Church history in the form of institutional history, and Gottfried Achenwall transformed statistics from its mere descriptive function into a historical-explanatory mode, there were many realms of knowledge and cognition that revealed a historicizing and secularizing process relating the past to the present. Johann Christoph Gatterer wrote in 1761:

> The times are past in which the essentials of history could be conveyed in a minute narration of wars, battles, murderous tales, fabled petty accounts, and the like. Now only that is accounted notable that brings to us a real gain in our major disciplines of learning or else in our objectives.[22]

Although this statement may be read as a thoroughly rationalist functional approach to history, it also reveals what the history of all must be for all, an assumption that might be applied in Gatterer's terms to the entire world, and in Justus Möser's terms representatively to the region of the city of Osnabrück.[23] This is not a plea for democracy, but the consequence of the premise that—in Leibniz's sense—everything is connected with all and forms a whole, and that therefore history must be not only cumulative history but world history reflecting a system. It is the task of this world history to bring order into the world of contingent experiences by means of the representation of connectedness. It is understood that Gatterer's program was realized only in fragments. His significance rests in his function as the pathfinder in a new, far-reaching perspective; as he put it:

> In effect, it [world history] is the history of the larger issues, of revolutions: whether they pertain to the human beings and the peoples per se, or their relationship to religion, the state, the disciplines of learning, the arts and crafts, whether they took place in the more distant or more recent ages.[24]

August Ludwig Schlözer pursued a similar program, with a focus on universal history, revealing a comparable discrepancy between its plan and its execution.[25] However, in order that plans such as those of Gatterer and Schlözer could be conceived in the first place, the idea of the "unity of humankind"[26] had to be accepted as the premise underlying the writing of history; yet, at the same time, humankind as a whole became also the "hypothetical agent" of history.[27]

Herder takes issue with all these new—and also with the older—positions of the historical literature of his day, and he finds his own point of view. Time and again, he reflects on the relation between the events of history, on the one hand, and their representation, on the other. These reflections—Chapters 1 to 8 of this anthology—help in the search for similar as well as differing principles governing history and its discourse, so that the two may theoretically be separated from one another and thus offered to enhance human cognition. Since Herder does not write the history of great names, but rather has in mind a history of factual relations determined by complex causation, his sources differ significantly from those of many historians. It is therefore of great importance to stress that Herder considers myths and mythological texts as historical sources, reflecting early *forms* of human efforts to assess the world in historical terms. He saw these sources not as documenting past relations of facts, but as documents of early forms of perception and representation (Chapters 9 and 10). The hermeneutic achievement that rests in this attention to form, in which the past encounters subsequent ages, consists above all in the acknowledgment of the peculiarity of the other, coupled with an intensified awareness of the self. Consequently, in Herder's view, history always treats of the past of the self. It does so even when it relates that which is long past and far away, for world history is the history of humankind—of which, in Herder's view, the individual's history is the abbreviated repetition—in a way a "phylogenetic basic law of intellectual history," as Friedrich Meinecke called it.[28] Hand in hand with the acknowledgment of the vantage points taken in earlier stages of human history, there goes the acknowledgment of the individual and particular dimensions in the various manifestations of the past, contextualized historically. The latter acknowledgment ought to be assessed on its own terms, and not on the basis of the ultimate perspective attained at any given point of development (the vantage point of the observer). However, the integration of the individual dimension into the totality of the world historical context is accomplished by Herder on the basis of the philosophy of history (Chapters 11 to 24). This is the core of his work and its theoretical foundation, the essential part of that which is to become and to be designated world history. In short, without philosophy of history, there is no world history.

Herder's "Reflections on World History" (Chapters 25 to 38) demonstrate how he, time and again pausing to reflect, aspires to take hold of the most varied streams of information coming his way. Part IV of this anthology presents a veritable stop-and-go process of knowledge gained and bound into the global and anthropological process. Time and again, the general reflections point back to the project of world history, until at last and briefly (Chapter 38)—as the *Ideen* remains a monumental fragment— general conclusions concerning the European sphere of life are reached. This "historical sense"[29] is not meant to rouse antiquarian interest and merely present the past; it is meant to teach. To avoid a misunderstanding here, it must be said that Herder does not conceive of history as teaching in the sense of the ancient topos of "the schoolmistress of life" (*historia magistra vitae*). The universal that makes world history possible in the first place rests for Herder on the one hand in anthropology, the unity of man and humankind in all its diversity. However, this is for Herder not a given, but precisely that which as *Humanität* can only come to the fore in history. On the other hand, the universality of world history rests in his assumption of the unity of the world. The totality of the world as such is not accessible to humankind; it is only either perceptible in symbolical representation or accessible by means of analogy. Herder's conception of world history thus entails a religious component—alluded to earlier—which compensates for the human incapacity to perceive totality immediately. The question that arises is, to whom is Herder's conception of world history directed? This question will be briefly touched upon in the following section.

III.

This overview of Herder's role in the human drama "On the Way to World History" concludes with a look at his worldview and objectives. These are revealed most clearly in his detailed accounts of human civilizations. Given the remarkable progress that has been made in the conceptualization and teaching of world history in the United States, due to the pioneering efforts of William McNeill, L.S. Stavrianos, Marshall G.S. Hodgson, and others, a review of Herder's writings on the subject 200 years ago is now of particular relevance. Our discussion of Herder's position in the context of the historiography, philosophy of history, and theoretical assumptions of his day has already pointed to his relevance to the conceptual foundations of modern world history. A sampling of his treatment of various areas of the world in his most mature work, the *Ideen,* will highlight his worldview and objectives, expressed in lessons to his countrymen as well as to a wider European public. This sampling will also provide students and teachers of history with food for thought, as they preview Herder's passage from concept to practice in his account of the currents of human civilization. As Herder traversed the continents, sketching remarkably clear images of the flaws and virtues of their inhabitants, his perception and presentation of the particular was rooted in and enhanced by the philosophy of history he had evolved "on the way to world history."

Upon concluding his account of ancient Rome in the *Ideen zur Philosophie der Geschichte der Menschheit,* Herder characterizes the Romans as "destroyers" who could not be "preservers," and he asserts that it would be futile for us to consider their state and their language as a bridge to the treasures of an earlier world. The account ends on a fatalistic and disillusioned note. However, before he turns, in the famous Sixteenth Book, to the Cisalpine world, he takes his countrymen, in the Fifteenth Book, on an impressive excursus on the progress of *Humanität* as the alpha and omega of human existence.[30] To set the stage, he confronts his readers with the apparent futility of human life and efforts, with the realization that no progress is discernible in the course of world history that has been presented by him up to this point, and with the fact that destruction obscures the change for the better that is ever present in renewal.[31] Yet he insists that reason and equity, the two pillars upon which rests the quality of *Humanität,* will sustain a doubting and despairing humanity in its quest for self-fulfillment.[32] In an effort to sketch Herder's worldview and objectives as they are revealed in his lessons for his countrymen from the pages of world history, his paean to *Humanität* in the Fifteenth Book of the *Ideen* constitutes the logical starting point. Everything he has said up to this point about the emergence and decay of humankind and human civilizations is measured against this standard. *Humanität,* likewise, is the beacon that guides him through the remaining and, unfortunately, incomplete part of the work, which covers the emerging modern world.

Specifically, what are the lessons for his countrymen offered by Herder from the pages of world history? To begin with, he establishes history as "the science of what is, not of what may possibly be according to hidden designs of fate." Speaking of Alexander the Great, he exclaims, "If we attributed his bold resolution to the secret purposes of a higher power, and his heroic achievements to a particular goddess of good fortune, we would run the danger of turning Alexander's recklessness into ultimate divine objectives, to diminish here his personal courage and military skill, while generally depriving the entire event of its natural form."[33] As the untiring educator of his nation, he points to the need, in every body politic, for "a class of men appointed to instruct, educate, and enlighten the rest; ... for wherever such teachers of the people were wanting, these people remained eternally mired in their ignorance and indolence."[34] Yet he also reminds his readers of the stages of development that in every nation must precede the ascent to rational autonomy. Speaking of theocracy as necessarily prevalent in ancient civilizations, from Egypt to China, he credits the Greeks with being the first to gradually separate legislation from religion, and he praises the Israelites who "alone distinguish themselves from all their neighbors in that they attribute neither the creation of the world nor that of humankind to their country."[35]

A rather remarkable set of lessons for his countrymen is offered in Herder's account of China. He sketches in admiring terms the virtues of the hierarchical structure of the Chinese state, the prevailing nobility of merit that gains for men of proven worth the positions of honor and the dignity that flows from that honor, the quality of Chinese law as unalterably rooted in the moral teachings of sacred books, and the guardianship of the son of Heaven, as the soul of the body politic, of ancient custom. He concludes by asking, "If each of these conditions were to prove effective and these principles be carried into actual practice, could one conceive of a more perfect political constitution? The empire would be the home of virtuous, well-bred, diligent, modest, and happy children and brothers."[36] Having thus set up his readers to share his admiration, he points out that there have also been negative assessments of the Chinese system and that "it would be regrettable if we could not find a middle way between the exaggerated praise and blame, which would thus probably point the correct path to truth."[37] This "middle way" leads Herder into a memorable admonition of his countrymen regarding the consequences of blind obedience.[38] He laments the "debilitating influence upon the entire structure of the state" that must necessarily come from this "childish confinement of human reason, strength, and sensibility," and he concludes by likening the empire to an embalmed mummy hardly to be expected to measure up to European standards in the sciences.[39] Although Herder insists that his negative assessment of Chinese civilization is not based on "hostile contempt" but drawn from accounts by writers favorably disposed to it, the contemporary observer cannot help but wonder whether the vehemence of Herder's indictment is not in some measure the product of his own impatience with his countrymen's fateful tendency to obedience.[40]

At any rate, Herder is not at all hostile to the qualities of gentleness, courtesy, and moderation in other peoples. This becomes evident in his account of India. Praising these qualities in the Indians and attributing them to the influence of the Brahmins, Herder concludes that, by comparison, the Europeans must often appear impure, inebriated, and deranged.[41] He is particularly impressed by the strength of the Hindu commitment to toleration and the absence of religious persecution, and he attributes the sorry lot of the pariahs to developments in the distant past that doomed the very poor, or those guilty of misdeeds, and the condemned and their innocent descendants, resulting in their willing submission to their fate and ultimate acceptance of it as heavenly punishment.[42] Herder is harshly critical of the Europeans, who enriched themselves among the Indians, concluding that all the reports and goods brought home by them do not compensate for the evils they heaped upon a people who had not offended them in any way.[43] However, there is an unresolved tension between Herder's repeated insistence that peoples become what they are capable of becoming in the context of their history and resources, ànd his negative assessment of their inability to transcend their limitations; and it is downright objectionable when he finds consolation in the fact that Asiatic despotism, "this oppressive burden of humankind, is found only among nations who are willing to bear it, that is, who feel its heavy weight to a lesser degree."[44]

In his account of Africa, Herder admonishes us to "lay aside our proud prejudices and consider the nature of this region with as much impartiality as if there were no other in the world."[45] He laments the scarcity of sources available to the student of African history, and he makes a valiant attempt to arrive at a scientific explanation of racial differences.[46] Even in the nations of which we have some knowledge, he observes, "the eye of the European seems to behold with too much tyrannical indifference to try to investigate the variations of national development in wretched black slaves. They are treated like cattle, and when they are purchased, they are set apart only by the conditions of their teeth."[47] "Thus," he concludes, "let us sympathize with the Negro, but not despise him, since the conditions of his climate could not grant him nobler gifts. . . . The materials were not wanting in him; but nature turned the shaping hand and created what was of greater need for him in his land and for the happiness of his life."[48]

The—to the modern ear—somewhat condescending note in his assessment ought not to obscure for us the genuine admiration he feels for the unvarnished *Humanität* of the peoples presently characterized as "developing nations." That admiration speaks to the reader in his assessment of the American Indians, whose "character stands alone on the globe, both in its vices and in its virtues."[49] Herder's account of the Mexican Indians does not deny the tempering of oppression by the Spaniards that has come with time, but he nevertheless sketches starkly the lasting effects of this "most unjust of all oppressions," which has shaped the Mexicans' character and left their souls "exhausted by servitude."[50] Asking whether there is discernible among the many American tribes one chief and central characteristic, he finds it in their "goodness of heart and childlike innocence, a character that their ancient establishments, their habits, their few arts, and above all their initial conduct towards the Europeans, confirm."[51]

Although Herder found much food for thought and many lessons for his countrymen in his survey of Asia, Africa, and the Americas, it was from the

Near East and from the Greco-Roman world that he drew his most penetrating insights. Introducing his account of the impact of the Near East on posterity, he concludes that "there is no other region of the world other than Greece and Rome that has invented and prepared as much for Europe and through it for all nations on earth."[52] Of the nations of the Near East, the Hebrews "had a greater impact on other peoples than any Asian nation; yes, to a certain extent, they have become, through Christianity as well as Mohammedanism, a source for the greatest proportion of the enlightenment of the world."[53]

To be sure, Herder finds much to say about the destructive empires of the Near and Middle East that ought to have given his countrymen pause to reflect. Although he admires Cyrus and the customs of the Persians sketched in Xenophon's *Cyropaedia,* and although he asks the Germans to rejoice in the probability of their kinship with this tribe, he nevertheless approaches the tomb of Cyrus wondering why he became so unyielding a conqueror, not realizing how much of a burden he thereby placed upon his successors. Cyrus's spirit of conquest gave them so grandiose a goal that they aspired to expand their empire even when it could be expanded no more. "If humaneness ever holds sway in the realm of humankind, its history will teach the renunciation of that mad spirit of conquest, that results necessarily within a few generations in self-destruction."[54] He compares the Phoenicians favorably to the conquering nations of the Near East, because they brought diligence and science to the regions in which they traded, and thus advanced *Humanität* in spite of themselves. They put to shame the later Europeans who, so much more amply endowed with the progress of civilization, discovered both of the Indies. While, under the sign of the cross, the Europeans enslaved others and exterminated them, the ancient Phoenicians traded and colonized in a manner that benefited the regions in which they held sway.[55]

Herder holds the civilization of Egypt in remarkably low esteem, concluding that, impressive as the gigantic Egyptian monuments are, the hieroglyphs that adorn them demonstrate rather the opposite of the profound wisdom one is led to expect to flow from them. When it comes to ancient writings, Herder extols the merit of the sacred Hebrew writings over all others. They are clearly superior to those produced by any other nation in history, including "the much more recent Koran of the Mohammedans, which after all utilized the precepts of the Jews and Christians."[56] Ultimately, Herder hears in the voices of the lawgivers of humankind a note of lament and sadness. So it was in the voice of Moses and also, as he turns to Greece, in that of Solon in the few fragments that have come down to us from them. They saw the changeable fate and fortune of humankind narrowly restricted by the laws of nature and hopelessly confused, and they lamented. It is in the ancient sages of Greece, rather than their philosophers and statesmen, that Herder sees the quality of gentle *Humanität* to which he aspires.[57] That ideal of a gentle *Humanität* is betrayed by the Romans, and Herder appeals to their great, beholding Rome from the heavens: "How unclean must appear your honor, how bloody your laurel, how low and hostile to humankind your stranglehold."[58]

While in Greece, "everything enduring and sound in its taste and in its constitution ... was caused by the felicitous equilibrium of its striving powers" and "the happy state of its institutions was more noble and permanent in proportion as they were founded on *humanity,* that is, reason and equity," we inherited from Rome "the fasces of the conquerors, which once chastised innocent nations."[59] Not even the pervasion of Rome by Christianity mitigates his harsh view of the Romans' grandeur, although he cherishes their law, rhetoric, and historical writings as "flowers of the intellect."[60]

To be sure, the Christianity Herder embraced, the teaching of which became "the business of his life," freed itself from its union with Rome. Herder's extensive writings on the Hebrew Bible, as well as those on the New Testament, blend the historian's and the theologian's tasks. He finds his concept of *Humanität,* the principal lesson to his countrymen, deeply rooted in the Hebrew and Christian traditions, but he is not by any means unaware of the peril that comes with blind captivity to tradition. Tradition in itself is for him "an excellent institution of nature," and he finds it indispensible. But, he emphasizes, "as soon as it fetters all power of thought both in practical politics and in education, and impedes all progress of human reason and all the improvements demanded by new circumstances and times, it is the true opium of the spirit for states as well as sects and individual human beings."[61]

Some of Herder's references to nonwestern peoples and European "minorities," such as the Jews and the faithful of religious persuasions other than his own, must be read in the historical context. Such a reading will reveal a penetrating comprehension of regions and peoples very distant from his own experience and accessible to him only through fragmentary travel accounts and other incomplete and unreliable sources. Such a reading will also reinforce the reader's awareness of Herder's humanism, which joins the best of the Hebrew Bible and the Christian tradition to the heritage of classical antiquity and the enlightenment of his own day.

In the currently prevalent and, it is to be feared, long-to-be-retained assessment of German history as culminating in the ultimate expression of inhumanity, Herder's lessons to his countrymen on the essence of *Humanität* demonstrate that a magnificent alternative was and continues to be available to them. Herder, the German thinker, teacher, and preacher, "On the Way to World History," transcended the limits of his homeland and became a European figure of the first rank. His key role in the evolution of historicism as a tool for providing access to the past on its own terms, and his finely balanced treatment of its universal and particular aspects, merits the translations offered in this anthology.

At certain points in the translations provided here, a recurrent image, of which Herder evidently was fond, is rendered in a phrase echoing his day: The term *Morgenland,* "Country of the Morning," is translated here as "the Morn" rather than as the conventional "East" or "Orient." Similarly, the German word *Aufklärung* for the Enlightenment seems appropriate for the purposes of setting off the particularly German characteristics of the age. In some instances, too, the length of Herder's sentences had to be retained, even at the risk of a loss of "clarity" in an end-of-the-twentieth-century sense. Here we were guided by Milan Kundera's recently stated creed for the art of translation: "For a translator, the supreme authority should be the author's personal style. But most translators obey another authority: that of the *conventional version* of 'good French' (or 'good German,' 'good English,' etc.) we learn in school. The translator considers himself the ambassador from that authority to the foreign author. That is the error: every author of some value *transgresses* against 'good style,' and in that transgression lies the originality (and hence the raison d'être) of his art."[62]

Part I

Principles of History—
Principles of Historiography

~ 1 ~

Early Leaves of *Critical Groves*

In this short text from 1767, Herder addresses the crucial question of the relationship between historiography and philosophy of history. As he frequently does, he begins his general reflections with a discussion of an individual "instance." The following text documents Herder's earliest discussion of the approach to art history of Johann Joachim Winckelmann (1717–68) and of Winckelmann's groundbreaking work entitled *History of Ancient Art* (*Geschichte der Kunst des Altertums*, 1764). The "Early Leaves" constitute a part of Herder's larger project entitled *Critical Groves*, three parts of which appeared in 1769; the fourth was published posthumously in 1843.

Portions of Herder's "Early Leaves" were published for the first time in 1963 by Hans Dietrich Irmscher.[*] The first complete annotated edition, prepared by Regine Otto, appeared in 1990.[**]

The plan according to which Mr. Winckelmann[1] intended to carry out his outstanding history of art, by his own account, is the following—and I concede that in the more recent literature an undertaking such as this has rarely been carried out in so grand a manner: "The History of Ancient Art which I have undertaken to write is not a mere chronicle of epochs, and of the changes which occurred within them. I use the term History in the more extended signification which it has in the Greek language; and it is my intention to attempt to present a system."[2]

I will leave it to certain philologists of my nation to gather together the

---

[*]Hans Dietrich Irmscher, "Probleme der Herder-Forschung," *Deutsche Vierteljahrsschrift für Literaturwissenschaft und Geistesgeschichte* 37 (1963), pp. 289–93.

[**]Johann Gottfried Herder, *Kritische Wälder* (Berlin and Weimar: Aufbau Verlag, 1990), (Johann Gottfried Herder, *Ausgewählte Werke in Einzelausgaben. Schriften zur Literatur*, vol. 2/1), pp. 641–52 (annotations in vol. 2/2, pp. 201–7).

various instances of the meanings of the word from a number of indices and dictionaries. In short, *history* in its Greek origin may mean "inspection, knowledge, science," and such is, after all, also a real story of things past.

But a system? Did the Greeks endeavor to erect such an edifice out of the pages of history? Is it possible to erect something like this, while allowing the work always to remain history?—For my purposes it amounts to the same thing whether history is a story of complicated events, or of simple makings, of data or of facts. Even the history of the thought, the higher learning, the art of a people, and of many peoples, remains, as simple as the subject matter may be, always a history of events, actions, transformations. Thus, if one historiographer is able to provide a system, each of them must be able to do so in his own fashion.

And why should he not be able to provide it? Each event, each fact in the world in its way is *a whole,* a whole that may be presented for the purposes of instruction; therefore, what is such a clear presentation, such a complete description of it for the instruction of others, if not a historical system? Each event, each fact in the world has its reasons to be and its causes that somehow brought it into being; as a being it also has consequences and a description of all this is, what else, then, but a historical system? Each event, finally, is nothing but a link in a chain, it is woven into connection with other events by means of attraction and repulsion,[3] it is effective in the interplay of things in the world. Is not a plan describing this connectedness, this universal system of effects a historical system? Is not a writer of history of such dimensions a philosopher, a pragmatic systematizer?[4]

More than likely! And among all philosophers, master craftsmen of didactic systems, and systematizers, such a universal philosopher—should he exist—would be for me the first and the greatest. But his very greatness means that I cannot touch his face; therefore, I cast my eyes downward and prefer to reflect.

If history were, in its simplest sense, nothing but the description of an event, of a process, the first mandate would be that the description be *complete,* that it exhaust the matter, that it show us the event from all sides. Even the annalist,[5] the writer of memoirs,[6] is bound to this completeness, and thus is obliged in a work standing by itself to create a "system." This is indeed so in a work standing by itself. Here a merely one-dimensional point of view is flawed, a one-sided portrayal of the same to be rejected. His historical datum should be for him an edifice to be inspected from all sides, and to be drawn from every vantage point. But I would like to see the writer of history who would *be able* to attain perfection even in this one instance. It is as impossible to represent on a level surface an entire body in the round that has been perceived without projection from one vantage point, as it is for the annalist and writer of memoirs to create out of his subject matter, and be it the most important, and be his discussion of detail nothing less than abundant, a historical system. There is always, even in the singular instance, even in the matter of mere external appearance, only the *attempt* at a system, and that is sufficient, indeed!

Sufficient for us human beings who perceive in one dimension, but not sufficient for his many-sided subject matter, and how much less yet for the *inner nature* of the same, for the causes of its genesis, for the state of its being! Here historical perception ceases and prophecy begins. Since I can never see cause as cause, effect as effect, but always must infer, conjecture, guess; since in this art of inference I have nothing for my witness but the similarity of cases, and since therefore my acuteness,[7] or my wit[8] in finding this similarity of one to another, this consequence of one through the other, is my only guarantor of the truth; since this guarantor, however, can be nothing but *my* acuteness, *my* wit, and since it therefore can be only a dubious witness, and a prophet of truth perhaps only *for me,* and a few of my brethren, it may be concluded that the writer of history and the philosopher of history cannot stand completely on the same ground. Place two spectators with telescopes of equal strength on the same spot and they will pretty much see the same; however, when it comes to passing judgment on what they have seen, to inferring, to conjecturing, they will no longer agree so fully. One seeks the causes of the event who knows where, and who knows how different in appearance, and just there and just as different in appearance does he indeed find them. This one and that one, each according to the position of his head, according to the house rules of his intellect and wit. And finally, there is the impact of the causation found, the more and less of difference in the impact—no human being can see this; each one must infer, conjecture, guess. Therefore, it is not the actual writer of history, it is not the eyewitness to the event who provides the causes, who judges why and to what extent something has come to be from them. Rather, it is no one else but the one who reflects on history, who seeks reasons, more or less true, more or less certain, more or less probable, who measures the tie between cause and effect, and who follows it.

Therefore, the writer of history should not be a systematizer or—why so contemptuously—a philosopher of history? Not so quick, my reader, we haven't come that far. I do not want to be a historical doubter, and I leave to our new Historical Society[9] the important examination of the questions, "to what extent is the sensus communis of judgment in things historical still the same in people of different estates and ways of living, or, more importantly, of varying composition of spiritual powers, or, most importantly yet, of differing degrees of education and its variables? How far may the humor of one's mind go to find in history, too, one's favorite views and one's favorite causes? How much may my humor contribute to the fact that I find in what I sought that, which I wanted to find, and find it more really the more often I try? How far may one persuade oneself to confuse experience and judgment, to believe as if one saw, and to subtilize opinion into experience? How much may the peculiarity of our thinking tie us to one or the other view, and how much may a certain historical disposition of our historical soul allow us to turn our thinking into the most appropriate, subsequently into the necessary, and ultimately into the one and only? From here must follow, with psychological dimensions, the determination of historical certainty, and of probability! From here must follow (and, strictly speaking, this last *from here* is for me) *the difference between history and judgment: history* and *system.* History must be believed; however, that which in it is intended to be seen as system, must be examined."

However, what in reference to a history may be considered a system is not merely the connection between *one* cause and effect, or secondly, of each individual cause and effect; rather, thirdly at last, it is the entire coordination of many events in terms of a plan, with a purpose, that constitutes a system. How is this so? Would it be possible, in terms of our theory of history, for a historicus par excellence to exist without this plan, without this coordinating of events that gives them a purpose? The mere raconteur is an annalist, a scribbler of memoirs and newspapers; the one who reasons about individual tales is a historical raisonneur; but the one who coordinates many events in terms of a plan, who gives them a purpose, he is, according to our art of history, the real historical artist, the painter of a grand portrait of the most fitting composition, he is the historical genius, the true creator of a *history*! And if that is so, history and system are one!

Very well! *creator, genius, painter,* and *artist* of history; but my simple mind, taught by Socrates to take time in arriving at a concept, is still so far behind that it is once more reminded of the original question: To what extent is the historical creator, who thought of a world of events, who wove together the connections and created, in accordance with this plan, a history, to what extent is he still a writer of history? It is readily apparent that I, once more, am back at the capital A.[10]

And since my memory is not sufficient to recall all the rules of historiography from Lucian to Abbt, and Gatterer,[11] and since, at any rate, examples of history preceded rules of history, how valuable would it be if I were to digress to a few of the oldest examples and examined, to what extent their history was a system. There is, for instance, the father of all, or at least of all Greek and Roman history, Herodotus.[12]

Herodotus' history, as confused as it may appear, with its episodes and transitions, is still after all an ordered edifice, as artfully created as ever in Egypt the hand of Daedalus was able to create a labyrinth which in the mind of the artist certainly was not a labyrinth. To a degree *Gatterer* has recently shown this,[13] and in his analysis (I do not speak here of the application to our day) has very well hit the mark as to the point of view from which Herodotus wrote, and from which he must be read. Still a son of the age attuned to hymns and Homeric tales, he worked out his history like an interlocking carmen,[14] placing, in the manner of the epopee, a theme at its basis, elaborating it with episodes and interjections almost like a historical rhapsodist: "I will sing to the Greece freed from the Persians!"[15] For this theme he takes as much from the world that preceded him and from his own world as was needed to elaborate it. Is it not the case, then, that he has worked out his history one-half as an historical epopee and one-half as a historical system?

None other but this! However, what if he had to do so only in deference to his age? What if such an edifice was only the result of the shortcomings of his age? What if, just because of this, he did not have among his successors anyone to emulate him? What if, for that reason, his history has been found flawed? Should the episodic edifice of his history then remain as much the model for our day as is assumed by the aforementioned famous teacher of history?—Herodotus did not have any historians to look back to; he, as the first, had to leap back further, and for each part of his history he had to refer back to the history of the most ancient of days. That was the foundation for *his* edifice of history; however, this is not the model of a plan for those who no longer may write as aboriginals. *Herodotus* wrote for a public which had been neither in Persia nor in Egypt and, moreover, did not know these countries, halfway or entirely out of a *Hübner*[16]; therefore, he had to become such a *Hübner,* and insert travel descriptions not because they belonged there, but because without them his history would have been incomprehensible to *his* Greece and—why shouldn't we say it—he also would have traveled in vain, and who would desire that? With these inserted patches of geography and alien history, he thus became for his age and for all succeeding ages so useful, so indispensable; nevertheless, in the manner of his *piecing together* of the composition, he still was not a model. *Herodotus,* finally, was an Asian, but an Asian Greek; therefore, the depiction of his nine muses *surrounding* his fatherland was exemplary; therefore, the national tone which prevails throughout, and which ought to be examined carefully by someone; therefore, his work became a reconstruction of history on the basis of Greek concepts, depicting it in terms of religion, politics, and way of life; therefore, his work became a *system* of history for his Greeks; yes, but not the model of a plan for the entire world.

Not even for the Greek ages succeeding him. *Thucydides,*[17] precisely the *Thucydides* who was awakened to become a historian by none other than *Herodotus,* the *Thucydides* who as a boy cried bitter tears of envy upon hearing the reading of the Herodotian history, he, as a mature man, as a writer of history—did not imitate it, but followed a concept seemingly unaware of Herodotus's work. So much the worse for him, it might be said. "That is also the reason why he does not have as significant a subject as Herodotus; that is also why he interjects such terribly long speeches, which are completely unknown in Herodotus; that is why he also does not have the gentle transition from one period of history to the next; that is why, we regret to say, we do not find him alongside other writers of history, but among the annalists." Perhaps it will not pain Thucydides very much to be found there, because he placed himself there of his own free will. His history does not reach for as wide a circle as does the Herodotian, and his introduction is not as splendid a portal as the vestibule of Herodotus with its Asiatic extensions; fair enough, for his intoduction was written by a statesman[18] who raised from ancient history only as much as he (not as much as he needed, for Herodotus was already there, but as much as he) wanted to improve or elucidate in regard to the prevailing prejudices concerning Greek antiquity. He organized his chronology in terms of winter and summer,[19] a natural way of accounting for the course of the war in his day, as appropriate for a general conducting a war as it was for a shepherdess to count her lifetime in terms of springs. He inserted speeches, the documentation and the mainsprings of that age, the collection and editing of which cost him so much, but which have the misfortune to be regarded by us as rhetorical exercises embraced by a great general. He often dwells at length, and at too great length, on matters of little significance. His history does not demonstrate sufficient proportionality with reference to the inherent significance of details to the total picture because—why should we not also say this—because he was still too close to the events, because he could not view them from an appropriate distance, allowing him to view them as a whole, because they were still pressing upon him, in a way *beneath,* not *before* his eyes. At the beginning of the war, he immediately decided to write his account of it; during the course of the war, he collected materials and ordered them; how could it be otherwise than that he had to write in segments, so that his history was completed not as a circle, as in the case of Herodotus, but in a straight line, as in a closeup, but with so much more *detailed* accuracy and decoration, everything not in parallel order, as in the case of Herodotus, but mixed up and sequential? But what do I say? *Completed?*[20] He did not complete it, and had he completed it, it could have become anything, but "not a *system* concerning the Peloponnesian War."

But now, the first among philosophers, who became a writer of history,[21] the amiable pupil of Socrates, who revealed to us the peculiarities of his teacher's soul, who was able to be philosopher and statesman in matters ranging from the raising of horses, the conduct of the hunt, and the art of budgeting, to the education of a prince and even to the counseling and the composition of encomia for rulers. When he proceeded to write history,[22] what else could it turn out to be but a system of statecraft and philosophy? How rich a range of opportunities was offered here to let the statesman, the general, the Socratic observer of humankind speak. Had Xenophon lived in our day, how different would his work have been? But now, too bad that, according to his understanding, a system and history apparently could not exist together; therefore, he isolated them completely. Wherever the states-man, the economist, the philosopher was meant to speak, well, there he let him speak, but not in the context of history. Whether he was the biographer or the reporter of a war, he was never less than the architect of the history of his hero, of his war; always nothing more than the most noble, the most gentle of writers of history. He was the writer of history who does not seem to be aware of a plan, of his own opinions, to whom it did not occur to arrange matters in accordance with these opinions and viewpoints; for him, the events seemed to fall into a certain order by themselves, the thoughts seemed to develop on their own, the history seemed to write itself. I do not believe that it is *one* of my favorite prejudices that ties me to Xenophon. But he is, at the point at which he meets the golden mean in his treatment of the vacillations of the age that preceded him and of the one that was to follow, for me the most classical of Greek writers of prose. He is a model, thus, of history; however, in whose work do we find history and the system further apart from each other than in his? And in whose work could they have been brought more completely together than in that of the author of the Cyropaedia, the teacher of the great Scipio, Lucullus,[23] and [empty space]

So much for Xenophon, but his successors hardly resembled him. The boundaries of this historical moderation became too confining for them; thus, they created for themselves a broader field. Writers of history turned into philosophers of individual histories. The clear procession of historical events within the context of quiet historical wisdom was too watery for their taste. The potion was spiced with philosophy, with doses ever larger, and finally of such potency that it could no longer be called history, but a philosophy composed at the occasion of a history, and now, of course, the history was indeed a system. The writer of history was no longer Xeno-phon, but Polybius[24]; I cannot offer a more complete example.

[portion struck out]

And so to avoid creating the appearance that I am selecting him to support my case, his latest British interpreter[25] may speak, who certainly knew him, and who even more certainly was more for him than against him: "Everywhere Polybius teaches in a didactic tone. Everywhere the official mien of the teacher, too sullen, too proud and condescending to make friends. This created in him the exaggerated eagerness to make himself clear, and clear again, resulting in repulsive repetitions and shaming the reader as if he were a pupil. Had Polybius written only for his countrymen, the Arcadians, so be it—however, not to be outdone, he raised himself to be the teacher of all of Greece, and he treats his readers as children. No writer of history of his day and of previous ages satisfies him, and he criticizes with utmost severity mistakes by others which he commits himself."[26] Hampton carries on, and even though he does not want to acknowledge that *Polybius,* aside from the main purpose of his history, *explicitly* had the subsidiary objective *promoting* the art of war, and even though he later praises him rather abundantly, he nevertheless cannot overlook the mien Polybius dared to adopt in regard to writers of history. To be sure, a statesman, a general, a philosopher who converses with us intimately in his study, and who, by means of thorough and profound reflections, enables us to learn from the misdeeds as well as from the prudence of past ages; by all means, the friend, the counselor, the companion of Scipio,[27] the teacher of Brutus, and even in our day the teacher of kings and heroes, as he should be in several matters other than the art of war, if he were to be read in terms other than those of Folard.[28] He was all this, to be sure, and yet much more than this as a writer of history. And whoever wants to be more than such a one, must necessarily come into situations in which he is no longer a genuine writer of history. So it is also with Polybius, whose history has already been called by others a philosophy stuffed with examples; and that, indeed, is a *didactic system.*

I skip the Romans,[29] and where will I find the moderns? Where I want to find them, partly in the company of mere and often pedantic raconteurs, partly among historical artists, who do nothing so gladly as paint, who guide us through historical periods as if they were tree-lined avenues, and provide us, to boot, with magnificent characters, portraits, and sketches that exist perhaps only in their brains; and practitioners of statecraft, at last, who manage to compose, on the basis of history, an entire didactic system for an entire nation in all its political dimensions. The first category probably will contain most of the Germans; the second will have the French, and the third the English and the Scots; and among the last, in particular, *Hume,*[30]— *Hume,* certainly one of the greatest minds of our age, always read by me with veneration. But read, may I say again, not as a writer of history, but as a philosopher of British history. He would not be worthy to be Hume's reader, who did not admire in him the clear-sighted statesman, the profound thinker, the penetrating narrator, the enlightening judge. However, as much as I wish to learn from him, the least among the plenty—is history. History is what Hume thinks of it, how the relationship of things appears to him, his judgment flowing from his perception, his perception of events and persons of the past, and how he positions them, but not necessarily how they happened and how they were.

I cite a British author because, among the Britons, there are the most noteworthy differences of mind and judgment regarding matters of national scope; therefore, the comparison of a variety of writers of history who think differently about an incident may demonstrate to us how wide a gap there is between history and a didactic system, between event and judgment.

Unexpectedly, thus, I have come in my Critical Grove to the point where I started, and what do I bring back with me from my mental stroll? It is roughly this:

A history may be a didactic system insofar as it presents to us *one* event, wholly, as if it were an edifice. However, if this event stands alone, it follows that such a presentation cannot be called a system.

Therefore, secondly, it must find out the causes of the event, the tie between cause and effect. This connection is not seen, but inferred, and the art of inference utilized is no longer history, but philosophy.

Finally, the third item. Should an extensive string of events be tied together with reference to *one* purpose, within *one* scheme, including the correspondence of the parts, the danger is so much the greater that this system, shaped according to the measure of one mind, will not be in every respect simple and clear history.

From these principles, which, if it were a matter of philosophical terminology, could be demonstrated rather conclusively, it would follow

that, as long as one believes in legitimate history, everything in it that might be considered system must be examined;

that the degrees of historical probability and the probability of the systematic part within it ought not to be confused;

that, the more plain it is and the more it is based upon obvious facts or data, the more probable is a history, and the more it is historical art, the more pragmatic it is, and the more instructive, perhaps, but also the more subject to examination;

that, to give a history to a nation, one ought never to proceed from the highest, the historical level, the pragmatic dimension of history, and so on, without first mastering the pure, clear, Herodotian way of writing and thinking. Should one proceed from the former, as for example in all six of the otherwise useful volumes[31] of the new historical Academy, one would be no further than in the conceptual stage (carrying out inquiries that might just as well not have been undertaken), and one would get as far as we have gotten with all the rules of the theater of the three unities[32] and the conceptual scheme, without caring a single crumb for the dramatic genius there and the historical genius here;

that historiography never deteriorates more than when it begins to be sophistry or even a system without historical foundation. In Germany, we have already made a good beginning at reasoning speciously, almost without knowing what about, of which, for example, Hausen's *History of the Protestants*[33] is evidence.

that, finally, that history is the best, in which what is history and what is system are quite distinct matters, connected indeed, but also clearly distinguished, and in which the author indicates to what degree he has drawn upon history and to what degree he has added his thoughts in the form of a system.—

Even if our present historical conjunctures in Germany had not led me along this trail of thoughts, it ought to be accepted as a self-examination to determine to what degree a reader, even in a history of art, has the twofold obligation to believe and to examine.

~ 2 ~

From *Journal of my Travels*

The following text is a document of Herder's enthusiasm for world history, as well as for cultures from all over the world. Frequent exclamation marks and somewhat abrupt syntax clearly demonstrate a new way of expression, which corresponds to a new way of thinking and feeling. This is one of several Herder texts that are considered crucial "triggers" of the German Storm-and-Stress movement of the early 1770s. The following is a programmatic passage from Herder's 1769 text, a kind of outline of his future historical and philosophical-historical writing.

Was the North or the South, the Morn or the Evening, the *vagina homi-num*?[1] Which was the origin of humankind, of inventions, arts, and religions? Did this originary force come suddenly upon the North from the Morn? Was it preserved there in the cold mountains like sea monsters under ice floes, and renewed in its giant's strength? Did it shape there its merciless religion in accordance with the climate, to fall upon Europe with its sword, with its law, and with its mores? If so, I see two streams, the one coming from the Orient through Greece and Italy, softly penetrating Southern Europe, thus giving rise to a gentle, southern religion; to a poetry of imaginative power; to the music, art, morality, and learning of the easterly southern regions. The second stream took the northern route from Asia to Europe, overwhelming the former in turn. Germany was part of that stream and, by right, this history of the North ought to be the subject of study in its fatherland: For, thank God, Germany became a troupe of southern colonies in formal learning only. If so, again, will the third stream not come rushing over from America, and the ultimate one, perhaps, from the Cape of Hope and from the world beyond it? How grand a story, the study of literature in its origins and spread, its revolutions up to now! And then to divine from America's mores, and Africa's, and from those of a new, superior southern world, the future shape of literature and world history! What a Newton does this task demand! Where is the point of departure? Eden or Arabia? China or Egypt? Abyssinia or Phoenicia? The decision between the first two will be made when it is shown that the Arabian language is a daughter of ancient Hebrew, and that the earliest monuments of humankind are not Arabian in disguise. The second question will be resolved when evidence is brought that China, in accordance with the de Guignes[2] hypothesis, is a daughter of Egypt, or when it is demonstrated, moreover, that she expanded first to India and to Persia, and only subsequently into Asia. The third option will be ruled out when it is shown that Abyssinia is merely a daughter of Egypt, and not the opposite, as Ludolf[3] and others argue; and, when Phoenicia will appear to be a daughter of Asia or Egypt, and not, as her alphabet appears to indicate, more ancient than Moses himself. How many ages of literature must have passed before we learned to know and to think? The Phoenician? Or the Egyptian, the Chinese, the Arabic, the Ethiopian? Or none of them? So that we, with our Moses, are in the proper place? How much more searching and discovering remains to be done! Our age grows equal to the task because of our de Guigneses, our Michaelises, and our Starkes.[4]—And that would take care only of the origins. Now the migrations. The *origines* of Greece—from Egypt or Phoenicia? Those of Etruria, from Egypt, Phoenicia, or from Greece?—And the *origines* of the North, from Asia, or India, or *aborigines*? And of the new Arabs? Of Tartar background or Chinese? And the nature and form of each, and further, the future shapes of American-African literature, religion, mores, manner of thought and laws.—A magnum opus of the human species, on the human spirit, the culture of this earth, of all regions, ages, peoples, forces, fusions, figures! Asian religion and chronology, and officialdom, and philosophy! Egyptian art, philosophy and government. Phoenician arithmetic, language, and luxury. All of Greece and Rome! Nordic religion, law, mores, war, honor! The papist age, monks, scholarship! Nordic-Asiatic crusaders, pilgrims, knights. Christian-heathen revival of scholarship! The French century! English, Dutch, German shapes!—Chinese, Japanese political life. The natural philosophy of a new world. American customs, and so on.—Grandiose theme: Humankind will not perish until everything is realized, until the genius of illumination has passed through this earth. Universal history of the world's formation!

~ 3 ~

From *This, too, a Philosophy of History*

This text, taken from Herder's programmatic first essay on the philosophy of history (1774), exposes in a nutshell Herder's methodological credo. The three parts concentrate on the past as firstly alterity and as secondly individuality, and on thirdly the history of the past as the art of integrating the first two in a totality. Herder explicitly rejects the idea of human history as a linear process of constant perfection, as well as the skeptical version of history as a chaotic movement.

This short excerpt is part of a text—*This, too, a Philosophy of History*—that became instrumental in the development of historicism, as well as in the fundamental criticism of the one-sided rationalism of the German *Aufklärung*.

I. No one in the world feels *the shortcomings of generalized characterizations* more acutely than I do. One portrays *an entire* people, epoch, region of the earth—*whom* has one portrayed? One compiles people and ages that *follow one another* in an *eternal alternation*, like the waves of the sea—whom has one portrayed? *Who* has been caught by the portraying word?— In the end, the many are still summed up in nothing but a *general term,* with each person perhaps thinking and feeling what he will—how imperfect a *means of portrayal,* how much one may be *misunderstood!*—

Whoever has noted, given the *uniqueness of one* human being, how *inexpressible a matter* it is to be able to express in a differentiating way what differentiates?[1] How he feels and lives? How *different* and *unique all things become for* him, after *his* eye sees them, *his* soul takes their measure, *his* heart feels them—how much *depth* there is in the character of even *one nation* that—no matter how often one has perceived and admired it—nevertheless *flees* from that characterization and, to say the least, in that characterization is so rarely recognizable *to everyone* to be grasped and truly felt—he will ask, is that the same as envisioning the ocean of entire peoples, ages and countries, of capturing them in *one glance, one sentiment, one word!* Faint, broken *phantom* of a word! The entire living portrait of the way of life, customs, needs, the characteristics of land and climate would have *to be added* or *would have to be provided beforehand;* one would first have to *sympathize* with the nation in order to feel a *singular one* of its *inclinations* and *actions, or all of them together,* to *find* one word, to *conceive* everything in the richness of that one word—or one will continue to read . . . merely *a word.*

All of us believe to this day that we still have *patriarchal, domestic,* and *human inclinations* like those possessed by the people of the Morn, that we are able to have *faithfulness* and *artistic diligence* like those possessed by the Egyptian; that we have *Phoenician agility, Greek love of liberty, Roman strength of soul*—who does not feel a *disposition* toward all this, if only there were *time, opportunity*—and . . . my reader, here we are. The most cowardly scoundrel doubtless still possesses a faint *disposition and potential* to be a magnanimous hero—but, between this faint disposition and *"the full awareness of being, of existence in such a character"*—a chasm! Thus, even if you lacked nothing but *time* and *opportunity* to transform your disposition to be like the people of the Morn, the Greek, the Roman, into *skills* and *genuine inclinations*—a chasm! Only inclinations and skills are talked about. But, to feel *the whole nature* of the soul that *pervades* all, that *shapes* all other inclinations and spiritual powers *in its image,* and *colors* the most indifferent of actions—to feel all of this, do not answer with words, but transport yourself into the age, into the region of the compass, into the entire history, feel your way into everything—only now are you on the way to understanding the word, only now will you escape from the notion that "all of this, taken singly or together, is within you!" Everything taken together within you? *The quintessence of all ages and peoples?* That alone shows the foolishness!

Character of the nations! Only *the data* of their *constitution* and *history* must determine it. Did not a patriarch "have inclinations *other* than those attributed to him by you? Or could have had?" I say *yes, indeed,* to both! Indeed, he had other, secondary characteristics, which are self-evident on the basis of what I have said or omitted, which are acknowledged by me, and by others who envision with me his history in the word that describes them; what's more, that he *could* have had far different characteristics—in *another* place, *at another time, with corresponding progress* of development, under *other circumstances*—if that is so, why then should not *Leonidas, Caesar,* and *Abraham* be *brave men of our century?* Could be!

But they weren't. On this question, inquire of *history—that is what we are talking about.*

Thus, considering the *mass of detail* of peoples and ages, I prepare myself likewise to encounter petty objections. That no people remained for *long* what it was, and could remain what it was; that *every people,* like every *art* and *science*—and what not in this world—*had its period of growth, flowering, and decline;* that each one of these changes lasted *only the minimum of time* that the wheel of human destiny could spare—that, finally, in this world *no two moments are the same*—that, therefore, Egyptians, Romans, and Greeks, too, were not the same at *all times*—I shudder when I think of the judicious objections that may be raised to this by people of wisdom, particularly those who know history! Greece consisted of *many city states; Athenians, Boeotians, Spartans, and Corinthians* were anything but the same—didn't they have agriculture in *Asia? Did not the* Egyptians once carry on trade as well as the *Phoenicians?* Were not the *Macedonians* conquerors as well as the *Romans?* Did not *Aristotle* have as speculative a mind as *Leibniz?* Did not our Nordic peoples surpass the *Romans in fortitude?* Were all *Egyptians, Greeks, Romans*—are all rats and mice alike?— No! Nevertheless they remain rats and mice!

How irksome it must come to be to address a public, from the *screaming* part of which (the nobler thinking part remains silent!) one must always expect *such* and even *worse* objections, and presented in *who knows what tone!* And that one must expect at the same time that the *large flock of sheep,* that doesn't know its right from left, so promptly follows suit! Can there be a *general picture* without *subordination* and *coordination?* Can there be a *broad view* without *elevation?* If you keep your face close to the picture, if you chisel away at the chip, pick at every dot of color, never will you see the *whole picture*—you will see anything but a picture! And if your head is full of images of a group to which you have taken a fancy, will your eyes be able to grasp the *totality of such changing epochs,* will they be able to *order them, gently pursue them,* sort out in each scene only the *main effects,* quietly accompany their *flowing together?* And now—to name it all! However, if you are unable to do any of this, history will flicker and flare before your eyes, a welter of scenes, peoples, epochs—read first and learn how to see! By the way, I know, just as well as you, that every *general picture,* that every *general concept,* is only an *abstraction*—the creator alone is able to conceive the total *unity of one, of all* nations in all their *manifoldness,* without thereby losing sight of their *unity.*

II. Therefore, let us move away from these petty objections, which miss the purpose and fail to see the point of view. Placed into the design of the grand totality—how miserable appear the "sundry *fashionable judgments of*

*our century concerning the merits, virtues, the happiness of nations so
distant, so changeable, based as they are merely on general scholastic
concepts!"*

If human nature, in reference to the good, is not *an autonomous divinity,*
it must *learn* everything, it must be cultivated in progressive steps, in a
gradual struggle it must *advance ever further;* if that is so, it will be shaped
most importantly, or even *exclusively,* by those *dimensions* which *move it*
toward virtue, struggle, and progress. In a certain sense, then, all of human
perfection is *national, secular,* and viewed most precisely, *individual.* Nothing is developed *unless the age, the climate, everyday needs, the world, the
destiny* provide the impetus; being separated from everything else, the inclinations and capacities that slumber in the heart can never turn into *skills;
therefore, the nation, given virtues of the most sublime kind on the one side,
on the other* may have *shortcomings,* may make *exceptions,* may reveal
contradictions and *perplexities* that will cause astonishment, but only in
him who brings with him his *own idealistic silhouette* of virtue drawn from
the compendium of his century, only in him who has sufficient philosophy
in himself to want to find in one spot on earth the entire globe—in no one
else! For anyone desiring to apprehend the human heart out of the *elements
of its living existence,* such *exceptions* and *contradictions* are entirely
human: Proportionality of energies and inclinations to reach a specific end,
which without them never could be *attained,* is therefore not at all the
exception, but *the rule.*

Let it be, my friend, that the childlike *religion of the Morn,* the *attachment* to the most gentle *sentiment* of human life, may reveal *weaknesses*
which, following the pattern of other ages, you condemn. A patriarch cannot be a Roman hero, a Greek *runner,* a *merchant* from the shores; nor can
he be that to which the ideal of your catheder, or your humor, has raised
him, in order to *give* him *false praise,* or *to condemn him bitterly.* Let it be
that he, compared to later standards, appears to you as *fearful, mortally shy,
weak, ignorant, idle, superstitious,* and if there is venom in your eye, *even
repulsive:* he is, what God, the climate, the age, and the world's epoch
could make him, a *patriarch!* He therefore possesses, in the face of the
shortcomings of later ages, *purity, the fear of God, humanity,* and possessing them he will be for every coming age eternally *a God!* What a figure,
compared to the *Egyptian, crawling, slavelike, a creature of the earth,
superstitious, and sad, severe* with *strangers, a thoughtless creature of
habit,* compared here with the *frivolous Greek, who shapes* everything *in
the image of beauty,* compared there with the *humanist in the grand style of
our century,* who carries all of wisdom in his head, and all the world in his
breast! Add to this the patriarch's *perseverance, faithfulness,* and *robust*

calm—can you compare this to the Greek *preference for boys* and *juvenile craving* for all that is *beautiful* and *pleasant?* And then again, should you want to adopt an ideal—I don't know whose—can you overlook the Greek's *frivolity, his dallying in religion, his lack* of steadiness in *love, modesty, and respectability?* However, was it possible for the *perfections* of the Greeks to be developed to this *extent* and to this *degree* without these *shortcomings?* You see, *Providence* herself did not demand it, she wanted to attain her purpose only in *change itself,* in the *advancement* through the arousal of *new energies and in the demise of others*—*philosopher* of the Nordic *earthly vale,* you who hold the *infant's scale of your century* in your hand, do you know more than Providence?

Powerful edicts of praise and chastisement, drawn by us from *a people we favored* in antiquity, to whom we took a fancy, and heaped by us upon all the world—upon which right are you founded? The Romans of old could be what they were like no other nation; they could do what *no one emulates,* they were *Romans.* They were atop a *pinnacle of the world,* and everything around them was *valley.* At the pinnacle of the world from the days of their youth, *shaped to think as Romans, they acted accordingly*—what wonder? And, what wonder that a *small people of shepherds and tillers of the soil* residing in one of the valleys of the earth was not the *iron-clawed animal*[2] able to act in this way. What wonder, then, that this people again possessed *virtues* not held by the noblest of Romans, and the noblest of Romans, in turn, at his pinnacle, under the duress of necessity, in cold blood could embark upon acts of *cruelty* that the shepherd in the *little valley,* again, did not harbor *in his soul.* At the pinnacle of that gigantic machine, such sacrifice, unfortunately, was often a *small matter,* often *necessity,* often (woe to humanity, how wretched you can be) a *blessing.* It was just this *machine,* which made possible *widely spread vices,* that *also raised virtue so high, spread its efficacy* so widely. Is humanity in *one* of its present states at all capable of attaining pure *perfection?* The pinnacle borders upon the valley. Surrounding noble *Spartans* there dwell *helots,* treated inhumanly. The Roman *triumphator,* colored by *divine purple,* is also invisibly *stained* by *blood. Brigandage, wantonness, and debauchery* surround his chariot; *suppression* before him, *misery and deprivation* in his train.—*Want and virtue,* in this sense, too, always dwell side by side in the human habitation.

Blessed *is the art of the poet,* magically it creates one of the earth's *favorite people* in godlike glow—the poet's art is *useful* also, for the human being is ennobled, too, by means of beautiful *prejudices*—but when the poet is a *historian,* a *philosopher,*[3] as most of them pretend to be, who thereupon, following the *one and only fashion* of their day—often a very petty and frail fashion—claim to *take the measure of all centuries*—*Humes!*

Voltaires! Robertsons! classical apparitions of twilight! What are you in the light *of truth?*

A *learned society of our day,* * without doubt with noble purpose, once presented the question: *"Which people in history was the most happy of all?"* And if I understand the question correctly, and if it does not lie *outside* the horizon of human capacity to respond, I would not know what else to say but, that at a certain time, and under certain circumstances, that point in time would come to every people, or there *never* was *one.* For if, again, human nature is not the vessel of an *absolute, autonomous, and unchangeable happiness,* as it is defined by the philosopher, it nevertheless absorbs everywhere *as much happiness as it can;* given the *flexible disposition* of human nature to *adapt to* the most varying conditions, needs, and trials, the appearance of happiness itself *changes* with every situation and point of the compass—(for, what else is it ever but the *sum of "the satisfaction of wants, the attainments of goals,* and *the gentle satisfaction of needs,"* which, after all, in each case grow out of *the land, the time, and the place?*); thus, at the root of it, all *comparison* becomes *precarious.* As soon as the internal *sense* of happiness, the *inclination,* has changed, the external *opportunities* and *needs transform* and *fortify* the *other* sense of happiness—who can compare the *differing modes of* satisfaction of *differing modes of* happiness in *differing* worlds? The shepherd and the patriarch of the Morn, the tiller of the soil and the artist, the sailor, the runner, the conqueror of the world—who can compare them? It is not the *laurel,* or the *sight of the blessed flock,* the *merchant vessel,* or the *captured banners* that matter, but the *soul* that *needed* it, *strove for* it, and now *attained* it, and did not *want* to attain anything else—each nation has the *center* of happiness *within itself,* as every sphere has its center of gravity!

Here, once more, the good mother has well provided. She placed the disposition toward *manifoldness* into the heart, but made each aspect of it so little *urgent* in itself, that, as long as only *a few* are satisfied, out of the notes that have been sounded the soul soon composes a *concert,* not perceiving the dormant notes, except insofar as they in turn *silently* and darkly *echo* the rising hymn. She placed the disposition toward *manifoldness* into the heart, and now spread *a part* of this manifoldness in a circle around us, at our disposal; now she *calmed* the human eye, so that after a little while of accommodation this circle became for it *horizon*—not *to look beyond;* hardly to *fathom* what is beyond! Everything that is still *akin* to my nature, what may be *assimilated* by it, I envy, aspire to, make it my own; *beyond*

---

*The gentlemen must have pursued a terribly high ideal for, as far as I know, they have never found a solution for their philosophical tasks.

that, benign nature has armed me with *insensitivity, coldness,* and blindness; it can even turn *into contempt* and *repugnance*—but has only the purpose to lead me back *to myself,* to let me rest at *the center,* upon which I stand. The Greek assumes as much from the Egyptian, the Roman from the Greek, as he needs for himself; he is *satisfied,* the rest *falls to the ground* and he does not reach for it! Or, when, in this development of *distinct national inclinations to distinct national happiness,* the *distance between people and people* has grown too far, behold how the Egyptian *hates* the shepherd, the nomad, how he *despises* the frivolous Greek! Thus any two nations whose inclinations and cycles of happiness *collide*—one calls it *prejudice, rudeness,* narrow *nationalism! Prejudice is* good—in its time, for it causes *happiness.* It forces peoples to rest in their *center,* attaches them more firmly to their *stems,* to flourish *in their own way,* makes them more ardent and thus also more happy in their *inclinations* and *purposes.* In this perspective, the most ignorant and most prejudiced nation often is the first one: the age of alien aspirations, and wishful ventures abroad is already *sickness, bloatedness, unhealthy profusion, premonition of death!*

III. Is it so, then, that the *universal, philosophical, philanthropic tenor of our century,* which grants to each distant nation, to each most distant epoch of the world "our own ideal" of *virtue* and *happiness,* is thus the sole judge of their customs, *to pass judgment* upon them by our standards alone, *to condemn them,* or to transform them *poetically?* Is not the good *dispersed* all over the earth? Because it could not be encompassed by one face of humankind, by one region of the compass, it was dispersed in a thousand faces, ever changing—an eternal Proteus—through all continents and centuries—and as Proteus changes and changes again, is it not higher *virtue* or the *happiness of the individual* toward which he strives? And yet, humankind remains humankind—though a *design of progress* becomes visible—this is my grand theme!

Those who, up to this point in time, have embarked upon representing the *progression of the centuries,* most of the time took along the favorite theme of the progression to *greater virtue* and *happiness* of *individual human beings.* In order for them to do so, facts were *enhanced* or *invented;* counterfacts were *shrunk* or *concealed;* entire aspects were *covered,* the meaning of words was *assumed, enlightenment* for *happiness,* some more refined *ideas* for *virtue*—and thus the *generally progressing improvement of the world* was turned into tales believed by no one, least of all by the genuine students of *history* and of the *human heart.*

Others who *saw the poverty of this dream,* and who did not know better, saw *vices* and *virtues alternate* like climates, perfections like a vernal tide of leaves *spring up* and *wilt again,* saw human customs and inclinations flutter like the *pages of destiny,* and turn—*no design, no progression, eternal revolution—weaving and tearing apart!—Penelope's labor!*—They fell into a *whirlpool,* embracing a skepticism in regard to all virtue, happiness, and the destiny of humankind, weaving it together with all of history, religion, and morality.—The newest fashionable tenor of the most recent, especially the *French philosophers,** is doubt! Doubt in a hundred *shapes,* but all with the dazzling title *"Based on the history of the world"!* Contradictions and oceanic waves, either one fails or whatever *is saved from being shipwrecked of morality and philosophy*—is hardly worth being mentioned.

Should there not be manifest *progress* and *development,* but in a higher sense than what has been assumed? Do you see this *stream* that flows on, as it issued from a tiny spring, grows, interrupted there, reappearing here, ever twisting and turning, digging further and deeper—and yet remaining *water! stream!* A drop remains ever only a drop, until it plunges into the sea— What if it were like that with humanity? Or do you see that growing *tree,* that striving human being? He must go through various *stages of life.* All clearly *progressing, a striving,* one upon the other in *continuity;* each separated from the other by apparent *pauses, revolutions, transformations,* and yet, each has the *center* of its happiness *within itself!* The youth is not *happier* than the innocent, blissful child, nor is the calm old man *unhappier* than the eagerly striving adult; the pendulum swings *with* always *equal force,* whether it reaches for its widest arc, and thus swings more quickly, or whether it swings in its slowest rhythm, and thus *approaches rest.* Nevertheless, there is yet an eternal striving. No one dwells in his age *by himself,* he builds upon that which *came before him,* and this again becomes nothing but the basis for the *future,* and it will not want to be anything but this— thus speaks *analogy in nature,* the eloquent *image of God* in *all works,* thus manifest in *humankind!* The Egyptians could not be what they were without the people of the Morn, the Greek stood upon the shoulders of the Egyptian, and the Roman mounted the saddle of the entire world—truly *progress, continuing development,* even though no individual might gain anything. The grand image tends toward totality. It becomes—that of which the history of empty hulls so gladly boasts, and of which it shows so little—*the stage of a guiding design on earth!* even if we should not see the ultimate design, the stage of the divinity, though only through the *openings* and *rubble of individual scenes.*

---

*The good and honest *Montaigne*[4] began it all; the dialectician *Bayle,*[5] a rationalizer whose contradictions as expressed in the reasoning of his Dictionary certainly could not be vouched for by *Crousaz*[6] and *Leibniz,* continued to have an impact on the century. And then the more recent philosophers, doubters of all with their own bold claims, *Voltaire, Hume,* even the *Diderots*—it is the grand century of doubt and wave-making.

At the least this vision is deeper than that philosophy which *muddles* things, which lingers only here and there, at the site of individual *conflagrations*, to turn everything into an *ants' play*, into the striving of individual *inclinations* and *energies*, without *purpose*, to turn everything into chaos, where one despairs of virtue, reason for being, and divinity. If I were to succeed in *tying together* the most disparate scenes without *confusing* them—to demonstrate how they *relate* to one another, how they *grow out of* one another, how they *lose themselves* within one another, all individually only moments in time, only through the progression *means to ends*—what a *vision*, what noble *application of human history*, what *encouragement to hope, to act, to believe*, even if one does *not* see *anything*, or *not everything!*—

~ 4 ~

Whether We Need to Know the End of History in Order to Write History

The following text constitutes the main part of the 122d letter of the *Letters Concerning the Advancement of Humanity* (1797). Herder explicitly addresses the analogy of ontogenesis and phylogenesis as a model of a philosophy of history. Moreover, it becomes very clear in these few paragraphs that Herder's fundamental assumption of "humanity" as the life of a species in the mode of asynchronic simultaneity *(Gleichzeitigkeit des Ungleichzeitigen)* is a significant critical assumption. This assumption has its basis in the system of Herder's thinking. World history, according to Herder, is the history of the differing manifestations of the potential of humanity—in the good as well as in the bad sense.

With this letter, Herder comments on James Burnett, Lord of Monboddo's *Ancient Metaphysics, or the Science of Universals.*[1]

You seem to believe that a history of humankind is not complete as long as one does not know the *outcome of things,* or, as it is said, one has not experienced the Last Judgment. I am not of this opinion. Whether the human species improves itself or worsens, whether it will turn at some time into angels or demons, sylphs or gnomes, we know what we have to do. *We* view the history of our species on the basis of the firm principles of our convictions regarding right and wrong, let the final act end as it may.

Monboddo, for example views humankind in his history and philosophy of humankind* as a system of vital energies, in which the elemental stage, plant life, animal life, and rational existence are set apart. Animal life, in his

---

*Ancient Metaphysics, vol. 3 (London: 1784). This part of the great work, because of the accumulated facts, would be well worth a German edition.

view, was at its highest stage when humans lived an animal-like existence. He finds echoes of this form of life in children. In his view, the stages through which the human passes as an individual also govern the course of life of the entire species. This is traced back by him to its first, naked condition in the open air, in the rain and in the cold, and he demonstrates the impact upon the human creature of clothing, the dwelling in houses, the use of fire, and of language. He shows the capacities possessed by this creature to swim, to walk upright, to exercise, and he finds in this condition the reason for the more extended span of human life, the larger bodies and their greater strength, of which primeval legends speak. On the basis of examples and reports he provides evidence that, because of the changing way of life, because of the consumption of meat and spirits, a sedentary mode of life in arts, crafts, and games, more delicate nourishment, sensual excesses and pastimes, the bodies of humans were weakened, became smaller, and life was shortened.—On the other hand he shows how social life and arts expanded the human mind, he shows how far the sagacity of natural man differed from the cleverness of civilized man, how all arts derived from imitation, and how the idea of the beautiful is unique to the condition of civilization. In both stages of human existence he finds nations, families, and individuals differing from one another, but the species in general *with declining animal powers,* and he has provided reflections on this topic which may be applied as one chooses.—

If we consider all this (as, after all, *Monboddo's* system, despite some of the peculiarities of the author, certainly does not deserve to be ridiculed), let us assume, what is also taught by history, that almost all peoples on earth at one time lived in a more primitive state, and that civilization was brought by only a few to others; what follows from this?

1. That, *on our mother earth all epochs of humankind do yet live and move.* There are peoples in the stage of childhood, youth, and adulthood, and they will probably be so for long, ere the seafaring grizzled old men of Europe, with their spirits, diseases, and slaving practices, transport them too into grizzled old age. Now, just as every humane duty obliges us not to disrupt the child's, the youth's stage of life, the energies and incentives that move him, the same mandate also prevails as to nations versus nations. I take great comfort in this respect from some conversations of Europeans, particularly missionaries, with foreign peoples, for example Indians, Americans; the most innocent responses, full of good spirits and sound reason, almost always were given by the foreigners. They responded child-like, to the point and correctly, whereas the Europeans with the imposition of their arts, customs, and doctrines usually played the role of jaded ancients who have completely forgotten what it is to be a child.

2. Since the differentiation of elementary, animalistic, vegetative, and rational energies takes place only on the conceptual plane, in which each human being consists of all of these, even though in different proportions, *one ought to beware to consider the one or the other nation as existing entirely on the animal level,* and to treat its people as beasts of burden. Pure intellect by itself does not require a beast of burden and as little as the most intellectual European can do without the vegetative and animalistic energies of his organism, as little does any nation exist entirely without rationality. The power of reason, of course, is manifold, depending on the sensibility that moves it in keeping with the distinct makeup of various peoples; nevertheless, it is and remains in all human manifestations *one and the same.* The *law of equity* is not alien to any nation; all have suffered for violating it, each in its own way.

3. If intellectual powers in various manifestations are the advantage of the Europeans, then *they can live up to this advantage in no other way but through reason and goodness* (both of which, fundamentally, are only one). If they act impotently, in furious passion, out of cold greed, in meanly-exalted pride, then *they* are the animals, the *demons* opposing their fellow humans. And who will guarantee to the Europeans that, some day, the same may not happen to them in several extremities of the earth, such as Abyssinia, China, or Japan?[2] The more their powers and polities in Europe age, the more unhappy Europeans some day leave that continent to make common cause here and there with the oppressed, the more intellectual and animalistic energies may join in a manner yet hardly imagined by us. Who can look into a future perhaps already carrying the seeds? Civilized states may develop where we hardly deem them possible; civilized states whither, though we considered them immortal.

4. Should reason in Europe some day, in ways not possible to be determined by us, gain so much in value, that it be joined with human kindness, *what a beautiful season for the members of the society of our entire species*! All nations would take part in it and enjoy this *autumn of reflectiveness.* As soon as the law of equity pervades trade and daily conduct everywhere on earth, all nations are brothers; the younger one readily will serve the older, the child the judicious elder, with all that is at its disposal.*

5. And would such an age be unimaginable? It seems to me that *it would have to appear in the course of necessity as well as calculation. Even our*

---

*Among many others I here once more recall *Le Vaillant's* recent voyage.[3] The difference noted by him between nations ruined by Europeans or maltreated, and autonomous peoples, is cutting. His principles, as to how to deal with these nations, are applicable to the entire globe.

excesses and vices must promote its appearance. In the discourse of the human species no rule should prevail, in its nature no nature dominate, unless such an epoch were brought about *by the inner laws of this species itself and by the dialectic of its powers.* Certain fevers and madnesses of humankind *must* diminish in the course of the centuries and stages of life. Europe *must* replace what it has wrongly taken, it must compensate for its wrongs, not as a matter of preference, but in keeping with the nature of things as they are. For, woe betide reason, if it were not to be reason everywhere, and the common good were not that which is the most commonly useful. The magnetic needle of our striving seeks this pole; after all the straying and wavering, it will and must find it.—

6. *So, let no one augur the decline and death of our entire species because of the graying of Europe!* What harm would it be to our species if a degenerate part of it were to perish? If a few withered branches and leaves fell from the tree that flows with sap? Others take the place of those that withered and flourish ever more freshly. Why should the western extremity of our Northern Hemisphere alone be the home of civilization? And is that really so?

7. *The greatest revolutions in the destiny of the human species up to this point in time have depended on inventions, or on revolutions of the earth;* in the immeasurable context of the ages, who knows all of these? Climates may change; owing to several causes many an inhabited country may become uninhabitable, many a colony may become a mother country. Only a few new inventions may cancel out many earlier ones; and since, at any rate, the highest exertion (unquestionably the hallmark of almost all European statecraft) of necessity must decline or be superseded, who can estimate the consequences? Our earth is probably an organism. We crawl about on the surface of this orange like tiny insects that are hardly noticeable, we torture one another and we settle down here and there. When heaven falls, the proverb says, what will happen to the sparrows? Should here or there a part of the orange rot, perhaps another generation will rise, even though the one that was replaced will not have passed away because of the intellectual dimension of its organism, its *reason.* Rather, it will have fallen victim to excess, vice, and the misuse of reason. It is certain that the cycles of nature in regard to *all* species on earth are related to one another, so that at the point when earth no longer provides warmth and nourishment for humankind, humankind here also will have attained its destiny. The blossom withers as soon as it has fully blossomed; but it also leaves fruit behind. Therefore, should the highest expression of intellectual energy be our destiny, it would be that energy which demands of us to leave to the future eon, unknown to us, a good seed, so that we do not die as cowardly murderers.

Monboddo regards our earth as an educational institution out of which our souls are saved. The individual human being can and should not view it differently, for he comes and he passes away. In the place at which, without willing it, he appears, he must help himself as well as he can, and he must learn how to organize *his* elemental and vegetative energies, *his* animalistic and intellectual energies. They gradually wane away, until his matured spirit disappears.—Here, too, *Monboddo's* system, incomplete as it is, is consequential, and I prefer it to many another *mercantile-political* history of humankind. A history of our species calls for mercantile-political considerations only in small part; its spirit is the *sensus humanitatis, sensibility and empathy for all of humankind.*

~ 5 ~

The Nemesis of History

In 1786, Herder published a lengthy and influential essay entitled "Nemesis. An Instructive Symbol,"* in which he gathered the different representations and meanings of the goddess Nemesis-Adrastea of antiquity. Beyond the investigation in the realm of mythology and iconography, Herder had in mind eventually to present Nemesis-Adrastea as the principle of measure, not only in the life of the individual but in the history of humankind as well. Herder repeatedly reminds his readers that Nemesis will be misunderstood if one interprets her as a deity of revenge or retaliation. As the symbol of the median between the extremes, she represents a principle not only of world history but also of historiography. In the following text, Herder concentrates on the role of Nemesis as a principle of human history in general.

It is a longstanding observation that the Father of Greek history, *Herodotus,* not only organized the course of history in accordance with Homer, but that the *thought* that *governs* the entire work, *its soul,* is that of the *epic.* That its soul could not be other than this, and what this term means for history, is presently the topic of our discourse.

1. Whatever is encountered by us in history grew from minute, unperceived, almost imperceptible beginnings; who sowed these sprouts? Who gave them seasons to thrive in, and drew from them blossoms and fruit, while others, as if through the power of a malicious destiny, perished, or took pains to grow?
2. That which in this matter depends on the will of man, compared to the

---

*See the excellent presentation of this text by Jürgen Brummack in Johann Gottfried Herder, *Schriften zu Philosophie, Literatur, Kunst und Altertum 1774–1787,* eds. Jürgen Brummack and Martin Bollacher (Johann Gottfried Herder, *Werke,* vol. 4) (Frankfurt am Main: Deutscher Klassiker Verlag, 1994), pp. 549–78, 1242–67.

invisible might that surrounds him, be it benignly or with hostility, is so little and so frail. The moment rushes past him. As if they were staged in an ambush, unforeseen and inescapable *"twists of fate"* burst forward; how may he prevail? How may he arm himself to face them?

3. And since the most weighty and sublime falls *first,* since everything terrestrial is frail, our eye turns to *splendid* ruins first, and dwells longest on them; since, finally, the *"struggle with fate"* (as it were, with invisible and resisting spirits) in the life of eminent, strong, and felicitous human beings is that which most attracts *sympathetic* contemplation, how else could it be but that in the history of human affairs it is this struggle that most concerns us?

4. If one now, fourthly, in reference to a Greek, adds to this that the wealth and the power of the barbarians, compared with the limitations and the sensibility of the Greeks, necessarily attracted them to a deity that brought down the barbarians' power and toppled their arrogance, it came about that, with or without being called so, a *Nemesis-Adrastea* became the guardian of Greek history, and is to this day the guardian goddess of *all human history,* essential to it, and inseparable from it. Let it be that she was perceived at first, in keeping with the course of civilization, by primitive humans as primitive, as enjoying human misfortune, as envious and pernicious; the more, as passions were tamed, reflective prudence and thoughtfulness also increased in the realm of history, the more brightly *this Nemesis* emerged on her triumphal chariot, revered by us as the *most just, the most patiently compassionate, the most swiftly ensnaring ruler of all human destiny.* Nowhere does she celebrate her triumph more calmly and splendidly than in history. Without invoking her name, the historian devotes himself to her; the guardian's chariot hovers above him, her step echoes in his ear as he observes the course of events. Either history is nothing but the retelling of external accidents, without rhyme or reason, or, should it not be accident, should there be *sense* within the accidents, making them the plaything of reason and absurdity, of good fortune and misfortune, what other deity could preside over history but *Nemesis-Adrastea,* the *daughter of Jupiter,* the astute observer, the strict avenger, the fairest, and the highly revered?

It would transgress the limits of this day to describe in greater detail the range of the homage paid by the historians of antiquity, *Herodotus, Thucydides, Polybius, Sallust, Livy, Tacitus, Plutarch, Herodian,*[1] *and others, to the deity who metes out;* homage paid by the one more rationally and more clear-sightedly, by the other more superstitiously; nevertheless, this much is certain: the more here, too, the fog of the *senseless-credulous* was lifted, and one recognized in the course of human events and destinies *order and regularity,* the more instructive and gratifying history came to be. Now that hostile *Ate,*[2] who enjoys human misfortune, no longer played arbitrarily upon the minds of humankind, but rather a lawgiver calmly penetrated the human breast, and checked the reins in keeping with a *rule,* it is at this point that the rational as well as the absurdly acting human, the rise and fall in the fortunes of empires consequent to the customs of the inhabitants, the *poco di più e poco di meno*[3] upon which in the context of things all depends, were subordinated to one *measure;* it is at this point that a *philosophy of world history* came to be. When human audacity, when ignorance and superstition clouded it, denied and twisted this measuring rod of truthfulness, the provocation carried with it, upon its own back, senselessness and sacrilege, deception and perdition.

Let it be granted to another age to contemplate the gradual path taken by *historical science* out of the darkness of monkish tales, absorbing with pain and difficulty this yardstick of Adrastea from the works of *Livy* and *Tacitus.* Italians, political Italians, were the people who, by separating morality and politics, raising distrust regarding the entire course of action in many of those who were wavering, making it longer and more difficult for themselves. For, there is *one* Nemesis, who guards *right* and *prudence* appropriate to humankind; or, should she be envisioned in the shape of two, they stand as sisters with equal attributes, as rulers of the world, beside each other upon *one* chariot. Though the time has not yet come that one would trust this truth, that "right is the highest prudence, that besides it there is no other," and act accordingly; it was considered a weakness in the venerable *Grotius*[4] that he believed in a *"Law of Humankind in War and Peace";* and historians who, based on principles of integrity, denied practical prejudices, in particular the *false honor* of their nation, usually were meanly repaid by the political hacks. The struggle between truth and error, however, is generally astir, and the decision as to whom victory should fall could not remain in doubt to even the most shallow doubter, since truth verifies itself.

There were two paths that joined in the end, that were pursued in the past century, even unintentionally, toward the objective of making history what it ought to be, *extending and narrowing* the view, yet *focusing* it upon even one point. At precisely the time that *Bossuet*[5] had completed his portrait of world history with splendor and good fortune, attaching all events to one "beloved people of God," *Pufendorf*[6] presented his *History of European States,* ordered by peoples and empires, in unvarnished shape, with dry *facts,* but well ordered. Laugh, if you wish, but at several German universities several texts of history as well as of statistics, written since then, have been given a degree of order, clarity, and usefulness, which were unattainable in the chaos of bygone ages. *Otto's* Republics, *Mascov's, Gebauer's,*

Achenwall's, Gatterer's, Schlözer's, Sprengel's, and Spittler's[7] basic texts present designs that cause me to be astonished at how much of significance and merit one is *capable* of saying about these matters with wisdom and kindness, without examining whether it was said consistently and whether it ought to be said for a mixed bunch of youthful pupils? The assemblage of states, peoples, and epochs of world history, however, in their alternation and competition with one another, constitutes a grand Olympia under the purview of impartial referees of the powers that govern the world: *Right* and *Prudence, Virtue and Fate.*

. . . The ultimate, and without doubt the greatest design of history, would be the design of Nemesis herself, representing the undiluted *history of humans* within all the concealments of states; with his perhaps most flawed work, *Voltaire* has earned indisputable merit pertaining to this history. For notwithstanding the many useless jests, the frequent gaps and incorrectness that may be contained in his *Universal History,* the freer view he cast around himself, the longer thread with which he tied everything together, above all the *principles of toleration,* the sentiments of *compassion* which he spread through all centuries, provide universal history with a standard that *Bossuet, Comenius,* and *Arnold* were unwilling to give to it. Travel accounts, maritime excursions, the passion for scientific discoveries, and the familiarity with the entire world benefited universal history; continuous and ever-growing in progressiveness, these efforts were in the long run able to teach humankind nothing but *humanity.* Whatever was perpetrated by Portugal in the East Indies through the Inquisition, by Spain in America with its treatment of the inhabitants, by both in Europe and in their own countries with the importation of gold and silver, what could not be accomplished by the slave trade, but only by the *rewarding of diligence,* by *mutual fairness,* by *common faithfulness,* what is wrought by wars, persecutions, uprisings, and revolutions, all of that has been demonstrated with incontestable proof by the history of the past century. Merit is earned by whoever places this history before the eyes of the beholder and who, with incontrovertible evidence, commands humankind to act with *humanity.* Subject to the brilliance of *justice and truth,* the consequences of vice and virtue, reason and unreason, love and hatred among human beings become the progressive *epos of human history.*

6

The "Querelle des anciens et des modernes"

In an article in the first volume (1801) of his periodical *Adrastea,* entitled "The Fine Arts under Louis XIV," Herder thematizes the famous "Querelle des anciens et des modernes." This dispute, which took place mainly in France during the second half of the seventeenth century, concentrated on the question of whether antiquity or the present could claim cultural supremacy. For Herder, this dispute has become obsolete insofar as it neglected the historical specificity of the multifaceted past; that is, Herder thus follows his concept of radically historicizing past and present.

The idle quarrel is well known which, throughout half a century, in France, England, and Germany, but preeminently in the first country, has been carried on regarding the *merits of the ancients and the moderns.* Even though much good was said in the process by both parties, the dispute could never come to an end because it was begun without a clear basis for the question, and it was almost always driven by vanity. Given such imprecise designations as the *ancients* and the *moderns,* without differentiation of the epochs in which they lived, the means they had at hand, the works they accomplished, their purpose in creating them, how was it possible to dispute over the question as it stands? In the end what mattered was the fact that the moderns, indeed, as they are, do not claim to be greater than the ancients, but suppose that they certainly *stand on a higher plane,* because they have lived through more epochs and experiences and possess a broader view of things before and around them, and so forth. It is said that, with the progression of the centuries, human reason and morality have matured. So let it continue to mature, and let it regenerate itself time and again, up to the

HISTORY

felicitous harvest. But the straw that is left behind ought not be considered a sacred relic; rather, it might be utilized productively.

If that were so, should the higher plane, the wider horizon, a learnedness drawn from broader experience be the advantage of the moderns, it follows from this by the same token that this advantage does not belong to any nation exclusively; for all of us are the latecomers, the ones taught often and amply by fate, all of us are the moderns. All of us are meant to have learned from these experiences; all of us are meant to utilize the higher plane of our existence with its broader vision for common purposes. In this regard, what do we care about a dispute about the ranking of nations and epochs? Whether the man who sang more beautifully, conceived nobler edifices, created with greater dignity was named *la Chapelle* or *Anacreon, Perrault* or *Palladio, Phidias* or *Girardon,* what does it matter? Should reason and morality have matured, let reason be shown precisely in the fact that peoples and epochs are forgotten and the best is learned the very best.

~ 7 ~

History

In this text, an excerpt from his periodical *Adrastea,* Herder points out the historic-ity of historiography. He does not write in indiscriminate support of all kinds of relativism, but he very distinctly makes his readers aware of the political and ideological determinants of historiography: reading old histories means reading them in their historical contexts. Another point in Herder's article is that history requires a certain form of publicity, in the modern sense of the term. Absolutism essentially does not need a public except for purposes of representation. History, according to Herder, presupposes a critical public.

Under Louis XIV it [i.e., history] did not exist. He used to remunerate historiographers; but they wisely neglected to carry out their task. He took them along into the field, to observe his deeds; *Boileau*[1] loudly trumpeted: "Great monarch, cease to be victorious, or else—I will cease to write" (Louis's ear was accustomed to this kind of praise); but he who ground out satires and odes did not write history. *Racine,*[2] the delicate, naive *Racine,* almost fainted when he unwisely mentioned the name of *Scarron*[3] in the presence of the king and Mme. Maintenon as that of a buffoon, and the king, in turn, referred to Racine most ungraciously in an anonymous memo-randum entrusted to Mme. Maintenon, concerning the then-prevailing mis-ery of France; the poor poet subsequently worried himself to death. *Racine,* in other words, did not write history. Pater *Daniel,*[4] a Jesuit, knew better how to handle this type of thing. In his history of France he made such prominent mention of the d'Aubigné family, of which Mme. de Maintenon claimed to be a member, that his book quickly gained currency among the courtiers, and through them in wider circles. He became the royal historiog-rapher, held his tongue, and enjoyed his pension.

How can anyone think that a monarch such as Louis during his lifetime would have a historian? If it is his first duty to tell the truth, to avoid telling falsehoods, and to remove with bold strokes luster and glitter wherever they distort the events or falsify characters, how was a historian thinkable at a court, under a government, which was all glitter, glitter of such numbing, blinding power that it transformed the world around it into a magic cave in which everywhere only the name of the grand monarch gleamed. The unique expression of Louis, "L'etat? c'est moi!" prohibited all manner of history in the presence of his eyes.

And how far did these eyes reach! He, who assaulted the Dutch, because of a few public mockeries on their part, with an awesome arsenal of armed power,[5] he, who banned *Bussy-Rabutin*[6] because of an impudent couplet, who for the sake of *Telemachus* was *Fénelon's*[7] irreconcilable enemy, a ruler such as he suffered no history.

At the least, he suffered no history other than the one that was presented to him from his own mementos, at his cost, a *metallic-gilded* history, made of memorial coins struck for him with inscriptions for the composition of which he had created his own academy, a full-scale, gilded history.

As a result, his enemies mocked him so much more maliciously, and those persecuted by him screamed so much the louder. From both sides, therefore, no history was to be expected which provides a calm assessment in toned-down light.

But the scenes move on, the times change and present themselves in their own consequences; only at this point does *comparative* history begin. Let no one despair that we or our descendants shall not learn in terms of history about the great events of our time. Our descendants, too, will gain the distance from which alone they will grant *an assessment with an unblemished* view. Whereas in the beginning of the eighteenth century *Louis, William, Eugene, Marlborough,*[8] and others were the heroes, there were others in the middle of the century; all have found their measure.

The most damaging disease of history is an *epidemic delusion of nation and epoch,* to which in all ages a frail humanity is inclined. Nothing is deemed more important by us than the present; nothing is rarer and greater than that which we experience. Should this narrow sentiment now be joined also by blossoming national pride, ancient prejudices of several kinds, contempt for other peoples and times, ambitious external endeavors, conquests, victories, above all, at last, that *comfortable or grand vanity,* that deems itself as the center of the world and the pinnacle of perfection and views everything under this premise, then this entire Chinese portrait is pervaded by a distortion of events and figures which, given appropriate talent on the part of the presenter indeed may entertain, perhaps even enchant, but in the end still will be quite tiresome. We feel deceived by the sparkling presentation and we are indignant because of this deception; for the subsequent period has stripped off the false veneer, rearranged the events, and *patterned* the figures *free of adornment*. How few are the histories of the previous century, and of those that preceded it, which may yet be read and found in agreement with our judgment of the merit of things! Presumptions, designs, battles, encomia, victories—at the end of the century everything has received a different measure; and who guarantees us, yes, who would be so presumptuous to think that he already possesses this measure, corresponding most certainly and clearly to the intentions and the original estimate of things? At any rate, we have progressed in the meantime.

The history of *William of Orange and Queen Anne* suffered the same fate, though for other reasons. The ferment of change among Whigs and Tories, who confounded a hundred things and altered their aspirations with every change of ministries, yes, who often did not themselves know what they wanted, for a long time made impossible an unvarnished view of events and characters. *Swift's* history of the last years of this queen[9] is the driest of his works, and though it aspires to be honest, it is yet also one-sided and partisan. An awakening is called for to bring order to the dream and the urgency of events, if it is—dreamed indeed.

How much is entailed, after all, in the readily spoken dictum—*History of the Modern Ages*. An estimable pedagogue assigned a rhetorical exercise on the thesis, "that modern history, though more pleasant, is, however, by far more uncertain than the ancient,"[10] and, as an eager admirer of ancient history, he advanced several reasons to strengthen his thesis. Aside from the uncertainty which is probably shared proportionally by ancient and modern history, modern history is much more complex and convoluted than the ancient. The conduct of our affairs, the tools and accessories to their realization, even more the designs and characteristics of the modern world have lost that *plain self-evidence* that magically attracts us in the history of the Greeks and Romans. All events on the European stage run into one another and their primary motives of action are often where one would least suspect them, in the darkest corner not, as one might think, of a cabinet, but of a servants' chamber or a room even more secretive. The organ stops of a state (called departments) often resound from such confusion, or else one of them, usually the war department, drowns out the others so loudly that a history of the period, that is, the drawing of a balance, could for certain be the attainment only of an Orpheus, an Amphion, or even a heavenly genius. For example, should *Boulainvilliers* have undertaken to draw a portrait on the basis of the forty-two folio-size volumes of reports on the state of France submitted at the order of the Duke of Burgundy,[11] how aristocratic it would have turned out to be! Had *Bossuet* written a history of his time, how clerical a shape it would have taken on, as, for example, the Abbot de Choisy turned his king into a veritable David and Solomon. The youngest, latest daughter of Mnemosyne is the muse of an authentic history[12]; when we come upon her or her predecessors by the middle or the end of the century, with how much joy will we greet her, with what rich hope in the prospects of future times do we want to embrace her!

∼ 8 ∼

Expectations for the Coming Century

The following text is another article taken from Herder's periodical *Adrastea,* this time from volume 3, published in 1802, one year before Herder's death. Prompted by the turn of the century, Herder questions the validity of any forecasting or predicting of the future. While clearly seeing a difference between the beginning and the end of the century, Herder admits various ways of predicting the future, but only if they are based on reason, experience, and knowledge of history. Thus, at the end of the life of the philosopher of history, this text once again puts the question of what kind of laws govern history and whether human beings are capable of recognizing them.

Toward the end of *each* century, humans, as we note from the pages of history, braced themselves to meet the new century with vigor. Feeling more or less clearly that they tarried unduly, they wanted to make up quickly for what they had neglected before the new century arrived, so that it might usher in a *new age.* The steeds of eager desires and wishes saw that they were close to a goal, a sheltered spot; they gathered their energies and snorted as they hurried along.

Thus, each new century embarked upon its course in *splendor.* One wanted to mark its entry with something new and grand; one adorned it beautifully, the *portal of hope.*

To demonstrate this for the entire course of the Christian era would be too extensive an excursion; with the more recent centuries, the impact of this *jubilation* becomes clearly visible. What agitation toward the end of the thirteenth, at the beginning of the fourteenth up to the eighteenth centuries in the minds and souls of humankind! To this agitation we owe, in part, *Petrarch, Hus, and Luther,* the revolution in the arts, the Reformation, and so many a design, foundation, endeavor, and initiative.

And in *our* age—who does not think of the waning of the eighteenth century with silent horror? Beginning in 1790 and up to 1800 there were occurrences not witnessed by the entire previous century, though the ground for much of this had long been prepared. But, how many of the unfortunate are no more, who, at the beginning of our century, hoped for a *new world*! In the world of politics and philosophy the aspirations and hopes gathered storm; the new century was to be the age of *autonomy,* in which everyone was to issue the laws for *himself.* Even a *new form of poetry* and *criticism* was to see the light of day; yes, one believed oneself to possess it already, a poetry and criticism which were said to have the advantage of not being tied to *any previous epoch,* but rather descended from the heavens to dwell *incarnate* in chosen individuals.[1] It was believed that, in the year 1804, the entire world would be turned to this new poetry, metaphysics, and criticism, yes, on its wings be converted to new forms of physics and medicine; nothing but *these* writings would be read.

What a strange contrast between the beginnings of the eighteenth and the nineteenth centuries! At the beginning of the former, everything was drawn from the heavens; according to the younger *Helmont,*[2] the millennium was to begin in 1734; according to *Petersen,* all things were to be *brought back to life* and he welcomed the blessed age with lovely voices.[*] One prepared for it through prayer, penitential sermons, and sharp rejection of abuses and vices; the chosen and the persecuted supported one another and lived in hope. At the end of the century, one renounced God, no longer expecting assistance from above; the fortune of humankind was to be based *on autonomy; on their own they were to* provide and maintain their due. In their day people such as these were called *enthusiasts, fanatics, and visionaries;* the names with which these people adorned themselves are remembered by everyone. *Autonomy* called for an exalted form of *egotism* even in the matter of designation.

How much fulfillment may be hoped for and not hoped for in centenary expectations must be told to us by reason, experience, and the history of bygone ages; for unfortunate is the youth who falls into such a whirlpool of confused ideas and coarse or refined presumptions. He finds salvation late or he drowns; at any rate, he always lost, along with the yardstick of his life, also his best years as well.

---

*Petersen's *Stimmen aus Zion* (1696).

Part II

Mythology and Historiography

*

The Will to Move

is

Wonder, the naming instinct;
but methods too so that the
syntax of linking to
equivalences had real

equivalences (measurement)
in time (cause) or space (mathematics)
the chaos of movement
the arbitrary unleashed →
the same, so that we might
move **beyond** yes. but were

~ 9 ~

On Monuments of the Distant Past

The following excerpts from a 1792 collection entitled *Zerstreute Blätter* (Scattered Leaves) demonstrate several principles of Herder's approach to documents of world history. Above all, the criticism of the sources requires an understanding of the documentary nature of the monuments of cultures from all ages and places. Each must be treated in the same differentiating way; the specificity of each source has to be maintained. On the other hand, Herder makes an implicit plea for comparative history in order to obtain reliable data to explain these documents in the context of the totality of human history. Finally, Herder takes the old monuments as witnesses to the youth of humankind. Thus, for Herder, world history becomes the name for human history in general. Herder ends his text of the *Zerstreute Blätter* with the following statement: "Just as the needle of the compass reacts differently at various locations on earth, and yet is subject to capital laws, so the power of imagination, the taste, the manner of composition of peoples varies, and yet everywhere it is and remains the same humankind."

Part I

When Pope begins his "Essay on Man" with the truth that in our limited life there is little left to do but "to look around and to die," it seems that he means by this *"look around"* a bit more than the mere *marveling* at things that some animals might have in common with us. Wonder is the first child of curiosity; however, curiosity must also become the mother of scrutiny. A traveler who would bring back from his pilgrimage among ruins and monuments nothing but the truth "that everything is in vain," and who would confer upon his thus gained indifference the air of a wise man's equanimity, would not have gained much thereby; rather he perhaps will have lost some of his former effectiveness within a more limited sphere. A melancholy pose upon the ruins of the distant past may look picturesque; but it is neither satisfying nor useful.

The human mind, therefore, in several ways is more effectively occupied when it takes note of the remnants of ancient revolutions affecting the inner makings of our earth as well as of the monuments of the distant past dispersed almost everywhere on its surface. In reference to the former there has not been a lack of hypotheses to arrange many of these manifestations together in a system, and to explain thereby the formation of our globe; in reference to the latter, one still proceeds more cautiously to collect individual facts and to explain others, and only a few bold spirits have dared to attempt a general synthesis. Who, indeed, would already venture to attempt one now, since so many documents remain undeciphered, others have hardly been reported or have been insufficiently described, and we completely lack knowledge of others that may be necessary links. Discoveries, in the meanwhile, proceed with great rapidity, and even the dullest person is compelled to take an interest. Yes, and what is even more noteworthy, the spirit of discovery of our age is evidently gaining in certainty, in impartial demonstration, in learned accuracy, and in veracity of the conclusions reached, because the centuries of ignorant monks or deceiving proselytizers are almost past. One traveler follows upon the footsteps of the other; one corrects, one ignores the other; and even when, as is to be expected, some secret reports which once concealed a selfish agenda will be made public, the *history of the monuments on the surface of the earth* will fall into the same pattern that has been quite vigorously followed for several decades in the study of the subterranean record of the distant past, and that no doubt will yield many a new result. The more slowly we proceed thereby with general hypotheses, the firmer the edifice will turn out to be.

Therefore, as a fellow wanderer among the plentiful ruins of our earth, I, too, will be granted permission to make a few comments which either will guide the thoughts of others, or may be improved upon by them.

1. First of all, it seems to me, one ought *not to base the entire exegesis of all the old and even the most ancient monuments left by all other peoples on the Hebraic legends of the primeval world,* but accept them merely for what they are, the reports of a pastoral people regarding the areas in which they lived. As little as the six days of creation will resolve for the geologist the question of the structure of the earth, as little may the family chronicles—indeed worthwhile in and of themselves—of this people provide satisfaction for all the peoples of the earth. The genealogy of Noah's sons appears to be nothing but a map of the regions which were known to the collector of the information, brought before us in a projection as he saw it and as he linked it to the progenitor of his people, according to characteristics which he does not name for us. So it is that, also at a later time, the

peoples dwelling around Palestine were connected with the Hebrews only in respect to kinship relations and referred to by them in terms either of honor or disgrace. To the researcher of the broader aspects of antique monuments this reference to kinship relations is an impediment rather than a help; it may lead him far astray and, in the end, he will have gained from it little more than Hebrew names. However, it is now common knowledge from all parts of the world, that peoples rarely, or almost never, call themselves what they are called by foreigners; much less that all peoples on earth should be known by names which were given to them by an isolated people on the basis of a kinship chart. What, for example, is gained by *Bruce* in calling his artful troglodytes *Cushites,*[1] except that he casts doubt for us upon the consistency of his hypothesis, and that he restricts the range of our vision. He might just as well have called them *Cainites* or *Kabyles,*[2] and thereby he would have given them more noble descent. Therefore, in reference to all monuments, the so-called Great Deluge ought to be forgotten, whether they were built previous to it or, as the Bedouins say of the Pyramids, before Adam's creation; unless there is other evidence giving the researcher doubts or disclosure, this chronology should neither satisfy him nor tempt him into a forced hypothesis running counter to other facts. Even less ought the researcher in this matter rely on the later recollection and so-called tradition of ignorant Arabs and other Mohammedans, since it is known how clouded the sources were from which their entire tradition flowed, with what lack of knowledge they accepted it, and compounded it with a thousand entanglements. Thus, when they show him here the tomb of Adam and Eve, there Job's and Abel's, these testimonies have as little documentary value as if they were pointing out to him the borders of the former Paradise. The primeval collector of the Hebraic tales already drew these from only one tradition, and he placed his Eden at the source of four streams, which nowhere on our earth spring from one and the same source. It is another matter with monuments that are exactly fixed on the basis of ancient written testimonies, or in reference to which oral tradition has managed to preserve itself on the basis of established circumstances of history. Otherwise, the name of Solomon in the legends of the Morn regarding the erection of their monuments is to be trusted as little as, in other regions, the name of Alexander or Julius Caesar.

2. *Rather, let each monument speak for itself, and explicate itself, where possible, in its location,* without our dragging in an explanation from a favorite region. If, for example, the rawest beginnings of hieroglyphic script in the form of human or animal figures or other symbols are encountered in Siberia or Mongolia, carved into rock and marked with red coloring, what is more natural than to conclude that here, too, a people once attempted what

was endeavored by almost all barbarians in any region of the world, and what daily is attempted by every child when it crudely sketches living figures and conveys with them any kind of remembrance? Such figures are noteworthy, but not miraculous; rather, one would have to wonder why such as these occur no more frequently on earth, even if the reason for this were not obvious. Since artistic culture in most regions of the old world is very ancient, childhood efforts such as these have long been lost, and they have been preserved only in the regions distant from the center of culture, in northern Asia, America, and perhaps inner Africa and on the islands. If they were someday brought together, it would be possible to discern in them too those epochs of progress in human dexterity and practice which particularly manifest themselves in all forms of art, for example in Chinese script, in the hieroglyphics of the Egyptians, and, yes, according to a comparative compilation of a few of those North Asiatic figures, *even in them.** In reference to the remote ages preceding our historical record, such efforts do not provide any conclusion; for, how easy it was to make the effort, and how many were the advanced peoples who were from times immemorial in contact with this stretch of northern Asia!

In Asia Minor, on the other hand, everything has deteriorated so much that, except for the ruins of Baalbek and Palmyra, which were protected by their desert, in Syria, Palestine, Mesopotamia, Assyria, and Chaldea, one encounters few or even no remains at all of the ancient wonders of the world and their capitals,** this again unfortunately is explained by the well-known history of these peoples, by the materials used in the construction of their cities and monuments, and finally by the changes even in the soil and in the climate of these regions. The seat of an idol carved in stone at Aradus, rock tombs, remains of aquaducts in the desert, leftover piles of baked bricks, partly marked with letters, in places where once the greatest splendor of the world prevailed, are in a way the minimum one might expect, and so much the more should one make use of this minimum. Wherever possible, no inscribed stone of these regions should be overlooked, yes, nowhere on earth should an undeciphered alphabet be underestimated; it can be compared to others, it can once be deciphered. Praiseworthy, therefore, is the effort expended, for example, by *Niebuhr*[5] in

---

*Strahlenberg,[3] tab. 16, 15, 14, 4.

**Oberlin's *Orbis antiqui monumentis suis illustrati primae literae,* Strassburg, 1790, may serve as a very useful inventory of the monuments of antiquity of the entire earth. Meiners, *Beschreibung alter Denkmale,* Nürnberg, 1786,[4] beginning with p. 12, covers only those monuments, "the originators of which are completely unknown and all of which point to the presence of more sizable and civilized peoples than were encountered at the time of the discovery of the New World at great distance from these monuments."

tracing the inscriptions at Persepolis, in Arabia, and in the part of Egypt traveled by him; had Bruce, who saw so many more hieroglyphs, been able to continue his effort, we would be farther along, since he himself counted the total of them at only 200 and some. If these efforts, then, should once be continued with reference to the monuments of Inner, South, and East Africa, Ceylon, in India, in western North America and wherever such characters are found, and should Europe be made their depository, it would be possible, at least here and there, to link them together in rows, and one would no longer need to make do with the obscure designations of unknown characters. An evocative monument may someday be for us a chapter of Genesis, a voice of the distant past.

3. *It is not beneficial for the elucidation of monuments when the peoples among whom they were erected are considered separately, as it were in isolation, as if no other were present any longer on earth.* The strained premise with which we are beset in this matter springs in part from the dearth of reports we have regarding the connectedness and commerce of the ancient world; even more, however, it springs from the distorted image which has been impressed upon us by the condition of Europe during its barbarian centuries. Fortunately, however, this condition was only a sorry interlude of history, which did not entirely suspend the extensive communication that was carried on between the peoples of Asia, Africa, and Europe even at that time,[*] and which least of all should be interpreted as a detriment to more distant ages. Our Genesis itself reveals, in its restricted realm of the patriarchs, a condition of the world in which there was necessarily much in common among the peoples with regard to crafts, the arts, even the sciences and luxuries;[**] and yet, after all it was the least of the concerns of migrating herdsmen to record things of this sort. Now, since the history of the Greeks is so early and distant, why would we not want to admit as witnesses *facts still manifestly present,* in the face of which, after all, a foreign, later writer of history disappears like a babbling breath. Was it possible to erect Persepolis, the tombs of the kings in its vicinity, the Indian temples at Ilura, on Salsetta, at Elephante, on Ceylon, the famous antiquities of Upper Egypt reaching deep into the desert and into Abyssinia, was it possible to erect all of these without the arts and luxury? It made me very glad, therefore, when I heard the truth proclaimed loud and clear to all his fellow scholars by a thinker who encompasses history broadly,[***] that "the

---

[*]See Fischer's *History of German Commerce,* part 1; Sprengel's *History of Geographical Discoveries;* Anderson; Bruce; Robertson; etc.[6]

[**]Gatterer's *Outline of World History,*[7] part 1, p. 31, has conveyed a brief sketch of this.

[***]Schlözer's *World History,*[8] part 1, pp. 85 ff.

human species is only One." That through all ages its parts have dwelled within one another, and will "and is meant to dwell within one another." For, as difficult as it is to make this apparent at every moment in the treatment of history and its monuments, it nevertheless is the embryo of the entire *living body of our history.* The human species is a whole; from its genesis it began to organize itself, and it shall consummate this organization.

A great revelation concerning the monuments of antiquity is therefore given, when the *ways in which peoples meet and interact with one another* are observed. Many monuments are evidently situated along the path of such communication, and they were probably created by it. Thus, the antiquities at the coast of eastern Africa; thus, perhaps, those others at the western coast of the Indian peninsula. Thus it was with Babylon, Damascus, Palmyra, Tyre; it does not appear to be any different with some of the remains in northern Asia, and I consider, for example, the city of *Madschar,* concerning the strange origins of which as from the wild Madschars, so much amazement has been expressed,[*] as nothing but a *site of commerce, a settlement of the Persians on a generally known route of world trade.* Should inscriptions be found there, and I hardly doubt it, they will clarify several issues. Even if some monuments should not be situated immediately along the trade routes of peoples, as long as they reflect wealth, trade, and therefore connectedness among nations, and even imitation in the arts, and if history should not shed light on the matter, then legends must take the place of history, and then, it seems to me, the ancient Egyptian, the Persian, and the Indian fable, as long as they are supported by authentic testimony, by the *monuments as such,* may always serve us in lieu of a Homer of those nations. At any rate, it seems that Asia, from the very outset, was a very vibrant region of the earth, and to this day it is the mother and the tomb of all world trade.

4. *Only the state of a dawning world may elucidate for us the resplendent monuments of high antiquity.* It evidently was their destiny to serve as *temples, palaces, and tombs.* Concerning temples, everyone knows what religion (at that time entirely a matter of the state) meant for all who initiated the construction and carried it out. The kings were gods on earth, and the priests were their tools or governors. The people lived frugally, and their needs were modest in those regions; they subordinated themselves willingly to mild laws, beholden to the discipline of kings and priests. To build for the gods a temple, for the king a mansion or a tomb, to them was

---

[*]See Büsching's *Magazin,*[9] part 5, p. 533. *Fischer,* one of the men most meritorious in regard to the history of the Northeast, already assumed the Persian origin of this town; my own hypothesis, however, does not fully correspond to his; the discovery of inscriptions would provide the best answer.

one and the same; for themselves, the people gladly dwelt in sheds which were not meant to be monuments. If one then presumes so orderly a state of the empire as that which, for example, is demonstrated by the figures on the walls of Persepolis, and adds a religion such as that of the Persians was by its essence, a religion which called for nothing but active life, the tilling of the soil, and the sustaining of the world with good fruit; if one should then, during the earliest dawn of the heroic age of the world, think of those fortunate conquests of which the Persian fable speaks, then it will be right here, at this place in the heart of Asia, between Egypt and India, upon an elevation which offered its own marble to the builders, where the power of the mountain, the mass of the people, the reverence for its king as the image of the deity could join with the arts of other countries as if it were the hub of all, it is here that monuments such as those at Persepolis become quite comprehensible. It was no different in India and Egypt, where probably, most of all in Egypt, the arts were much more at home. The segregation of the people into castes, the strict subordination of these to laws, prescriptions, and priests, the fixation of specific occupations, the contentedness of the people under their benign sky, subject to a mildly despotic government; the way of life of the Egyptians, at last, among whom everything proceeded from caves, and whose art preeminently consisted of rounding out these caves and of decorating them, of shaping protruding rocks into the images of gods, sphinxes, and obelisks; only a constellation of such conditions in such an age made possible monuments such as these. Today we are as little able to build pyramids as we are to build obelisks. Even the age of our great Gothic cathedrals in Europe appears to have ended; our diligence, our statecraft turns toward a greater number of objectives which are completed more quickly and are often also more useful. That so much effort was expended upon the *tombs of kings* in itself fully demonstrates the youth of the world. One enjoyed life on earth, one wished for immortality, and one had not yet dared to secure it beyond the grave, so one sought it *in the tomb*. The man, for whom during a short life the world stood at his command, built for himself the most splendid *eternal dwelling,* into which he slipped as a corpse, according to legend often with much treasure, by way of a secret corridor known only to the priests, to seek there eternal rest or an eternal life in the tomb. All of this breathes the spirit of the dawn of the world's ages. *He* was the giant who built these monuments.

5. *In regard to all monuments of the distant past, one must look not only back to the causes that advanced them, but also at the effects which came to be because of them; for no work of art stands lifeless in the history of humankind.* Everyone is familiar with the more recent hypotheses by means of which attempts have been made to reach back to a primeval people of

arts and inventions; these efforts have been made ever since the box of Noah was relegated to utter uselessness. An impartial researcher of the most ancient monuments need not be troubled for the time being by any such hypothesis; for him the first primeval people is rooted in the *cooperation of the peoples,* in the diverse *efforts at organizing them;* and in viewing the chain of things, he looks not only at that which preceded, but also at that which followed. More than of anything else, he takes note here of *human nature,* in a way *created for the second time,* that is to say, he takes note of the enormous attachment that binds each of the most ancient peoples even after millennia, to its region of the earth, to its religion, and to its political constitution. No European tie may bind the peoples as, for example, the Ganges binds the Indians to their sacred places and pagodas. The Persians with their temples of fire were less tied to a fatherland, since the *palace of Dschemschid* appears to have been merely a sanctuary of their political constitution. And yet, how very strong has been the influence of this people, especially in its original dwelling places, continuing to make itself felt in ways partly unrecognized to this day! *The caves and temples of Upper Egypt* have long since become the dwelling places of nocturnal birds and brigands; their impact, however, their reputed wisdom, their secrets, their symbols, how far abroad have they been dispersed, in what forms have they been metamorphosed! Finally, the miserable *crypts of the Jewish Land,* originally caves of the troglodytes, subsequently tombs of the kings and the rich, how much have they caused to come about that, without them, would hardly ever have been spread among so many peoples! In these subterranean tombs, there came to be an assemblage of the patriarchs, a realm of the dead *(Scheol),* filled with the eternal life of shadows. Here flowed the rivers of Belial, here death gnawed; here, in these rocky chasms, resurrection was revealed. Had the bodies been burned in Asia Minor as they were in India, the concept of the transmigration of the souls probably would have evolved or been perpetuated here, too, and providence would have chosen another spot on earth as the birthplace of consoling hopes needed by an oppressed humanity. Thus everywhere the same. Nothing that touched the heart of humankind through the impact of eternal monuments has failed its purpose. . . .

So I will be permitted, then, on the basis of the principles established here, to engage in reflections concerning this or that monument of the distant past and, wherever concise history does not suffice, to give expression to some conjectures. Following our unimpeded path, we will come in good time to the monuments of Greece and Italy, monuments with which the imagination, at any rate, is most readily occupied.

Part II

In order to avoid all strife concerning the most distant antiquity of primeval peoples, we will begin our examination with the monuments not of a mountain nation, but of a people living in the most beautiful climate, along the banks of the *Ganges,* and farther down on the Indian peninsula. Even if the Brahmans, as legend has it, have come from the North, this North shall trouble us as little as the chronology of their antiquity; a few monuments of the Indian religion are before us; they shall guide us.

To be sure, we still lack a great deal in this matter. The ancient monuments and temples of India itself still are little known to us, not to mention professionally sound reports about their setting, figures, and inscriptions; only along the western rim of the peninsula, on the island of Elephanta, in Salsette, the caves of Canara, and a few other sites, do we know the antiquities a bit better, whereby we have to thank our compatriot *Niebuhr* for the most distinct report and illustration regarding them.[*] On the other side of the peninsula, at the site of the renowned temple of *Jagannatha,* at the monuments at Madras[**] and farther up, along the Ganges, we still are deeply in the dark with reference to statuary, temple architecture, carved legends of the gods, inscriptions, and so forth; for, even if travelers here and there report something in brief words, this, though always instructive, is rarely satisfactory. The best we hope for in this regard should come from the Learned Society of Calcutta, which in a more exact description of some antiquities—though still without drawings—has already made a beginning.[***] Should a Briton be struck by the passionate desire to undertake a

---

[*]Niebuhr, *Reisebeschreibung,* part 2, pp. 16 f.

[**]In the Danish Mission Reports (parts 2, 3, 5, 6) there are, here and there, a few good, though still insufficient, reports given of, for example, the Pagoda at Sidambaram, the monuments at Madras, etc. In the *Sketches Chiefly Relating to the History of Indostan* (London: 1790), pp. 94 ff.,[10] a number of noteworthy monuments are merely listed, and in Tieffenthaler's *Description of Hindostan*[11] they are largely cast aside with great contempt as heathen rubbish. I have not yet seen the English publication *A Comparative View of the Ancient Monuments of India* (1785)[12]; according to the announcement, it supposedly deals exclusively with the monuments of Salsette. Riem's *Monuments of Indian History and Art* (Berlin: 1789)[13] contains, in part 1, the tombs of the emperors Akbar and Sher Shah, thus samples not really of Indian, but of Arabic architecture. *Tavernier, Grose, Anquetil,*[14] and several travel accounts contain much that is good, yet remain seriously insufficient.

[***]Above all, I take note of W. Chamber's *Account of the Sculptures and Ruins of Mavalipuram,* in part 1 of *Asiatick Researches,*[15] pp. 145 f. Part 2 is said to contain reports of other monuments; the same goes for vol. 7 of the *British Archeology, Descriptions of the Antiquities at Bombay;* I have not yet had the opportunity to make use of either one of these books.

journey through India, exploring its architecture and painting, or should it please Mr. *Hastings,* who already has earned great merit in Europe on behalf of Indian literature, also to make available drawings and reports of ancient monuments—if he has collected such, which is probable—we would at once be much further ahead.

However, on the basis of what we know up to now of India's monuments, it follows that the style that prevails in them, as well as their entire purpose, *reflects extremely local as well as national characteristics,* so that, regardless of where the seeds of art and religion may have come from to the Ganges, they have assumed along its banks an entirely distinctive nature. Let us, on the basis of a few pieces, develop these attributes in terms of merits and deficiencies.

1.

Most of India's monuments are rooted in religion; for we know how mightily religion rules to this day over all the tribes of the people. In it are rooted those wondrous cave temples, filled with carved legends of the gods, those numerous pagodas in which are also found the statues of the god or the deities to whom they are consecrated as dwelling places. Rooted in religion are the portraits of the gods and their deeds which are carried around in processions. Rooted in religion, at last, are the innumerable resting places and colonnades with which the Indians decorate and surround their sacred ponds, so that for more than one reason many a restless European marvels at this land as the seat of the most ancient repose, goodness, and gentleness. Now, since many of their divine legends are so delicately conceived, since their mythology is so fully a metaphysics of the life of flowers and plants, one would have to expect as a result the most beautiful artistic images.[*] *Brahman,* the Indian symbol of creation, appears on a lotus leaf, drifting on the surface of the calm sea; his wife *Sarasvati,* the goddess of science and harmony, holds a book or plays the sitar. *Vishnu,* the preserving power in the world, manifests himself in his twenty-one incarnations, though several times in horrifying, but sometimes also in quite pleasing shapes. Appearing as the beautiful Mojeni, he bewitched the great destroyer himself. In the incarnation of Rama he appeared as a handsome youth, holding a bow and arrow, liberating the world from monsters and giants. In the figures of Balapatrem and Parsurama, he taught humankind diligence and virtue; in

---

[*]See *Die Mythologie der Indier* by Baldaeus, Sonnerat,[16] and W. Jones, *On the Gods of Greece, Italy, and India;* in the *Asiatick Researches,* vol. 1, Forster's *Anmerkungen zur Sakontala,*[17] the translated Bhāgavata Purāna, etc.

the former incarnation, he himself did not know that he was *Vishnu,* and he carried the ploughshare. As Krishna he entered the world to overthrow cruel and proud kings. All of the gods were at the ready to worship him, they sang his praises and bedecked him with flowers. The harmonies of the angels resounded and all the stars looked down, dispensing good fortune. Raised by a shepherdess, he watched the flock as the shepherd; the melodious sounds of his shepherd's flute attracted the wild animals to him, bewitching shepherdesses and shepherds; nine maidens enchanted by love are in his train, and he dances and jests with them. He slew the monstrous snake Kalija, protected the virtuous king Dharma-Rama; everywhere he found followers and friends, and he lived a joyful life until his self-determined death. He is the beloved God of Indian women; images portray him above all Ramas as crowned with flowers, adorned with precious stones, at ease and joyful. There are several more of such representations of *Vishnu,* and his spouse as well as one of his sons, also is an image of beauty. *Lakshmi,* his wife, the goddess of riches, together with the goddess of science and harmony, hailed from the sea of milk; Vishnu found her in a rose of one hundred and eight leaves, and one thousand and eight smaller leaves, and with her he begot *Kama,* or *Manmadi,* the God of love who gnaws at the human heart. He appears as a child, carrying the quiver on his back, the bow and arrows in his hand; his bow is made of sugarcane, adorned with flowers; his pasture is a swarm of bees, his arrows are sharpened flowers; he rides on a female parrot. His beautiful wife, Rati, representing tenderness, kneels on a charging horse as she shoots an arrow. Even *Iswara,* or *Shiva,* the destroyer, does not appear everywhere in horrifying shapes; appearing as a very handsome beggar, he once knew how to enchant virtuous women with his love, so that their otherwise pure vows and sacrifices were no longer valid. These are the major deities of the Indians; aside from them, there are yet a number of subordinate deities, portrayed in literature as quite attractive figures. *Indra,* the god of the skies, though carrying the thunderbolt, is not a furious god; as the ruler of the bright and good spirits, he dwells in the heavenly paradise, the master of the three parts of the world. Gently his chariot touches upon the mountains of earth, and with the thunderbolt he carries a flower in his hand. *Varuna,* the God of the Sea, rides a fish; the goddess of the river *Ganges* walks on the waters of the quiet stream, bearing two waterflowers in her hands. *Arun* is the wagonmaster of the sun; by the power of the God Surya, who sits behind him destroying the shadows of the night, he holds the reins of twelve or seven horses. *Narada,* *Brahma's* son, a lawgiver, skilled in the arts of war and peace, carries the *Wina,* the Aeolian harp which is moved by the harmonious spirit of the ether. The *Indian muses and nymphs* at last, the personifications of the most innocent and most beautiful emanations of nature, the trees, plants, flowers, the seasons, yes, even the musical sounds, are perhaps the most tender buds of any poetic expression. Inspired by emanations such as these, imagine what may be expressed on canvas, and in representative art as well as in the melodious words of poetry.

If we now add that the Indians, particularly in the more advanced tribes, are a well-shaped, musically inclined people, and that the women among them, according to the most trustworthy travelers, are in their childhood and during their younger years, of a very delicate constitution; if we add further the religion of the Brahmans, which, coming from the North, not far from the borders of Kashmir, established its first mythological dwelling in the center of Asia's beauty, and that Krishna upon his appearance selected for himself the most beautiful and joyful tribes; if we take into consideration the delicate, sensuous taste of the Brahmans, which, avoiding wine and meat, enjoys flowers and water more delicately than any other nation, retains in greater purity the capacity to feel, the senses, and imagination, and does not know the stormy passions of the soul that run through generations. If we take note that, among all the nations on earth, the Indians are the only people who have made sensual lust into a fine, yes even a worshipful art[*]; and if we then add the delicate exactness, the religious diligence, the untiring attention with which perhaps they alone were able to create works of art as if they were duties requiring the most painstaking diligence, may we not expect such refined literary expressions to be reflected also in paintings and other artistic representations? And if we had the opportunity to see contemporary Indian paintings or other works of art, produced during times of general oppression and decay, and observe their splendid colors, and the subtle diligence and delicate soul that characterize them, who would not be curious to see the monuments of their better and best times! Who would not wish to find at Mount Meru a Parnassus, in Agra's fields a Thessaly, and at the banks of the Ganges an Asiatic Athens?

Perhaps this expectation will not entirely deceive us; and should the monuments of art and literature of those regions be presented to us at some future time as were those of Greece, it will come to pass after a number of other indications that one at least will have doubts about continuing to place the Indians below the Egyptians in matters of art and literature, and to regard them, who among the nations on earth are perhaps the least barbarous, as crude barbarians. *Niebuhr*,[**] who has observed many Egyptian

---

[*]In this regard, see *Grose, de Pagès, Mackintosh, Sketches Relating to the Manners of the Hindoos*,[18] and the report of any traveler not prejudiced against this nation.
[**]Niebuhr's *Reisebeschreibung*, part 2, pp. 32 ff.

monuments, finds the bas-reliefs and statuary in the temple of Elephanta greatly superior in drawing and composition to the Egyptian figures; he observes in several of the former the expression of anger and anxiousness, and he is of the overall opinion that these enormous temples carved into rock required no less toil and much more art than the Egyptian pyramids. *W. Hunter** praises in several of these giant figures "the very finely shaped details, conveying well the bulging muscles and various emotions, for example the profound and quiet grief in some, contempt and contrariness in others; he finds that in most there is appropriate proportionality of the limbs, and he observes in reference to the caves of Canara that, since they do not contain deformed figures such as occur on Elephanta and at Ambola, their works of art are perhaps the most ancient representations of all, and that they were created at a time during which the taste and mythology of the people had not yet been corrupted." Could it be that we now have satisfactory descriptions—I will not say pictures of Indian monuments of the upper country—in order to trace in some measure the *history of art* of this people and to give the reasons how, where, and when the disformed figures were introduced into paintings, and when they were discontinued? If we were to know with a measure of exactitude the images of the gods and heroes in their *various regions, sects, and temples,* it would become easier to differentiate where, for example, the thick lips and other strange features of the body and dress are to be found or not to be found, and how they have mingled or paired with the undisputed history, mythology, and development of the Indian nation. At this point, however, we are completely in the dark about this matter. We do not even know from where the best-known images of the Indian gods, which we have seen in the works cited above,** were taken. Even less do we know where others are located, which are remembered by *Jones* in his poems and commentary. And a history of the mythology, art, and poetry of this people still lies far in the future. How should we already dare to think of such a history at this point, when the monuments not far from Bombay, Madras, and Pondicherry, which for centuries were so near to the Europeans, have hardly been noted in the most recent times, or described? And we only very recently, for example, have received some reports of the most remarkable so-called seven pagodas at Mavalipuram?***

---

*In Ebeling's *Sammlung von Reisebeschreibungen,* part 9 (Hamburg: 1787), pp. 466 ff.

**Those in *Baldaeus, Holwell,* and *Jones*[19] appear to me the most original, as the Indian paintings—certainly originals—in the museum of Cardinal Borgia in Veletri correspond very much with the earliest of these. From where might *Jones* have received his? Did he perhaps simplify them?

***Asiatick Researches, vol. 1, p. 145.

If we were told of monuments in Greece upon which the gods and heroes of Homer are carved in stone, what a sensation would be created by this! It was there that the most exalted stories of the first Indian epic poem, the Mahabharata, were represented, it is there that the beds of Dharma-Raja, of Vishnu, and so forth, still remain entirely unexamined, just a few miles from a major settlement of the British and the French; how would it be now if one were to study the pagodas, in which usually one divinity is revered in a strictly localized way, throughout all of India? Much, of course, has been destroyed by time; even more has been desolated by the Mohammedan princes on behalf of their God and Mohammed, or turned into mosques; what remains was looked on by the missionaries as disgraceful idolatry, and the Europeans in their greed for money despised it most deeply. There remains for us only one wish, that the fancy of wealthy Britons be directed toward a depictive exploration of the antiquities of India as far as the religion of the Brahmans reached. At the moment, we speak only, with few exceptions, of mythological *calendar illustrations* and reports based on hearsay.

2.

If it is permissible to speak of these, then, above all, *the obstacles* must *be cited, which appear to stand in the way of the art of the Indians;* should my assumptions be proved wrong in the course of time, I will gladly be proved wrong.

The main obstacle, to wit, was the very source of their art, *their religion, and all that came with it.* Their gods originate *from symbolic concepts,* which were also retained as symbols in their monuments—which for that reason, however, also severely constrained their art. Their customary position is to be seated, for they are kings, masters of the universe; this position, placing the feet closely together in the fashion of the Morn, is not conducive to the plastic arts. An embossed figure arises from the carpet, or the flower, upon which it sits; the feet appear as if added on, lifeless limbs. No vital energy, no striving growth may be visualized in the representation. When, then, the head of the god carries the pyramid crown, when his ear is adorned with ornaments, his breast with pearls, his gown with sundry jewels of the Orient, the figure appears rich indeed, but less beautiful in terms of art.[*] A

---

[*]This adornment appeared to them to be so inseparable from the figure of the god, that the embodied god could otherwise hardly reveal himself to humankind. When Krishna was born, the Bāgavata Purāna says, he brought with him into the world four hands, a gown adorned with rubies, and ornaments for the ears decorated with splendid pearls. He appeared dressed in crimson, carrying arms and a crown upon his head. His body was sky-blue, thus his name. See *Sammlung Asiatischer Original-Schriften* (Zürich: 1791), p. 178.

painting that expresses this decorative assembly with fresh and living colors may compete with nature; the bas-relief, however, and the statuary lag behind. Now, since standing figures, as a matter of course, are also burdened with this type of adornment, which even ties up the feet, art is hereby deprived of its main purpose, the representative shaping of the body. Future reports may demonstrate sometime how Krishna with his playmates, and Kama, the god of love, with his mother and spouse, are playfully introduced; otherwise, the image of Vishnu, as he sleeps, resting upon a snake or in the lap of his wife, does not represent by our standards an attractive likeness of a god. When, at last, horrifying manifestations of Vishnu had to be represented, how he, in the form of a fish, had to retrieve the book of laws from the bottom of the sea, how, in the form of a turtle, he had to support the sinking earth, how, now as a wild boar, he charged the giant, and then again, as a monster, broke free from the confinement of a column, it is the taste of the art that determined the way it treated this fable. I know of beautiful as well as repulsive representations of this*; authentic reports will reveal which were the most popular or the most frequent representations, and how they change in respect to context and time. Equally difficult to represent in the plastic arts are some of the animals ridden by Indian gods. In the fairy tale it sounds pleasant to hear of the God of Love riding a parrot; of Shiva riding a cow, the symbol of virtue; Supramanier, a peacock; Sani, the God of Punishments, a raven; the Ruler of the Netherworld, a buffalo; and the Ruler of the Spirits introduced as riding an elephant; the significance of this in each case can nowhere be mistaken; to the eye, meanwhile, except for the portrait in colors, it does not present as satisfying and solid a proportionality of art as is given when the God of Fire rides a ram; the God of the Sea, a crocodile; the God of the Wind, a mountain goat; the God of Plenty, a white charger adorned with wreaths; and the Goddess of Discord and Misery, a black horse, holding the standard of the raven. It is everywhere noticeable, however, that *symbolic allegory* had overcome art; it was beholden to religious designation and legend.

This may be observed even more clearly in the *attributes with which the sacred legend burdened its gods in the world of art also;* in order merely to reveal these attributes, she gave them many hands, many heads. Thus, by means of this divine disfigurement, legend of course had rich opportunity to sustain and repeat itself; with each symbol, each arm, each head, a story, an attribute of the deity could be related, and in one singular figure the teacher as well as the student, in a way, had before him the entire epopee of the

---

*Compare, for example, *Baldaeus, Dapper,*[20] *Sonnerat, Jones;* the first and the last contain the most passable figures.

god, a complete inventory of his relations and deeds. *Everything* regarding him was important, and I doubt whether the symbolic dimension of art is more fully expounded in any people on earth than the Indians. The symbolism of the Egyptians appears so simple against theirs, that it is to be wondered how the two could be confused, or be held equal to one another. Each of them is focused on the locale, and in each there prevails an altogether different spirit of composition.

So it seems that the entire art of the Indians originated in books; so it was that Vishnu, in his first metamorphosis, already recovered the lost vedas; that is why I would like to see for this aspect of symbolic art translations of a great many Indian poems, fairy tales, and legends. An entirely different path was taken by Greek art. At the outset, it served the priests, but not for too long. Soon they deprived Bacchus of his horns, other gods of their oppressive symbols, and *symbolized the gods themselves into lasting, eternal characters.* The forehead of a Jupiter, a Hercules, an Apollo, or a Bacchus characterizes the entire figure; the same goes for the other parts of the body. The art of Greece was shaped to speak as art, without alien attributes, without the letters of the sacred legend; under the tutelage of the Brahmans, the art of the Indians could hardly mature to this point. The caste of the artists was a subordinate one; the caste of the Brahmans was its ruler. The former could contribute diligence and effort to the work; the latter provided for it the governing thoughts.

3.

Therefore, even if—though I do not endorse this—the art of the Indians is not accorded any value as art, in the history of humankind it now and ever will retain value as the *monument of a philosophical system,* which perhaps could originate only along the Ganges, and at its banks also appears to be imperishable. I mark out a few axioms of this remarkable philosophy and relate them to Indian art.

1. A *creative, preserving, and destroying power* was the foundation of this system, a system that recommends itself as much to sensuous perception as to deeper intellectual contemplation. To be sure, much that is true and good could be tied to the *principles of light and darkness* of the Persians, to the systems of *active and passive forces of nature* of other nations; but I doubt whether one of these measures up to this triad of powers in terms of providing a vision at once encompassing, ethereal, and full of grace. Every flower teaches us this system (the Indians loved flowers), and what they taught was confirmed by the flowers of heaven, the solar sys-

tems, the milky ways, all parts of the universum; creation, preservation, and decline are the three points of its transcendent as well as its particular existence. The creative power, Brahma, soon was pushed into the shadows by the Indians and deprived of the most prominent part of its veneration (for, how little do we know of creation!); Vishnu and Shiva, the pervasive preserver and the destroyer of things, in the meanwhile, share the throne of world dominion. An attribute of the great beauty of this poem of the universe was also that the *procreation* of beings became a focal point uniting all three of the powers, as they encounter one another, as they appear to suspend one another, and articulate precisely thereby further the chain of nature.* Fertility destroys the flower, and yet all its powers strive toward this flowering; whatever destroys it, preserves creation. So it is that *Vishnu's avatars* are also in a sense the sum of all *events of human history;* for, what does history show us but decline and resurgence, the customary oppressions of all kinds, and further, here and there, perhaps a new altar of Rama, the incarnate, richly sustaining deity.

2. *The migration of souls* was rooted in this system, if not essentially, then as if it were a dream; a pleasant or horrifying dream for beings entirely unable of themselves to penetrate the region of the invisible powers. The immolation of the body probably helped to create the basis for this concept, and it is incredible how deeply it has been rooted in the impressionable sensibility of the Indians. The concept of the migration of the souls by itself would demonstrate (if there were no other evidence) what may be made of a human being through illusion and faith; but, by the same token, it also demonstrates that the Brahmanic system is a quite carefully thought out system, a fact that is then quite satisfactorily verified by its refined arrangement of the elements composing the world, of the senses and the powers of the soul, of virtues and vices, yes, of the most delicate effects of the human spirit.** If we knew the rich literature of the Brahmans in the context of their ancient and more recent history, we would be enlightened on several issues.***

3. The *being that was first and primal* was not Brahma, Vishnu, or Iswara, but *Brahman, self-sufficiency;* Indian philosophy has endeavored to present it to us in such distant majesty, but at the same time also in such intimate closeness to us, that it may hardly be surpassed in either regard. "It

---

*Iswara wanted to destroy the world with fire; Vishnu captured him; Brahma supports both; from there the lingam.[21] See *Sonnerat,* 4th ed. (Zurich: 1783), p. 152.
**See in this regard especially the Bhagavad Gita (London: 1785).
***See in this regard the *Essay XVIII On the Literature of the Hindoos, Asiatick Researches,* vol. 1, p. 340.

was, it is what is now, it endures. Outside of it creation is *Maya,* delusion; creation is present only in our senses, in our minds. Far more intimate than the great elements is the *being of beings in All;* the All, however, is not this being itself; no thing is a part of it, all things are within it, they are its reflection. The heart may seek him, *the one who is,* by means of principles which are, like him, everywhere the one and only." And they have sought him, these strange sages, and they are still seeking him along stringent paths of asceticism, seclusion, and concentration of the powers of heart and mind. Have they found him? May he be found along this path? *We,* least of all, ought to decide, we, who with our way of life, our diversions and cravings, perhaps do not have even a notion of the more refined *Maya* (delusion), which, under the idea of the *being of being,* deceives those human beings who are set apart from wine, sanguinity, and passion.

These exalted speculations had a powerful influence on the art of the Indians, in that they determined the veneration of sacred images, places, and elements, that is to say, the entire makeup of sacred monuments. They say, "as the eye is pervaded and animated by the light, the vessel by fire, iron by the magnet, so also is the universe enriched with powers by the eternal spirit, and the human soul by the most noble powers. Sacred images are merely recollections of the divine which are found in their innermost essence *within the self,* in a pure mind and heart." With this principle, the limits of their religious art were determined, and by means of the threefold personification of the most sublime God their entire journey was predetermined; for the idea of the most sublime God was not representable in an image. . . .

～ 10 ～

On the Earliest Documents of Humankind

The following text constitutes the introductory part of a manuscript which Günter Arnold of Weimar, Germany, discovered in 1980. Rudolf Smend edited it for the first time in 1993.[*]

According to Smend, Herder finished this text in 1769. In the following excerpts, Herder prepares the ground for his interpretation of the first eleven chapters of Genesis by presenting his new understanding of the Old Testament and developing his methodological approach to the Bible. More than the theological aspect of Herder's text, what is important in this context is Herder's idea of reading these passages of the Old Testament as an historical document, with its traces of local, national, and poetic elements of the old times, on the one hand, and its account of the origin of humanity, on the other. This document of the origin of world history, according to Herder, must be accepted not as something "sacred" that is exempt from time and eludes human access through human hermeneutics, but as historical in the strict sense of the word. It requires an historical contextualization that has its foundation in the "sensate cognition" of the text. In other words, the older the documents of history, the more poetic they are—but they are nevertheless *documents* of history.

[First Part]

Yes

The peoples of the earth, like individual human beings, are more similar to one another in their childhood than in the later stages of developed character. As long as they search to satisfy their basic needs and give labored

---

[*]Cf. Johann Gottfried Herder, *Schriften zum alten Testament*, ed. Rudolf Smend. (Johann Gottfried Herder, *Werke in zehn Bänden*, vol. 5) (Frankfurt am Main: Deutscher Klassiker Verlag 1993, pp. 9–178). The text included here is on pp. 11–30.

utterance to their first concepts and their unconcealed cravings, there is revealed in all of them, and in almost identical manner, a kindred soul. Thus it is that, among all the peoples of the world of whom we know through individual reports and fables drawn from the conditions of their youth, their primary attention has directed itself at almost the same kinds of things and, in all of them, in almost one and the same way.

Up to this point they had been barbarian, ignorant, and unfamiliar with the nature of things, at each new encounter victims of surprise, at each new terrifying encounter victims of fear, of terror. Each monster encountered had caused them to tremble, the experience or threat of misfortune had made them fearful and superstitious in turn; therefore, they had invented for themselves a number of mostly fearsome or fear-dispelling gods, had created for themselves a religion to appease the affects of these deities. So it was that all of nature, which could harm or serve them, in all its parts and individual changes and destinies, appeared as *deity*—as a pantheon of living beings who worked for or against humankind, and their entire religion the fear and superstition of these beings.

The philosopher *Hume*[1] has proved the truth of this statement on the basis of history and human nature; the philosopher *Michaelis*[2] has accepted it with appropriate modification; and the earliest fables found in the case of almost every nation, as well as all instances of comparison of the childhoods of individual humans, confirm it.

However, as they gradually escaped from these days of oppression, toil, and privation, as they—a bit more familiar with the nature of things—celebrated somehow the first sabbath of their thoughts, the first day of rest, a more reflective question *concerning the origin of things* became natural. One wanted now to obtain a clearer account: *How did the world, how did human beings,* how did the present condition of the world, of humankind, *how did the individual particularities and inventions,* how in particular did the *nation* of which one was part, with its *language, customs,* and *mentality,* come to be? This, more or less, was the catechism of every nation, as it arose from raw superstition to early self-consciousness.

Each people thus came to think of a *cosmogony, an anthropogenesis, a philosophy* concerning the evil and the good of the world, especially of its own regions, a *genealogy* and *history* of its ancestors, customs, and habits, in order to possess, what are called "Origines—original documents." Thus, there followed upon the earliest primitive religion which in almost all languages derived its name from fear, a kind of historico-physical philosophy.

Nothing in nature, however, proceeds in leaps and bounds, and so the change from the condition of barbarian mythology to the earliest, more brightly lit philosophy, did not come about in one leap. When a human soul is nurtured through its entire youth by concepts of a strong, raw, and sensuous kind, and all of its thinking is shaped by them, it still incorporates these materials even while it endeavors to think independently. So it was, also, that no people could think about the causes and origins of the matters raised other than on the basis of the materials and premises of that people's previous condition. It stripped off the uppermost, rough layer of skin, but it was unable to transform at once the entire body that had been shaped by such mythology.

The teaching of previous times, tradition,[3] thus became its first source for providing answers to such questions. It is known how much *those* people, who do not—as we do—live on the basis of knowledge, but on the basis of experience, make of this source of wisdom. The voice of their fathers, the saga of previous ages, is for them the treasure closest to omniscience. And, where should tradition, after all, have been examined more closely, than in that which bears the name tradition itself, *in matters of origin*. The answer, therefore, turned out to be in keeping with the spirit of the previous age, *mythical*.

Each nation thus conceived the creation of the world and of humankind, its own condition, and its peoplehood in *terms of religion:* everything assumed *theological coloring;* for, as mentioned above, they had hardly left the age of wonders and signs, and divine deeds, and the appeasement of the deities, and still thought in terms of the concepts of their fathers. Each nation thus charged its own god, or its gods, as well as it could, with the building of the world, with the shaping of humankind, with the earliest housekeeping of the world, with the earliest misfortunes of their fathers, with the institution of the covenant and the mores of its state. Everywhere, the theological garment was the sacred veil of concealment, the sacred adornment of the manifestation and the dignity of the origin.

It was natural that these theological traditions had to be as national as anything in the world. Everyone spoke after the tongue of his fathers, he beheld the world that was around him, he gained insights into the things that appeared before him as the most noteworthy, in accordance with the reasons that best explained them on the basis of his climate, of his nation, and of his previous guidance; he drew conclusions in keeping with his interest and in accordance with the mentality, language, and customs of his people. The world and humankind, and the people, therefore were created in line with the ideas of his age, his nation, and his culture, national and local at once, in the most minute sense as well as in the most grandiose. The Scandinavian built for himself a world drawn from and shaped by the giants of frost, the earth from the corpse of Ymer, the sea from his blood, and the sky from his skull. He created his humans from pieces of drifting wood; he explained for himself the evils of the world by drawing upon the wolf *Fenris* and the great snake of Midgar; thus he conceived for himself the nature of things and of the heavens; everything was giant, monster, and magic. The Iroquois[4] turned turtles and otters, the Indian elephants, the Negro at last a cow's horn filled with dung into the engines of what they wished to explain. Here, all antiquities and travel accounts are full of sagas and traditions, of local poetry and national fairy tales. Whoever wishes to do so, let him bring order, light, and openings into this infinite and so wildly overgrown forest.

Everywhere, thus, these ancient theological-philosophical-historical national traditions were enwrapped in a sensuous, image-rich language, which could arouse the curiosity of the people, charge its imagination, guide its inclinations, and amuse its ear. The fathers taught their children, the lawgivers and so-called wise men taught the public, which was called the people. Each one thus had to find images drawn from his own world, poetry suitable to his own soul, enduring characteristics to suit his own heart, among which he had been raised, which lived within him and needed only to be aroused to live in him forever. Everywhere documents of this kind are found composed in a strong, image-rich language full of fantasy. These documents, therefore, could be none other than very poetic. They were concerned with the most interesting matters pertaining to a nation; they were drawn from the most lively and the most vigorous ideas of the primitive times, which in a way had been nothing but image, sensation, and affect; these documents absorbed for themselves all that was sacred and terrifying in the religion of the fathers; they flowed from the mouth of a venerable distant past; they were so shaped that children and the people at large would master them, and would make them into their favorite songs and sayings of wisdom; they were meant to guide the public and preserve it to be true to its origin and aware of the national tradition. The language in which they were presented was full of images, full of sensuous expressions; it was devoid of abstractions and scholarly concepts; and in this instance it assumed in addition both the venerable seal of most ancient traditions and the new, which must be marked by a style of elucidation unknown heretofore; moreover, it had to be to the highest degree a popular and sensuous language. How poetic such documents had to become.

And they became consummate poetry. At a time when an art of letters and writing could hardly be thought of, the voice of tradition was to preserve them. Hence, they had to be brief, filled with few, strong, and chosen words, filled with certain, in a way inseparable, eternal chains of words, filled with passages and pauses of stark consistency; in a way they had to be a living art of memory. In addition, since nothing was to be patched onto them, nor anything taken from them, since they were to remain whole and eternal in the voice of the people and of the nymph Echo—who is always apt to shorten and distort—it became even more necessary to dress them in the whole cloth of a drama that could not be deprived of any of its parts, and that would soon betray any additions. An arrangement of strophes and στίχοις,[5] a kind of repetitive rhythm, of rhymes, wordplays, analogies, and a hundred other items became ever so many measuring rods of memory and a living poetry. And if in that age language was, after all, lively, rousing, full of falling and rising sounds, full of song in speech, what was more natural than that it assumed the modulation of a rough chant, poetic also in the structure of the words, the verses, the strophes, the arrangement of the whole.

Now, music is to be added, to enliven these sounds and images in a way to lull them into the ear, to embed them eternally in the soul through the melody of the song. If now is added a form of declamation corresponding to the upheavals and excessive movement of that time, a raw form of dancing will result; now, there are the νόμοι,[6] the laws, the archaic documents, the chants, which make the trees dance and the oaks assume life.

I have traced the mentality of the nations and, without recourse to a system or to excessive pondering, this is what I arrived at: that each of them *has created for itself documents corresponding to the religion of its land, to the tradition of its fathers, and to the concepts governing the nation; that these documents appeared in a poetic language, in poetic dress, and in poetic rhythm—that is to say, "in mythological national songs of the origins of their most ancient memories worthy of note."*

And each nation of antiquity that raised itself without foreign assistance in the pursuit of its own culture, even if ever so slightly above the stage of barbarism, possessed such songs. Wherever there are remains or reports of the past, there also are the ruins of such documents. The Edda of the Celts and ... of the Indians, the cosmogonies, theogonies, and heroic chants of the most ancient Greeks, and the common reports of the Spanish, the Gauls, the Germans, and all who were called barbarians, all resound with the wholeness of one voice, one singular sound of suchlike poetic documents, of bygone ages.

Whoever wishes to infuse life into Iselin's history of humankind[7] pertaining to so noteworthy a moment in time, let him return all these national sagas, mythological envelopments, and fragments of documents into the naked, deprived human soul which then began to shape itself in this way, and along with the general panorama of regions, peoples, and ages, let him sift from barbarism "a spirit of documentary traditions and mythological chants," as Montesquieu—though a thousand times more useful for bourgeois society—collected a spirit of the laws. There, at least, are found everywhere the evocative features shaping the image of the human spirit and heart, not found by us in our cultured and unnatural age. The true shape of sensuous man, the entire gymnasium of imaginative power and poetry, the earliest and strong politics of wit and acumen, the simple wellsprings of the passions and national prejudices—all of what we find in our more refined epoch only in weak and dark outlines, is alive in the documents of this age of the world. Our century is too refined, too political, and too philosophical; or, we are another species of humankind that represents nothing but collecting scribblers and thoughtless antiquaries, too much so for us to have yet had a philosophical history of this poetic point in time; for, how many people are there who in their philosophical, politic, mature years are not ashamed of the childhood of their days? And yet, how much might still be learned from that time?

Second Part

Yet, in all of these traditions, where is genuine truth, history, where are firm dates? Poetic envelopments, lively, moving, popular images may deceive; tales of the nation may bewitch the entire nation and guide it; the rhythm of poetry may preempt the ear and the mind, and with its melody it may embed forever into the memory of humankind the imperishable oratory— but where is truth and where is conviction? I grope around among the peoples of the earth as if I were in a romantic grove full of magical chants and gripping voices; but where—not to be enclosed by the magic circle— where is a firm and certain voice of eternal truth?

Most of these matters are of the kind about which in *human* terms no certain reports may be received. Who knows the beginnings of God's ways? And who knows how the innermost of things was called from nothingness? Who witnessed God's creation of man, and who was the guardian of man in the childhood of his life?—This *either-or* should already present us with the twofold question, do you want to know nothing, with all of your suppositions know nothing, or do you want to wait for a higher voice? As long as no earthly spirit penetrated the innermost recesses of nature in order to know the true nature of things, how could he conjecture its *coming to be*? And as long as we do not know ourselves *as we are today,* how can we know the day on which we *came to be*? Thus, there is called for and indispensable in this matter, as in a thousand other matters pertaining to the childhood of humankind, a direct instruction by the Divine.

By the same token, the roots of the origins of each nation are as much hidden in the chain of events as the roots of a tree and the source of the river within the earth. Everything that happened before the age that is imaginable to us is as if it never happened, and where, after all, do we place in the history of peoples the time when they were not and came into existence, the time when reflection was rare and articulate speech even more so, and since speech was constrained, how much less was written, written of history, and the history of truth? Either one seeks the excuse not to know of all of this, thus to wander about eternally in this labyrinth of innumerable suppositions concerning the creation of the world, the origin of humankind, of inventions and nations—or, let one search whether a divine voice has deemed us worthy of instruction.

This voice has indeed deemed us worthy, and there are some oriental, Hebrew documents that have been perpetuated in the Jewish tradition, which the founder of our religion, himself raised in the thought of the Jews, has confirmed by accepting them; his successors have placed them among the main pillars of our religion, and they have been established also in our own day as canonical writings of divine appearance. I would say that even in terms of form alone, the unmythological nature of their conceptions, the exaltedness and nobility of their ideas, testify to their divine origin, unless doubters were able to explain on the basis of national particularities these external perfections as well as they explain imperfections in others; so it is better not to use reeds as reasons, as long as stronger evidence is at hand.

I do not want to excerpt this evidence from our dogmatic tracts and biblical commentaries; rather, I want to stay with my thesis that the more representative, ancient, and authentic these documents are, the more diligence and accuracy they merit in the process of elucidation. Literary or, as it is said, physical impact they have sufficiently had upon the chain of peoples; after all, they have spread widely over the lands of the Morn, and for a long time they have left traces in the thought of the Sabaeans, Arabs, Persians, and Indians; in the form of Christianity they have taken root in a large part of the world, and, considered as the basis of the faith of nations at least, they have overcome all the pondering about these matters of origin by Greek and other philosophers, never mind how much literature in Christian lands has fused in other respects with heathen elements; during the Middle Ages they imbued Mohammedism with rotted branches, and over so many centuries gave birth in many nations and languages to mystical and physical, philosophical and dogmatic exegeses. Therefore, they have affected infinitely more than other documents the spirit of humankind, the direction of our thought, the chain of literatures in Europe.—How noteworthy for us are these few documents, coming from so distant an age, of such great, memorable happenings, which are inexplicable in any other way, which came from the original instruction of God, and which have done so much for the chain of thought of so many nations, centuries, and religions!

But now the other side: how many demeaning misfortunes have they encountered, more demeaning than encountered by any document of secular antiquity. During the finest days of the Jewish religion and language, during the golden centuries of Moses, David, Solomon, and some of the prophets, they have contributed uncommonly much to the nobility of the great thought that manifests itself from that time in Holy Scripture. Were we not so very accustomed to consider also the canon of the Old Testament as a book written by one single author, at one time and from one pen, the striking vision would have been pursued for a long time and more intensively as to what the contents of these documents have contributed to the makeup of the Jewish religion in general, and what greatness and distinction they have contributed in particular, in the context of the various epochs, situations, persons, and points of view from Moses to Isaiah, from David to Jeremiah, and considered with due attention to the individual genius of each writer. At any rate, we have probably given only half of the noble, critical attention to the golden age of the Hebrews that we have given in such amplitude to the golden ages of the Greeks, the Romans, and I do not know what other nations. During these golden ages, then, these national documents also stimulated on the whole the spirit of Jewish prophecy.

But, immediately following upon the Babylonian captivity—what a change of spirit in all! And, as time moved on, how much more of a change there was! Until finally, among the Jews, the thought of Hellenism arose full and square, a rhapsody of tongues, languages, nations, and generations. And how far one strayed in embracing this thought from the spirit of those Mosaic and pre-Mosaic documents, to understand them no more, nor to feel them in the right sense—that is documented by citations, allusions, and accommodations of various kinds taken from the writings of this particular point in time. In this thought is rooted the cause that was to ruin entirely the pure imagery of the Morn, to distort it, and to transplant it a hundred times to strange and foreign soils to the point of wild confusion.

The spirit governing the fates mandated that this path of transplantation was to stretch much too far, through regions, ages, and peoples. Christianity was sown in the soil of Greek and Roman thought and with its roots drew into itself infinitely much from these foreign regions and ways of thinking; where did the ancient poetic spirit go that welled within Moses and in all that he assembled? Mystical, or at least quite barbarously edifying, and idiomatic-dogmatic interpretations almost completely pervaded the spirit of the century—who can count all of these rare and peculiar interpreters in Asia, Europe, and Africa?

Like the dove of Noah, not finding a place to rest, I want to pass over the monkish centuries, and, notwithstanding all more recent achievements in the awakening of the ancient Hebrew literature, why did the unfortunate spirit of the day have to be such that all was at once fitted into a dogma, and if it did not want to fit, why did it have to be beaten into it? Nothing on earth has been more harmful to the Bible than this systematizing and differentiating spirit of scholasticism; during the times in which it arose, it represented what remained of and connected with the preceding century; but now, have we not advanced sufficiently to be free of it? It ruins and tears apart the works of sacred antiquity, which it ought to interpret in the spirit of their own age and their originators. It chops into pieces, as Turks and Tartars do to this day, the most precious monuments, to make of them millstones and mosques.—How much damage has been done also to these documents in that they came to be such significant articles of an orthodox dogmatics, *regarding creation and the state of innocence* and *of sinfulness* and what else? Who can name passages of scripture that are burdened more oppressively by this dogmatic yoke than these (as much as I venerate dogmatics)?

At the same time they were captured by the philosophical-materialistic, and in the further course of history by the genealogical-historical spirit that arose in Europe. What physical hypotheses about the first chapter of Genesis! What geographical hypotheses about the second and the tenth! What philosophical ones about the third, chronological about the fifth, and grammatical about the eleventh! And, as for the other, what more can I say? I value each of these handmaidens in her own place, but what happens when they turn into mistresses of the house? Furies, who ruin and tear apart the text, diverting it so far from the original simplicity and nobility of the Morn that, in the end, nothing is left but contributions to the indulgence of this or that mad mind. Whoever cares to do so, let him count all these learned, recognized and unrecognized sins, brought by each one from the specialty of his studies into the opening chapters of the Bible. Thus, there was erected a splendid palace of the Morn; the portal and the courtyard—in keeping with the oriental manner—were to reflect the name and the glory of the prince, and, behold, they are filled with the baggage of brigandage.

Up to our own day, yet, they have still found strong objection who dared to look past all of this baggage, endeavoring to climb back across all the centuries with their peaks and valleys, to come to the proper place where these precious monuments, this dear firstborn of the human spirit originally was formed. They have frequently been called heretical, and I will therefore not call them by name.—It has been my only purpose to transport myself, who stand behind a dividing wall of so many interludes of ways of thought, opinions, and languages of exegesis, to the place where these documents were revealed, where they were collected from the lips of the people, and where they had life. God of the Morn, who revealed them, you speak and your servant listens! But transform also my spirit, so that I may hear you at the place and in the language in which you spoke!

Third Part

No one will doubt that the first Mosaic chapters are *documents, Origines*[8]; for they contain reports of the most ancient matters of humankind. However, not all are of the same mind regarding whether they are separate documents, or whether they represent a coherent story or regarding much else that follows from this. And yet, nothing appears more obvious to me than that they cannot be a coherent story.

Of how many things do we fail to receive reports, though they ought not to be missing in a story? Of how many things do we receive reports, though they are not part of the story? Where is the tie among them all? And what about pieces of contradictory content? Whence come many a repetition, insertion, recapitulation, giving rise to the grossest misunderstandings when all is supposed to be a coherent story, composed by one pen and for one purpose, to be the most ancient history of humankind. I present here only a few examples; the rest will appear later. Following upon the completion of the seven days of creation, how many individual insertions and recapitulations are there in the second chapter of Genesis, which, given a coherent story, would have each belonged in their place and particular day. Pre-Adamites, black and red Adams, twofold creations, a thousand questions concerning the time of the naming of the animals, the Fall, the birth of Cain, and so forth. Doubts and misinterpretations have arisen, and must come about, if everything is to be a coherent Mosaic history. Thus the dogmatists would then be given an open field, to make something new of every word that is repeated in the course of the chapters, to place the image of Adam against the image of God, and to discover whole items of proof. Thus the mystics would then be given an open field, to discover the secret meanings of words that appear twice, and each time want to be new; and, on the other hand, to prophesy the sublime reasons why it pleased God to enlighten us only about these, and no other matters of origin, and why about these in so fragmentary a way, and so full of gaps—a wide field for the mystical counselors of God in this earliest of stories. And finally, the writers of history par excellence, the scientists, the philosophers, the writers—what piles of dreams, fables, suppositions, fairy tales, hypotheses have they heaped together everywhere to fill the gaps, to turn Moses into the pragmatic writer of the history of the world, of its peoples, of learning and art, with due attention to causation and consequences and all that goes along with them. What in the work of Moses are merely some solid gold coins, how far has this been drawn out in gilded threads by others?

Individually separate documents! These and nothing else are before us in every part of the story. The report of the days of creation is complete; one clearly sees in every part that it was conceived to be one individual whole composed of seven pieces and nothing more. It ends, therefore, with the third verse of the second chapter; and yet already, even in the style of writing, yes, and even in the name given to God, it sets itself apart from that which follows. Now, individual reports of the primal condition of the world, of the creation of man, of Eden, of the creation of woman—each viewed as individual fragments; thus and in no other way does it stand in its place. These anecdotes proceed from verse 7–23, or, if one cares, from 4–24. Then follows the story of the seduction by the snake and the transformed state of humankind—evidently an entity from the last verse of the second to the nineteenth verse of the third chapter; and a few items belonging there are appended. Now, from verse 3 to verse 15 of the fourth, the story moves obviously and without diversion to an account of the first fratricide; and individual accounts of memorable family matters enter the flow. Then, from the third verse to the end of the fifth chapter, there follows another entity, the account of genealogy. And now, a song of the corruption of the world and of the Great Flood, of the preservation of the patriarch Noah, told in a few paragraphs and subdivisions, up to the account of his blessing, and the beautiful symbol of the rainbow as concluding matters worthy of remembrance—whereupon the connecting tie is torn again. It follows a family anecdote of Noah and his sons, ending abruptly and forming a whole in itself; the genealogy is broken off and forms a whole; the pronounced hypothesis of the multitude of the peoples and languages—broken off and forming a whole—then follows yet another genealogy and only now the more connected account of the patriarchs. What? Ought it not be discernible whether in each piece, with each word and circumstance, and coloring, the individual subject is brought out, or whether everything is introduced only insofar as it contributes to the whole of the story? Is it not so that in the case of all of these individual documents each one has a singular theme, a singular interest, a singular center, to which each word and image rushes? Does not everything then also become a distorted figure when each part is torn from its individual drama, from its singular existence, to be coupled with others, thus producing a thing—I do not know what to call it—in which each individual aspect is misplaced, in which everything is cast out into the false light of a certain generality? Here nothing retains its own color and size and shape; one sees distorted and obscured figures.

This, then, has been my primary purpose, *to see each document in the particular light* in which it stands; and in this approach I have more than one predecessor. The great philologist of the Morn, *Michaelis,* has in many instances found individual sayings and beginnings of songs, and thereby cast them in remarkable clarity. Someone else,[9] whose book and its review I have not had the opportunity to see, has presented suppositions that Moses used more ancient documents in the composition of his story. And a third one,[10] whom, by the way, I do not want to place with his dreams next to the first one, is not on the whole wrong when he says that these partial pieces must be elucidated as such, even though he does not present in his own example anything that is wholesome. So it is obvious that others before me have raised their voices; will I succeed in putting them together in my own fashion, and spelling them out? I continue:

These documents are of the Morn; they were composed not only in this language, but, what is more important, in the mentality of the Morn. They are not Egyptian, as is so much in the Book of Job, in the later books of Moses, and in the entire Mosaic constitution; I find in them a certain entirely pure manner of thinking characteristic of the Morn, and perhaps this distinction will later provide us with additional insights regarding the author of the same, and so forth. They were, however, not conceived or written at all in a Kabbalistic vein, and if these pieces were written after the Babylonian captivity, Hardouin[11] would be right in all his madness. Nor were they conceived or written at all in a Hellenistic vein, and even less in the vein preferred in recent times as modes of representation and explanation. We are placed in the wake of the commentaries of so many centuries; in the elucidation of these pieces, too, Hellenism has mingled with a dogmatic-mystical-homiletic-philosophical spirit and fermented; who is there willing to throw himself into the bright air of the Morn, to listen to its voices?

Those who do, caught by the thought of the Morn, love images, the forms in which they are couched, and figurative speeches; and then, if one places the land into the context of the age, the poetic gown will become more visible. The voices of the Morn come from the age of traditions, and at that time everything turned to the poetic. They were meant to remain on the lips of the common people and to dwell in their soul; thus, with each footstep, there were sensuous modes of thought and of the imagination. The entire internal makeup, the parts of the whole are easy to behold; the spirit of the tale reflects the sacred throughout, as did the sagas of earlier times; the entire impression is not didactic, nor a dry account, but rather romantically enchanting; its melody sings us into the realm of earlier events. Add to this in some instances the evident rhythm, the plays on words, allusions, changes of pace—I do not know what more would be called for to evoke the poetic spirit.

I will not say that they are all equally poetic, that they are all complete poems or songs. We will encounter only a few of those; the others, however, are remnants, pieces of the poetic tradition, all of them reflecting poetic spirit—as is the case in the most ancient documents of all nations, coming from times governed by sensate perception. But I do not set them apart so thoroughly from that which followed, as if, for example, with the story of Abraham an altogether different spirit had all at once arisen. That story, too, and those of a much later time, reveal poetic sparks, but evidently much less frequently, in a more singular way, since here the form in which they are garbed and the tone of the poetry often govern everything from the detail to the whole. They were thus poetic documents of the Morn, drawn from the sagas of earlier times!—That is how they ought to be read; do not take any image further than is called for by the makeup of the whole, any further than is demanded by its part in the poetic meaning with its flow and context; do not transplant the figurative expressions into the soil of rigid demonstration or historical documentation; give your ear to the tone of the piece—that is how one reads in a manner worthy of the matter.

Moreover, I do not wish to push any further the similarity of these to the songs of the origins of other peoples. This similarity ought to do nothing more than preserve in us the intuitive spirit that will feel the poetic national tone as much here in its dignity as it feels it elsewhere in its meanness. The divine history of creation, of the transformation of the world, of the first misfortunes and memorable tribal matters must absolutely appear in the national light, as do the cosmogonies of the Greeks, as does the account of the origin of evil among the Iroquois, and the story of earlier great deluges and national distinctiveness among the Arabs. Here it is everywhere the man of the Morn, the son of Adam, of Seth, Noah, Shem, the Hebrew, the Jew; he must speak in the voice of his fathers, he must speak in the spirit of the sacred legends of earlier times—any more general, less focused projection is a distortion, false and confusing. It is clear that I do not demean the renown of the pieces, but that I confirm it.

During the childhood of the world, everything bears witness to the fact that God came to the assistance of the first human beings in their need, as they knew little in these matters and could not know more, as a revealing God with fatherly instruction. This instruction—even if I view it as national tradition, as the legends of previous ages—always remains divine in its origin, and it remains divine even when it is composed in national songs; I will explain further.

The presence of God in scripture never means as much as if God, in order to gain a concept of this matter or that, thinks in this manner and with the words in which his revelation presented itself. Nothing is more childish and more objectionable to God than the shadow of this claim; and how? Have not many disputations concerning the nature of theopneusty,[12] concerning the degree of divinity in thoughts and words, come so close to this childishness, that I would not be able to place a straw in between? No word in the Bible is divine in the sense that by its means we now know how the gods speak in the heavens, how God thinks himself of the matters which lie in this sphere, and through which images, in which order, and in which manner he perceives them for himself?—Nothing is more childish than this thought. With our God there is no sequence of thoughts, no abstraction of general concepts, no thread of historical representations; and how should there be images? Additional figurative representations? Rhetorical adornments? Poetic deception? The ringing sound of words?—I am ashamed to go on writing; with God everything is one eternal, consummate thought; and to call, in this sense, one thought, one word of the Bible divine represents the greatest hyperbole of anthropomorphism.

Far from us be, therefore, the illusionary kind of imagination, as if God in His presence for one single moment had so powerfully taken hold of the soul of the writer in the course of its thoughts that all its human thinking in that moment was destroyed, and that, in a way, God thought His thoughts into that soul, and through it conceived the world. That would be the destruction, the annihilation, or, what is just as senseless, the deification of a human soul—a fanatic thought which is contradicted by all conceptions of God and of our nature, the entire makeup of Holy Scripture, and all common sense. What kind of childishness is it, to have elucidated for oneself by God in a divine way how He created the world? How the essence of things became real through his potential? And so on, and concerning all of this God is to instruct us in the way in which He thinks of everything?—Miserable, childish arrogance! Senselessness exceeded by nothing in the world! One can take the philosophy of ten thousand millions of Newtons in their intensity, and present it to a student who is ten thousand million times more ignorant than the most ignorant of peasant boys—we still do not have the relation of ourselves to God! Here, we will always have similarity, assimilation; there, we will have no relation at all, nothing commensurable. God thinks without words, without symbols, without sequentiality, without images, without any external aspect of representation; and we?—frail human, write on—how do you think?

In this sense, everything in the Bible is thoroughly human. The thought and the word, the sequence and the manner of representation, all are human. A human soul produced each thought written down, and since there is no other way for us to learn to think, beginning with our youth, but through words, each thought at once appeared in the world in its human symbolic shape, in the form of the word that expressed it. It came to be out of the chain of previous thoughts, shaped by the way of thought of its writer and the treasure of his personal culture. So it came about that his composed or written work bore the imprint of its originator, of his location, of his time, of his nation, of his language; and the entire manner of exegesis of the same was to be human therefore. The spirit may read as if God were speaking, for, after all, the original source of tradition rests in Him; but the exegete ought to forget that it is God who is speaking. It is he, as a human being, and from a human being, and in a human language, who receives the word; and as long as we do not have a divine grammar, a divine logic, and a divine metaphysics, so long do we also want to practice exegesis in human terms. Language, epochs, customs, nation, author, coherence—everything is as if it were in a book by human hands.

The canonization of these books to the level of divine provenance, therefore, has a more exalted nature than to determine the art of exegesis. For there is no nobility in the perception of God's spirit by those who endow him with the excellent position of a professor of poetry, with that of an exalted stylist, and thereby even derive a Mohammedan justification for the divinity of their Jewish or Christian Koran. To arouse humanity's power of imagination, to compete for it with all of the crowned poets, to exceed them all in the stirring and exalted quality of the style—truly, a poor challenge for the spirit of God, who would surely have had the traditions of His book written without all figurative imprecision, if His authors, and their disciples, had grasped the brightness of this language, if the genius of those ages could have heard them. What an error, to take as a hallmark of the divine that which, instead, is nothing but the weakness of humankind, and the cinders of the sensate century; and how much is there to come to the monumental conclusion: so much greatness, purity, exaltedness is attainable through the powers of a human being, the greatest spirit of the Morn; but, precisely at this point, nothing more: this instance of beauty, and that image, and this mode of presentation are plainly superhuman, heavenly, divine! How much is there to the monumental conclusion!

So there is neither proof for the divinity of Holy Scripture (which serves dogmatic purposes and there indeed is verified), nor is the furor poeticus a piece of theopneusty; nor ought it to disturb our human ways of interpretation. I consider these pieces *"sacred, most ancient, poetic, national documents of the Morn"*: That is how I want to read them!

Part III

Philosophy of History

⁓ 11 ⁓

On the Character of Humankind

This text is the twenty-fifth letter in Herder's collection *Letters Concerning the Advancement of Humanity* (1793). It is one of those rare texts in which Herder formulates his general "credo" about humanity, in the very specific sense in which he uses the term. "Humanity" is the potential of every human being. It is the foundation of human history and must not be confused with sentimental applications like humanitarian efforts. "Humanity" *(Humanität)* is the power of human beings to form their history, for good or ill. World history is the development of humanity, which is not something each human being is endowed with by birth. The goal of world history is the attainment of the greatest possible human diversity; thus, history is a never-ending process. It proceeds in accordance with and is based on natural laws, which are analogically valid on the level of human culture and history; as Herder put it, "the nature of the human being is art." Hence, world history is an open process of self-aware perfection as an activity, not as a result: the present—as Leibniz, who is omnipresent in Herder's oeuvre, put it—is pregnant with the future, and the future is seen as a positive one. Herder as philosopher of history is an optimist. As a background for this text, we have to keep in mind that the French Revolution was just entering the phase of terror.

All your questions concerning the progress of our species, which really would call for a book in response, are answered, it seems to me, by one word, *humanity, to be human.* Were the question to be whether the human being could become, and should become, more than human, a superman, a human being beyond the realm of the species, every line written in response would be in vain. Now, however, since only the *laws governing his nature,* the *ineradicable character of his kind and species* are under discussion, allow me to write a few paragraphs.

On the Character of Humankind

1. *Perfection* in an object is found in nothing but that the thing is what it is meant to be and what it is capable of being.

2. Perfection in an *individual* human being, therefore, is found in that he, in the course of his existence, be himself and continue to become himself. That he utilize the powers nature has given him as his heritage; that he strive with them to profit himself and others.

3. *Survival, life, and individual well-being* are the foundation of these powers; whatever weakens this foundation, or takes away from it, whatever victimizes human beings, or mutilates them—whatever its name—is inhuman.

4. The *education* of the human being begins with the inception of life; for, though he brings his powers and limbs into the world, he must learn how to use these powers and limbs, how to use and to develop them. A condition of society, thus, which neglects education, or moves it in the wrong direction, or favors this wrong direction, or, finally, renders the education of humankind difficult or impossible, insofar is an inhuman condition. Such a condition deprives itself of its limbs and of what is best about them—the realization of their powers. For what other purpose would humans have joined together, but that thereby they might become more perfect, better, happier human beings?

5. *Distorted* human beings, that is to say, humans who are *flawed in their development,* demonstrate in their miserable existence nothing other than that they lived, from their childhood on, in a society beset by misfortune; for, in order to become human, each one brings with him a potential that is sufficient.

6. No human being can live *for himself, alone,* much as he might wish to do so. The capacities which he attains, the virtues or vices which he acts out, to a lesser or greater degree will bring pain or joy to others.

7. To provide for and to facilitate in each individual case *the mutually most beneficial impact of one human being upon the other,* that, and that alone can be the purpose *of all human community.* Whatever interferes with, hinders, or voids this purpose is inhuman. Whether the human being lives briefly or for a long time, in this estate or that, he is meant to enjoy his existence and to convey the best of that existence to others; to that end, the society that he has joined is meant to assist him.

8. Once a human being passes away, he takes with him nothing but the consciousness of having satisfied, to a greater or lesser degree, his duty to be human. Everything else he leaves behind, for humankind. The skills perfected by him, all the interest accumulated on the capital of his powers,

which far exceeds the heritage loaned to him at the outset, all this falls *to his kind.*

9. His place is taken by young, vigorous human beings, who *continue to utilize* this heritage; they in turn step from the stage, and others come to take their place. Humans die, but humankind lives on immortally. Its principal good, the capacity to use its powers, the formation of its capacities, is a common, a lasting good, and it must, in a natural and continuous way, *grow further.*

10. Practice *increases* powers, not only in the individual, but immensely more so among the many in discourse with one another. Humans create for themselves ever more and better tools; they learn ever more and to their greater advantage to use one another as tools. The *physical power of humankind,* therefore, increases; the mass of that which must be moved becomes greater; the machines which are to move it become more highly developed, more artful, more adroit, and more refined.

11. For the nature of the human being is *art.*[1] Everything to which he is disposed, can and must in time become art.

12. All *objects* that fall into his realm (and his realm is as wide as the earth) invite him to this task. These objects are subject to his ends, and are not being explored, recognized, and utilized according to their nature in itself. There is no one who could put limits upon his activity, not even death. For humankind renews itself with ever-new perceptions of things, with eternally young powers.

13. Infinite are the combinations with one another into which the objects of nature may be brought; the spirit of inventiveness in their utilization, therefore, *is unlimited* and *progressive.* One invention gives rise to the next; one activity arouses the other. Often, with one discovery, cause is given for a thousand new activities, and ten thousand more are founded upon them.

14. Now, let one imagine the *line of this progress* not as straight, nor as uniform, but as stretching in all directions, with all manner of turns and twists. Neither the asymptote, nor the ellipse, nor the cycloid can portray the course of nature.[2] Now humans eagerly fall upon an object; now they leave it in the middle of the task, either tired of it or because they have been torn away by another, newer object. When this new one has become too old for them, they will return to the former; or it may even be that the new will lead them back to the old. For, in human affairs, everything is connected with nature, because the human being is no more than human, and it is only with *his* organs that he sees and uses nature.

15. From all this there springs a *competition* of human powers which must *increase* by the same token as the sphere of discovery and practice grows. Elements and nations come into contact with one another which

otherwise did not seem to know each other; the more intense the conflict in which they are engaged, the more they gradually rub off their sides against each other, and at last there come into being some common endeavors of several peoples.

16. A *conflict*[3] *among all the peoples on our earth* is indeed conceivable; in effect, the ground for such has already been prepared.

17. It should not be surprising that nature calls for much time, for many transformations, to carry out these tasks; for nature, no time is too long, no movement too intricate. *Everything* that is capable of happening and is meant to happen may come to be only in the context of *all* of time, and in the context of *all* of space[4]; whatever does not come to be today, because it cannot come to be, will come to be tomorrow.

18. The human being is indeed the first, but not the only creature on earth; he governs the world, but he is not the universe. *Thus, he is often confronted by the forces of nature,* and he therefore struggles with them. Fire destroys his works; floods cover his land; storms destroy his ships; and diseases murder his kind. All this is put into his way, *so that he may overcome it.*

19. He carries the weapons for doing so *within himself.* His intelligence has mastered animals, and he uses them to his ends; his caution has set limits to fire, and forces the storm to serve him; he puts dikes in the way of the floods, and he walks upon their waves; he knows how to steer the course of diseases, and even the ravaging of death. To the *greatest of his goods* the human being has come by *accident,* and a thousand discoveries would have remained hidden to him, had not necessity invented them. She is the weight of the clock, which drives all its wheels.

20. It is the same with the storms within our breasts, with the *passions of humankind.* Nature has rendered the characters of our kind as diverse as they might possibly have been, so that what is innermost in humankind may be brought out, so that all its powers may be realized.

21. Just as there are among the animals *destructive* as well as *preserving* kinds, so it is among humans. But, among the former as well as among the latter, the destructive passions are *fewer in number*[5]; they can and they must be constrained and mastered by the preserving tendencies of our nature; though not eliminated, they must be brought under control.

22. This control is *reason;* in terms of action, it is *equity and goodness.* A blind power, devoid of reason, in the end is always an impotent power; it either destroys itself or must at last be subordinate to the mind.

23. It is by the same token, that genuine reason is always tied to *equity and goodness;* the one always leads to the others and vice versa, reason and goodness are the two poles around the axis on which the sphere of humanity revolves.

ON THE CHARACTER OF HUMANKIND 103

24. Wherever they appear to run counter to one another, there one or another matter does not sit right; but it is precisely *this divergence* that makes *the flaws visible,* and that brings the focus of the interest of our species ever more into accord with rectitude and certainty. Each more delicate flaw that is revealed gives rise to a *new, higher rule of pure, all-encompassing goodness and truth.*

25. All the vices and flaws of our species, therefore, must *in the end* serve *the whole to the best.* All the misery that comes from prejudices, lethargy, and ignorance will at last serve only to teach the human being more of its condition; all excesses to the right and to the left in the end push him back onto his own center.

26. The more obstinate, stubborn, and lethargic the human species, the more harm it does to itself; this harm it must bear, it must atone for it and make amends; and so much later it will reach its destiny.

27. To place this destiny exclusively *beyond* the grave is not beneficial to humankind, but harmful. Only that can grow there which has been planted here, and to deprive a human being of his existence here, to reward him for it with one beyond our world, means to defraud him of his existence.

28. Yes, to distort for the entire human species thus deceived the end point of its destiny, means to twist from humans' hands the sting of their effectiveness, and to maintain them in a fraud.

29. The purer a *religion* was, the more it was compelled to and was determined to advance humanity, the essence of what it means to be human. This is the touchstone even of the mythologies of the diverse religions.

30. *The religion of Christ,* which was represented by Himself, taught by Him and practiced by Him, was this *humanity.* It was nothing but this; but it was this also in the widest sense, in the purest source, and in the most effective application. Christ knew for himself no nobler name than when he called himself the *son of man,* that is to say, a human being.

31. The better the state, the more appropriately and felicitously it *nurtures* within it this *humanity;* the less humane it is, the more unfortunate and worse it will be in its conduct. This pervades all its members and associations, from the cottage to the throne.

32. For politics, the human being is a *means;* for morality he is *the end;* both sciences must become one, or they will both be harmful to one another. All disparities appearing in the process, in the meanwhile, must instruct human beings, so that they, at the very least, learn from their own mistakes.

33. Just as each attentive *individual* human being is guided by the law of nature to humanity—his rough edges are rubbed off, he must overcome

himself, give in to others, and learn to use his powers for the benefit of others—so it is that the *diverse characters and mentalities* work for the benefit of the larger whole. Each feels the evils of the world *in accordance with his own situation;* he is therefore under the duty to address these evils from that vantage point, to come to the assistance of the flawed, the weak, and the oppressed at that point to which *his* mind and *his* heart direct him. If he succeeds, he will thereby have within himself his most particular joy; if he does not now succeed, someone else at another time will do so. But he has done what he had to do and what he was able to do.

34. If the state is, as it is meant to be, *the eye of general reason, the ear and the heart of general fairness and goodness,* it will listen to each of these voices, and it will arouse and encourage the activity of humans in keeping with their diverse tendencies, sensibilities, weaknesses, and needs.

35. It is only *one edifice* that is meant to be completed, the simplest, the greatest; it stretches across all the centuries and nations; as it is in the physical, so it is also in the moral and political sphere, that *humankind is engaged in eternal progress and striving.*

36. *Perfectibility,* therefore, is not a deception; it is the means and final end to all that is called for and made possible by the character of our kind, by our *humanity.*

Raise your eyes and see. Everywhere the seed is sown; here it rots and germinates, there it grows and ripens to a new seed. There it lies under snow and ice; be consoled, the ice melts, the snow warms and covers the seed. No evil that is encountered by humankind can be or is meant to be other than conducive to humankind. It would, after all, be their own responsibility if things were otherwise—for even the vices, flaws, and weaknesses of humans, as manifestations of nature, are governed by rules and are being, or are subject to being, calculated. This is my *creed. Speremus atque agamus.*[6]

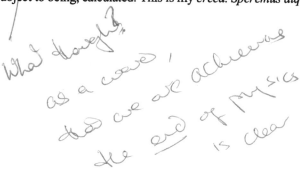

~ 12 ~

On the Term and the Concept "Humanity"

The twenty-seventh and twenty-eighth letters of Herder's collection *Letters Concerning the Advancement of Humanity* (1794) constitute the following text. It is a core text regarding the central term of Herder's idea of history: humanity. Herder insists on using the term *Humanität*, although he is of course highly aware of the fact that the term is a foreign word in the German language. In doing so, he distances himself from anything that might weaken or sentimentalize the quality he captures with the word "humanity." It is not something given; rather, it is a specific human quality in gestation. Human history is the process of its development. To be passive is to urge human history to surrender to contingent circumstances and to fall below the already-attained level of humanity. In other words, humanity develops as activity in history.

You[1] fear that one might mark the word humanity with a stain; could we not change the word and say *humankind, humaneness, human rights, human duties, human dignity, love of humankind*?

Humans we all are, and, to that extent, we carry with us *the quality of being human,* or in other words, we are part of *humankind.* Unfortunately, in our language [i.e., German], the term *human being,* and even more so the compassionate word *humaneness,* have been given the subsidiary connotation of lowness, weakness, and false pity, so much so that one has become accustomed to utter the former only with a glance of contempt, the latter with a shrug. *"That Human Being!"** we exclaim, with a tone of moaning and contempt, and we believe thereby to let off lightly a good man with the expression, "that he might have been overcome by *humaneness.*" No reasonable person will condone the idea that the character of our kind, of which we are part, be demeaned so barbarously; such conduct was more imprudent than if one had turned the name of one's city or kinship association into a despicable term. We, therefore, want to beware that we do not write letters on the advancement of such kind of *humaneness.*

The expression *human rights* cannot be used without reference to *human duties;* both relate to one another, and we seek for both just one word.

The same is true for *human dignity* and *love of humankind.* The human species, as it now is and as it probably will remain for a long time, in its largest part does not have dignity; one may rather pity than venerate it. However, in order to live up to the *potential of its kind,* and for the sake of its *worth* and *dignity,* humankind is meant to be developed. The beautiful expression *love of humanity* has become so trivial that one rather loves all in order not to love any one human being among them effectively. All of these words contain partial concepts pertaining to our purpose, which we would like to express in *one* term.

Thus, we want to stay with the word *humanity,* to which, among the ancients and the moderns, the best authors have tied such noble concepts. The word humanity stands for the *character of our kind;* but we are born with this character only in terms of disposition, and, to become actual, it must be developed. We do not bring this character with us ready-made into the world; but, in this world, it is to be the goal of our strivings, the sum of our endeavors, of our *worthiness;* for we do not know of something *angelic* in the human being, and when the demon that governs us is not a humane demon, we become the scourge of man. The *divine* in our kind is thus constituted by the *ascent to humanity;* every great and good human being, lawgivers, inventors, philosophers, poets, artists, each noble human in keeping with his estate, in raising his children, in observing his duties, by means of example, work, institution, and teaching, has contributed to it. Humanity is the treasure and the yield of all human efforts, it is, in a way, what amounts to *art in our kind.* The effort to attain this quality is a task that must be carried on incessantly, or we will sink back, whether we be of higher or lower estate, to raw animality, to *brutality.*

Should it be so, then, that the word humanity demeans our language? All cultured nations have added it to their tongue; and should our letters fall

---

Adelung even had to find room for a long article on the banishable neuter form of the term *"it, the human being."*[2]

into the hands of a stranger, they should at the very least appear harmless to him; for no man of integrity will want to have written *Letters on the Advancement of Brutality.*

Gladly I welcome with you . . . the word *humanity* into our language; because the concept conveyed by it, but even more the *history* of that concept, appears to entitle it to its rights as a citizen.

As long as the human being, this marvelous riddle of creation, reflected upon himself in his visible state, and in so doing measured himself against that which dwelt within him, against his potential and the powers of his will, or even against the external objects of enduring nature, he was oppressed by a feeling of *frailty,* of *weakness* and *disease;* it is for this reason that in several writings of the Morn this perception was originally attached to the name given to our kind. In those terms, the human being is *made of clay,* he is a vessel, *frail* and *glued together,* touched by a fleeting breath; his life is a *phantom,* his destiny is *toil on earth.*

This perception by itself led to *humaneness*—that is, to the compassionate feeling for the suffering of others, to the taking part in the imperfections of their nature, with the accompanying effort to cope with those imperfections, or to assist in overcoming them. The people of the Morn are so rich in moral expressions and couched ways of driving home this human feeling as a duty, or of recommending it to our kind as an indispensable virtue, that it would be very unjust to deny them humanity just because they did not possess this word.

The Greeks had a nobler name for the human being, ανθρωπος, *one who looks upward,* who directs his face and his eyes upward, or, as elucidated even more artfully by *Plato,* one who in the act of seeing also sums up and calculates. But, by the same token, the Greeks could not help but observe in this upward-looking, rational species all the flaws that eventually cause pitying compassion, that is to say, bring about humanity and companionship. In Homer and in all their poets, the most tender lament concerning the destiny of humankind is voiced. Recall the words of Apollo, in describing the mortals,

> —as they, like the leaves of the tree, now greening and fresh,/ nurtured by the fruits of the earth; but then shortly/ wilting, soullessly falling by the wayside—[3]

Or, when Jupiter himself pities the immortal steeds of Achilles, as they mourn their master:

—He spoke in his innermost soul:
Pitiful you, why did we give you to King Peleus,
to a mortal, you, who never age and die?
Was it to see you suffer with the miserable humans?
For, nowhere is a more miserable being, than man;
none of all who move above the earth and breathe.—[4]

Their lyrical poets sing in the same vein.

Next to self-preservation, it was thus the first duty of humankind to assist our neighbors in their weakness and to protect them from the evils of nature or from the raw passions of their own kind. It is to that end that the care of their lawgivers and wise men was directed, that in word and custom they urged upon human beings these indispensable and sacred duties to their fellow humans, thereby founding the most ancient *human law and law of peoples*. It was religion that caused man to abstain from murder, to assist the weak, to bring the strayed back to the right path, to care for the wounded, and to bury the dead. Religion gave shape to the duties of wedded life, of parents toward children, of children toward parents, of the native toward the stranger, and gradually extended this compassion also to the enemy. What was begun by poetry and the wisdom of the lawgivers was developed further by philosophy; and we are indebted in particular to the Socratic School, that *the knowledge of the nature of man, of his essential relations and duties* became the subject of study of so many of the most exquisite spirits and in so many systems of thought. What Socrates did among the Greeks was done by others among other peoples; *Confucius,* for example, is the Socrates of the Chinese, *Manu,* of the Indians; for, generally speaking, the laws governing human obligations have not remained unknown to any people on earth. But in every public constitution, depending upon location and time, these laws governing human obligations have been promoted in part, and in part hindered and despoiled, by the so-called *public interest.*

It was among the Romans, therefore, to whom the word *humanity* actually belongs, that the concept found occasion to be more specifically developed. Rome had rigid laws concerning servants, children, strangers, enemies; the upper classes had rights vis-à-vis the people, and so forth. Whoever observed the laws with utmost rigidity could be *just,* but not thereby also *humane.* The man of nobility, who on his own did not make use of these rights where they were not fair, who did not act toward children, slaves, the lowly, strangers, and enemies as the Roman citizen or patrician, but as a human being, was *humanus, humanissimus,* not only in

---

Heyne has superbly demonstrated this as the purpose of ancient Greek institutions in several of his *opuscul. academic.*[5]

conversation and social discourse, but also in matters of business, in domestic customs, in the entire sphere of conduct. And since the study of and love for Greek philosophy has contributed much to this end, in that it made the rough and rigid Roman more yielding, more gentle, more pleasing, and more fair in his way of thinking, what more beautiful name could have been given to the disciplines of learning devoted to edification than that of the *liberal arts*? To be sure, philosophy was not excluded from them *; rather, it was the instructor and companion of these edifying disciplines of learning, sometimes their mother, and at others their daughter.

Since *humanity,* in these terms, gained a name among the Romans first of all as the mistress subduing rigid civil laws and prerogatives, as the real daughter of philosophy and the liberal arts, a name which was passed on by them to posterity, so let us pay respect to the name as well as to the subject matter. Even in the most superstitious and darkest ages, the term *humaniora* recalls the serious and beautiful purpose that the disciplines of higher learning are meant to serve; since we cannot very well call them *human* sciences, still we want never to forget, or to give up this purpose, with and without the word humanity. We are in need of this word as much as the Romans were.

For if you were now to take a further look into history, there was a time when the word human being (*homo*) assumed an altogether different meaning; it came to mean *he who bears an obligation, a subject, a vassal, a servant.* Whoever was not within these categories enjoyed no rights, his life was not secure; and those to whom these serving humans belonged, they were *superior beings.* The oath with which one pledged oneself to them was called *human duty (homagium),* and whoever wanted to be a free man, had to demonstrate by means of the letter certifying his being a free man, that he was not a *homo,* not a human being. Are you now surprised that so low an image is attached to the word human in our language? By its very heritage the word connotes nothing but a despised man, a Mennisk,[7] a little man.**

Also, the words *Leute* [people] and *Leutlein* [little people] conveyed only the image of attachment to the land which they were bound to till, and on which they died. The prince, the noble was master over and owner of land and people; and his treasurers, clerks, caplans, vassals, and clients were *homines, humans,* or *little humans,* with sundry anxilary attributes that merely explicated the degree to which they belonged to *Him.*

Ernesti's address *de humanitatis disciplina* is known in this regard.[6]

**Neither *Wachter* nor *Adelung* has observed the origin of this ending in the word *Mennisk;* but it appears to be the genuine one, for, if one pronounces the word *Mensch* in the low Saxon dialect, that is, in the ancient and genuine manner, it is pronounced *Mens=ch (Mensk),* that is, a miserable and unarmed man, a little man.

~ 13 ~

Preface to the *Reflections on the Philosophy of the History of Humankind*

In the following text, Herder introduces his readers to his project of a philosophy of history, and he asks his readers for benevolence. This *captatio benevolentiae* was necessary in 1784, when the first volume of his great Weimar philosophy history—*Reflections on the Philosophy of the History of Humankind*—was published, because philosophy of history as a discipline was then of very recent origin. Voltaire had coined the term, and only a few authors had ventured into this new field. The goal of philosophy of history was to develop a perspective on human history as a totality that is essentially governed by rules, as is nature. It has to be noted, however, that Herder was not aiming at a quantifying system of laws, such as exists in the modern natural sciences. He is interested in an approach to world history and human culture that allows us to see individual facts, epochs, and persons in their own essence, and at the same time to formulate very general rules and laws that presumably govern the complexity of history. The framework for this assumed—hypothetical—totality of history is provided by Herder's belief in God. Thus, faith confirms the ultimate totality of world history. Yet Herder is anything but an unquestioning Christian believer. In his perspective, nothing specifically human is simply "given" to the human being, neither nature nor culture, neither the other nor the self. Knowledge has to be developed, as the organs for acquiring knowledge have to be developed by experience. World history for Herder is exactly this: the never-ending process of the development of the human faculties in coordination with nature.

If this book is to live up to its title, it should probe much more deeply from the outset and embrace a much wider compass of ideas. What is human happiness? How far does it exist in this world? How far is it to be found, considering the great differences among all the beings upon earth, and especially of humankind, under every form of government, in every climate, in every change of circumstance, stage of life, and the times? Is there a standard governing these various conditions of life, and has Providence reckoned on the well-being of her creatures, in all these situations, as her ultimate and grand purpose? All these questions had to be examined, they had to be pursued and assessed throughout the unruly course of the ages and forms of government, before a general result for all of humankind could be produced. Thus, there was a wide field to be traversed, and profound depth to be explored. I had read almost everything that was written upon the subject; and, from my youth, every new book that appeared relative to the history of humankind, and in which I hoped to find material for my grand work, was for me a treasure discovered. I rejoiced that, in recent times, this philosophy rose to greater prominence, and I made use of every assistance that fortune sent my way.

An author, who presents his book, as long as it contains thoughts which, though he did not invent them—for how little is there in our day that may be newly invented—he, at least *found* and made his own, yes, in which he dwelt for years as in the property of his spirit and heart, an author such as this, I say, for better or for worse, in a way presents to the public with his book a part of his soul. He not only reveals the subjects that have employed his thoughts at certain periods, the doubts and resolutions that have come to him thereby in the course of his life, that troubled him or relieved him; rather, he also counts on—for what other attraction would there be to become an author and to reveal matters of the heart to an unruly multitude?—some like-minded souls, perhaps only a few, to whom in the labyrinth of their years these or kindred ideas have come to be of importance. With those he converses unseen, and to those he imparts his sentiments, expecting from them in return their more valuable thoughts and advice when they have advanced beyond him. This great commerce of spirits and hearts is the singular and the greatest benefit of printing, which otherwise would have brought as much harm as usefulness to literary nations. The author thought of himself as being part of the circle of those who truly felt an interest in what he wrote, and from whom he therefore wanted to elicit their engaged and constructive thoughts. This is the highest merit of authorship, and a well-disposed person will find much greater joy in what he excites in others than in what he says himself. He who reflects on how opportunely this or that book, or merely this or that hint in a book, has sometimes come his way; what joy it has afforded him to find another and distant spirit—yet near to himself in his pursuit of his own or yet a better trail—and how such a thought has occupied him for years and led him on, he will consider an author who speaks to him and imparts to him his innermost thoughts, not as one who labors for hire, but as a friend, who trustfully also reveals unfinished thoughts, so that the more experienced reader may think in concert with him and lead his imperfections nearer to perfection.

On a subject like mine, *the History of Humankind, the Philosophy of their History,* such a disposition to the quality of *humanity* in the reader appears to me a prime and pleasing duty. He who wrote it was a human being and you who read it are a human being too. He was liable to error, and has perhaps erred; you have acquired knowledge which he did not and could not possess; make use, therefore, of what you find useful, and accept his good will; yet do not confine yourself to reproach, but improve it and extend it. With feeble hands he has laid a few foundation stones of a building, which only the course of centuries may and will complete; bliss will prevail once these stones are covered with earth, and he who laid them is forgotten, when, over them or even in another place, only the more beautiful edifice remains.

But I have unwittingly wandered too far from the design with which I set out, and which was to give an account of the manner of my falling upon this subject, and turning to it again among other occupations and duties of a very different nature. Already at an early age, when the meadows of higher learning were still lying before me in the beauty of the morning, which is so greatly diminished by the noon of our life, the thought frequently occurred to me, *whether, as everything in the world has its philosophy and science, there must not also be a philosophy and science of what concerns us most closely, of the history of humankind at large?* Everything called this to my attention, metaphysics and morals, physics and natural history, and lastly, religion above all. Shall the God who has ordered everything in nature by measure, number, and weight, who has so regulated according to these the essence of things, their forms and their relations, their course and their subsistence, that only one system, one goodness and one power prevail, from the grand edifice of the universe to the speck of dust, from the power that holds the planets and suns together to the thread of the spider's web, shall He, who has conceived so sublimely and divinely of everything in the human body and within the powers of the human soul, so that when we dare if ever so distantly to emulate in thought this *Singular Wisdom,* we lose ourselves in the abyss of His thought; how, I said to myself, shall this God in the general destination and disposition of the totality of our kind depart from His goodness and to that end not have a plan? Or should he want to hide this plan from us, even though he has displayed so much of the laws of his eternal purpose in regard to the inferior part of creation, which is of less concern to us? What is the whole of humankind other than a herd without a shepherd? Or, in the words of the lamenting prophet: *are they not left to their own ways, as the fishes of the sea, as the creeping things that have no ruler over them?*[1]—Or did they not need to know the plan? This I am inclined to believe; for what human being grasps even the little purpose of the individual life? And yet, he sees as far as he is meant to see, and he knows enough to direct his own steps; and yet, does not even this very ignorance serve as a pretext for great abuses? How many are there who, because they perceive no plan, actually deny that there is one, or, at the least, think of it with trembling dread, and believe in doubting, and doubt in believing! They constrain themselves mightily from considering the human species as an anthill, where the foot of one stronger, who in his strange shape is himself an ant, crushes thousands under his foot, annihilates thousands in their minute and their great endeavors, yes, where lastly the two grand tyrants of the earth, chance and time, sweep away the entire pile without trace and leave the empty space for another industrious community, which in turn will be removed without leaving a trace.—The proud human being refuses to consider his kind as such outcropping of the earth, as the prey of all-consuming decay; and yet, do not history and experience force this image upon him? What whole is completed upon earth? What is whole upon it? Is not time ordained as well as space? And the two are, after all, twin offspring of one destiny. The one is full of wisdom, the other of apparent disorder; and yet, the human being is evidently formed to seek after order, to master a speck of time within the ages, so that posterity may build upon the past; for, to this end he is furnished with memory and reflection. And does not this building of one age upon another render the whole of our species a deformed gigantic edifice, where one pulls down what the other built up, where what never should have been erected is left standing, and where in the course of centuries all becomes a heap of ever more decaying ruins, under which timid mortals dwell with ever more increasing confidence?—I will pursue no further this chain of doubt, and the contradictions of humankind within itself, with one another, and in conflict with all the rest of creation; suffice it that I have sought for *a philosophy of the history of humankind* wherever I could seek it.

Whether I have found it, let this work, but not its first part, decide. This part contains only the foundation, partly in the form of a general overview of our dwelling places, partly in the form of an examination of the organized beings who, subject to us and with us, enjoy the light of this sun. No one, I trust, will think this course too long, or beginning at too remote a distance; for there can be no other if the destiny of humankind is to be read from the book of creation, and it cannot be explored too carefully and from too many points of view. Whoever wishes for mere metaphysical speculations may come to them by a shorter route; but these, divorced from experience and the analogy of nature, appear to me aerial flights that seldom lead to an end. The ways of God in nature, the intentions which the Eternal has actually displayed to us in the chain of his works, they are the Holy Writ, the letters of which I have endeavored to spell, with skill inferior to that of an apprentice, but at least faithfully and with zeal. Were I to be so fortunate as to impart to only one of my readers something of the sweet impression of the eternal wisdom and goodness of the unexplored creator in his workings, which I have felt with a confidence for which I know not a name, this impression of confidence would be the guiding thread to lead us in the pursuit of the work through the labyrinth of human history. Everywhere the great analogy of nature has led me to religious truths, which I had to suppress—with effort—for I did not want to deprive myself of them preemptively, but rather step by step remain faithful to the light, which everywhere beams upon me from the hidden presence of the creator in his works. It will be so much the greater pleasure both to my readers and to myself when, as we proceed on our way, this obscurely dawning light rises upon us at last as the flame and brightness of an unclouded sun.

Let no one be misled, therefore, by my occasionally employing the term nature, personified. Nature is not a self-sufficient entity; rather, *God is all in His works;* yet I was desirous at least not to abuse this sacred name, which no creature under the sun ought to pronounce without the deepest reverence, by employing it too frequently, since I could not introduce it with sufficient solemnity at all occasions. Let him, to whom the term "nature" has been demeaned and rendered meaningless by many writings of our day, conceive of it instead as *that almighty power, goodness, and wisdom,* and in his soul name that invisible being for which no language on Earth can find an expression.

It is the same when I speak of the *organic powers* of creation; I do not believe that they will be considered *qualitates occultas* since their operations are apparent to us, and I know not how to give them a more precise and determinate name. At some future period I intend to enter more fully into these and other subjects, at which I must here give no more than a cursory glance.

In the meanwhile I rejoice that my apprentice undertaking has been made in an age when the hands of masters have labored and gathered within so many individual disciplines of learning and knowledge, to which it was necessary for me to have recourse. These, I am assured, will not despise the esoteric efforts of one uninitiated in their arts, but improve them; for I have constantly observed that, the more real and firmly grounded a science is, so much the less empty altercation occurs among those who are attached to it and cultivate it. Verbal disputes are left by them to those who are learned only in words. Most parts of my book show that a philosophy of the history of humankind cannot yet be written but that it may perhaps be written at the end of our century or our millennium.

Thus, great being, invisible and sublime genius of our kind, I lay at your feet the most imperfect work that mortal ever wrote, in which he dared to trace and follow in thought thy steps. Its leaves may decay and its letters vanish; the forms and formulas will also vanish, in which I have discerned traces of thee, and endeavored to exhibit them to my brethren; but thy intentions will remain, and thou wilt gradually unfold them to thy creatures, and exhibit them in nobler forms. Bliss, if then these leaves shall be swallowed up in the stream of oblivion, and in their stead clearer ideas rise in the souls of humankind.

Weimar, 23 April, 1784.

~ 14 ~

The Human Being Is Predisposed to the Power of Reason

The following text contains Herder's basic anthropological assumption, which explains why human beings have been able to develop their specific type of culture. This foundation lies not in the fact that human beings developed language, but in the fact that they walk and stand upright.* Thus Herder found the specific distinction in a criterion provided by a disposition of nature. The consequences of this natural human condition direct evolution to the development of what is deemed specifically human: culture. According to his general principle that history, like nature, must be based on laws, Herder finds the most fundamental conditions of human history in the realm of the human body, which he analyzes according to the principles of comparative anatomy as he found it in contemporary research.

Internally and externally, the orangutan resembles man. Its brain has the form of ours; it has a broad chest, flat shoulders, a similar face, and a similarly shaped skull; its heart, lungs, liver, spleen, stomach, and intestines are like those of man. *Tyson*** has pointed out forty-eight parts, in which it resembles our species more than the ape; and the accounts of its behavior, even its follies and vices, perhaps also its menstruation, suggest similarity to humankind.

Certainly, therefore, in its inner being, in the manifestation of its soul, it must have some resemblance to humankind; and those philosophers, who

---

*Let us note in passing that even most recent anthropological research tries to prove empirically what Herder discovered more than 200 years ago—without being aware of him. As can be seen from the sources quoted or referred to by Herder, he is familiar with his contemporary research and formulates his own position by discussing the conclusions of other scholars of his time.—Ed.

**Tyson's *Anatomy of a Pygmy compared with that of a Monkey, an ape and a man* (London: 1751), pp. 92–94.[1]

would debase it to the level of the small, more instinctive animals, seem to me to lack the standard of comparison. The beaver builds, but instinctively; its whole mechanism is constructed for this; but it can do nothing more; it is incapable of associating with humans, of taking part in their thoughts and passions. The ape, on the contrary, no longer has a fixed instinct; its power of thinking stands close to the brink of reason, at the pitiful edge of imitation. It imitates everything, and therefore its brain must be suited to a thousand combinations of sensory images of which no other animal is capable; for, neither the wise elephant nor the adaptable dog does what the ape is able to do; *it would perfect itself.* But this it cannot; the door is locked against it; it is impossible for its brain to connect its own ideas to those of others and to take ownership of that which was imitated. The female ape described by *Bontius*[2] possessed a sense of modesty and covered herself with her hand when a stranger approached; she wept, sighed, and appeared to perform human functions. The apes described by *Battel*[3] move about in social groups, arm themselves with clubs, chase the elephants from their territory; they attack the Negroes and gather around their fire, but they do not have the intellect to keep it going. The ape of *de la Brosse*[4] sat down at table, used the knife and fork, became angry, expressed sadness, and possessed all human emotions. The love of the mothers for their children, their raising and accommodation to the arts and tricks of the ape's life, the order of their commonwealth and their order when moving about, the punishments they inflict on their malefactors, even their droll artifices and malice, in addition to a number of other, incontestable traits, are sufficient proof that they are creatures resembling humans in their inner being as much as their external appearance indicates. *Buffon*[5] wastes the stream of his eloquence when he disputes the correspondence of the inner and the outer organism of nature with reference to these animals; the facts collected by Buffon himself regarding them are sufficient to contradict him, and the correspondence of the internal and the external in the organism of nature, correctly defined, remains undeniable in all manifestations of life.

What, then, is lacking in the manlike creature, that it did not become human? Was it, perhaps, language alone? But men have taken pains to raise several apes; and, had this animal, which imitates everything, been capable of speech, it certainly would have imitated this first, and waited for no instruction. Or does it depend solely on its organs? Not that either; for, though apes may readily grasp the content of human speech, no ape has yet, despite his continuous gesticulating, gained for himself the facility to converse with his master in pantomime and to discourse with him on human terms by means of gesticulation. It must be something else, therefore, that closed the door of human reason to the poor creature, leaving it, perhaps, with the faint sense of being so near and yet not belonging.

What was this something? It is strange that almost all the difference appearing upon dissection should seem to consist in *the parts appropriate to walking*. The ape is so formed as to be able to walk erect, and it is therein more like the human than its brethren; but it is not formed entirely to this end, and this difference seems to deprive it of everything. Let us pursue this point of view, and nature herself will guide us to the paths along which we will have to search for the earliest disposition to human dignity.

The orangutan[*] has long arms, large hands, short legs, and large feet with long toes; but the thumb of its hand and the great toe of its foot are small; thus *Buffon,* and earlier *Tyson,* on this account termed the ape species quadrimanous; and, with these small members, the ape evidently lacks the basis that enables the human to stand firm. The hind part of its body is slender, its knee broader than in the human and not so low; the muscles that move the knee are rooted lower in the thigh than in the human, so that the animal can never stand perfectly upright, but, with bent knees, always seems to be learning to stand. The head of the thighbone hangs in its socket without a ligament; the bones of the pelvis stand like those of quadrupeds; the last five vertebrae of the neck have long pointed processes, which prevent the head from being bent backward; thus, the creature is not formed to stand in the upright position, and the consequences of this condition are disastrous. Its neck is short and the clavicles are long, so that the head appears to be stuck between the shoulders.[**] Thence, its forepart is enlarged, it has prominent jaws and a flat nose; the eyes stand close together; the ball of the eye is small, so that none of the white around the pupil is seen. The mouth, on the other hand, is large, the belly thick, the breasts long; and the back appears feeble. The ears stick out as in animals. The orbits of the eyes approach each other; the head is articulated posteriorly, as in animals, and not centrally, as in the human. The upper jaw is protruded forward, and the insertion of the intermaxillary bone *(os intermaxillare)* peculiar to the ape completes its separation from the human face.[***] Now,

---

[*]See Camper's *Kort Berigt wegens de Ontleding van verschiedene Orang-Outangs (Brief Account on the Dissection of Different Orangutans)* (Amsterdam: 1780). I know this account only from the copious extract in the *Göttingische Gelehrte Anzeigen* (Zugabe, St. 29, 1780), and it is hoped that it, and the essay *On the Organs of Speech in Apes* in the *Transactions,* will be inserted in the collection of the tracts of this celebrated anatomist (Leipzig: 1781).[6]

[**]See the front and the back views of this wretched figure in *Tyson.*

[***]See an illustration of this bone in [Johann Friedrich] Blumenbach, *De generis humani varietate nativa . . . ,* Tab. 1, fig. 2. Yet not all apes appear to have this *os intermaxillare* in the same degree, as *Tyson,* in his account of the dissection, plainly says it was not found.

from this formation of the head, the lower part projecting forward, with the back of the head hanging; from this location of it on the neck, from the entire sweep of the vertebrae corresponding to the position of the head, the ape remains always only an animal, however great its resemblance to the human.

To prepare ourselves for this conclusion, let us consider countenances appearing to border on those of animals, however distantly. What makes them like the animal? What gives them this debased, crude appearance? The protruding jaw, the pushed-back head; in short, the remotest resemblance to the quadrupedal organization. The moment the center of gravity on which the human skull rests in its exalted arch is shifted, the head seems fixed to the spine, the toothy jaws project forward, and the nose flattens out to the nostril of the beast. Above, the orbits of the eyes draw closer together, the forehead recedes and receives from both sides the deadening pressure of the ape's skull. The head becomes pointed on top and in the rear, and the cavity of the skull narrows—and all of this because the thrust of the figure appears to have been shifted away from the beautiful, free carriage of the head that facilitates the erect posture of the human.

Shift this point in another way, and the entire bearing becomes beautiful and noble. Rich with thought, the forehead will thrust forward, and the skull will rise vaultlike, with exalted, calm dignity. The broad nose of the beast will contract into a higher and more delicate shape. The retreating mouth will be more attractively covered, and thus will be formed the lips of the human, which are lacking in the most clever of apes. The chin will sink to round the fine perpendicular oval; the cheek gently rises; The eye will look from beneath the thrusting forehead as from a sacred temple of thought. And how did all of this come about? Through the shaping of the head so as to facilitate *the upright posture,* through the internal and external disposition of the same to a *perpendicular center of gravity.** Let those who doubt survey the skulls of apes and humans, and no shadow of their doubt will remain.

All external form in nature is a representation of its inner workings; and thus, great mother, we approach the most sacred of your terrestrial creations, the laboratory of the human mind.

Great pains have been taken to compare the size of the human brain with the brain mass of other species of animals, and thus to weigh the animal and

---

*Daubenton's[7] treatise *Sur les différences de la situation du grand trou occipital dans l'homme & dans les animaux* in the *Memoires de l'Académie de Paris* 1764, which I found mentioned in Blumenbach, I have not yet read; I therefore also do not know where his thought goes and how far he carries it. My opinion is drawn from the animal and human skulls lying before me.

the human brain against each other. But this mode of weighing and calculating can give no accurate result for three reasons.

1. Because one link of the relation, the mass of the body, is too indeterminate, and does not provide pure proportionality to the other so finely shaped link, the brain itself. How varied are the things which give weight to a body! And how varied may be the relation to each other which nature assigned to them. Nature knew to lighten the heavy burden of the elephant's body and head by means of air; and, though its brain is not overly large, it is the wisest of the animals. What weighs most in the body of an animal? The bones; but to these the brain is not immediately proportioned.

2. Unquestionably it matters a great deal, to what purposes of the body the brain is employed, and to what functions of life it sends its nerval impulses. If, therefore, the brain and the nervous system were weighed against each other, a finer and yet not a pure proportionality would be given, for the weight of both would indicate neither the fineness of the nerves nor the purpose of their paths.

3. Thus, ultimately all depends on the *more delicate elaboration,* on the *more proportionate relation of the parts in respect to one another,* and, it seems, most importantly on the *extensive and unconstrained arena* in which the impressions and perceptions of all the nerves may be tied together with the greatest power, with the most incisive truth, and lastly also with the freest interplay of variety, to be firmly fused together into the unknown divine oneness we call *thought,* concerning which the size of the brain gives us no information.

Nevertheless, these quantitative assessments* are valuable and afford us, if not the ultimate, nonetheless some instructive and intermediate results. Some of these I dare to adduce here, to show the ascending uniformity of nature's course.

1. In the smaller animals, in which the circulation and organic warmth are yet imperfect, we find a smaller brain and fewer nerves. Nature, as we have already remarked, has made up to them by means of pervasive and finely distributed instinct what she was obliged to deny them in sensibility; for it is probable that the developing organism of these creatures could neither produce nor support a larger brain.

---

*We find a copious collection in *Haller's* major work on physiology[8]; and it would be desirable if Professor *Wrisberg* were to publish his rich findings, to which he refers in his commentary to *Haller's* smaller work on physiology[9]; for, as we shall soon see, the *specific gravity* of the brain, which he has investigated, is a finer standard than that employed in preceding assessments.

2. In animals with warmer blood, the mass of the brain increases in proportion to their more elaborate functions, but immediately there appear other factors that seem to govern in particular the proportion between the nerves and the musculature. In beasts of prey the brain is smaller; in these, the muscular powers predominate, to which, and to the stimulation of the animal's instincts, they are largely subservient. In the calmer, grazing animals, the brain is larger, though even in these it seems principally employed to be utilized in sensory nervous functions. Birds have much brain mass; for, in their colder element warmer blood is necessary. The circulation is arranged in a more compact fashion, corresponding to their proportionately mostly smaller bodies; so it is that in the lovestruck sparrow the brain fills the entire head and constitutes one fifth of the weight of its body.

3. In young creatures, the brain is larger than in full-grown ones; evidently, this is so because it is more soft and tender, and therefore occupies a larger space, but is not on that account heavier. Within it, there still is the ample supply of special fluids needed for the operations of life and internal development, enabling the creature in its youth to become functional, a process requiring much effort. Over the course of years, the brain grows more firm and dry; for capacities are then acquired, and the human being as well as the animal is no longer susceptible to such light, graceful, fleeting impressions. In short, the size of the brain in a creature appears to be a necessary collateral condition, but not the primary one, for the enhancement of capacities and cerebral activity. Of all the animals, as the ancients already knew, the human being has proportionally the largest brain; yet in this point the ape is not inferior to him; yes the horse in this regard is exceeded by the ass.

Thus, there must be another factor that physiologically enhances the more refined thinking capacity of the creature; and, according to the scale of organization that Nature has placed before our eyes, what else could it be but the *structure of the brain* itself, the more perfect *elaboration* of its parts and fluids, and finally its more appropriate *placement and proportion,* facilitating the reception of mental stimuli and ideas in the most felicitous glow of life. Let us then turn over the leaves of Nature's book to the finest pages she ever wrote, the tablets of the brain itself; for, as the end of her workings are the sensibility, the well-being, the general happiness of the creature, the *head* must be the most secure repository in which we find her thoughts.

1. In creatures in which cerebral development hardly exists, the brain appears very simple; it is as a bud, or a pair of buds of the spouting spinal marrow, providing nervous impulses to only the most essential sensory

functions. In fish and birds, the brains of which, according to a comment of *Willis,*[10] are similar in general structure, the number of protuberances increases, and they are also more distinct. Finally, in warm-blooded animals the cerebrum and the cerebellum are evidently distinguishable; the lobes of the latter unfold, corresponding to the organization of the creature, and the individual parts relate to each other precisely in keeping with the objective. Nature, thus, as in the whole formation of her species, so in their ultimate embodiment and end, the brain, has only one *prototype,* which she employs in the meanest worm and insect, which she does indeed alter in minor ways in all species according to their varied external makeup, but in altering them develops further, enlarges, and shapes, at last to perfect it fully in the human being. Nature completed the cerebellum sooner than the brain itself, because the former in its origin is closer and more closely related to the spinal marrow, and, therefore, more uniform in the several species in which the shape of the cerebrum still varies considerably. And this ought not to come as a surprise, since such vital nerves for the animal functions proceed from the cerebellum that Nature, in the development of the most refined powers of reason, had to take its course from the spine to the anterior parts.

2. The lobes of the cerebrum show greater elaboration in more than one respect in the development of their more precious parts. Not only are the convolutions more deeply and more distinctively marked, more numerous and more diverse in humans than in any other creature; not only is the cortex of the human brain its most refined and delicate part, reduced to a twenty-fifth of its original weight upon exsiccation, but the treasure that is covered and interlaced with cortex, the medulla, is more distinct, more clearly defined, and comparatively greater in the more highly developed animals, especially in the human, than in all other creatures. In the human, the cerebrum far outweighs the cerebellum, and its superior weight indicates its internal amplitude and greater elaboration.

3. Now, all the experiments hitherto collected by *Haller,* the most learned physiologist any nation has yet produced, show how futile it would be to seek to discover *the indivisible work of the formation of ideas* substantively and in their diversity in the individual physical parts of the brain; yes, it seems to me that even if all these experiments were available, the very manner of the formation of ideas would have led to the same conclusion. Why is it that we name the powers of our thought according to their different functions—now imagination and memory, now wit and reason? That we distinguish the impulse of desire from the will as such, and that finally, we set apart the capacity to feel from that of motion? Even the minimum of serious reflection shows that these faculties cannot be separated from one another in terms of location, as if reason resided in one region of the brain,

memory and imagination in another, and the passions and sensory powers in yet another; for the thought inhabiting our soul is undivided, and each of these effects is a fruit of the thoughts. It would, therefore, appear all but senseless to attempt to dissect abstract relations as if they were a body and to tear apart the soul as Medea did the limbs of her brother. If we are unable to detect in the coarsest of our senses the matter that conveys feeling, which is so different a matter from the nervous fluid—if there is such a thing—how much less will we be capable of perceiving the mental connection of all the senses and sensibilities, so that we would be able not only to see and to hear them, but that we could also arouse them in the various parts of the brain as readily as we can finger the keys of a harpsichord. Even the ideal of expecting this is strange to me.

4. The thought appears even stranger to me when I consider the structure of the brain and its nerves. How different here is the economy of nature from what our abstract psychology of the senses and the faculties of the soul would suppose! Who would infer from metaphysics that the nervous system originates, diversifies, and connects in a certain way, and yet these are the only regions of the brain the organic functions of which we know, as their effects are placed before our eye. Nothing remains for us, then, but to consider this sacred laboratory of ideas, the innermost brain, where the senses converge, as the womb in which the embryonic thought is fashioned invisibly and undivided. If that womb be sound and healthy, and afford the embryo not merely due cerebral and vital warmth, but also that amplitude of space—the appropriate facility within which the invisible organic power that here pervades everything, can embrace the perceptions of the senses and of the whole body and combine them, if I may be allowed the metaphor, in that *luminous point,* which is called *reflectiveness*—then the finely organized creature becomes capable of reason, if aided by external circumstances of instruction and the development of ideas. If this is not the case, if the brain is deficient in essential parts or in the more delicate fluids, if coarser senses crowd the space or the brain finds itself, at last, in a twisted, compressed condition, what will be the consequence? As that refined focusing of the rays of thought does not take place, the creature remains a captive of the senses.

5. The construction of the brains of various animals evidently appears to demonstrate this, and it is from this construction, compared with the external organization and way of life of the animal, that it may be reckoned why nature, which everywhere aimed at one model, could not always attain it and was compelled to vary from it, here in one way, and there in another. The chief sense of many animals is that of smell; it is the most necessary to sustain them and to guide their instinct. Observe how the nose protrudes in

the face of the animal; in like manner, the olfactory nerves project in their brains, as if the anterior part of the head were made for them alone. Broad, fulsome, and clearly defined, they push forward as if they were protuberances of the ventricles of the brain; and in some species the frontal sinuses extend very high, perhaps to strengthen the sense of smell, so that, if I may use the expression, a great part of the animal soul is *olfactory*. The optic nerves follow next in order, the sense of sight being the most necessary to the animal after that of smell. They already reach farther into the central region of the brain, as they also serve a more refined purpose. The other nerves, which I will not here enumerate, follow in proportion as the external and internal organization require a connection of the parts, so that, for example, the nerves of the occiput support and animate the mouth, the jaws, and so on. Thus they finish, as it were, the countenance, and thus frame the external figure to a whole, as the internal is framed by the proportion of the internal powers. This proportionality, however, ought not to be assessed exclusively in regard to the facial features, but should be applied to the entire body. It is quite pleasing to examine comparatively the varying proportions of diverse figures and to contemplate the internal particularities provided by nature for each creature. Where nature withheld, she compensated; where she was compelled to render complex, she did so wisely, that is to say, in keeping with the external organization of the creature and in harmony with its entire way of life. Yet still she had her model ever in view, and deviated from it unwillingly, because a certain *analogical sensibility and cognition* constituted the great end to which she sought to fashion all terrestrial creation. In the cases of birds, fish, and the most diverse kinds of land animals, this may be shown in one progressive analogy.

6. Thus we come to the superiority of the human in the structure of the brain. And on what does this depend? Evidently, on his *more perfect organization in the whole* and ultimately on his *erect posture*. Every animal brain is formed after the shape of its head; or, more likely, the latter is shaped after the former, as nature works from the inside to the outside. To whatever gait, to whatever proportion of the parts to one another, to whatever *habitus,* at last, she destined the creature, to these she compounded, to these she adapted its organic powers. And thus, in keeping with these powers and with the degree to which they affected one another, the brain turned out to be large or small, broad or narrow, heavy or light, complex or simple. Consequently, the senses of the creature were strong or weak, predominant or subservient. Cavities and musculature of the forehead and the occiput fashioned themselves as the lymph gravitated, in short, according to the *angle of the organic direction of the head.* Of numerous proofs in support of this, which might be adduced from various genera and species, I shall

mention only two or three. What produces the organic difference between our head and the head of an ape? The angle of the direction of the head. The ape has every part of the brain that is possessed by humans, but it has them in a location pushed backward, in keeping with the shape of its skull, which again is due to the different angle at which it is formed, not designed for upright gait. Hence, all the organic powers operated in a different manner; the head did not turn out to be as high, as broad, as long as ours; the inferior senses became prominent with the protruding lower part of the face, and it became the countenance of an animal, just as its pushed-back brain always remained only an animal brain. Thus, even if it has all the parts of the human brain, it has them in a different location and in different proportion. The Parisian anatomists found the anterior parts in the apes they dissected to be similar to those of the human; but the internal, from the cerebellum, were proportionately deeper. The pineal gland was conical, with its point turned toward the back of the skull, and so on.—Thus there is a manifest relation between the angle of the head and the gait, the posture of the figure, and the way of life. The ape dissected by *Blumenbach,*[*] had still more of the brute, probably because it was of an inferior genus, thus its larger *cerebellum,* thus the other missing distinctions in the most important regions. These are not present in the orangutan, because its head is less turned back, its brain is less pushed back, though still pushed back when compared with the rising and rounded free vault of the human brain, the solitary, beautiful chamber for the formation of rational ideas. Why does the horse not have the *rete mirabile,* as do the other animals? Because its head stands erect, and the carotid artery rises in some measure like that of the human, precluding the obstructions prevalent in animals with lowered heads. Accordingly, it came to be a nobler, swifter, more courageous animal, with higher body temperature and in need of little sleep; on the other hand, in animals with lowered heads, nature had so many other dispositions in the structure of the brain that it separated its major parts by a bony partition. Everything thus depended on the *direction* in which and for which the head was formed, corresponding to the organization of the entire body. I will not adduce additional examples, hoping that inquisitive anatomists will turn their attention, particularly in dissecting animals resembling humans, to this inner relationship of the parts *to their relationship with respect to each other and to the direction of the head in its relation to the whole.* Here, I believe, resides the difference among organisms in regard to this or that instinct, with the result of an animal or a human soul; for, every creature is in all its parts a living, comprehensively functioning whole.

---

[*]Blumenbach, *De varietate nativa generis humani,* p. 32.

7. Even the degree of human handsomeness or deformity may be determined by this simple and general law regarding the shaping of the head for the purposes of erect posture. For, as this shaping of the head, this expansion of the brain into its wide and beautiful hemisphere, and with that this internal disposition to reason and freedom, was consistent only with the erect posture, as the proportion and the gravitation of the parts themselves, the degree of the body temperature, and the nature of the blood circulation demonstrate, so it was that nothing other than the perfection of the human shape could derive from this inner proportionality. Why does the crown of the Grecian head incline so pleasingly forward? Because it contains the amplest space for an unconfined brain, revealing ample, wholesome cavities of the forehead, a temple thus of *youthfully precious and pure human thoughts*. The back of the head, by contrast, is small, so that the animal cerebellum might not preponderate. So it is with the other parts of the face; as organs of sense, they indicate the finest proportion of the sensory faculties of the brain; and any deviation from this proportion would produce the likeness of an animal. I am certain that on the agreement of these parts one day will be erected a valuable science, to which physiognomy with its conjecturing can by itself hardly grant us access. The basis for the external shape is rooted within, because the organic powers shaped everything from the inside out, and nature has made every creature a complete whole, as if she had never created anything else.

Look up to heaven then, human creature, and rejoice, in awe of your immeasurable advantage, which the creator of the world attached to so simple a principle, your erect posture. Were your gait that of a bowed-down animal, were your head shaped with voraciously protruding mouth and nostrils, and your members shaped accordingly, where would be your superior power of mind, the image of the divine that invisibly descended into you? Those miserable wretches who were raised among animals have lost it; as their heads were deformed, their internal powers ran wild; coarser senses drew the creature down to the earth. But now, owing to the shaping of your members to the upright posture, the head has received its beautiful position and direction; with that, the brain, this delicate, ethereal sprout of heaven, gained ample room to spread out and to let its branches descend. Rich with thought, the forehead arched, the animal organs receded, and a human shape emerged. As the skull rose higher, the ear was seated lower; it became more closely connected with the eye, and the two senses gained more intimate access to the sacred chamber in which ideas are formed. The cerebellum, the sprouting blossom of the spine and of the sensual powers of life, predominant in animals, came into a subordinated and more subdued relationship with the cerebrum. The rays of the wonderfully beautiful *cor-*

pora striata in the human came to be more distinct and delicate, a hint of the infinitely finer light concentrated in this central region and proceeding outward from there. Thus it came to be, if I may speak figuratively, that the flower was formed which merely sprouted from the extension of the spinal cord, but arches forward in the form of a plant rich in ethereal powers that could be generated only by this aspiring tree. . . .

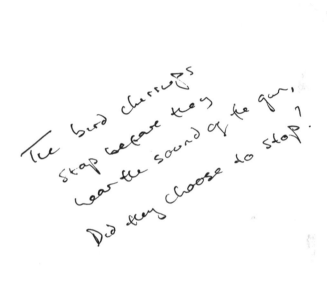

$$\sim 15 \sim$$

Specifically Human Predispositions
Besides Reason

In the following series of five texts, Herder continues to confirm the anthropological foundation of his philosophy of history as a theoretical framework for his world historical perspective. The most striking aspect of his undertaking may be his capability to outline the all-encompassing quality of God's creation, which integrates even destructive moments into the dynamics of this irreducible totality. In this optimistic view of the universe, every thing and every event has its own right, place, and function, from the most minute element in inorganic nature to the most elaborate cultural event. The human being is the first freedman of creation, hence endowed with the power to say no—but also with the power to make wrong decisions. This capability implies moral responsibility and opens the way to understanding of the specificity of human history.

(1) The Human Being Is Predisposed
to Refined Sensibility, Art, and Language

While nearer to the ground, all the senses of the human being were more limited in scope, and the lower senses dominated over the higher ones, as demonstrated by the example of humans raised in the wild. Smell and taste, as in the animal, gave direction.—Raised above the earth and plants, it is not smell that now dominates, but the eye; it has a wider realm around it and is exercised from infancy in the finest geometry of lines and colors. The ear, placed deep below the projecting skull, comes closer to the inner chamber where ideas are gathered, whereas in the animal it extends upward, listening, in many of them by its very shape doing so intensely.

With the erect gait, the human being becomes a creature disposed to art;

for through the erect gait, the first and the most difficult of the skills learned, the human being is initiated to acquire all of them, to become, as it were, a living work of art. Behold the animal! To some degree it already has fingers like the human being; but here they are confined in a hoof, there in a claw, or in some other form, and impaired by callouses. By attaining erect posture, the human being acquired free and sensitive hands; tools for the most delicate of operations and a ceaseless groping for new and clear ideas. The view of *Helvétius*[1] was correct that the hand was for the human being a great aid in attaining reason; for how much does the elephant acquire by means of his trunk! Yes, this delicate sensitivity of the hands pervades the entire body, and mutilated human beings have often fashioned works of art with their toes when fingers were lacking to execute them. The minute thumb, the great toe, which are so particularly fashioned in their muscular structure, though they appear to us contemptible limbs, are for us the most essential assistants, disposing us to stand, walk, grasp, and carry out all the functions of a soul pervaded by art.

It has often been said that the human being was created defenseless, and that one of its distinguishing characteristics was to be capable of nothing. But this is not so; it has weapons of defense, as do all creatures. The ape, for one, handles the club and defends itself with dirt and stones; it climbs trees and escapes from the snake, its greatest enemy; it removes the roofs of houses and may even kill humans. The wild maid of *Songi*[2] knocked her sister over the head with a club and compensated with climbing and swiftness for what she lacked in strength. Thus, even the human being raised in the wild, by its makeup, is not defenseless; but once he stands fully upright and has acquired the rudiments of civilization, what animal has the multifaceted tools of art possessed by the human being in the arm, the hand, the dexterity of the body, in all its powers? Art is the most powerful weapon, and the human being is all art, is a weapon through and through. The human lacks only claws and teeth for attack; designed to be a peaceable and gentle creature, the human being was not meant to be a cannibal.

What depths of artistic sensibility lie hidden in each of the human senses, disclosed here and there mostly by necessity, want, disease, the absence of another sense, deformation from birth, or accident, suggesting to us what other senses, undisclosed in this world, may lie within us. If some blind people have raised their sense of feeling or hearing, their memory, or their power of computation, to a degree that appears fabulous to humans of ordinary faculties, undiscovered worlds of diversity and delicacy may reside in other senses, not developed in our complex organism. What delicacy of perception the human being has already attained in the eye and the ear, and surely will extend still farther in a higher state, since, as *Berkeley*[3] observes, light is the language of divinity, which our finest sense but continually spells in a thousand forms and colors. Melody, which the human ear perceives, and art only develops, is the purest mathematics, which the soul practices obscurely through the sense,[4] as it demonstrates the most refined geometry through the eye, by letting the ray of light play upon it. Infinitely will we marvel when, having progressed one step further in our existence, we see clearly what we practiced darkly with our senses and faculties in our complex, divine organism, what the animal practices in a preliminary way, in a manner suitable to its makeup.

Still, all these implements of art, brain, senses, and hands would have remained ineffective even in our upright posture, if the creator had not given us a spring to set them all in motion, *the divine gift of speech.* Speech alone awakens slumbering reason; or rather, the bare capacity of reason, which of itself would have remained eternally dead, through language acquires living power and efficacy. By speech alone, the eye and the ear, the perception of all the senses becomes one and through them unites itself in the creative thought, which alone instructs the work of art of the hands and the other members. The example of those who are born deaf and dumb shows how far speechless humans are from attaining rational ideas even among other humans, and in what primitive wildness all their instincts remain. Such a being imitates what it sees, whether good or bad, and it imitates less perfectly than the ape, because it wants the internal criterion of discrimination, yes, even sympathy with its own species. There has been more than one instance* of a person born deaf and dumb who murdered his brother in consequence of having seen a pig killed, and tore out his bowel with cold pleasure, merely in imitation of what he saw; a dreadful proof of how little our much-praised human reason and the sensibility of our species may do *of and by themselves.* The delicate organs of speech, therefore, must be considered the rudder of our reason, and speech as the heavenly spark that gradually kindles our thoughts and senses to a flame.

In animals we perceive preliminary indications of speech; and here too nature works from the bottom up, ultimately to perfect this art in the human being. The function of breathing requires the entire chest, with its bones, ligaments, and muscles, the diaphragm, and even parts of the abdomen, the neck, and the upper arms; for this great task, nature has constructed the whole spinal column with its ligaments and ribs, muscles and vessels; she has given the parts of the thorax the stability and flexibility that it requires, and proceeded from the lower creatures to the higher ones in creating more

---

*I remember such a case related in Sack's *Vertheidigtem Glauben der Christen,*[5] and I recollect having seen more in other works.

perfect lungs and trachea. The newborn animal greedily inhales the first breath, yes, it reaches for it as if it could hardly wait for it. Marvelously diverse are the parts provided for this task; for almost all parts of the body need air to thrive with efficacy. Yet, greedy as all creatures are for this divine breath of life, not everyone is endowed with voice and speech, which are ultimately produced by those small tools, the head of the trachea, a few cartilages and muscles, and that simple *member, the tongue.* Most simple is the appearance of this thousandfold artificer of all divine thoughts and words which, with a bit of air pressed through a narrow opening, not only put into motion the entire realm of human ideas, but effected everything achieved by humans on earth. It is infinitely beautiful to observe the gradation with which nature, beginning with the voiceless fish, the worm, and the insect, slowly advanced the creature to sound and voice. The bird rejoices in its song as the most artful of functions, as well as the most splendid of advantages given to it by the creator; the animal, provided with a voice, calls upon it as soon as it feels the inclination and the inner state of its being wants release, in joy or in suffering. It gesticulates little, and those animals speak only by signs to whom the living sound is comparatively denied. The tongue of some is so formed as even to enable them to repeat human words, but without understanding their meaning; the external organization, particularly when tutored by man, rushes ahead of the internal capacity. But here the door is shut, and the manlike ape, in a way deliberately and forcibly, is deprived of speech by the pouches nature has placed at the sides of the windpipe.*

Why has the father of human speech done this? Why did he not want to allow the creature that imitates everything to imitate specifically this criterion of humankind, inexorably closing the way to it by peculiar obstacles? Visit a hospital for the insane and attend to their discourse; listen to the speech of some of those born deformed or extremely simple-minded, and you need not be told the cause. How painful to us is their utterance, and the profaning of the gift of human speech! And how much more would it be profaned in the mouth of the lascivious, coarse, bestial ape, if it were able to ape human words, with the half-human understanding that I have no doubt it possesses! A disgusting tangle of humanlike sounds and the thoughts of an ape—no, the divine faculty of speech was not to be thus debased, and the ape was rendered dumb, more dumb than other animals, each of which, down to the frog and the lizard, has its own peculiar sound.

But nature has constructed the human being to be lingual; to this end as

---

*See [Petrus] Camper's *Essay on the Organs of Speech in Apes; Philosophical Transactions [of the Royal Society of London],* 1779, vol. 1, pp. 139–59.

well, he is framed erect and his chest arches from a rising column. Human beings who have been raised among animals lost not only speech itself, but in some measure the capacity to acquire it; an evident proof that their throats were deformed and that human speech is consistent only with erect gait. For, although several animals have organs of speech resembling those of humans, not one is capable of that *continuous* stream of speech that issues from the free, exalted, human breast, from our more narrow, artfully closed mouth. The human being, on the contrary, is not only able to imitate all their sounds and tones, so that, as *Monboddo*[6] says, he is the *mocking-bird* of terrestrial creatures, but a deity has taught the human being also to coin ideas in tones, to designate figures by means of sounds, and to rule the earth by the words of his mouth. Human reason and culture begin with speech, for by it alone the human governs himself also, and becomes capable of reflection and choice, of which his organization renders only him capable. There may, there must be superior creatures, whose reason is aroused through the eye, a feature observed being sufficient for them to form ideas and to fix them in a differentiated manner; the human terrestrial creature is still tutored by the ear, by which he gradually begins to learn to understand the language of light. The differences among things must be imprinted in his soul first by the assistance of another; from this he learned to communicate his own thoughts, first perhaps by gentle and heavy breathing, then by vocal sound and chant. Expressive of this is the name given by the people of the Morn to the animals they call *the silent ones of the Earth;* it was only in being organized with the capacity for speech that the human being received the breath of divinity, the seed of reason and eternal perfection, an echo of that creative voice to rule the Earth, in a word, the *divine art of ideas,* the mother of all arts.

(2) The Human Being Is Predisposed to More Refined Instincts, and Thus to Freedom

It is passed on from one to another, that the human being is void of instinct, and that this constitutes the character of the species; he does have all the instincts possessed by any highly developed animal around him; only, in conformity to his organization, he has them moderated to a more delicate proportion.

The infant in the mother's womb seems under a necessity of going through every state that is appropriate to a terrestrial creature. It floats in water; it lies prone with open mouth; its jaws are large, before the lips, which are not formed till late, can cover them; no sooner does it come into the world than it gasps for air, and sucking is its first untaught function. The entire process of digestion and nutrition, of hunger and thirst, goes on instinctively, or through some still more obscure impulse. The muscular and procreative powers strive in like manner to develop themselves; and the human being need only be deprived of reason, by passion or disease, to reveal to the observer all the animal instincts. In a human being, yes, in entire nations, that lead a savage life, privation and danger unfold the capacities, senses, and powers of beasts.

Thus, it is not so much that the human being is deprived of instincts as that they are *suppressed,* and made *subordinate* to the control of the nerves and the finer senses. Without them, the creature, who is still in great measure an animal, could not live.

But how are they suppressed? How does nature bring them under the control of the nerves? Let us contemplate their progress from infancy; this will show us in a very different light what humans have often so foolishly lamented as human weakness.

The young of the human species comes into the world weaker than that of any animal; this evidently is so because it is fashioned to a proportion that could not be developed within the mother's womb. The four-footed animal acquired the quadruped figure in the matrix; and it ultimately attained complete proportionality, although at first its head was as disproportionate as that of the human. In the animals that have a rich nervous system and thus bring their young into the world feeble, the relationship of the powers comes into balance within a few weeks or days. The human being alone remains feeble for a long time; for, if I may use this expression, his limb structure is *fashioned to the head,* which was formed disproportionately large in the womb and comes thus into the world. The other limbs, which require earthly nutriment, air, and movement for their growth, grow long before they measure up to it, although through all of the years of childhood and youth they grow to gain proportionality, and the head does not grow in the same measure. The feeble child, thus, is an invalid, as I may say, of its superior powers, and nature develops these incessantly and from the earliest beginning. Before the child learns to walk, it learns to see, to hear, to grasp, and to exercise the most delicate mechanism and gauging of these senses. Like the animal, it exercises these faculties instinctively, only in a more refined manner, not by innate ability and art; for all the artful dexterity of animals is the consequence of coarser stimuli; and were these present in a dominant way from childhood on, the human being would remain an animal and would, knowing all before learning it, acquire nothing human. Thus, either reason had to be born with him as an instinct, which appears a contradiction in terms, or the human being had to come into the world feeble, *in order to acquire reason.*

He acquires reason from infancy, being formed to it, to freedom, and to human speech through art, as he is to his ingenious mode of movement. The suckling at the mother's breast reposes on her heart; the fruit of her womb becomes the novice in her arms. His finest senses, the eye and the ear, awake first, guided by the images of figures and by sounds; bliss, if they be guided felicitously. The capacity to see unfolds gradually, absorbed by the eyes of those around, as the ear is caught by the language of humans, and by their help learns to distinguish the first concepts. Thus the hand learns gradually to grasp, and only now do the limbs strive after their appropriate exercise. The human being was first the apprentice of the two finest senses; for the artful instinct to be formed within is *reason, humanity, the mode of life peculiar to humankind,* not possessed or acquired by any animal. Even domesticated animals acquire some things from humans, but they do so as animals; they do not become human.

Hence it becomes clear what human reason is: a designation so often used in modern writings to imply an innate automaton, in which sense it can lead only to misinterpretation. Theoretically and practically, reason is nothing but something *received,* an acquired proportionality and direction of ideas and faculties, to which the human being is formed by its organization and mode of life. We know nothing of a reason of angels, any more than we are capable of having an intimate perception of the internal state of a creature beneath us; the reason of humans is *human.* From infancy, the human being compares the ideas and impressions of the finer senses, basing the comparison on the refinement and veracity with which they are conveyed, the number received, and the quickness of mind with which he learns to connect them. The entity derived from this is the thought, and the sundry linkages of these thoughts and perceptions, resulting in judgments of what is true and false, good and bad, happiness or misfortune, this is reason, the progressive work of the formation of human life. Reason is not innate, but acquired; thus, according to the impressions gained by the human being, the models followed, the internal faculties and energy used to tie these sundry impressions proportionately to the innermost being, individual reason is rich or poor, deficient or sound, stunted or well-grown, as is the body. Should nature deceive us by means of the perceptions of the senses, we would have to suffer ourselves to be deceived in her way; yet, only as many humans as possessed the same senses would be deceived in the same manner. Should humans deceive us, and we not have organs or faculty to detect the deception, and to gather the impressions to a more appropriate proportion, our reason would become crippled and often remain so for life's duration. It is because the human being must learn everything, indeed, because it is its instinct and destination to learn all, as it learned its upright gait, that it learns to walk by falling, and often comes to truth by erring, whereas the animal moves securely in its quadrupedal gait, guided by its more strongly developed proportion of senses and instincts. The human being enjoys the royal prerogative of seeing far and wide with head erect; yet, with that comes also the fact that much is seen darkly and falsely, that in fact steps are often missed and the human being must be reminded by stumbling how narrow is the foundation on which rests the mental and emotional edifice of human concepts and judgments; still, the human being is and remains, in keeping with its high *rational destination,* what is not given to any other creature on earth, a son of the gods, a sovereign of the earth.

In order to feel the preeminence of this destination, let us consider what is included in the great gifts of *reason* and *freedom,* and how much nature ventured, as it were, when it entrusted them to such a feeble, complicated, terrestrial creature as the human. The animal is but a stooping slave, though some of the nobler species carry the head erect, or at least with craned necks yearn for freedom. Their souls, not yet ripened into reason, must be subservient to the impulses of necessity, and in this service must prepare themselves from afar for the proper use of the senses and appetites. The human is the first *freedman* in creation; he stands erect. The balance of good and evil, of falsehood and truth, hangs suspended within him, enabling him to explore, requiring him to make choices. As nature has given him two free hands as instruments and a surveying eye to guide his movement, she has given him the power not only of placing the weights, but also, if I may say so, of *being a weight* on the scale. He can give credence to the most delusive error, and be voluntarily deceived; he can learn in time to love the chains with which he is fettered, contrary to his nature, and adorn them with sundry flowers. As it was with deluded reason, so it was also with abused or shackled freedom; in most human beings, it represents the relation of powers and propensities, as fixed by convenience and habit. The human being rarely looks beyond these, and is capable of becoming worse than a beast, when fettered by mean propensities and execrable habits.

Still he is, in regard to his freedom also, even when he most severely abuses it, a king. He may still make choices, even though he chooses the worst; he is his own master, even though he destines himself, by his own choice, to the lowest. Before the Omniscient, however, who conferred on him these powers, reason as well as freedom are limited; and they are happily limited; for the one who created the source had to know and foresee every one of its channels, and had to be able to guide them in such manner that the most turbulent brook would never escape the reach of his hands; none of this, however, changes anything in the matter itself, or in the nature of humankind. The human being is and remains in himself a free creature, though all-comprehending goodness embraces him even in his follies, and turns these both to his own and the general good. As no projectile can escape the atmosphere into which it is shot, and as it is governed, when it falls back, by one and the same laws of nature, so is the human being, in error and in truth, in rising and in falling still human; a feeble child, indeed, but a freeborn nevertheless; though not yet rational, yet capable of superior reason; though not yet formed to humanity, yet endowed to be so formed. The New Zealand cannibal and a *Fénelon*, the wretched Fuegians[7] and a *Newton* are creatures of one and the same species.

It seems, indeed, as if every possible variety were also to be found upon our earth in the use of these gifts; and a progressive scale becomes visible, from the human who borders on the beast to the purest genius in the image of the human. Nor should this make us wonder, as we see the great gradation of animals below us, and the long road nature had to take, to prepare in us the little budding flower of reason and freedom, providing order. It seems that everything was meant to be on earth that was possible to be, and we shall be able sufficiently to explain the order and wisdom of this ample richness only when, advanced a step further, we perceive the end for which such variety was ordained to spring up in the great garden of nature. Here we see little more than the laws of necessity prevail; for the whole earth was to be inhabited, even in its remotest wilderness; and only he who stretched it out so far knows the reason why he admitted to this, his world, both Fuegians and New Zealanders. Even to those who feel the greatest contempt for humankind, it is undeniable that, notwithstanding the many wild branches, reason and freedom sprung up among the children of humankind, and that under the celestial beams of the sun these noble plants also bore beautiful fruits. It would be almost beyond belief, were it not for the testimony of history, to what heights human *reason* has ventured, endeavoring not only to trace the creating, sustaining deity, but also to emulate it, providing for order. In the chaos of beings revealed by the senses, the human being sought and found unity and reason, laws providing for order, and beauty. The most hidden powers, their inner springs not known to him at all, he has observed in their external appearance, and explored their movement, number, measure, life, yes, even their very existence, wherever he has perceived them in the heavens or upon earth. All of these endeavors, even when erroneous or mere dreams, are evidence of his majesty, of a godlike power and preeminence. The being which created everything has indeed placed a ray of his light, a stamp of the power most peculiar to him, in our feeble makeup; and, low as the human is, he can say to himself, "I have something in common with God; I possess faculties that the supreme, whom I know in his works, must also possess; for he has revealed them all around me." Evidently, this *similitude with him* was *itself* the sum of all his creation on earth. On this stage, he could reach no higher; but he also did not neglect to ascend to this level, and to lead the sequence of his created beings to this highest point. That is why the ascent to this point is so uniform, notwithstanding the diversity of the figures.

In like manner, *freedom* also has produced noble fruits in humankind, and displayed its merits both in what it has rejected and in what it has pursued. That humans have renounced the unsteady reins of blind instinct, and voluntarily assumed the *bonds of matrimony,* of social friendship, succor, and fidelity, for the duration of *life and death;* that they have given up their own wills and chosen to be governed by *laws,* so as to establish and defend with their life's blood *the rule of men over men,* although it still remains far from perfection; that noble-minded men have sacrificed themselves for their *fatherland,* and not only offered their lives in one tumultuous moment, but, what is far more magnanimous, night and day, for years and years, through the stages of life, have without hesitation unceasingly given the whole effort of their lives in order to confer upon a blind and ungrateful multitude what constitutes, at least from their point of view, well-being and peace; that philosophers filled with the spirit of God, at last, out of the noble longing for *truth, freedom, and happiness* of our kind, have willingly submitted to slander and persecution, poverty and want, and have held on to the thought that they had obtained or advanced for their brothers the noblest good of which they were capable; if all of these do not represent great human virtues and the most powerful strivings for the *self-determination* that rests within us, I do not know of any other. It is true, the number of those was small who have been in the vanguard of the great multitude and as physicians imposed upon them what they not yet were able to choose for themselves; yet these few have been the flower of humankind, the immortal, free sons of the gods on earth. Their individual names outweigh those of millions.

(3) The Human Being Is Predisposed to Most Delicate Health, Yet at the Same Time to the Most Enduring Fortitude, so as to Spread Over the Earth

With erect posture, the human being acquired a delicacy, warmth, and strength that could not be attained by any animal. In the savage state, the human would be largely covered with hair, especially on his back; and that then would be the blanket, for the deprivation of which the elder Pliny has accused nature so moanfully.[8] The benevolent mother of all has given the human a more beautiful covering, the delicate and yet so durable skin, capable of withstanding the unpredictability of each season, the changes of climate, when aided by a bit of artfulness, which is second nature to this creature.

And to this artfulness the human being was not to be led solely by naked necessity, but by something more human and more beautiful, blessed *shame*. Whatever some philosophers may say, shame is natural to the human, indeed, even hinted at vaguely in some species of animals, for the female ape covers herself, and the elephant retires for copulation to the dark and solitary forest. We hardly know of any nation, however close to the animal stage,* which does not, especially in the female, beginning with the period when the passions awake, prefer some kind of veil, particularly since the sensitive delicacy of these parts and other circumstances call for a covering. Thus, even before the human sought to protect the other limbs from the fury of the elements, from the sting of insects by means of clothing or salves, a sort of *sensual economy* of the most impetuous and necessary of the instincts led to the veil. Among all the more noble animals, the female will be sought, and does not offer herself; in this, she unconsciously fulfills the purposes of nature, and among humans it is the more delicate woman who is also the wise guardian of blessed shame, which, given the erect posture, was bound to develop at an early stage.—

Thus, the human being received clothing, and soon after the acquisition of this and of some other artfulness, was capable of enduring any climate on earth, and of taking possession of it. Few animals, among them almost only the dog, were able to follow the human into all regions, and those only with such changes of figure, with such deviation of their innate temperaments! The human has changed the least, and has not changed at all in essential parts. It is astonishing how fully and uniformly human nature has been preserved in comparison with the deviations among his wandering relatives in the animal world. The delicate nature of the human being is so consti- tuted, so consummately organized—that it stands at the highest stage—so that few variations, which may not even be called anomalies, were found possible.

Whence came all of this? Once more, from the erect posture, and from nothing else. Were we to walk on all fours, like the bear and the ape, there is no doubt that the human races (if I were allowed to use that ignoble word) would have their more constricted fatherland, and would never leave

---

*I am familiar with only two entirely naked nations, and they live in a manner alike to that of animal wildness, the Fuegians at the uttermost tip of South America, an execra- tion of other nations, and a wild people in the vicinity of *Arakan* and *Pegu,*[9] in regions that remain a mystery to me still, though I find them confirmed in the most recent travel reports (Mackintosh's *Travels,* vol. 1 [London: 1782], p. 341).

it. The human bear would love the cold, the human ape the warm fatherland; so as we learn to this day, the closer a nation is to the stage of the animal, the more it is attached with the ties of body and soul to land and climate.

As nature exalted the human, it was exaltation to dominion over the earth. The upright posture with its finely organized structure also provided for a more elaborate blood circulation, a more diverse mixture of the vital fluids, and with that also that *more intrinsic and fixed temperature of vital warmth,* which alone could make possible the inhabitation of both Siberia and Africa. Nothing but the erect, more artful organic structure made possible the endurance of the extremes of heat and cold not achieved by any other creature on earth, and which, nevertheless, bring about only the most minute measure of change within the human.

Now it came about that with this more delicate structure, and all the consequences arising from it, the door was opened to a series of diseases, with which no animal is acquainted, and which *Moscati** has eloquently enumerated. The blood that carries on its circulation within a perpendicular engine, the heart pressed into an oblique position, and the intestines that perform their function in an upright situation, must be exposed to more danger of being disarranged than they are in the body of an animal. The female sex in particular, it would seem, must pay more dearly than we for its greater delicacy.—Yet, here too the beneficence of nature compensates and mitigates in a thousand ways; for, our health, our well-being, all our perceptions and excitements are more refined and spiritual. No animal enjoys a single moment of human health and joy; it does not taste a drop of the flowing nectar drunk by man; yes, considered merely with respect to the body, the diseases of the animal are fewer, it is true, because its bodily structure is coarser, but then again they are also the more persistent and severe. Its cellular membrane, the coatings of its nerves, its arteries, bones, and even its brain, are harder than ours; whence all the land animals around humankind, the elephant alone perhaps excepted, whose life span approaches that of the human, live a shorter time, and die a natural death, the death of indurating age, much sooner than the human being. Thus nature has assigned to the human being the life most extended, and with that, the life most healthy and rich in joy possible in a terrestrial frame. Nothing finds succor within itself more readily and in more various ways than the many-sided human nature; and it took all the excesses of madness and vice, of which indeed no animal is capable, to enfeeble and despoil our organism

---

Vom körperlichen wesentlichen Unterschiede der Thiere und Menschen (Göttingen: 1771).[10]

to the degree that it is in some cases enfeebled and despoiled. Nature has benevolently bestowed on every climate the herbs that heal the diseases to which it is subject, and nothing but the confounding of all climates could have converted Europe into that sink of evils, experienced by no people living according to the dictates of nature. Yet even for this self-made evil it has given us a self-made good, the only one of which we were worthy, the *physician* who enhances nature as long as he abides by it, and who, if he is incapable of or prevented from abiding by it, at least buries the sick in a sanitary way.

Further, behold the maternal care and wisdom of the divine economy that determined also the stages of our life and the duration of our kind! All living creatures here on earth that must quickly reach full development, also grow rapidly; they mature early and quickly reach the goal of life. The human being, planted upright like a tree of heaven, grows slowly. Like the elephant, the human remains longest in the womb; the time of youth lasts long, incomparably longer than that of any animal. Nature has spun out as long as she could the happy time in which to learn, to grow, to enjoy life, and to savor it in the most innocent manner. Many animals reach full development within a few years, days, yes, almost in the moment of birth; but they are also so much the more imperfect, and die the earlier. The human being must learn the longest because he has the most to acquire; for everything in human existence depends on self-gained dexterity, reason, and art. Even if life be shortened later by the innumerable host of accidents and dangers, there was the carefree, extended time of youth, when, with the body and spirit the world around also grew, when, with the slowly rising and ever-extending sphere of vision, the orbit of human hopes also widened, and the heart, in the nobility of youth, in impetuous curiosity and impatient longing, learned to beat ever more strongly for all that is great, good, and beautiful. The flowering of the sexual drive comes about later in a sound and unsoiled human being than in any other animal, for the human is intended to live long, and not to dissipate too early the most precious nectar of the spiritual and physical powers. The insect, submitting to love early, also passes away early. All the chaste species of animals who pair for life live longer than those who do not. The lustful rooster dies early; the constant dove of the forest may live for fifty years. For the favorite of nature here on earth, thus, marriage is ordained, and the earliest, freshest years of life are meant to be lived for the self, as if encapsuled within a bud of innocence. Thereupon follow long years of masculine and carefree powers in which reason ripens, reason, which flourishes in humans, together with the urge of procreation, into an advanced age unknown to animals, until at last death comes gently to release the settling dust, as well as the spirit it held captive, from their strange union. Thus nature has showered upon the fragile abode of the human body all the art an earthly creature can encompass; and, even in what shortens and enfeebles life, she has compensated for the *brevity* of enjoyment with greater *sensibility*, for the *weariness* with the power of *deeper feeling*.

(4) The Human Being Is Predisposed to Humanity and Religion

I wish I could encompass within the word *humanity* all that I have said thus far about the noble formation of the human being to reason and freedom, to the finer senses and appetites, to the most delicate and robust health, to the peopling of and dominion over the earth; for the human being has no nobler word for its destiny than the one that designates itself, the word in which the image of the creator of our earth lives imprinted, as visible as it could become here. In order to present the most noble duties of humankind, we need only to delineate the human form.

[1.] All the appetites of a living being may be traced to the need for *self-preservation* and the need to *take part* or *communicate with* others; the organic structure of the human being, when subject to higher guidance, provides the most exquisite order for these inclinations. Just as the straight line is the most stable, so for its protection the human being has the most limited circumference on the outside, and the most manifold quickness of response within. The human being stands upon the most narrowly circumscribed basis and thus can most readily protect its limbs. The point of gravity falls between the most flexible and strongest pelvic joints possessed by any earthly creature; no animal shows in this area the supple strength of the human. The more compact, hardened chest and the utility of the arms as they are situated provide the widest orbit of protection, to preserve the heart and to shield the most precious parts of the body from the head down to the knees. It is no fable that humans have fought with lions and overcome them; the African takes on more than one when he combines circumspection with cunning and force. Nevertheless, it is true that the makeup of the human being preeminently facilitates defense rather than attack; in the latter he needs assistance from ingenuity; in the former he is by nature the strongest creature on earth. His very form thus disposes him to *peacefulness*, the preeminent hallmark of humanity, not the ravages of rapine and murder.

2. Among the appetites directed toward others, the *sexual urge* is the most powerful; in humankind, it too is subordinate to the enhancement of humanity. What in the four-footed animal, even in the modest elephant, is

copulation, in human beings is, in keeping with their basic makeup, kiss and embrace. No animal has human lips, the delicate rim of which is the last part of the face formed in the womb; it is in a way the ultimate sign of the finger of love that these lips should close so beautifully, reflecting the richness of reason. The old saying, he *knew* his wife, is applicable to no brute. The ancient fable says that the two sexes were once androgynous, like flowers, to be separated later. These and other meaningful poetic evocations in the fable were meant to be a veiled expression of the superiority of human love over the love of animals. By the same token, the fact that the human urge is not, like that of animals, subject merely to the seasons of the year, demonstrates obviously (though the cycles to which the human body is subject in this regard have not up to now been competently studied) that it is governed not by compulsion but by the attraction of love, that it remains subordinate to reason and the moderation of free will, as does everything pertaining to the human person. Thus, love in humankind was meant to be *humane;* to that end, nature destined, in addition to the basic makeup, also the later development, the duration, and the proportionality of the drive in both sexes; indeed, nature placed the sex drive under the law of a *communal, voluntary covenant* and the most friendly communion of two beings with one another, who feel themselves united in one for life.

3. Since, except for communicative love, all other tender affections are content with *participation,* nature has formed the human being, of all living creatures, as the one *most eager to share,* fashioning it out of all the rest, shaping it to be akin to all the realms of creation to the degree called for by empathy with all. The fabric of the human organism is so elastic, fine, and delicate, and the nervous system is so intricately tied to all parts of the vibrant being that, as the analogue of the all-feeling deity, the human may slip imaginatively into almost any other creature, to empathize with it to the degree needed by the other creature, without suffering personal disruption, even if the danger is there. Our organism feels empathy even with a tree, as long as it is a growing, greening tree; and there are human beings who cannot physically endure the felling or mutilation of the tree in its greening youth. It pains us to see its withered crown; we lament a lovely flower that is wilting. Even the writhing of a squashed worm does not leave a tender-hearted human indifferent, and the more perfect the animal, the closer it is in its organization to ours, the more sympathy it arouses with its suffering. Strong nerves were called for to open a living creature and to watch its internal palpitations; only the insatiable thirst for fame and science could gradually deaden this organic empathy. Women, being more delicate, cannot even bear the dissection of a dead body; they feel pain with every member that is forcibly destroyed before their eyes, the more so the more

delicate and precious the parts turn out to be. Ransacked intestines evoke horror and revulsion; a cut-open heart, a split-apart lung, a destroyed brain cut and pierce like knives into our own limbs. We still feel empathy with the corpse of a beloved person already in the grave, we feel the chill of the pit not felt by him, and we shudder when we as much as touch the body. So sympathetic a disposition was woven into the human body by the universal mother, who took everything from within herself and who feels the most intense sympathy with all. The vibrant fibers of the human organism, its empathetic nervous system, need not the appeal of reason; they are ahead of reason, in fact, they often run powerfully and perversely counter to its appeal. Discourse with the mentally deranged, for whom we feel, causes madness in turn, and it occurs the sooner, the more the human being fears it.

It is strange that the ear should arouse and intensify this compassion so much more than the eye. The sigh of an animal, the cry forced from it by its bodily suffering, draws closer all that are akin to it, who, as has frequently been observed, mournfully gather around the whimpering sufferer, and would willingly lend assistance. In humans, too, the visual perception of suffering is more apt to cause fear and tremor than tender compassion. But no sooner does one sound of the sufferer reach us than we lose composure and hasten to be near, as if our souls were pierced. Is it that the sound converts the image painted by the eye into a living being, that it recalls and concentrates in one point all of the recollections of one's own feelings and those of others? Or is there yet, as I believe, a deeper organic cause? Enough, the experience is genuine, and it demonstrates in the human being *voice and speech* as the source of the greater compassion. We feel less compassion for that which cannot sigh, because it is destitute of lungs, a less perfect creature, less akin to us in organization. Some who were born deaf and dumb have given the most horrible examples of lack of sympathy and compassion for humans and animals; and we will observe yet more instances of the same among savage nations. Yet even among these the law of nature is not imperceptible. Fathers, who are compelled by hunger and want to sacrifice their children, doom them to death in the womb before their eye has seen them, before they have heard their voices, and many a killer of her own child has confessed that nothing rested more heavily upon her, that nothing remained longer in her memory, than the first feeble cry, the whimpering plea of the child.

4. Beautiful is the chain with which the all-feeling mother binds the reciprocal feelings of her children, enhancing them link by link. As long as the creature was crude and callous, hardly capable of sustaining itself, it was also not entrusted with the care for its offspring. The feathered inhabitants of the air hatch and raise their young with maternal love; the senseless

ostrich, on the other hand, deposits its eggs in the sand. "It forgets," relates an ancient book, "that a claw may tread upon them, or that a wild beast may destroy them, for God has deprived it of wisdom, and imparted to it no understanding." The one and the same organic cause from which the creature receives more brain also provides it with more warmth and enables it to give birth to or hatch living young, nurse them, and give them motherly love. The creature that comes into the world alive is, as it were, a plexus of the mother's own nerves; the child nursed by the mother is a sprout of the mother plant that nurtures it as part of itself. On this most intimate reciprocal feeling are founded all the more tender affections in the organism of the animal, to which nature could exalt its species.

In the human species, maternal love is of a higher kind, a sprout of the humanity of the upright posture. The nursing infant rests in the mother's lap beneath her eyes and drinks the richest and most delicate fluid. It is a brutal custom, and one that even tends to deform the body, for women to nurse their children on their backs, which in some countries they are compelled to do by necessity. The father's affection and domestic love tame the worst of savages; even the lioness is affectionate toward her young. The first society arose in the paternal habitation, bound together by the ties of blood, mutual trust, and love. Thus, to break the wildness of humankind and to accustom it to domestic intercourse, the childhood of our species was destined to last long years; nature compelled and held our kind together by tender ties, so that we could not, like the more quickly maturing animals, disperse and forget one another. Now the father became the tutor of the son, as the mother had been his nurse; thus a new link of humanity was formed. For here lies the ground of a necessary *human society,* without which no human being could grow up, without which humankind could not increase in numbers. The human being, thus, is *born* to live in society; this is learned from the compassion of the parents and from the long years of childhood.

5. However, since the mere compassion of humankind is incapable of being universally extended, and could in this limited and complex being, be only an obscure and feeble guide with reference to everything distant, it came to be that the correctly guiding mother of all gathered together its manifold and lightly twined branches under a more unerring standard, that of the *rule of justice and truth.* The human being is created upright; and as everything in the human figure is subject to the head, as the two eyes see only one object, the two ears hear but one sound, and as nature in all external respects has everywhere connected symmetry with unity, and placed unity in the center, so that the twofold always pointed to the center, the great law of equity and balance became also the standard of humankind in regard to the internal: *What you do not wish others to do unto you, also*

do not unto them; what you wish those to do unto you, do also unto them. This incontestable rule is also written in the breast of the savage, for, when he eats the flesh of others, he expects to be eaten in turn. It is the rule of truth and falsehood, of the *idem et idem,* founded on the structure of all our senses, yes, I might say, of the upright posture of the human itself. If we were to see obliquely, or the light struck us in an oblique direction, we should have no idea of a straight line. Were our organization without unity, our thoughts without reflectiveness, we would also roam in our actions in irregular serpentines, and human life would know neither reason nor purpose. The law of equity and truth makes faithful fellows and brothers; yes, when it gains ground, it even makes out of enemies friends. The one whom I embrace also embraces me; the one for whom I sacrifice my life also will sacrifice his for me. The uniformity of attitudes, thus, the unity of purpose among different persons, uniform loyalty in one covenant, has founded all *human law, the law of nations, and the law of animals*—for even animals who live in social organization observe the law of equity—and humans who divert from it by cunning or force are the *most inhuman* creatures, even though they be the kings and monarchs of the world. No reason, no humanity, is conceivable without strict equity and truth.

6. The upright and beautiful figure of the human being forms him to *decorum,* for it is the fair friend and servant of truth and justice. Decorum of the body is for it to stand as it ought, as God fashioned it; genuine beauty is nothing more than the pleasing expression of internal perfection and health. Consider the divine image of the human being disfigured by negligence and false makeup; the beautiful hair torn out or transformed into lumps, the nose and ears pierced and weighted down, the neck and the other parts of the body deformed in themselves or by the dress that covers them; who, envisioning this, even if the most capricious fashion were the judge, will still find here the decorum of the upright and beautiful human frame? It is no different with manners and gestures, no different with customs, arts, and human language. All these are pervaded by one and the same *humanity,* which was attained by few peoples on earth, and despoiled by a hundred through barbarism and false arts. To trace this humanity is the genuinely *human philosophy,* which that sage called down from heaven,[11] and which reveals itself in social intercourse as in politics, in the sciences as in all the arts.

[7.] Finally, *religion* is the highest expression of humanity in humankind, and let no one wonder why I rank it so. If the intellect is the highest endowment of the human being, it is the business of the intellect to detect the connection between cause and effect, and to divine it where it does not see it. The human intellect does this in regard to all matters, activities, and arts; for even when it pursued an *acquired* skill, an antecedent intellect must have determined the connection between cause and effect, thus initiating this particular ability. Now it is true that we do not concede to nature any innermost cause; we do not really know ourselves and do not know the wellsprings of anything within us. Thus it is that, in respect to all effects outside us everything is only a dream, only conjecture, name; yet it is a true dream, as long as we frequently and consistently observe the same effects connected with the same causes. This is the course of philosophy, and the first and ultimate philosophy has always been religion. Even the most savage nations have practiced it; for no people on earth is completely without it, any more than any is without the human capacity for reason and human figure, language and connubial bonds, or some manners and customs proper to humankind. Where they saw no visible author, they believed in an invisible one, and thus always still searched for the causes of things, although they be obscure. It is true, they attended more to the phenomena than to the essence of nature; and contemplated the horrifying and transitory more than the pleasing and enduring dimensions; also, they rarely came to the point of subordinating all causes to one cause. Yet, even this first effort was also religion, and it means little to say that it was *fear* that among most peoples invented the deities. Fear, as such, does not invent anything; it merely alerts the intellect, to conjecture and to suppose something true or false. Thus, as soon as the human being learned to use the intellect subject to even the slightest impulse, that is, as soon as the human being beheld the world in a manner different from the animal, it had to conjecture invisible and more powerful beings that either helped or harmed. These the human being sought to make into friends or to keep as friends, and thus religion became, guided by truth or falsehood, rightly or wrongly, the tutor of humankind, the comforting guide in a life so dark, labyrinthine, and full of danger.

No! Eternal source of all life, all being, and all form, you have not failed to manifest yourself to your creatures. The prone beast dimly perceives your power and goodness, as it uses its powers and follows its inclinations in keeping with its organization; for it the human being is the visible deity on earth. But it was the human being who was raised by you, without knowing or willing it, to search for the causes of things, to divine their connections, and thus to find *You,* the great bond of all things, being of beings! The human being does not know your innermost nature, for it does not see the essence of any power on earth; yes, and if it were the human endeavor to give you shape, it was in error and necessarily so, for you are without shape, though the first and only cause of all shapes. Yet even each slightest false glimmer of you still is light, and each false altar erected by humankind to you is an incontestable monument not only of your existence, but also of the human power to know and worship you. Thus religion, even considered merely as an exercise of the intellect, reflects the highest humanity, is the most exalted blossom of the human soul.

But it is more than this; it is an exercise of the human heart, and the purest direction of its capacities and powers. If the human being is created to be free and on earth subject to no law but the self-imposed, it must turn into the most savage of all creatures, unless the law of God in nature is soon recognized and the child emulates the perfection of the father. Animals are born servants in the great mansion of the terrestrial household; slavish fear of laws and punishments is also the most certain hallmark of the animal in humankind. The true human being is free and obeys from goodness and love; for all laws of nature, wherever they are observed, are good, and where they are not understood by humankind, the way is shown to abide by them in childlike simplicity. If you do not go willingly, the sages say, still you must go; the law of nature will not change on your account; but the more you come to know its perfection, goodness, and beauty, the more this living form will also shape you in your earthly life to the *image of the deity*. True religion thus is a childlike worship of God, an emulation of the highest and the most beautiful in the human realm, and thus the most intensive satisfaction, the most effective goodness and human love.

Thus it also becomes apparent why in all religions on earth the greater or lesser kinship of God to humans had to be found, either in that the human was raised to the level of the divine, or in that the father of the world was dragged down to the image of the human. A more exalted figure than ours we do not know; and, whatever is meant to move the human being and humanize it, must be conceived and felt in human terms. A nation governed by the senses thus enhanced the human figure to divine beauty; others, more spiritually disposed, produced symbols for the human eye to convey the perfections of the invisible. Even when the deity wanted to reveal itself to us, it spoke and acted among us in *a human manner* appropriate to each and every age. Nothing has so much ennobled our form and our nature as religion, solely because it has led them back to their purest destination.

That the hope for and belief in immortality was thus also connected with religion and by it established among humans is again rooted in the nature of things, almost inseparable from the concept of God and humankind. How? We are children of the eternal, whom we are meant here on earth to know and to love by emulating him, to the knowledge of whom we are aroused by everything, to emulate whom we are compelled by love and suffering, and yet we know him but so dimly; we emulate him so feebly and childishly; indeed, we even perceive the reasons why we, in our present state, cannot know him and emulate him in any other way. And if there is no other state of being possible for us? If there is for our most definite and finest disposition no real progress? For, just these, our most ennobled powers, are meant so little for this world; they strive beyond it because here, everything is governed by the needs of our nature. And still we feel our nobler parts incessantly contending with these wants; precisely that which seems to be the end of human organization finds on earth indeed the place of its birth, but not its consummation. Has the deity, then, broken the thread, and with all these preparations in the human frame produced at last an immature creature, deceived about all of its destination? All things upon earth are fragments; and shall they remain forever and ever imperfect fragments, and the human race a mere herd of shadows chasing after dreams? Here religion has tied together all the wants and hopes of humans into *faith,* and woven an *immortal* crown for humankind.

(5) The Human Being Is Predisposed to the Hope of Immortality

Let the reader not expect here any metaphysical proof of the immortality of the soul, from the simplicity of its nature, its spirituality, or the like. Natural science knows nothing of this simplicity, and would rather incline to raise doubts about it, as we are acquainted with our soul only through its workings in a complex organization, which appear to spring from a diversity of stimuli and perceptions. The most common thought is merely the result of innumerable individual perceptions, and the mistress of our body acts upon the innumerable host of subordinate powers as if she were present beside them—.

Neither can *Bonnet's* philosophy,[12] as it is called, the system of germs, be our guide here; for, in respect to the transition to a new existence, it is partly devoid of proof, partly inapplicable. No one has discovered in our brain a spiritual brain, the germ of a new existence; not even the slightest analogy to this is discernible in its structure. The brain of the dead remains with us, and if the seed of our immortality possessed no other powers, it would lie down and be consumed to dust. Yes, this philosophy, it appears to me, is entirely inapplicable to this subject; for we do not speak here of a creature begetting young of the same kind, but of a withering creature springing to a new existence; rather, this philosophy, even if it were true exclusively with regard to the terrestrial generation, and all hope rested upon it, it would oppose insuperable doubts to this hope. If it is determined for eternity that the flower shall remain flower, the animal animal, and that from the onset of creation everything rested in predetermined mechanical design, then farewell enchanting hope of a superior existence. Predetermined to my present state, and to no higher existence, I have lain a germ from all eternity; all that was destined to spring from me are the preformed germs of my children; and when the tree dies, all the philosophy of germs dies with it.

If we, therefore, do not wish to deceive ourselves with pleasing words on this important question, we must begin deeper, and from a wider sphere, and take account of the entire *analogy of nature*. We cannot penetrate the innermost recesses of her powers; it would thus be in vain, as well as unnecessary, to desire from her profound, essential *revelations* regarding any state of being whatsoever. But the effects and forms of her powers lie before us; these therefore we can compare, and perhaps gather *hopes* from the progress of nature here below, and from its general prevailing character.

～ 16 ～

The Nature of Humankind Manifests Itself in a System of Spiritual Powers

This and the following text are taken from the 1784 part of Herder's Weimar philosophy of history. Herder reveals a spiritual core to his concept of humanity, thus opposing materialistic theories of his time, and he conceives of the whole of history as a manifestation of spiritual processes. The soul is that part or aspect of the human being which allows participation in this totality. Immanuel Kant very harshly criticized this part of Herder's *Reflections*, as well as the following one.

The principal doubt usually raised about the immortality of organic powers is deduced from the implements with which they operate; and I may venture to assert that for us the illumination of this doubt will throw the greatest light, not merely on the hope for, but also on the confidence in, eternal continuance of activity. No flower blossoms by means of the external dust, the coarse component that makes up its structure; much less does an animal, ever growing anew, reproduce itself the same way, and still less is thinking, by an internal power of such multifarious complexity as our soul, possible on the basis of the component parts into which a brain may be dissolved. Even physiology convinces us of this. The external picture that draws itself within the eye comes not to the brain; the sound that refracts within our ear does not enter our soul as sound. No nerve lies extended so as to vibrate to a central point; in some animals not even the two optic nerves fuse into one, and there is no creature in which the nerves of all the senses come together so as to unite within one visible point. Even less does this apply to the nerves of the entire body, though the soul feels itself present and acts in its minutest member. To imagine the brain, therefore, to be self-cogitative, the nervous fluid self-sentient, is a feeble, unphysiological notion; rather, consistent with all experience, there are *peculiar psychological laws,* subject to which the soul carries out its functions and joins its concepts. That this takes place in each case in conformity with her organs, and in harmony with them, that, when the tools are defective, the artist can do nothing, and the like, all of this cannot be doubted; but it also does not alter anything in the matter as such. What comes under consideration here is the *manner* in which the soul operates, the *essence of what it conceives.*

1. And with regard to this point it is undeniable, that the *thought,* even the first perception, with which the soul envisions an external object, is *something totally different from what the sense offers to it.* We call it an image, yet it is not the image, the speck of light, that is pictured in the eye, and that does not reach the brain at all; the image in the soul is a spiritual being, created by itself at the impetus of the senses. From the chaos of things surrounding it, the soul calls forth a figure on which it fixes its attention, and thus, by its intrinsic power, it forms out of the many a whole that belongs to itself alone. This it is able to restore for itself even when the figure is no longer present; the dream and the fictional capacity can combine it according to laws very different from those under which the senses represented it, and do so in reality. The fury of the deranged, so often adduced as witnesses to the materiality of the soul, attest actually to its immateriality. Listen to the lunatic and take note of the course taken by his soul. He proceeds from the idea that touched him too deeply and thus unhinged his mental tools and disturbed the connection with other sensations. He now refers everything to this idea, because it is the dominant one and he cannot get away from it; with reference to it, he creates for himself a world of his own, a peculiar concatenation of thoughts, and each of his deviations in the linking of ideas is to the highest degree *spiritual.* He does not conceptualize according to the chambers of the brain, not even in sequence to the sensory stimuli, but rather in keeping with other ideas that are akin to his, and in keeping with his ability to make those his own. All the associations of our thoughts proceed in the same way; they belong to a being which by its own energy, and often with a strange idiosyncrasy, calls up recollections and ties together ideas not on the basis of an external mechanics, but in keeping with internal love or disaffection. I wish that honest people, in this regard, would make known the protocol of their hearts, and that acute observers, in particular physicians, would make known the particularities observed in their patients; if this were done, I am convinced, we should have clear proofs of the operation of a being, organic it is true, yet acting of itself, and according to the laws of spiritual bounds.

2. The same thing is demonstrated by the *artificial formation of our*

ideas from childhood on, and by the *tedious course,* through which the soul arrives only late at a consciousness of itself, and with considerable labor learns to make use of its senses. More than one psychologist has observed the ingenious twists with which a child obtains conceptions of color, shape, size, and distance, and by which it *learns to see.* The physical sense learns nothing, for the image draws itself upon the eye on the first day, as it will also draw itself on the last day of life; but the soul learns to measure, to compare, and to perceive spirituality, by means of the sense. In this it is assisted by the ear; and language is certainly a spiritual, not a physical means of forming ideas. Only one devoid of sense can take sound and word for the same thing, and just as these two differ, so do body and soul, organ and power. The word recalls the idea, and transfers it from the mind of another to us; but the word is not the idea itself, just as the material organ is not the thought. As the body is increased by food, so is our mind enlarged by ideas; indeed, we observe in it the same laws of *assimilation, growth,* and *generation,* only not in a physical manner, but in a manner particular to itself. The mind too may gorge itself with nourishment, so that it will be unable to absorb it and to transform it within itself; the mind too has a symmetry of its powers, every deviation from which becomes disease, either asthenic or sthenic, that is, derangement; finally, the mind carries out this business of its internal life with a genial power in which love and hatred, inclination to what is of its own nature and aversion to what is dissimilar to it, display themselves as in terrestrial life. In short, and put plainly, an *internal spiritual human being* is formed within us, which has a nature of its own, and uses the body only as an implement, indeed, which will act according to its own nature, notwithstanding even the worst disorder of the physical organs. The more the soul is separated from the body by disease or the compulsive state of passions, and thus in a way compelled to roam in its own world of ideas, the more singular will be the manifestations we note of its peculiar power and energy in the creation and linking of ideas. In desperation it now roams among the scenes of its earlier existence, and since it is unable by its very nature to cease in its task of forming ideas, it now prepares for itself a new, *wild creation.*

3. The clearer mode of *consciousness,* this great asset of the human soul, was *brought into it only gradually, in a spiritual manner, and by means of humanity.* A child possesses little consciousness, though its soul is incessantly exercising itself to attain it, and to become conscious of itself by means of all the senses. All its striving for concepts has the purpose of becoming aware of the self in God's world, and enjoying its existence with human energy. The animal still roams in the darkness of a dream; its consciousness is pervaded by so many stimuli of the body and so strongly

enwrapped by them, that its makeup does not allow for that bright awakening that leads to a consistent generation of ideas. The human being, too, is conscious of its *sensual* state only through the medium of the senses, and as soon as these suffer, it is no wonder that a dominant idea will deprive it of its self-awareness, playing out within the self a sad or mirthful drama. But even this rushing into a land of vibrant ideas reveals an internal energy in which the power of consciousness, of self-determination, often manifests itself in the most deviant ways. Nothing renders a human being so peculiarly sensible of its own existence as cognition; cognition of a truth which we gained ourselves, which is akin to our innermost nature, and which, in being beheld, often fades for us from visibility. The human being becomes oblivious of the self, loses track of time and of the sensory powers when called by a higher thought and in pursuit of it. The most awful tortures of the body have been shown to be suppressed by a single vital idea which at the time prevailed in the soul. Humans who were gripped by an affect, specifically by the most vibrant and purest affect of all, the love of God, have been found to disregard life and death, and in this abyss of all ideas have felt as if in heaven. The most ordinary task comes to be difficult for us, as long as it is carried out only by the body; but love eases the most burdensome business, and gives us wings for the most toilsome and far-reaching exertion. Space and time vanish before her; she is ever in her element, in her own ideal region. This nature of the mind displays itself even among the most savage people; it matters not for what they fight; they fight in the throng of ideas. Even the cannibal, impelled by audacity and thirst for revenge, strives, though in abominable ways, for a *spiritual* pleasure.

4. All the states, diseases, and peculiarities of the organ thus can never mislead us, not to feel *primitively* the power that dwells within them. Memory, for example, depending on the varied makeup of humans, differs among them; in some it is formed and sustained by images, in others by symbols of abstraction, by words, or even numbers. In youth, while the brain is soft, it is vivid; in age, when the brain hardens, it becomes sluggish and adheres to old ideas. It is the same with the other faculties of the soul, and it cannot be otherwise as long as a power functions organically. However, here too the *laws of the retention and renewal of ideas* should be taken note of; they are altogether spiritual, and not physical. There have been humans who have lost the memory of certain years, even, of certain parts of speech, of names, persons, and things, even individual letters and symbols; the memory of the previous years, the recollection of other parts of speech and their unimpaired usage, remained with them; the soul was fettered only in the one part in which the organ suffered. Were the chain of her ideas material, the soul, in keeping with these manifestations, would either have

to move about within the brain and keep specific protocols for certain years, substantives, and names; or, were the ideas to be hardened with the brain, all of them would have to be hardened, and yet the memory of youth still remains especially vivid among the old. At a time when the soul, in keeping with its organ, can no longer combine quickly, or think with rapid facility, it holds so much more firmly to the goods it attained in its finest years, controlling over them as if they were its property. Immediately before death, as it feels less fettered by the body, this memory reawakens with all the vividness of youthful joy and the bliss of age; the rapture of the dying rests largely on this. From the commencement of life, our soul appears to have but one task, that of attaining *internal shape, the form of humanity,* and to feel herself sound and joyful within it, as the body does in its own shape and form. To this end it strives incessantly, and with as much cohesion of all its powers as the body may ever exert for its health, as it feels at once when any part of it suffers, and supplies fluids as best it can to repair the breach and to heal the wound. In the same manner does the soul labor for her always precarious and often illusory health, endeavoring to soothe and augment it, sometimes by proper remedies, at other times by delusive ones. Marvelous to behold is the art it employs to this end, and immeasurable is the supply of resources and cures it knows how to provide for itself. If the *semiotics of the soul*[1] should once be studied in the same manner as the semiotics of the body, the spiritual nature so particular to it will be apparent in all its diseases that the conclusions of the materialists will vanish like the mists before the sun. Yes, for the one who is convinced of *this internal life of the self,* all external states, in which, like all matter, the body is unceasingly changing, are in time only transitions, which do not pertain to its essence; such a person will pass from this world to that as imperceptibly as he passes from night to day and from one stage of life to the next.

Each day the creator has provided us with an experience unique to us, revealing to us how little everything in our machine is inseparable from us as well how little one part is inseparable from the other; this experience is the brother of death, the balm of sleep. The gentle touch of its finger separates the most important functions of our existence; nerves and muscles rest; sensual perception ceases; and yet the soul continues to think in her own domain. It is no more separated from the body than it was in the state of wakefulness, as demonstrated by the perceptions interwoven by the dream; and yet it acts according to its own laws even in the deepest sleep, the dreams of which we do not recollect unless a sudden awakening brings them to mind. A number of people have observed that in undisturbed dreams their soul pursues the same series of ideas uninterruptedly, in a manner different from what it does in a waking state, wandering always in an ever youthful, lively, and beautiful world. The perceptions of the dream are more vivid for us, its affects more passionate; the connections of thoughts and possibilities in the dream have greater facility; our outlook is more cheerful; and the light that surrounds us more brilliant. In healthy sleep, our walk often turns into flight, our shapes are larger, our resolution is firmer, our actions are less restrained. And all this depends on the body, as even the most minute aspect of the soul must necessarily harmonize with it as long as its powers function within such intimate incorporation. Yet, experience of sleep and dream, which is certainly quite strange in itself and would greatly astonish us were we not used to it, demonstrates that not every part of our body belongs to us in the same manner, indeed, that certain organs of our machine may be unstrung, and that the superior power, based on mere recollections, functions in a more ideal, vivid, and free manner. Now, since all the causes that induce sleep and all its physical symptoms not only in a manner of speaking, but physiologically and really, are *analogues of death,* why should this not also be true of its spiritual symptoms? And so there remains for us, when the sleep of death falls upon us from disease or weariness, the hope that it too, like ordinary sleep, will only soothe the fever of life, that it will gently redirect the movement that was too uniform for too long, that it will heal some of the wounds incurable in this life, and that it will bring the soul to a joyful awakening, to the enjoyment of a new and youthful Morn. Just as in the dream my thoughts return to my youth, just as I, only halfway freed from some of my organs, but more concentrated upon the self, feel myself in the dream freer and more active, so you too, refreshing dream of death, will pleasingly bring back the youth of my life, the most beautiful and strongest moments of my existence, till I awake in that image, or rather in the more beautiful image of a celestial youth.

17

The Present State of Humankind Is Probably the Connecting Link between Two Worlds

With the following part of his philosophy of history, Herder comes to the end of his reflections on the nature of the human being as an agent of history. The conclusion might read that the human being, as a "middle being," is the mediator between the animal on the one side and presumed celestial creatures on the other. But the human being is not limited to the role of a mediator. Herder insists on the human dialectics of freedom and determination as a condition for human history. In large portions of this far-reaching exploration of philosophical and even theological ideas, Herder is very much indebted to Leibniz and Gotthold Ephraim Lessing.

Everything in nature is connected; one stage strives toward the next and prepares it. If then the human being is the last and highest link, closing the chain of terrestrial organization, it also, and by the same token, begins the chain of a higher species of creatures as its lowest link, and is therefore probably the central link between two interlocking systems of creation. The human being cannot pass into any other organization on earth without regressing and wandering in circles; to stand still is impossible, since no living power in the realm of the most effective goodness can be in a state of rest; thus, the human being must anticipate a stage so proximate, and yet again so exalted above, just as the human, endowed with the most noble of advantages, resides at the edge of the animal world. This prospect, which is supported by all the laws of nature, alone gives us the key to the wonderful phenomenon of the human being, and at the same time to the only *philosophy of human history*. For thus,

1. The singular *contradiction* of the human condition becomes clear. As an animal, the human tends to the earth and is attached to it as its habitation; the human side holds the seed of immortality within, which demands to be planted in another soil. As an animal, the human being is able to satisfy its needs, and humans who are content with these satisfactions feel themselves quite happy here below; but those who seek a nobler destination will find imperfections and piecework everywhere; what is noblest is never accomplished upon earth, what is purest has rarely attained stability and duration; for this theater is always, for the powers of our minds and hearts, merely a place for exercise and trial. The history of our kind, with what it has attempted and what has befallen it, the endeavors it has undertaken and the revolutions it has undergone, sufficiently proves this. Now and then, a philosopher, a good man, arose and scattered thoughts, precepts, and actions on the flood of time; the water formed some rings around them, but the stream soon carried them away, washing away any trace of them; the jewel of their noble purpose sank to the bottom. Fools prevailed over the council of the wise, and spendthrifts inherited the treasures of wisdom gathered by their parents. As far as is the life of the human here below from being calculated for eternity, equally far is the incessantly revolving sphere of the earth from being a studio of enduring works of art, a garden of never-fading plants, a pleasure seat of eternal dwelling. We come and go; every moment brings thousands into the world and takes thousands out of it; it is a hospice for wanderers, an errant planet on which birds of passage rest themselves and from which they hasten away. The animal lives out its life; and even if its years be too few to attain higher ends, its inmost purpose is accomplished; its capacities are fulfilled, and it is what it is meant to be. The human being alone is in contradiction with the self and with the earth; for, the most highly developed creature among all its organisms, it is at the same time the least developed in terms of its higher disposition, although it may leave this world sated with life. The cause of this, evidently, is that the present stage of human existence, the last for this earth, is at the same time the first for another existence, in the face of which the human here appears as a child in its earliest efforts. The human thus represents two worlds at once, and that makes for the apparent duplicity of his being.

2. It immediately becomes clear which part must predominate in most humans here below. The greatest number of humans is of the animal kind, brought into the world with only the potential for humanity, which must be first formed by diligence and labor. In how few is it rightly formed! And how frail and delicate is the divine plant even in the best! Throughout life the animal strives to predominate over the human, and most permit it to hold sway as it pleases. Thus the animal incessantly drags down, while the

spirit strives upward, while the heart longs for a freer sphere; and since, for a sensuous creature, the present is always more vivid than the distant, and since the visible has a more powerful effect upon it than the invisible, it is easy to conjecture which way the balance will incline. Of how little pure delight, of how little pure knowledge and virtue, is the human being capable! And were the capability there, to how little of these is the human accustomed. The noblest ties here below are disturbed by inferior propensities, as the voyage of life is perplexed by contrary winds, and the creator, merciful-severe, has related the two causes of disorder to one another, to tame the one by means of the other, and to raise within us the first step to immortality more through raging storms than through pleasing breezes. An often-tempted human has learned much; a lethargic, idle one does not know what is within, much less the joyful satisfaction of how far the human powers extend. Thus, life is a conflict, and the garland of pure, immortal humanity is attained with difficulty. The goal is before the runners; those who fight for virtue will win the palm in death.

3. Thus, if superior creatures look down upon us, they may view us in the same light as we do the *middle species,* with which nature makes the transition from one element to another. The ostrich flaps its feeble wings not to fly but to gain assistance in running; its heavy body draws it to the ground. But even for the ostrich, and for all the middle creatures, Mother Nature has made provision; they too are perfect within themselves, and appear deformed only to our eyes. So it is with our human nature here below; its deformity is hardly noticed by an earthly spirit; but a higher spirit, looking into the internal and capable of seeing several links of the chain as they are fitted together, may feel pity for us, but not contempt. For it sees why humans must depart from this world in so many diverse states, young and old, foolish and wise, as greybeards in their second childhood, or even as the unborn. Madness and deformity, all stages of culture, all the aberrations of humanity were encompassed by the omnipotent Good, and there is ample balm in its storehouse to heal the wounds that death alone can mitigate. Since the future state probably springs out of the present, as does our organization from inferior ones, the business of the future is no doubt more closely connected than we imagine with our existence here. The garden above blooms only with plants of which the seeds sprang forth here, sprouting under coarser husks. If then, as we have seen, sociability, friendship, and active participation are but the principal end to which the quality of humanity has been directed in its whole development among humankind, this finest flower of human life must necessarily attain there the renewing form, the height that leaves all in its shadow, for which our heart thirsts in vain in all earthly endeavors. Our brethren above, therefore, love us with

more intensity and purity than we can feel for them; for they see our state more clearly, to them the moment of time is no more, all discrepancies are harmonized, and in us they are perhaps educating, unseen, partners of their bliss and companions of their labors. But one step farther, and the oppressed spirit can breathe more freely, the wounded heart is healed; they are aware of the approaching step and with a strong grip help the stumbling.

4. Since therefore we are of a middle species between two orders, and in some measure partake of both, I cannot conceive that the future state is so remote from the present, and so incommunicable with it, as the animal part of the human is inclined to suppose; rather, many steps and attainments in the history of our kind are to me incomprehensible without assistance from above. For instance, that the human being should have come of itself to the road of cultural advancement, and invented language and the first science without guidance from above, appears to me inexplicable, and the more so the longer the human is supposed to have remained in the coarseness of animal life. A divine economy has certainly ruled over the human species from its first origin, facilitating entry into its course. But the more the human powers have been exercised, the less have they required this assistance from above, or were capable of appreciating it, although even in later times the greatest events in the world have arisen from inexplicable causes, or have been accompanied by circumstances which we cannot explain. Even diseases have often been their instruments; for when an organ loses its proportion to others, and thus becomes useless in the ordinary course of life, it seems that the restless internal energy should direct itself to other dimensions of the universe and perhaps receive impressions there, unattainable by an undisturbed organization, but also not required by it. Be this as it may, it is certainly a benign veil that separates this world from the next; and it is not without reason that it is so still and mute around the grave of the dead. The ordinary human being in the course of life is kept from impressions, one of which would break the whole sphere of ideas, rendering it useless for this world. The human being, formed for freedom, was not intended to be the imitative ape of superior beings, but rather, even under tutelage, was meant to live in the blissful delusion of acting autonomously. To appease the self, and its noble pride upon which human destiny rests, the human being was deprived of the sight of more exalted beings; for it is probable that we would despise ourselves were we acquainted with them. The human being, therefore, was not to anticipate the future state, but to arrive there through faith.

5. This much is certain, that there dwells an infinity in each of the human powers which cannot be developed here only because they are repressed by other powers, by animal senses and appetites, and lie bound, as it

were, to the state of terrestrial life. Particular instances of memory, of the imagination, indeed, even of prophecy and premonition, have discovered wonders of that hidden treasure that reposes in the human soul; and indeed, the senses are not to be excluded from this observation. That these treasures usually revealed themselves to be due to diseases and corresponding defects does not change anything in the nature of the matter, since this very dispro-portion was necessary to give to the one weight that matters on the scale its freedom and to demonstrate its power. The expression of *Leibniz,* that the soul is a mirror of the universe,[1] contains perhaps a more profound truth than has usually been elicited from it; for the powers of the universe also appear to lie hidden within the soul, and it requires merely an organization, or a series of organizations, to activate and exercise them. The All-Good will not deny to the soul these organizations, and he tutors it like a child, gradually to prepare it for the fullness of ever-increasing enjoyment, under the delusion that its powers and senses are self-acquired. Even under the present fetters, *space* and *time* are empty words for it; they measure and designate proportions of the body, but not of the inner capacity, which reaches beyond space and time when it acts in the full intensity of joy. Give yourself no concern for the place and hour of your future existence; the sun that brightens your days provides the measure of your dwelling and your business on earth, and in doing so it obscures for you the other celestial bodies. When it sets, the world appears in its greater dimension; the sacred night that once enveloped you, and that will envelope you again, covers your earth with shade and will open for you in the heavens the splendid tomes of immortality. There you find dwellings, worlds, and expanses—

In the fullness of youth they glitter,
though millennia have passed by,
the tides of time deprive them not
of the light that glows upon their cheeks.

But here, before our eyes,
all is decay and passing:
The splendor of the earth, its happiness
is threatened by decline.[2]

The earth itself will be no more when you will continue to exist and, in other abodes and organized differently, take joyful part in *God* and His creation. On earth you have enjoyed much that is good. Here you have attained the state of being in which you learned, as a child of heaven, to cast your eyes around you and above you. Thus, depart from her happily, and bless her as the meadow upon which you played as the child of immortality and as the school in which you were raised by suffering and joy to man-hood. You have no further claim on her, she has no further claim on you; crowned with the cap of freedom, and girded with the belt of the heavens, cheerfully set your staff forward.

Thus, as the flower stood there, in its upright posture closing off the realm of the subterranean, inert inanimate creation, to enjoy the coming of life in the face of the sun, the human being stands once more erect above all those bent to the earth. With uplifted eye and raised hands, he stands as a son of the house, awaiting his father's call.

18

The Nature of Peoples in the Vicinity of the North Pole

With the following six parts, Herder comes to the description of the concrete realization and manifestation of the human being in different places on earth. In accordance with his fundamental assumption that history is the development of the greatest possible variety in the totality of time and space, Herder starts with a profile of the individualizing characteristics of different peoples living in different regions of the world.

No navigator has yet been able to set his foot on the axis of the earth[*] and draw from the North Pole some perhaps more accurate conclusions respecting its general structure; in the meanwhile, we have proceeded far beyond the habitable parts of the globe, and described regions that may be termed the cold and bare ice-throne of nature. Here may be seen wonders of the creation incredible to an inhabitant of the equator, those immense masses of beautifully colored rocks of ice, those splendid northern lights, astonishing deceptions of the eye by the air, and the frequently warm caverns of the earth despite the severity of the cold from above.[**] The steep broken rocks of naked granite appear to extend much farther here than they could toward the South Pole, as, in general, the greater part of the habitable earth rests in the northern hemisphere. And as the sea was the first abode of living creatures, the Northern sea, with its bounty of inhabitants, may still be considered the womb of life, and its shores as the rim, along which the

---

[*]The hopes of our countryman, *Samuel Engel*,[1] on this subject, are well known; and one of the latest northern adventurers, *Pagès*, seems to have weakened the supposition of their impracticability.

[**]See Phipps, *Voyages;* Cranz, *Geschichte von Grönland*[2]; etc.

organization of terrestrial creatures commenced in mosses, insects, and worms. Waterfowl welcome the land, that as yet fosters few birds of its own; aquatic animals and amphibians crawl on the strand, to find warmth in the rare rays of the sun. Amidst the liveliest turbulence of the waves, as it were, the limits of created life on earth are revealed.

How has the organization of the human being preserved itself under these limitations? All that the cold could effect upon the human body was to compress it in some measure and thus, as it were, constrain the circulation of the blood. The Greenlanders usually grow to less than five feet, and the Eskimo, their brethren, grow smaller, the farther north they live.* But, as the vital power works from within to without, it has compensated in warm and durable thickness what it could not bestow in aspiring height. The head is large in proportion to the body, the face broad and flat; for nature, which brings forth beauty only in moderation and in the mean between extremes, could not here round a soft oval, and still less could allow the ornament of the face, the beam of the balance, the nose, to project. As the cheeks occupy the greater breadth of the face, the mouth is small and round; the hair is stiff, for the fine, rising nectar that makes for soft and silky hair is wanting; the eye does not reflect the soul. In like manner, the shoulders grow broad, the limbs large, the body sanguine and corpulent; only the hands and feet have remained small and delicate, the branches and extremities, so to speak, of the creation. As with the external form, so it is with the stimuli and the household of the fluids within. The blood circulates more slowly, and the heart beats less vigorously; thus, here the sexual drive, which grows so immensely with the increasing warmth of other lands, is weaker. It awakens later; the unmarried live modestly, and the women almost require compulsion to take upon themselves the troubles of married life. They give birth to fewer children, so that they compare the prolific and passionate Europeans to dogs. In their connubial state, as in their general way of life, a calm sobriety, a tenacious containment of the passions, prevails. Unable to feel those stimuli which in a warmer climate also produce more volatile spirits, they live and die quietly and peaceably, indifferently content, and active only from necessity. The father raises the son in and to that equilibrium, which he esteems the grand virtue and happiness of life, and the mother nurses her infant for a long time, and with all the deep and tenacious affection of animal maternity. What nature has denied them in elasticity and responsiveness to stimuli, it has given them in enduring, indefatigable strength, enveloping them with that warming fatty tissue, with that abundance of blood, which render their vapor suffocatingly hot in close habitations.

---

*See Cranz, Ellis, Egede, Roger Curtis's *Nachricht von der Küste Labrador,*[3] etc.

No one, it seems to me, can fail to observe here the equalizing hand of mother nature, who acts uniformly in all her works. If the human stature be retarded in those regions, vegetation is stunted even more; few and small trees grow there; mosses and shrubs crawl close to the earth. Frost even contracts the measuring rod lined with iron, and shall it not stunt the growth of human fiber, despite its inherent organic vitality? But that vitality can only be constrained and, so to speak, enclosed in a smaller sphere of growth, another analogy of the effect in every kind of organization. The extremities of the marine animals and other creatures of the frigid zone are small and delicate; nature has, as much as possible, kept everything in the sphere of internal warmth; there the birds are supplied with thick plumage, the beasts with enveloping fat, as are the humans with their warm sanguine-ous covering. Nature has also necessarily, and indeed from one and the same principle of all terrestrial organization, denied them in externals what is unsuitable to this constitution. Spices would be destructive to their bod-ies, which are prone to internal putrefaction, just as the liquor of madness, brandy, which has been introduced to them, has put to an end so many. Thus, the climate has denied them these stimuli. It compels them from the outside in their meager existence and with their great inclination to rest, which is rooted in their inner makeup to the active and physically demand-ing life, upon which all their laws and institutions are founded. The few herbs that grow here are such as purify the blood, and thus are precisely adapted to their wants. The atmosphere is in a high degree devoid of phlo-giston,* so that it counteracts putrefaction even in dead bodies and promotes longevity.[4] The dry cold does not allow for poisonous animals, and the people are protected from troublesome insects by their own natural insensi-bility, by smoke, and by the long winter. Thus does nature indemnify and act harmoniously in all her operations.

After describing this first nation, it will not be necessary to dwell as extensively on those that resemble it. The *Eskimo* of America are the brethren of the Greenlanders in figure, as well as in language and customs. But, as these poor wretches are pushed northward as bearded strangers by the beardless Americans, their mode of life is in general severely toilsome and precarious; yes, so hard is their fate that in winter they are often obliged to sustain themselves in their caves by sucking their own blood.** Here, and in a few other parts of the earth, dire necessity sits on her loftiest throne and

---

*See Wilson's *Beobachtungen über den Einfluß des Klima auf Pflanzen und Thiere* (Leipzig: 1781); and Cranz's *Historie von Grönland,* vol. 2, p. 275.

**See Roger Curtis's *Nachricht von Labrador,* in Forster and Sprengel's *Beiträge zur Völkerkunde,* vol. 1, pp. 105 ff.

compels humans to lead almost the life of the bear. Yet everywhere the quality of humanity is preserved; for even in what appear to be the features of the greatest inhumanity among these people, their humanity is evident when they are closely examined. Nature endeavored to test what forced circumstances the human species could endure, and humanity has stood the test.

The *Laplanders* inhabit a comparatively milder climate, and they are a milder people.* The size of the human figure increases; the flat rotundity of the face diminishes; the cheeks are lengthened; the color of the eyes turns dark gray; the straight black hair becomes carroty; and the internal organization of the person expands with the external frame, like the bud that unfolds beneath the beam of a more genial sun.** The Mountain Laplander grazes his reindeer, which neither the Eskimo nor the Greenlander can do, and obtains from them food and raiment, coverings for his dwelling and his bed, conveniences and enjoyments which the Greenlander, living at the edge of the earth, is compelled to seek mostly from the sea. Thus the human being acquired an animal as friend and servant, and hence learned arts and a more domestic mode of life. His feet thus were inured to the chase, his arm to the guidance of the rein, his mind to a taste for acquisition and permanent property; at the same time, the possession of the animal fosters the human's love of freedom and accustoms the ear to alert watchfulness, which we observe in many nations in a similar condition. Cautious as his animal, the Laplander listens and is startled at the slightest sound; he loves his way of life and, upon the return of the sun, he casts his eyes to the mountains, as does his reindeer; he speaks to his animal and it understands him; he cares for it as he would for his own wealth and the members of his household. Thus, with the first tamable land animal that nature bestowed upon these regions, she gave the human being a guide to a more human mode of life.

Of the people that dwell by the Arctic Ocean, along the wide extent of the Russian Empire, in addition to the many modern well-known travel accounts in which they are described, we have a collection of portraits of them, the contemplation of which says more than my description could do.*** Huddled together and isolated as some of these people dwell, we still see even the people of the most diverse ancestry brought under the same yoke of the Nordic environment and, so to speak, forged by a chain to the

---

*It is well known that *Sajnovics* found the language of the Laplanders to resemble the Hungarian. See [Janos] Sajnovics, *Demonstratio, idioma Ungarorum et Lapponum idem esse* (Copenhagen: 1770).

**On the subject of the Laplanders, see *Hoegström, Leem, Klingstedt,*[5] Georgi's *Beschreibung der Nationen des russischen Reiches.* . . .

***Georgi, *Beschreibung der Nationen des Russischen Reiches* . . . (St. Petersburg: 1776).

North Pole. The *Samoyed* has the round, broad, flat face, the rough black hair, the squat, sanguineous body stature of the northern mold; but his lips are fuller, his nose broader and more open, his beard diminished and continually decreasing along the immense tract of land to the eastward. The Samoyeds are thus, so to speak, the Negroes among the peoples of the North; and their great sensitivity to stimuli, the early puberty of the females in the eleventh or twelfth year,* yes, if the account be true, their black nipples, and other circumstances, render them still more similar to the Negroes, notwithstanding the coldness of their climate. Yet in spite of their warm and delicate constitution, which they probably brought with them as a national character, and which, it may be presumed, even the climate itself could not subdue, their makeup is on the whole that of the North. The *Tungus,*** who dwell farther to the south show some resemblance to the Mongolian tribe, although they are as distinct from them in language and race as the Samoyeds and Ostyaks are from the Laplanders and Greenlanders. Their bodies are more pleasingly shaped and more slender; the cut of their eye is narrower, like that of the Mongols; their lips are thin, their hair softer, yet their faces retain the flat northern shape. It is the same with the Yakut and the Yukaghir, who appear to take after the Tatars to the point of kinship, as the former took after the Mongolians. In the vicinity of the Black Sea and the Caspian, in the Caucasus and Urals, parts of which form the most temperate regions on earth, the appearance of the Tatars comes closer to beauty. Their bodies become slender and more lean; the head loses its plump rotundity for a more attractive oval; the coloring becomes vivid; the nose protrudes boldly and is well-shaped; the eye becomes lively, the hair turns dark brown, the step is alert, the countenance is pleasingly modest and shy; thus, the nearer we come to the regions where nature is most profuse of life, the more exquisite and better proportioned is the organization of humankind. The more we proceed to the north again, or the further we move into the Kalmuck steppe, the more flat and barbarous we find the features, in the northern or Kalmuck mold. In this, however, much must be attributed to the way of life of the people, to their descent and ethnic mix, and to the condition of the soil. The mountain Tatars preserve the clean lines of their features better than those that dwell in the plains; hordes that

---

*See Klingstedt, *Mémoires sur les Samojedes et sur les Lappons.*

**For an account of all these peoples, see Georgi *Beschreibung der Nationen des russischen Reiches; Pallas;* the travel accounts of the elder *Gmelin;* etc. The most remarkable circumstances relating to the different peoples have been extracted from *Pallas's* travel accounts and *Georgi's* commentary and published separately, in *Merkwürdigkeiten der verschiednen Völker* (Frankfurt and Leipzig: 1773–77).[6]

live near settlements and towns are more marked by other influences in customs as well as facial features. The less a people is displaced, the more it is compelled to remain faithful to its rough and simple way of life, the more it will also preserve its original makeup. As on this great plain of Tatary, inclining as it does to the sea, so much roaming has gone on and so many upheavals have taken place, causing more mingling than mountains, deserts, and rivers could set apart, the exceptions to the rule cannot fail to be observed; but the rule is confirmed by these very exceptions, for the Northern, Tatar, and Mongol characteristics divide the whole among them.

19

The Nature of the Peoples Along the Asian Spine of the Earth

As there are many probabilities that the first abode of the human species was along this spine of the earth, one might be inclined to seek on it the most beautiful kind of humans; how very much are we deceived in this expectation! The appearance of the Kalmucks and Mongols is well known; with a middling stature, they have, marginally at least, the flatness of the face, the thin beard, the brownish coloring of the northern climate; but they are distinguishable by the shallow angle of the eye cut obliquely to the nose, by narrow, black, slightly arched brows, by a small, flat nose, too broad toward the forehead, by large, protruding ears, by bowed lower legs and thighs, and by white and prominent teeth, which, together with the rest of the features, appear to characterize a beast of prey among humans. Where do these characteristics come from? The bowed knees and legs find their primary cause in the people's way of life. From childhood on, they are sedentary or cling to the back of a horse; they divide their time between sitting and riding, and the only activity that gives the human foot its finely straightened shape, that of walking, is unknown to them, except for a few steps here and there. Should it not be, then, that several other features of their way of life are also reflected in their makeup? The protruding, animal-like ear, in a way always watchfully listening; the narrow, sharp eye, capable of perceiving in the farthest distance the smallest sign of smoke or dust,

---

*See Pallas's *Sammlungen über die mongolischen Völkerschaften,* vol. 1, pp. 98, 171 ff; Georgi's *Beschreibung der Nationen des rußischen Reichs,* vol. 4 (St. Petersburg: 1780); Schnitscher's *Nachricht von den ajukischen Kalmucken,* in Müller's *Sammlung zur rußischen Geschichte,* vol. 4, part 4; Schlözer's *Auszug aus Schober's Memorabilia Russico-Asiatica,* in the same collection, vol. 7, part 1; etc.[1]

the white, projecting, bone-gnawing tooth; the thick neck and the backward reclining position of the head on it—are these features not concretized gestures and characteristics of their way of life? If we now add to this, as *Pallas* observes, that their children, even to the age of ten, frequently have deformed, puffed-up faces and a cacochymic appearance[2] until they become better shaped as they grow up; if we consider that extensive tracts of their country lack rain, and have little water, or at least none that is pure, and that thus from their infancy they scarcely know what it is to bathe; if we reflect on the salt lakes and swamps, and the saline nature of the soil upon which they dwell, the alkaline taste they relish in their food and even in the deluges of tea with which they daily enfeeble their digestive faculty; if we add to these the elevation of the country they inhabit, the thinner air, dry winds, alkaline effluvia, and long winters spent in the smoke of their huts, and with snow continually before their eyes, and a few other, lesser conditions; is it not probable that their makeup originated from these causes some thousands of years ago, when many of them were perhaps even more intensely effective, and thus gradually became their hereditary nature? Nothing invigorates our bodies more, and contributes more to their growth and firmness, than washing and bathing in water; particularly if to these be added walking, running, wrestling, and other bodily exercises. Nothing tends to debilitate the body more than the drinking of warm fluids; and these they gulp down in immoderate quantities, seasoned too with corrugating alkaline salts. Hence, as already observed by *Pallas,* the feeble, effeminate figures of the Mongols and Burats, five or six of whom, with their utmost exertions, cannot do what a single Russian can perform; hence the extreme lightness of their bodies, with which on their little horses they seem to fly, or skim along the surface of the ground; hence, lastly, the cacochymic habit transmitted to their children. Even some of the neighboring Tatar tribes are born with Mongolian features, which disappear as they grow up, and this renders it more probable that some of the causes are climatic, which are more or less engrafted into the frame of the people by their mode of life and descent, and rendered hereditary. When Russians or Tatars intermix with the Mongols, it is reported, handsome children are produced, being, in Mongol terms, of delicate and well-proportioned shape.[*] Here too, nature has thus remained true to herself in their organization; nomadic people under this sky, in this region of the earth, and with these modes of living, had to become this sort of light birds of prey.

And traces of their makeup spread far and wide; for, whither have not these birds of prey extended their flight? More than once have their victori-

---

[*]Pallas in the *Sammlungen zur Geschichte der mongolischen Völkerschaften, Reisen,* vol. 1, p. 304, [vol.] 2, etc.

ous excursions overrun parts of the globe. Thus, Mongols have established themselves in many countries of Asia, and they have ennobled their makeup by the features of other nations. Moreover, much before these warlike expeditions there were those ancient migrations from this highest spine of the earth, the site of early human settlement, into many surrounding countries. Perhaps it is for this reason that the eastern regions of the world, extending to Kamchatka as well as across Tibet, through the Indian subcontinent beyond the Ganges, are characterized by Mongol features. Let us take a view of this sector of the earth, in which appears much that is singular.

Most of the refinements of the Chinese with regard to their physical shape bear Mongol characteristics. We have observed the misshapen feet and ears of the Mongols; it was probably a similar defect, aided by a wrong turn of culture, that gave occasion to that unnatural confinement of the foot and that frightful distortion of the ears common to many nations in this region. People were ashamed of their appearance and, wishing to alter it, affected parts that yielded to change and ultimately became hereditary as repulsive marks of beauty. As far as the great differences of their provinces and modes of life permit, the *Chinese* display evident oriental features, which happen to be most striking to the eye only in the Mongolian latitudes. Climate has merely reduced the broad face, the narrow black eyes, the stump nose and thin beard to a softer, rounder figure; and the taste of the Chinese seems to be as much a consequence of ill-constructed organs as their wisdom and form of government carry the seeds of despotism and barbarism within. The *Japanese,* a people of Chinese culture,* are almost universally ill-proportioned, with large heads, narrow eyes, stump noses, flat cheeks, and scarcely any beards; and they are generally bandy-legged. Their form of government and philosophy abounds with violent restrictions, thoroughly suitable only to their country. A third form of despotism prevails in *Tibet,* the religion of which extends far into the barbarian steppes.

Oriental characteristics** move along the mountains beyond the Ganges down into the subcontinent, with the peoples probably following the same mountainous route. The kingdom of Assam, which borders on Tatary, if we may trust the reports of travelers,*** is marked by people with goiter and

---

* *Allgemeine Sammlung der Reisen,* vol. 2, p. 595. Charlevoix. *Von den Sineson,* see Olof Toree, *Reisen nach Surate und China,* p. 68, *Allgemeine Reisen,* vol. 6, p. 130.[3]

**The more ancient accounts describe the Tibetans as ill-shaped. See *Allgemeine Reisen,* vol. 7, p. 382. More recent reports (Pallas, *Nordische Beiträge,* vol. 4, p. 280) moderate this description, thereby also providing a more favorable image of their geographic situation. They probably represent a rough-edged intermediate step to Hindostan culture.[4]

***See *Allgemeine Reisen,* vol. 10, p. 557, from Tavernier.[5]

flat noses. The ill-shaped ornaments affixed to their stretched earlobes, the coarseness of their food, and their nudity, given the mildness of their climate, are characteristic of the barbarism of an uncultivated people. The Arrakanese, with their wide, open nostrils, low foreheads, narrow eyes, and earlobes extending down to their shoulders, represent just this deformity of the Oriental regions.[*] The Barmas of Ava and Pegu are as inveterate enemies of even the slightest appearance of beard as the Tibetans and other more elevated nations; they do not want to be deprived of their Tatar beardlessness even by a more bountiful natural environment. It is the same, with some differences according to the people and climate, even in the islands further south.[**]

To the north it is no different, even to the Koryacs and Kamchadales at the outer limits of the Oriental world. The language of the latter is reported still to bear some resemblance to the Chinese-Mongolic, although they must have been separated from these peoples in very ancient times, since they remained ignorant of the use of iron; nor does their physical makeup belie their region of descent.[***] Their hair is black, their faces broad and flat, and their noses and eyes deeply embedded; and their intellectual disposition, an apparent anomaly in this cold and inhospitable climate, still must be considered appropriate to it. Lastly, the Koryacs, the Tsushimaans, the Kurile Islanders, and the inhabitants of islands farther east[†] appear to me to be gradual transitions from the Mongol to the American mold; and if we would obtain an acquaintance with the northwestern end of America, which remains for the most part unknown to us, and with the interior part of Jedso and the great expanses toward New Mexico, of which we know as little as of the heart of Africa, it seems to me that we will see, as indicated by the last journey of *Cook*,[‡] rather distinctive shades increasingly blending into one another.

So far-flung is the extent of the partially distorted, but generally more or less beardless Oriental influence; and the diversity of the languages and customs of the nations testifies to the fact that this Oriental influence is not

[*] *Allgemeine Reisen,* vol. 10, p. 67, from Ovington.[6]
[**]See Marsden, *Beschreibung von Sumatra,* p. 62. *Allgemeine Reisen,* vol. 2, p. 487.[7]
[***]*Allgemeine Reisen,* vol. 20, p. 289, from Steller.[8]
[†]See Georgi, *Beschreibung der Nationen des rußischen Reichs,* vol. 3.[9]
[‡]See Ellis's *Nachricht von der Cookschen dritten Reise,* p. 114. *Tagebuch der Entdeckungsreise,* tr. by Forster, p. 231, with which the older accounts about the islands between Asia and America should be compared. See *Neue Nachricht von den neuentdeckten Inseln,* Hamburg and Leipzig: 1776. See also the accounts in Pallas's *Nordischen Beiträgen,* Müller's rußischen Sammlungen, and the *Beiträge zur Völker- und Landeskunde,* etc.[10]

due to descent from one particular nation. What then would be its cause? What, for example, has emboldened the various peoples to take issue with the beard, to stretch the earlobes, or to pierce the nose and lips? It seems to me that an original deformity must have given rise to it, which afterward called for assistance from a barbarian form of art, and at length became an ancient custom of the forefathers. The degeneracy of animals reveals itself in the hair and the ears before it takes hold of the rest of the body; further down it reveals itself in the feet, just as the transformation of the visage is marked first by the alignment of its features, the profile. When the geneal-ogy of these peoples, the general condition of these faraway regions and countries, but, most important, the divergences among the internal physiol-ogies of these peoples will have been examined more thoroughly, we shall not fail to reach more appropriate conclusions on these questions too. And ought not *Pallas,* skilled in science and acquainted with nations, be the first to give us a *spicilegium anthropologicum?*[11]

～ 20 ～

The Nature of Peoples Favored by the Temperate Zone

On the bosom of the highest mountains lies the kingdom of Kashmir, hidden like a paradise. Its fertile and pleasant hills are surrounded by mountains rising higher and higher still, until the summits of the ultimate, covered with eternal snow, ascend to the clouds. Here gush pellucid rivulets and streams; the earth adorns itself with salubrious herbs and fruits; islands and gardens are clad in refreshing green; pastures are spread throughout; venomous and savage animals are banned from this paradise. These may be fitly named the mountains of innocence, as *Bernier* says, which flow with milk and honey; and the branch of humankind dwelling there is not unworthy of the place. The Kashmirs are deemed to be the most clever and ingenious people of India, equally capable of excelling in poetry and science, in arts and manufactures, the men most finely formed and the women often models of beauty.[*]

How happy might Hindustan have been if the hands of humans had not combined to desolate the garden of nature and to torture the most innocent of human beings with superstition and tyranny. The *Hindus* are the gentlest race of humankind. They intentionally injure nothing that breathes; they respect everything that bears life and sustain themselves with the most innocent of nourishments, milk, rice, the fruit of trees, and health-bringing herbs, offered to them by their mother country. "Their figure," observes a more recent traveler,[**] "is straight, slender, and attractive, their limbs are finely proportioned, their fingers long and delicately sensitive to feeling, their faces open and pleasing; their features reveal in the women the most

---

[*] *Allgemeine Reisen,* vol. 2, p. 116, from *Bernier.*[1]
[**] Mackintosh, *Travels,* vol. 1, p. 231.

delicate lines of beauty, in the men a masculine-gentle soul. Their gait and their whole bearing are in the highest degree graceful and attractive." The thighs and lower extremities, which in all northeastern countries were misshapen or shortened like those of apes, are lengthened here and present an aspiring human beauty. Even the Mongol influence, which was wedded to this human kind, has transformed itself into dignity and pleasantness. And the original disposition of their minds is consonant with the frame of their bodies. So indeed is their manner of life, when considered apart from the yoke of slavery and superstition. Temperance and quiet, gentle feelings and a still profundity of the soul characterize their work and their leisure, their moral teaching and their mythology, their arts and even their tolerance under the most extreme yoke of human tyranny. Happy lambs, why could not nature sustain you carefree and undisturbed on your native plains!

The ancient *Persians* were an unattractive mountain people, as demonstrated by their remnant, the Gaurs.* However, since scarcely any country has been so much exposed to incursions as Persia, and as it lies immediately beneath nations of well-formed people, a compound has resulted, which in the nobler Persians combines dignity with beauty. On the one hand lies Circassia, the mother of beauty; on the other side of the Caspian Sea dwell Tatar tribes, who have already improved their appearance in their favorable climate, and have spread their numbers. Further to the east is India, and the Persian blood has been improved by maidens purchased in this country and in Circassia. Their cast of mind has adapted to this ennobling environment of humankind: for the quick and penetrating capacity to think, the fertile and lively imagination of the Persians, with their supple, courteous manner, their propensity to vanity, pomp, and pleasure, yes, their disposition to romantic love, are perhaps the most precious attributes fostering a balance of passions and features. Instead of those barbarous embellishments with which deformed nations endeavored to cover the defects of their bodies, thereby increasing them, more agreeable customs have been adopted here, which enhanced physical beauty. The lack of water compels the Mongol to be uncleanly; the soft Indian bathes; the voluptuous Persian anoints himself. The Mongol sits on his heels when he does not cling to his horse; the gentle Indian rests; the romantic Persian divides his time between amusements and games. The Persian tints his eyebrows; he dresses so as to enhance his stature. Beautiful figure! Gentle equilibrium of the passions and the powers

---

*Chardin, *Voyages en Perse,* vol. 3, chap. 9, seq. In Le Brun (Bruyns), *Voyages en Perse,* vol. 1, chap. 42, no. 86–88, there is a description of the Persians that may be compared with that of the blacks immediately following (no. 89, 90), that of the coarse Samoyeds (chap. 2, no. 7, 8), that of the savage southern Negroes (no. 197), and that of the gentle people of Benin (no. 109).

of the soul, why could you not communicate yourself throughout the globe?

We have already observed that some *Tatar* tribes originally belonged to the well-formed peoples on earth, and that they have deteriorated only in the northern countries, or in the steppes; both shores of the Caspian Sea display this enhanced beauty. The female inhabitants of Uzbekistan are described as tall, well-formed, and agreeable*; they accompany their men to battle; their eyes, the account continues, are large, black, and lively, their hair black and fine; the bearing of the men commands respect and reflects a kind of refined dignity. Similar praise is extended to the Bokharans; the beauty of the female Circassians, the silken-black string of their eyebrows, their fiery black eyes, their smooth foreheads, their small mouths, and their rounded chins are known and praised far and wide.** One might be tempted to believe that the dial of the balance of human beauty stood here precisely in the middle, while the scales extended east and west to India and Greece. Fortunately for us, Europe lay at no great distance from this center of human beauty, and many peoples that dwelt in this part of the globe either remained for some time in, or slowly traversed, the regions between the Caspian and the Black seas. At least we are thus no antipodes to the land of beauty.

All the peoples who pushed their way into this region of beautiful human formation and stayed there for some time have softened their features. The *Turks,* originally an unattractive people, refined their appearance, because, as the conquerors of extensive regions, they profited from the proximity of well-formed peoples; to this the commandments of the Koran have probably contributed, by which they were enjoined ablution, cleanliness, and temperance, while they were allowed voluptuous leisure and sensual pleasure. The *Hebrews,* whose ancestors likewise came from the heights of Asia, led a nomadic life, sometimes in arid Egypt, sometimes in the deserts of Arabia; even though they were never able, in their narrow country and under the oppressive yoke of the law, to raise themselves to an ideal that is called for by a life of freer activity and greater sensual indulgence, they still bear, even in their present extensive dispersion and their deep wretchedness, the imprint of the Asiatic makeup. Neither do the hardy *Arabs* constitute an exception; for though nature has formed their peninsula more for a land of freedom than a land of beauty, and neither the desert nor the nomadic life can possibly be the best nurse of physical beauty, at the same time this hardy and brave people is one marked by physical beauty; its broad impact on three continents will be seen in subsequent pages.***

---

*Allgemeine Reisen, vol. 7, p. 316, [3]18.

**See a few portrayals by Le Brun, *Voyages au Levant,* vol. 1, chap. 10, no. 34–37.

***See portrayals of them in *Niebuhr,* vol. 2; Le Brun, *Voyages au Levant,* no. 90, no. 91.

At last, human beauty found a site along the coasts of the Mediterranean Sea,* at which it was able to fuse with the spirit, and thus could become visible, in all the attractiveness of terrestrial and heavenly beauty, not only to the eye but also to the soul; this was Greece threefold, in Asia Minor and on the islands, in Greece proper, and along the shores of the other countries of the Occident. Gentle zephyrs fanned the creatures gradually transplanted here from the heights of Asia, breathing life into every part. Time and destiny assisted ever more in exalting their vitality and giving them the crown that continued to be enthusiastically admired by everyone in the ideals of Greek art and wisdom. Here figures were conceived and created which no connoisseur of Circassian beauties, no Indian or Kashmirian artist could have designed. The human form ascended Olympus and clothed itself in divine beauty.

I shall not stray farther into Europe. It so abounds in forms and mixtures, it has changed nature in so many ways through its cultures and arts, that I not dare generalize with regard to its splendid, intermingling nations. Rather, I will look back once more from the last shore of the quarter of the globe we traversed together and, after an observation or two, proceed to black Africa.

In the first place, it is obvious to everyone that the region of the most perfectly formed people is a middle region of the earth, lying, like beauty itself, between two extremes. It is not subject to the constricting cold experienced by the Samoyedes or the saline steppe winds of Mongolia; on the other hand, it is equally a stranger to the burning heat of the sandy African deserts and the humidity and violent changes of the American climate. It lies neither on the utmost height of the equator nor on the declivity toward the pole; rather, it is protected on one side by the lofty walls of the Tatar and Mongol mountains, and on the other it is cooled by the sea breeze. Its seasons change with regularity, yet without that violence that prevails along the equator; and, as Hippocrates once observed, that a mild regularity of the seasons appeared to have great influence in tempering the passions, it has no less in the mirror and imprint of our souls. The predatory Turcomans,[2] who roam the deserts or the mountains, retain a hideous countenance even in the mildest climate; were they to settle down in peace, and to indulge their lives in softer pleasures and activity that would connect them with other, more cultured nations, their features, as well as their customs, would in time assimilate with those of their neighbors. The beauty of the world is

---

*Portrayals in Le Brun, *Voyages au Levant,* chap. 7, no. 17–20; in Choiseul Gouffier, *Voyages pittoresque;* etc. The monuments of ancient Greek art exceed all these representations.

intended for peaceful enjoyment only; by means of this alone it imparts itself to humans and is embodied by them.

In the second place, it was of no small advantage to the human species not only to have commenced its existence in this region of perfect forms, but from this region to have spread culture beneficently to other nations. As the deity could not make the whole earth the seat of beauty, it allowed humankind at least to enter onto the stage through the portal of beauty and, having absorbed its features for a considerable time, to have its peoples seek other regions. Moreover, it was one and the same principle of nature that by the same token turned these well-formed nations into those having the most beneficent impact upon others; for she gave them the alertness and elasticity of spirit that are an integral part of this bodily makeup, as well as of the beneficent function of influencing other nations. The Tunguses and the Eskimos sit eternally in their dwellings, and give themselves no concern about other nations, be it for good or ill. The Negro has invented nothing for the European; it has never entered his mind to bring happiness to Europe, or to wage war against it. From the region of well-formed peoples we have derived our religion, our art, our sciences, the entire makeup of our culture and humanity, however much or little it may be. In this region has been invented, imagined, and executed, at least in its rudiments, everything that could enhance and shape humankind. The history of human culture will incontestably prove this, and in my view our own experience bears it out. We northern Europeans would be barbarians still, had not the kind breath of fate wafted us at least some flowers of the spirit of these peoples, to impregnate the savage tribes with the branch of beauty, to ennoble them over the course of time.

The Nature of the African Peoples

It is only fair, when we proceed to the country of the blacks, that we lay aside our proud prejudices and consider the nature of this region with as much impartiality as if there were no other in the world. The Negro, whom we consider a cursed son of Ham[1] and the image of the fiend, has equal right to call his cruel despoilers albinos and white satans who so degenerated only because of a flaw of nature, just as several animal species living near the North Pole degenerated to whiteness. "I," he could say, "I, the black, am the original human being. I, more than any other creature, have been sustained by the source of life, the sun; within me and everywhere around me this source has exerted itself most profoundly and with the greatest vitality. Behold my land, rich in gold and the fruits of the earth, my trees reaching to the heavens, my robust animals! Here each element teems with life, and I have become the center of this vital agency." Thus might the Negro say; so let us humbly tread upon the soil so peculiarly his.

On the very isthmus that joins Africa to Asia, we meet with a singular nation, the Egyptians. Large, strong, corpulent (for the Nile bestows this opulence on them), big-boned, and of a yellow-brown complexion, they are at the same time healthy and prolific, temperate and long-lived. Though now indolent, they once were industrious and diligent; evidently, it took a people of such frame and general constitution[*] to bring about the admired arts and institutions of the ancient Egyptians. A people of a finer mold would have hardly undertaken the task.

Of the inhabitants of Nubia and the interior regions of Africa further south, we yet know but little. If, however, we may trust the preliminary

---

[*] See the statues of their ancient art, their mummies, and the drawings of them on the cases.

communications of *Bruce*,[*] no Negro tribes dwelt upon the whole of this elevated region, but instead they were confined to the east and west coasts of this quarter of the globe, where the land is lowest and the heat is most intense. "Even under the equator," Bruce says, "on these temperate and rainy heights, we find none but white or yellow-brown complexions." Remarkable as low altitude and intense heat would be in explaining the origin of the Negro blackness, it is even more to our purpose that the figure of the people in these parts also displays a gradual declension to the Negro form. We know that the Abyssinians were originally of Arab descent, and the two nations have been frequently and long connected; yet, if we may judge from the representations in *Ludolf*[**] and others, how much harsher are the features we meet here than those among the Arabs and more distant Asian peoples! They approach those of the Negro, though yet remotely, and the great diversity of the country, with its lofty mountains and pleasant plains, the variations of the climate, with its storms, heat and cold, and temperate times, in addition to a number of other causes, appear to explain these harshly composed features. In a diversified quarter of the globe, a diversified branch of humankind had to come to be, with a character of great vitality, and great endurance, which, however, also seems to represent a transition to the most extreme of forms, approaching that of animals. The culture and the form of government of the Abyssinians conforms to their physical makeup as well as to the general condition of their country, a coarse mixture of Christendom and heathenism, ranging from untrammeled freedom to barbarian despotism.

On the other side of Africa, in like manner, we know too little of the *Berbers*, or *Brebers*, to be able to form a judgment of them. Their residence in the Atlas mountains and their hardy and active way of life have preserved in them that well-proportioned, light, and flexible makeup by which they are also distinguishable from the Arabs.[***] Consequently, they are as little of Negro descent as are the Moors, for these latter are of Arab descent mixed with other peoples. A handsome people, says a recent observer,[†] with fine facial features, long oval faces, beautiful, large, and fiery eyes, elongated and not broad or flat noses, framed by fine, slightly curled black hair; thus, in the midst of Africa, they reflect an Asian makeup.

---

[*]Buffon, *Supplemens à l'histoire naturelle*, vol. 4, pp. 494–95. *Lobo* says, at least, that the blacks there are neither ugly nor dull-witted, but ingenious, delicate, and possessed of some taste (*Relation historique d'Abissinie*, p. 85). As all accounts of this country are ancient and lack certainty, the publication of Bruce's *Travels*, if he did visit Abyssinia, is much to be wished.[2]

[**] Ludolf's *Historia Aethiopica*, here and there.[3]

[***]Höst, *Nachrichten von Marokos*, p. 141; compare with pp. 132–33.[4]

[†]Schott's *Nachrichten Über den Zustand vom Senega*, in the *Beiträge zur Völker- und Länderkunde*, vol. 1, p. 47.[5]

The Negro race properly begins with the Gambia and Senegal rivers, but here too in a gradual transition.* The *Jolofs* or *Wolofs*[6] do not yet have the flat noses and thick lips of the ordinary Negroes. But they, and the smaller, more nimble *Fulah*,[7] who according to some accounts spend their lives in mirth, dancing, and the most harmonious order, with their limbs well shaped, their hair sleek and but little woolly, their countenances open and inclined to oval, are models of beauty compared to the *Mandingos*.[8] Thus the thick lips and flat noses of the Negro form, which spreads far down through innumerable varieties of small tribes in Guinea, Loango, Congo, and Angola, do not begin until we cross the Senegal. In Congo and Angola, for instance, the black skin assumes an olive hue, the woolly hair turns reddish, the pupils become green, the lips are less prominent, and the figures are smaller. In Zanguebar, on the opposite coast of Africa, this same olive coloring is found, but in larger figures of more even shape. The Hottentots and Kaffirs, at last, are regressions of the Negroes to other configurations. The nose of the former begins to lose some of the flattened form and the lips some of the swollen thickness; the hair is halfway between the woolliness of the Negroes and that of other peoples; the coloring is light brown; the figure is like that of most Europeans, except for the smaller hands and feet.** If we now had knowledge of the many tribes that dwell beyond these arid regions in the heart of Africa, as far as Abyssinia, and among whom, from many indications on their borders, fertility of the land, physical beauty, vigor, culture, and art are enhanced, we might master the shadings of the portrait of the peoples of this great continent, with perhaps no gaps remaining.

But how deficient we are in authentic information about this region of the earth! We barely know the coastal areas of the country, and even these often no further than the reach of European cannon. No contemporary Europeans have traversed the interior of Africa, which is being done so frequently by Arab caravans***; what we know of it is either from the tales of the blacks or from rather ancient reports by a few fortunate or unfortunate adventurers.† Even the nations that, as things are, we might know, the eye of the European seems to behold with too tyrannical indifference to try to investigate the variations of national development in wretched black slaves. They are treated like cattle, and when they are purchased, they are set apart

---

*See Schott's *Nachrichten vom Senega*, p. 50, *Allgemeine Reisen*, vols. 3–5.[9]
**Sparrmann's *Reisen*, p. 172.[10]
*** See Schott's *Nachrichten vom Senega*, pp. 40, 50.
†Zimmermann's "Vergleichung der bekannten und unbekannten Theile," a treatise full of learning and good judgment, in the *Geographische Geschichte des Menschen*, vol. 3, pp. 104–5.

only by the condition of their teeth. A Moravian missionary,[*] writing in another part of the world, has given us more accurate discriminations of the Negro peoples than many a traveler in Africa skirting along the shores. How fortunate it would have been for the studies of nature and of humankind, if a company of persons endowed with *Forster's* cast of mind and *Sparrmann's* patience, and the learning of both, had traversed this unexplored country! The accounts that are given of the cannibal Jagas and Anzicans[11] are certainly exaggerated when they are extended to include all the peoples of interior Africa. The Jagas appear to be an alliance of robbers, an artificial nation so to speak, a mixture of the outcasts of several peoples turning into pirates on solid ground, and to this end inured to cruel and barbarous practices.[**] The Anzicans are mountain people, perhaps the Mongols and Kalmucks of this region; but how many happy and peaceful nations may dwell at the feet of the Mountains of the Moon![12] Europeans are unworthy to behold their happiness, for they have unpardonably sinned, and still continue to sin, against this quarter of the globe. The quietly trading Arabs, in the meanwhile, traverse the country and have planted colonies far and wide.

But I forget that I meant to speak of the makeup of the Negroes as a branch of humankind; and it would be well if natural philosophy had applied its attention to all the varieties of our species as much as to this one. I put forth a few results of these studies.

1. The black color of the Negroes is no more to be wondered at than the white, brown, yellow, or reddish colors of other nations. Neither the blood nor the brain nor the semen of the Negroes is black, but the reticular membrane beneath the cuticle, that is common to us all, at least in some parts and under certain circumstances, is more or less colored. *Camper* has demonstrated this,[***] and according to him we all have the potential of becoming Negroes. Even in the cold of the Samoyed country, the ring around the nipples of the female breast has been noted; the germ of Negro blackness could not be further developed in that climate.

2. All depends, therefore, on the cause enabling it to unfold here, and analogy instructs us once more that sun and air must have a great share in it. For what makes us brown? What differentiates the two sexes in almost every country? What has rendered the descendants of the Portuguese peo-

---

[*]Oldendorp's *Mißionsgeschichte auf St. Thomas*, pp. 270 f.[13]
[**]See Proyart's *Geschichte von Laongo, Cacongo*, etc., to the German translation of which (Leipzig: 1770) is added a competent collection of accounts respecting the Jagas.[14]
[***]See Camper's *Kleine Schriften*, vol. 1, pp. 24 f.[15]

ple, after dwelling for centuries in Africa so similar in color to the Negroes? Yes, what sets the Negro so vastly apart from one another in Africa? The climate, in the widest sense of that word, so as to include the way of life and diet. It is precisely the region to which the eastern wind brings the greatest heat over the entire countryside that is inhabited by the blackest Negro tribes; where the heat decreases, or is cooled by the sea breezes, blackness pales to a shade of yellow. The cool heights are inhabited by white or whitish people, while in the close lower regions the oil that occasions the black appearance beneath the cuticle is rendered more adust by the heat of the sun. Now if we reflect that these blacks have resided for ages in this quarter of the world, and completely adapted themselves to it by their mode of life; if we consider that some of the causes that operate now more feebly must have acted with greater power in earlier periods, when all the elements were in their primary and rude force; and if we take into the account that so many thousands of years must have brought about a complete revolution, as it were, of the wheel of contingencies, which in one period or another turns up everything that can take place upon this earth; we shall not wonder at the trifling circumstance that the skin of some nations is black. Nature, in her progressive, hidden operations, has produced much greater deviations than these.

3. And how did she effect this minor change? To me, the thing seems to speak for itself. It is an oil that colors the reticular membrane. The sweat of the Negroes, and even of Europeans in this country, frequently has a yellow color. The skin of the blacks is a thick soft velvet, not as taut and dry as that of the whites; the heat of the sun having drawn from their inner parts an oil that rose to the surface as far as it could, has softened their cuticle and colored the membrane beneath it. Most of the diseases of this country are related to the gall bladder, and if we read the descriptions of them,* we shall not wonder at the yellow or black complexion of the inhabitants.

4. The woolly hair of the Negro may be accounted for on similar principles. Since the hair is nourished only by the fine juices of the skin and is generated, seemingly contrary to nature, within its fat, the hair curls in proportion to the nourishment it receives, and it dies where this is deficient. Thus, in the coarser makeup of animals, we find their wool changed into bristling hair in countries uncongenial to their nature, where the flowing juices cannot be absorbed. The more refined makeup of the human being on the other hand, intended for all climates, was able, owing to the abundance of this oil that moistens the skin, to change the hair into wool.

---

*See Schott's *Observations on the Synochus atrabiliosa,* in excerpts, *Göttingisches Magazin,* vol. 3, part 6, pp. 729 f.[16]

5. But more than all of this is demonstrated by the particular formation of the parts of the human body; and it seems to me that this formation too is elucidated by the African makeup. According to various physiological evidence, the lips, the breasts, and the sexual organs are exactly proportionate to each other; since nature, in keeping with the simple principle governing her creative art, had to provide these peoples, whom she deprived of nobler gifts, with a correspondingly ampler measure of sensual enjoyment, this had to be expressed in physiological form. The fullness of the lips, even among whites, is considered by physiognomy as the sign of a very sensuous disposition, just as lips appearing as a fine, purple thread are considered the characteristic of a refined, cold disposition, not to speak of other attributes. What wonder then, that in nations for whom the sensual appetite is the height of happiness in life, external marks of it should appear? A Negro child is born white; the skin first becomes colored around the nails, the nipples, and the sexual organs; and the same correspondence of parts in the disposition to color is observable among other peoples. A hundred children are as nothing to a Negro, and the old man who had no more than seventy, lamented his fate with tears.

6. With this oil-rich makeup, disposing the individual to sensual pleasure, the profile and the entire frame of the body were bound to change. As the mouth protruded, the nose as a result was reduced to being snubbed and small; the forehead receded and the face at a distance assumed resemblance to that of an ape. Conformable to this would be the position of the neck, the transition to the occiput, and the elastic structure of the entire body, which is formed, even to the nose and skin, for sensual animal enjoyment.[*] As in this quarter of the earth, as in this native land of the sun's warmth, the most succulent and loftiest trees arise; as here herds of the largest, strongest, and most lively animals are teeming, particularly among them enormous numbers of apes, so that air and water, the sea and the sands swarm with life and fertility; the nature of human beings in the course of its development, with respect to its animal dimension, could not but follow this universal simple principle of the creative powers. The more refined intellectuality that, under this burning sun, within this breast boiling with passions, had to be denied to this creature, was compensated for by the makeup of the fibrous system that did not allow for these kinds of perceptions. Thus, let us sympathize with the Negro, but not despise him, since the conditions of his climate could not grant him nobler gifts, and let us honor mother nature, who gives

---

[*]Camper is said to have shown, in the Haarlem *Acta,* that the Negro has the centers of motion nearer together than the European, and in consequence possesses greater elasticity of body.

in denying. He lives a carefree life in a land that offers him his nourishment with abundant liberality. His limber body moves in the water as if it had been made for that element; he runs and climbs as if each were his sport; and constituted strong and healthy as well as nimble and alert, he bears up with his distinctive makeup under all the accidents and diseases of his climate, from which so many Europeans perish. What good would be to him the tormenting sensations of higher joys for which he was not made? The materials were not wanting in him; but nature turned the shaping hand and created what was of greater need for him in his land and for the happiness of his life. Either nature ought not to have created Africa, or it was requisite that Negroes should be made to inhabit it.

~ **22** ~

The Nature of the Peoples on the Islands of the Tropical Zone

Nothing is more difficult than to characterize the main features of the countries scattered over the bosom of the ocean. For as they are remote from one another, and have been peopled for the most part by different migrants from near or far regions and at different points in time, and each, therefore, in a way constitutes its own little world, they represent to the intellect in the study of nations as multicolored a picture as they do to the eye on the map. Yet even here the principal features can never be denied when it comes to the general order of nature.

1. On most of the Asiatic islands, we meet with a kind of Negroid people who appear to be their most original inhabitants.* They are, depending on the variety of the region in which they live, of varying shades of blackness, with frizzy, woolly hair; here and there appear the protruding lips, the flat nose, and the white teeth, and, what is noteworthy, with this physical makeup there also is found the temperament of the Negro. The same raw and robust strength, the carefree mind, the boisterous sensuality, which we observed in the blacks of the continent, are evident also in the Negrilloes of the islands, yet everywhere proportionate to their climate and mode of living. Many of these peoples are still at the lowest stage of development, because they were pushed up into the mountains by later arrivals who now live on the shores and in the plains; thus there is little genuine and reliable information about them available.**

---

*Sprengel's *Geschichte der Philippinen,* Forster's *Nachrichten von Borneo u.a.* [und anderen] *Inseln* in the *Beiträgen zur Völker- und Länderkunde,* vol. 2, pp. 57, 237 f; *Allgemeine Reisen,* vol. 2, p. 393; Le Gentil's *Reisen,* in Ebeling's *Sammlung,* vol. 4, p. 70.[1]
**See *Reisen um die Welt,* vol. 1 (Leipzig: 1775), p. 554.[2]

Now, where does this resemblance to the Negro form on such remote islands come from? Certainly not because they were peopled ages ago by colonists from Africa; rather, it is because nature works everywhere uniformly. This, too, is the region of the hottest climate, cooled only by the sea breeze; why, then, should there not also be Negrilloes of the islands, as there are Negroes on the continent? Especially since, as the original inhabitants of the islands, they must also reflect in their makeup the most penetrating impact of nature in this region of the earth. To these must be added the Igorots of the Philippine Islands[3] and blacks of similar kind in most of the other islands; also the savages of the western coast of New Holland,[4] described by *Dampier*[5] as one of the most wretched tribes of humankind, and who appear to be the lowest class of this type of people in one of the most desolate areas of the earth.

2. In later times, other people whose makeup is less striking have settled on these islands. Such, according to *Forster*,[*] are the *Biajoos* of *Borneo;* the *Alfoories* in some of the Moluccas; the *Subadoes* of Mindanao; and the inhabitants of the Ladrone Islands, the Carolines, and others farther south in the Pacific Ocean. They are said to have a great degree of similarity in language, complexion, makeup, and customs; their hair is long and straight, and we know from recent voyages to what a level of beauty this strain of humans has been capable of attaining on Tahiti and some islands near it. Yet this beauty is still totally sensual, and the somewhat snubbed noses of the female Tahitians appear to reflect the enduring imprint of the shaping climate.

3. The Malays, Arabs, Chinese, Japanese, and some others are still later arrivals on many of these islands, thus bearing still clearer traces of their descent. In short, this array of islands may be considered as a repository of human forms, variously modified according to the character they bear, the land they inhabit, the time of their residence, and the way of life they have enjoyed, so that often in the closest proximity the most singular diversity may be encountered. The New Hollanders seen by *Dampier,* and the inhabitants of Mallicollo, appear to be of the coarsest makeup; and the people of the New Hebrides, New Caledonia, New Zealand, and so on, rise gradually above these. The Ulysses of these regions, *Reinhold Forster,*[**] has given us such a learned and intelligent account of the types and subtypes of humankind there, that we cannot but wish we had similar materials for a *philosophical-physical geography* of other parts of the world, as foundation for a history of humankind. I now turn to the last and most difficult quarter of the globe.

---

[*]*Beiträge zur Völkerkunde,* vol. 2, p. 238.
[**]Forster's *Bemerkungen auf seiner Reise um die Welt,* chap. 6.[6]

∽ 23 ∽

The Nature of the Americans

It is well known that America extends through all the zones of the compass, and combines not only the extremes of heat and cold but the most sudden changes of weather, while at the same time its surface exhibits the loftiest and steepest mountains as well as the most level and extensive plains. It is also common knowledge that this long, extended continent, deeply indented with large bays on the eastern side, has a chain of mountains stretching from north to south, so that its climate and the products of nature bear little similarity to those of the Old World. All of this calls our attention to the type of humans dwelling there as to the progeny of an opposite hemisphere.

On the other hand, it results from the very situation of America that this enormous region, so widely separated from the rest of the world, could not be peopled from many different points. Extensive oceans and winds separate it from Europe, Africa, and southern Asia, and there is no short passage to it from the Old World, except on its northwestern side. This diminishes to a certain degree the expectation we may have been led to form of a great diversity in it; for if the original and the majority of its inhabitants came from one and the same region, with perhaps only little intermingling with other arrivals, and gradually moved down through the continent, eventually filling the whole country, the makeup and disposition of its inhabitants would display a certain uniformity, to which there would be few exceptions, notwithstanding the diversity of climates. And this the various accounts of North and South America confirm; that indeed, notwithstanding the great variety of regions of the compass and peoples who often made violent efforts to set themselves apart from one another, the makeup of humankind there, on the whole, lies under an imprint of uniformity that is not even found in the land of the Negroes. An understanding of the nature of the

187

Americans thus, in a way, constitutes a clearer task than the examination of another quarter of the globe with a more mixed population. And the solution of the problem cannot begin anywhere but at the site of the probable crossover.

The nations touched upon by *Cook*[*] ranged from medium size to six feet in height. Their complexions inclined to copper color, the shape of their faces squarish, with rather protruding cheekbones and little beard. The hair is long and black; the structure of the limbs is strong, and only the feet are flawed. Whoever is familiar with the nations of East Asia and the neighboring islands will observe the gradual transition, feature by feature. I do not draw this conclusion from a single nation, for it is probable that many, coming from various tribes, crossed over; but they were all Oriental peoples, as demonstrated by their makeup, even their flaws, but most of all their ornaments and their arbitrary customs. Were we once to have a complete overview of the entire northwestern coast of America, of which we now know only a few landing sites, and were we to have of its inhabitants portraits as faithful as those that *Cook,* for example, has given us of the chiefs in Alaska and other places, a number of things would be elucidated. It would be resolved whether, further down along the great coast not yet known by us, Japanese and Chinese also have crossed over, and what we are to make of the legend of a civilized, bearded nation dwelling along this western dimension. The Spaniards would indeed have the best opportunity of making these discoveries from Mexico, if they shared with the two greatest maritime nations of Europe, the English and the French, the glorious spirit of conquest for the advancement of science. In the meantime, at least *Laxmann's* visit to the northern coast, and the attempts of the English from Canada, may procure for us some new and valuable information.

It is singular that so many accounts agree in representing the western nations of North America as the most civilized. The *Assiniboins*[2] are famous for their size, strength, and agility; the *Cristinaux*[3] for their loquacious liveliness.[**] We have little information, however, respecting these nations, and the people of the plains in general, that can be deemed much better than fable; our more authentic accounts begin properly with the Sioux. With these, the Chippewa, and the Winnebago, *Carver*[***] has made us acquainted; with the Cherokees, Chickasaws, and Muskhogean, *Adair,*[†] with the Five Nations, as they are called, *Colden, Rogers,* and *Timberlake,*[5]

---

[*]W. Ellis, *Nachrichten von Cooks dritter Reise,* pp. 114 ff.[1]

[**]*Allgemeine Reisen,* vol. 16, p. 646.

[***]Ebeling's *Sammlung von Reisebeschreibungen,* vol. 1 (Hamburg: 1780).

[†]Adair, *Geschichte der Nordamerikanischen Indianer* (Breslau: 1782).[4]

with those to the North, the French missionaries; and amid all their variety, who is not left with the impression of one predominant form, as well as of one chief characteristic? This, to wit, consists in that sound and steady strength, the fiercely proud love of freedom and war, which informs their way of life and domestic affairs, their education and government, their occupations and customs both in peace and war. A character that stands alone on the globe, both in its vices and in its virtues.

And how was this character acquired? It appears to me that here too much is explained by the gradualness of their migration from northern Asia and by the conditions of life in this new area of the world. They were coarse and hardened nations at the time of their crossing; they were conditioned by storms and mountains; once they had mastered the shores and found before them the great, free, and more beautiful country, must not their character in time have molded itself to this country? Between these great lakes and rivers, in these forests, on these plains, other nations were formed than on those rough and frigid slopes to the sea. As the lakes, mountains, and rivers divided, so did the nations; tribes engaged in fierce conflict with one another, thus evoking even among the most placid nations that warlike hostility, making it a predominant characteristic. They turned into martial people and they left their mark on all aspects of the land that their *Great Spirit* had given them. They practice the shamanistic religion of the people of northern Asia, but in an American vein. Their healthy air, the verdure of the meadows and woods, and the refreshing waters of their lakes and streams inspired them with the breath of freedom and the sense of ownership in this country. All the nations of Siberia have allowed themselves to fall under the yoke of a heap of miserable Russians, all the way to Kamchatka! These firmer savages of America have given ground on occasion, it is true, but they have never bowed their necks to the yoke.

As their character may be traced to this origin, so may their singular taste in ornamenting themselves. All nations in America eradicate the beard; consequently, they must have migrated from some region where little beard was generated, and thus they were disinclined to deviate from their fathers' custom. That region is the eastern portion of Asia. Thus, even in a climate conducive to its growth, they were and continue to be averse to beardedness, and plucked out the facial hair from childhood on. The peoples of the north of Asia had round heads, while more to the east the features became more squarish; what was more natural than the desire of the Americans to retain these ancestral features and thus to shape their faces? They probably dreaded the softer oval as an effeminate form, and they thus endeavored to retain the compressed warlike features by forceful makeup. Those with Nordic round heads gave their faces a round shape in keeping with the makeup of the more northern regions; others tended to give their faces a more squarish appearance, or pushed the head between the shoulders, that the new climate might effect no change in either their countenance or stature. No country, except the east of Asia, affords examples of such violent attempts at embellishment; and, as we have seen, probably for the same purpose, to preserve the appearance of the tribe in distant regions; it is even likely that they brought with them to America the taste for this mode of beautifying themselves.

Lastly, the red copper color of the Americans is least capable of misleading us; for already in the east of Asia the complexion of the peoples had shaded into brownish red, and it was probably the air of another continent, the ointments and other things, that here enhanced the coloring. I wonder as little that the Negro is black as I do that the American is red, since they, so different from one another, have lived for millennia in regions of the compass so diverse that I would be more likely to wonder, if everyone on this globe were snow-white or brown. Do we not see that, in the coarser makeup of animals in diverse regions of the world even the major parts of the body are transformed with the change of climate? And which is more to be wondered at, an alteration of the limbs of the body in their general proportion and bearing, or a little more or less color in the membrane beneath the skin?

After this introduction, let us accompany the peoples of America down through the continent and observe how the uniformity of their original character has been variously modified, yet never lost.

The most northern Americans were described as small and robust; in the middle parts of the continent dwelt the tallest and most handsome tribes; those living further south in the flats of Florida were compelled to yield to the former in strength and courage. "It is remarkable," says *Georg Forster,*[*] "that despite the characteristic diversity of the various North Americans depicted in *Cook's* work, one general cast of countenance prevails through the whole, which was familiar to me, and which, if my memory does not deceive me, I observed actually in the Fuegians of Tierra del Fuego."

Of New Mexico we know little. The Spaniards found the inhabitants of this country well-clothed, industrious, and neat, their lands cultivated with care, and their towns built with stone. Unfortunate nations, what are you now, unless you have preserved yourselves, like *los bravos gentes,* in the safety of the mountains. The Apaches proved themselves as a swift and brave people, whom the Spaniards were unable to harm. And how superior does *Pagès*[**] find the Choctaws,[6] the Yataches, and the Tekaws!

---

[*]*Göttingisches Magazin* (1783), p. 929.
[**]Pagès, *Voyage autour du Monde* (Paris: 1783), pp. 17, 18, 26, 40, 52, 54, etc.

Mexico now is a sad reflection of what it was under its kings; scarcely a tenth part of its inhabitants remain.* And how has their character been changed by the most unjust of oppressions! I do not believe there exists on the face of the earth a deeper, more inveterate hatred than that which the suffering American cherishes against his oppressor, the Spaniard; for however highly *Pagès,* for example,** extols the greater mildness the Spaniards now display toward those they oppressed, he cannot avoid taking note in other parts of the book of the misery of the oppressed and the barbarity exercised toward those who have maintained their freedom. The Mexicans are described as of a deep olive complexion, attractive and with pleasing countenances, their eyes large, lively, and sparkling, their senses alert, their limbs agile, with only their souls exhausted by servitude.

In Central America, where everything suffers under the humid heat and the Europeans lead the most miserable of lives, the pliant nature of the American did not succumb. *Waffer,**** who, having escaped from the buccaneers, resided some time among the savages of Terra Firma,[7] relates the friendly reception they gave him and describes their makeup and way of life thus: "The men were from five to six feet in height, big boned, broad-chested, and well-proportioned. There was not a cripple or a deformed person to be seen among them. Their joints are supple, they are agile, and they run with great speed. Their eyes are gray and lively, their faces round, their lips thin, mouths small, and chins well-formed. Their hair is long and black, and they take delight in combing it frequently. Their teeth are white and evenly spaced; they ornament and paint themselves as do most Indians."—Are these the people that are represented to us as an enervated, unfinished outcropping of humankind? And they dwelt in the most enervating region of the isthmus!

Fermin, a faithful explorer of nature, describes the Indians of Surinam as well-formed human beings, of a cleanliness hardly found anywhere else on the face of the earth:† "They bathe as soon as they arise in the morning, and their women anoint themselves with oil, partly to care for their skin, partly to protect themselves against the sting of the mosquitoes. They have a cinnamon coloring, shading into red, though they are as fair as we at birth. A limping or deformed person is not found among them. Their long, pitch-black hair turns white only with most extreme age. They have black eyes,

---

Storia antica del Messico, excerpt in the *Göttingische gelehrte Anzeigen* (1781), Supplements 35, 36; and an even richer contribution in *Kielsches Magazin,* vol. 2, 1, pp. 38 f.

**Pp. 88 ff.

***Allgemeine Reisen,* vol. 15, pp. 263 f.

†Fermin's *Beschreibung von Surinam,* vol. 1, pp. 39, 41.

sharp facial features, little or no beard at all, plucking it out by the roots as fast as it appears. Their fine white teeth remain sound into extreme old age, and their women, as delicate as they may appear, are of robust health." It seems to me that, upon reading *Bancroft's* description* of the brave Caribs, the indolent Worrows, the purposeful Accawaws, the social Arawaks,[8] and so on, the prejudiced notion of the feeble frames and the worthless character of these Indians will be given up, even in the most sultry climate in the world.

If we proceed southward to the innumerable tribes of Brazil, what a number of nations, languages, and characters shall we find! Yet, ancient as well as more recent travelers have described them as similar to one another.** "Their hair never turns gray," says *Lery,* "they are ever alert and happy, as their fields are continually green." The brave Tupinambs, to avoid the Portuguese oppression, withdrew into the unexplored and impenetrable woods, as several other warlike nations have done. Others, whom the missions of Paraguay knew to attract, given their obedient disposition, were almost bound to degenerate to childishness; yet this, too, was a natural consequence, and neither they nor their valiant neighbors may on this account be deemed the dregs of humankind.***

But we are approaching the throne of nature, and the most wicked tyranny, the kingdom of Peru, rich in silver mines and cruelty. Here the poor Indians are most severely oppressed, and their oppressors are clerics and Europeans who have become effeminate living among women. All the powers of these tender children of nature, who once lived so happily under their Incas, are now reduced to the singular capacity to suffer and endure with constrained hatred. "At first sight," says *Pinto,*[†] governor of Brazil, "a South American appears gentle and harmless; but upon closer scrutiny one will detect in his face something savage, mistrustful, gloomy, and morose." May not all this be accounted for by the fate of the people? They were gentle and harmless when you visited them; and you should have refined the untutored wildness of these good natured creatures, enabling them to become what they were capable of being. Now, can you expect anything else but that they be mistrustful and gloomy, nourishing the deepest moroseness inextinguishably in their hearts? They are bruised worms, that appear hateful to our eyes, because

---

*Bancroft's *Naturgeschichte von Guiana,* third letter.

**Acunha, Gumilla, Lery, Marggraf, Condamine,* etc.[9]

***Dobritshoffer, *Geschichte der Abiponer* (Vienna: 1783). See the description of several nations in Fr. Gumilla's *Orinoco illustrado,* etc.[10]

†Robertson's *Geschichte von Amerika,* vol. 1, p. 537.

we have crushed them with our feet. The Negro slave in Peru is a lordly creature, compared with the oppressed wretches to whom the country belongs by right.

Yet it is not taken wholly from them, for fortunately the Cordilleras, and the deserts of Chile, are there to bestow freedom on many valiant nations. Such, for instance, are the unconquered Moluches, Puelches, and Araucanians, and the Patagonian Telhuelhets,[11] or the gigantic southern people, six feet tall, big and strong. "Their appearance is not disagreeable; they have round faces, somewhat flat, lively eyes, white teeth, and long black hair. I saw some," says *Commerson,*[*] "with long but not very thick whiskers. Their skin is copper colored, as in most of the Americans. They roam over the extensive plains of South America, constantly on horseback, tracking the game." *Falkner* and *Vidaure*[**] have given us the best accounts of these, and beyond them nothing remains but the cold, barren verge of the land, Tierra del Fuego, and in it the Fuegians, probably the lowest species of humankind.[***] Diminutive, ugly, and of an unbearable body odor, they sustain themselves on mussels, clothe themselves in sealskins, freeze all the year in the most dismal winter, and though they have plenty of woods, they lack solid houses as well as warming fire. Happy it is that compassionate nature has suffered the land toward the South Pole to terminate here; had it extended farther, what wretched semblances of humankind would have dozed away their lives in benumbing frost!

These, then, are some of the principal features of the peoples of America; and what may be inferred from them for the whole?

In the first place, that we should as seldom as possible speak in generalities about the nations of a quarter of the globe that extends through all the zones. Whoever says that America is warm, healthy, wet, low-lying, and fertile is correct; and if another should say the opposite, he would also be correct, that is, with respect to different seasons and places. So it is with the American nations; for they are humans inhabiting an entire hemisphere throughout all zones. At one extremity and at the other there are dwarfs, and close by the dwarfs are giants; in the central parts there dwell intermediate-sized, and more or less well-formed peoples, gentle and warlike, indolent and alert, of diverse ways of life and of every cast of character.

Secondly, there is nothing to prevent this many-branched trunk of hu-

---

[*]*Journal encyclopédique* (1772). Several testimonies are brought together in Zimmermann's *Geschichte der Menschheit,* vol. 1, p. 59; and in Robertson's *History of America,* vol. 1, p. 540.[12]

[**]Falkner's *Beschreibung von Patagonien* (Gotha: 1775). Vidaure, *Geschichte des Königreiches Chili,* in Ebeling's *Sammlung von Reisen,* vol. 4, p. 108.[13]

[***] See Forster's *Reisen,* vol. 2, p. 392; *Cavendish; Bougainville;* et al.

mankind, with all its twigs, from having arisen from one single root, and consequently displaying a uniformity in its progeny. And this is what is meant when people speak of the prevailing facial features and appearance of the Americans.* *Ulloa* observes in the central regions particularly narrow foreheads covered with hair, small eyes, thin hooked noses, broad faces, large ears, well-formed limbs, small feet, and squat figures; and these characteristics extend beyond Mexico. *Pinto* adds that the noses are somewhat flat, the faces round, that the eyes are black or chestnut-brown and piercing despite their smallness, and that the ears are set far back from the rest of the face;** the same features are observable in representations of peoples dwelling in very remote regions. This dominant physiognomy, which changes in its finer points according to zones and peoples, appears to be a family trait even in the most diverse of tribes, and it indeed points to a rather uniform origin. Had peoples from all quarters of the globe come to America at very different points in time, whether they mingled with one another or remained unmixed, the diversity among humankind here would have had to be much greater. Blue eyes and blond hair are not to be found throughout this entire region of the world; the blue-eyed Cessares[15] of Chile and the Acansas of Florida have disappeared in modern times.

Thirdly, if, after this description, we were to ascribe to the Americans a dominant or central character, it would be goodness of heart and childlike innocence; a character that their ancient establishments, their habits, their few arts, and above all their initial conduct toward the Europeans, confirm. Springing from a savage land and unsupported by any assistance from the civilized world, all the progress they made was their own; and in their feeble beginnings of civilization, they exhibit a very instructive picture of humankind.

Beautiful.

---

*Robertson's *History of America*, vol. 1, p. 539.[14]
**Ibid., p. 537.

The Search for the Origin of Humankind and the Beginning of History on the Basis of Written Sources

As he had previously done (see Chapters 9 and 10 of this volume), Herder again scrutinizes ancient documents from different cultures in order to obtain information about the beginning of history. The approach here, however, is unlike his approach in those two chapters, in that here he does not concentrate on the contextually and culturally determined mode of linguistic and literary representation. Instead, he compares different myths and mythologies from all over the world and confronts them with results of the most recent research in those times in fields such as biology, geology, anthropology, ethnology, and geography. He thus relates the metaphorical representation and the narrative way of presenting ancient experiences of humankind to the findings of contemporary science. One of his conclusions is that it is impossible to determine a precise place on earth where the one and only origin of humankind may have occurred. Another is that human history displays comparable steps of development, so that—and this, again, is Herder's basic assumption—humanity is similar, although not uniform, all over the globe. Space, time, and circumstances modify the appearance of humankind, and this process of modified individualization is at the core of world history.

1. Our Earth Is an Earth Peculiarly Formed
for Its Animate Creation

The philosopher is much in the dark respecting the origin of human history, and peculiarities already become apparent in its remotest periods, which this one and that were unable to fit into their systems. Therefore, philosophers fell upon the despairing method of cutting the knot and not only regarding the earth as the ruins of a former habitation but also regarding the human species as a surviving remnant. The remnant had eluded this general accounting, perhaps in mountains and caves, after the planet in another state, so to speak, had experienced its last judgment. ["]The human rationality, art, and tradition of this remnant are considered the saved booty of a fallen prehistoric world*; for that reason, this remnant, on the one hand, is supposed to show from the outset a brilliance based on the experiences of many millennia, but, on the other hand, can never be brought to the light of day, as through these surviving humans, serving as an isthmus, the cultures of two worlds are entangled and bound together." If this opinion were true, there could be no such thing as a pure philosophy of the history of humankind; for our species itself and all its arts would be nothing more than the slag remaining after the destruction of a previous world. Let us inquire what foundation there is for a hypothesis that makes an inexplicable chaos of our earth itself and of its human history.

In the original formation of our earth, it seems to me, this hypothesis has no foundation; for the earliest apparent ravages and revolutions of the earth do not presuppose preexisting human history; rather, they are part of the creative cycle that made our earth habitable in the first place.** The ancient granite, the inner core of our globe, exhibits, as far as we have any knowledge of it, no trace of extinct organic beings; it does not contain them, nor do its component parts presuppose their existence. It is probable that the ancient granite's highest peaks rose above the waters of creation, since they do not reveal any trace of an impact of the sea; but on these naked heights a human creature could as little breathe as it could find nourishment. The atmosphere surrounding this mass was not yet separated from water and fire; pregnant with the several components of matter, which would settle upon the foundation of the earth only in multifarious compounds over periods of time, and gradually give it shape, this atmosphere could neither give nor sustain the breath of life of the most refined of the terrestrial creatures. Thus, the earliest formation of life occurred in water; and it came to be with the force of a primal creative power, which could not yet assert itself anywhere else, and thus manifested itself in the infinite number of shellfish, the

---

*See in particular the acute essay *Versuch über den Ursprung der Erkenntniß der Wahrheit und der Wissenschaften* (Berlin: 1781).[1] The hypothesis that our globe is formed from the ruins of another world is held in common by several natural scientists, for very different reasons.

**The facts on which the following assertions are built, are scattered through various modern books of geology, and are in part so well known, through *Buffon* and others, that I shall not bother to parade a string of quotations.

only beings capable of living in this pregnant sea. In the progressive formation of the earth, they frequently perished, and their destroyed parts became the source of more refined compounds. The more the primal rock was separated from the water and fertilized by its sediments, that is, with the elements and compounds that pervaded it, the more the creation of plants hastened after the creative life of the water, until upon every bared stretch of earth there vegetated what could vegetate. But even in the greenhouse of this realm, no terrestrial animal could survive. On heights upon which the plants of Lapland now grow, we find petrified plants of the most torrid zone of the earth, a clear proof that their atmosphere once had this climate. Yet this atmosphere must already have been rendered to a considerable degree more pure, because so many sediments had settled from it and the tender plant requires light to live; since, however, in these petrified images of plants, terrestrial creatures, not to speak of human bones, are yet nowhere to be found, it becomes probable that they did not yet exist on earth, since neither the stuff requisite for their formation nor that for their sustenance was present. So it went, through various revolutions, until finally in the uppermost strata of clay and sand, the elephant and rhinoceros skeletons appear; for what have been regarded as human forms in more deeply seated petrifications are altogether dubious and have been explained by more accurate natural scientists as the skeletons of sea creatures. On earth too, nature began with the formations of the warmest climate, and, as it appears, with those of the greatest bulk, as in the sea it first produced the mailed shellfish and the large *cornu ammonis;* at least it is certain that, among the numerous skeletons of elephants, which have been washed together at a late period and in some places preserved even with their skins intact, snakes, marine animals, and the like have been found, but no human bodies. And even had human bodies been discovered, they would have been unquestionably of a very modern date compared with the ancient mountains, in which no remnants of these kinds of living beings are to be found. Thus speaks the oldest book on earth, with its leaves of clay, slate, marble, lime, and sand; and what would it thereby say regarding a transformation of the earth, which supposedly was survived by a species of humankind, the remnants of which we are said to be? All it says tends rather to prove that our earth has fashioned itself from its chaos of substances and powers, under the animating warmth of the creative spirit, through a series of preparatory revolutions, to a particular and original whole, until at last the crown of its creation, the exquisite and delicate human creature, was enabled to appear. Those systems, therefore, that speak of tenfold transformations of the regions of the world and its poles, of the hundredfold overturning of an inhabited and cultivated soil, of the expulsion of humans from one region into another or even from their graves under rocks and seas, and depict nothing but horror and terror in all of ancient history, run counter to the makeup of the earth, or are at least unsupported by it, notwithstanding all the revolutions it has unquestionably undergone. The fissures and veins in the ancient rock, or its collapsed walls, say nothing of a habitable earth before the present; indeed, had the ancient mass melted down through some such fate, assuredly no living remnant of the primeval world would have survived for us. The earth as it is now, as well as the history of everything that lives on it, remains for the researcher a singular and complete problem to be solved. As we approach this end, we ask:

2. Where Was the Place of Formation and the Most Ancient Abode of Humankind?

That this place could not have been a late-formed edge of the land requires no proof; we proceed immediately, therefore, to the summits of the eternal, primeval mountains and the land that gradually accumulated alongside them. Did humans come into being everywhere, as shellfish came everywhere to be? Did the Mountains of the Moon[2] give birth to the Negro, the Andes to the American, the Urals to the Asian, the European Alps to the European? And does every major mountain region of the world indeed have its own variety of humankind? As every region of the earth has its peculiar species of animals, which cannot live elsewhere, and consequently must have been born in it, why should it not have its own variety of humankind? And would not the varieties of national features, customs, and character, and particularly the great difference in languages, be proof of this? Every one of my readers knows how brilliantly these arguments have been adduced by several learned and astute researchers of history, so that at last it was considered the most strained hypothesis, that nature indeed was able to create apes and bears everywhere, but not humans, and thus, in complete contradiction to the course of her other operations, exposed the most delicate of her creatures to a thousand perils by this singular frugality of creating only a single pair. "Behold even now," they say, "the prodigality of all-teeming nature! What innumerable seeds of plants and outcroppings, of animals and humans, does she scatter into the lap of destruction! And is it possible that at the very juncture when the human species was to be produced, our prolific mother, whose virgin youth was so rich in the seeds of all beings and forms that, as the structure of the earth shows, she could sacrifice millions of living creatures at one revolution in order to produce new kinds, should at that time have exhausted herself with inferior beings and have completed her wild labyrinth of life with two feeble human creatures?" Let us see to what extent this apparently brilliant hypothesis corresponds to the course of the culture and history of our kind, and is consistent with its form, its character, and its relation to the other living creatures of the earth.

In the first place, it is evidently contrary to nature that all living beings should have received life in equal number or at the same time; the structure of the earth and the internal constitution of the creatures, render this impossible. Elephants and worms, lions and animalcules, do not exist in equal number; from their essence, also, they could not be created originally in like proportions, or at the same time. Millions of testaceous creatures had to perish before the bare rock of our earth could become the seedbed of more refined life; a world of plants perishes annually so that the life of higher beings may be sustained. Thus, even if one sets aside entirely the ultimate causes of creation, it is rooted in the very substance of nature that it makes one out of the many, and that through the cycling wheel of creation it had to destroy an infinite number that a group smaller in number, but nobler in being, might live. Thus she proceeded on an ascending scale, and, in leaving everywhere sufficient seed to preserve the species she wanted to endure, she paved the way for more exquisite, refined, and higher species. If the human being was meant to be the crown of creation, it could not share with the fish, the pregnant slime of the sea, one mass, one day of birth, one place, and one site of habitation. The blood of humans was not meant to be water; the life-giving warmth of nature thus had to be purified to a point, its essence so refined, that it reddened human blood. All the human vascular tissues and fibers and the skeletal structure itself were to be of the finest clay, and since the almighty nature never works without second causes, it had to provide for itself the substances requisite to the task. This course was followed even in the creation of the coarser animals; when and where every animal could arise, it arose; energies thronged through every gate and formed themselves to life. The *cornu ammonis* existed before the fish, the plant before the animal, which could not live without it; the crocodile and the cayman crawled as the sagacious elephant arrived to select his food and to wave his trunk. Carnivorous animals required a numerous and already much increased progeny of those that were to provide their nourishment; consequently, they could not come into existence at the same time and in equal numbers with these. Humans too, if they were to be the inhabitants of earth and masters of creation, had to find their realm and dwelling prepared; necessarily therefore, they had to appear later and in smaller numbers than those over whom they were to hold sway. Had nature been able to produce from the original substance in its earthly workshop something higher, purer, and more beautiful than the human being, why would she not have done so?

And that she did not do so demonstrates that with the human being she closed her workshop and her formations, which she had begun with richest abundance in the bed of the sea and now completed with the most exquisite frugality. "God created man," says the most ancient written tradition of the peoples, "in his own image; in the likeness of God he created him, one man and one woman; after the multitudes he had created, the smallest number; there he rested, and created nothing more."[3] The living pyramid thereby was completed at its summit.

Now where could this summit be placed? Where did this pearl of the completed earth engender itself? Necessarily in the center of the most active organic powers, where, if I may put it this way, creation had progressed farthest, had developed most extensively and with the greatest refinement, and where could this be but in Asia, as already made probable by the very structure of the earth? It was in Asia that our globe had that great and extensive elevation never covered by water, stretching its rocky spine over the range of the compass in diverse chains. Here also was manifested the most intense mutual attraction of creative powers, the friction and cycles of the electric current, here the substances of the fertile chaos settled in greatest fullness. Around these mountains there came to be the greatest continent, as demonstrated by its dimension; and upon and alongside these mountains there live the largest number of species of living animal creation, which probably roamed over them in the enjoyment of existence while the rest of the world lay under water, scarcely breaking the surface with forests or naked mountaintops. The mountain imagined by *Linnaeus** as the mountain of creation does exist in nature; but not merely as a mountain, rather as an extensive amphitheater, a constellation of mountains, the arms of which extend into various climates. "I must observe," says *Pallas,*** "that all animals which have been tamed in the countries of the north and the south are found in the wild in the temperate climate of Central Asia (the dromedary excepted, neither species of which thrives out of Africa, or can be brought to endure the climate of Asia without difficulty). The native places of the wild ox and the buffalo, of the musimon, from which our sheep are descended, of the bezoar goat and the ibex, the intermixture of which has produced the fertile race of our domesticated goats, are found in the mountainous chains that extend over the central part of Asia and a part of Europe. The reindeer abound on the high mountains that skirt Siberia and cover its

---

Linnaei amoenitates academicae, vol. 2, p. 439. *Oratio de terra habitabili;* the speech has been translated frequently.[4]

**Bemerkungen über die Berge,* translated in the *Beiträge zur physikalischen Erdbeschreibung,* vol. 3, p. 250, and elsewhere.[5]

eastern extension, and they frequently serve there as beasts of burden and draft animals. They are also found in the Ural chain, whence they have spread to the more northern countries. The camel with two humps is to be found in the deserts between Tibet and China. Wild pigs inhabit the woods and morasses throughout all the temperate parts of Asia. The wild cat, from which our domestic cat is derived, is sufficiently known. Lastly, the major breed of our domestic dogs is certainly descended from the jackal, though I do not think its blood wholly uncontaminated, but believe that it has been intermixed, from a very remote period, with that of the common wolf, the fox, and even the hyena, which has occasioned the extreme variety of sizes and shapes of dogs, etc." Thus *Pallas*. And who does not know the wealth of Asia, particulary of its southern countries, in the products of nature? It is as if this loftiest of the world's heights has surrounded itself not only with the most extensive but also with the richest land, that from the beginning drew into itself the greatest abundance of organic warmth. The wisest elephants, the cleverest apes, the most active animals are nourished by Asia. Indeed, notwithstanding its decline, perhaps it has, with regard to genetic potential, the most ingenious and exalted of human beings.

But what about the other continents? That Europe was supplied both with humans and animals chiefly from Asia, and that it was probably still largely covered with water, or with forests and morasses, when the more elevated land of Asia was already cultivated, is already verifiable by the record of history. With the interior of Africa we have yet too little acquaintance; both the shape and the altitude of its central ridge of mountains in particular are totally unknown to us; yet it is on many accounts probable that this arid continent, lowland over wide stretches, does not measure up with its ridge of mountains to the height and breadth of Asia. Thus, Africa too was probably covered with water for a longer period, and though the torrid zone there has not denied its own powerful characteristic to the budding life of plants and animals, it still appears that Africa and Europe are more like offspring, beholden to the womb of mother Asia. Most of the animals have these three continents in common, and they form on the whole but one continent.

Lastly, when we consider the ridge of steep mountains, too lofty to be inhabited, that stretch through America, their still raging volcanoes, the lowland at their feet, large tracts of which are on a level with the sea, and its living creation, which consists primarily of plants, amphibians, insects, and birds, with fewer species of the more perfect and active land animals enjoyed by the Old World; and when to these we add the immature and simple constitutions of its tribes, it will be difficult to imagine that this continent was the earliest inhabited. Rather, it is compared with the other hemisphere, a rich subject of study for the explorer of nature, regarding the differences between two contrasting hemispheres. Thus, even the beautiful valley of Quito could hardly be considered the birthplace of the original pair of human beings, as much as I would like to grant this honor to it and to the Mountains of the Moon in Africa, and as little as I care to contradict those who might find evidence to support this assertion.

But enough of mere conjecture, which I wish not to be abused, so as to deny the Omnipotent the power and the substance to create human beings wherever he pleased. The voice that everywhere planted land and sea with appropriate inhabitants could also have given each continent its native lord, had it thought fit. But is not the reason discoverable in the character of humankind as hitherto unfolded, why it did not choose to do so? We have seen that our reason and our quality of humanity depend on education, language, and tradition, and that in this respect our species differs totally from the animal, which brings its infallible instinct into the world with it. If this is so, the human being could not, by nature of its specific character, have been generally dispersed over the desert world like the beasts. The tree that could everywhere be propagated only by being tended, was meant rather to spring from one root, in a place where it could flourish best, where he who planted it could foster it himself. Humankind, destined to possess the quality of humanity, from its origin was meant to form a kinship of brothers, of one blood, guided by one shaping tradition, and so the totality came into being, just as to this day every family comes to be, branches of one trunk, sprouts of one original nursery. It seems to me that this distinguishing plan of God for our species, which sets it apart from the animal even in terms of origin, must appear to be the most appropriate, the most beautiful, and the most dignified to everyone who takes into account the characteristics of our nature, the makeup and quality of our reason, the manner in which we form concepts and develop humanity within us. With this design, we became the favorites of nature, produced by her as the fruit of her most mature industry, or, if you please, as the sons of her ripe age, in the place best suited for these tender latecomers. Here she raised them with maternal hand, having surrounded them with that which from the very outset could facilitate the cultural formation of their human character. Just as only one kind of human reason was possible on earth, and nature, therefore, produced only one species of creatures capable of reason, so it also placed these beings capable of reason into one school of language and tradition, and undertook this task of education through a succession of generations from one origin.

3. The Course of Civilization and History Provides Historical Evidence that the Human Species Originated in Asia

Where did all the peoples of Europe originate? In Asia. Of most of them we know this with certainty; we know the origins of the Laplanders, the Finns, the Germans and the Goths, the Gauls, the Slavs, the Celts, the Cimbri, and so on. Partly through their languages, or the remains of their languages, and partly through accounts of their ancient settlements, we can trace their origins a considerable distance to the Black Sea or into Tartary, where some remains of their languages still exist. We know less of the descent of other peoples, because we know less of their most ancient history; for it is only the ignorance of earlier times that makes for autochthons. If *Büttner*,[6] the historian of ancient and modern peoples most learned in the study of languages, would reveal to us the treasures of his accumulated readings, as he could, and provide us with the parentage of a number of peoples of which they themselves are ignorant, he would confer no small benefit on humankind.*

The origins of the Africans and the Americans, to be honest, are more obscure to us; from what we know of the upper rim of the former and a comparison of its most ancient traditions, it is Asiatic. Farther south, we must be satisfied to find nothing in the figure and color of the Negroes contradicting this origin, but rather a progressive portrait of national formations based on climate, as Book Six of this work endeavored to show. It is the same with America, which was settled later; its settlement from the East of Asia is made probable already by the uniform makeup of its peoples.

But we learn more from the languages of the peoples than from these formations; and where on the earth do we find the languages that were cultivated in the most distant past? In Asia. If you want to behold the marvel of peoples speaking nothing but monosyllabic languages over thousands of miles across the range of the compass, look to Asia. The peoples inhabiting the areas beyond the Ganges, Tibet, China, Pegu, Ava, Arracan,[7] Burma, Tonkin, Laos, Cochin China, Cambodia, and Siam, speak nothing but uninflected monosyllabic words. It is probable that the earliest rules of their linguistic culture and writing fixed this; for in this corner of Asia almost all the most ancient institutions have remained virtually unchanged in every respect. If you wish to see languages whose great and almost overflowing richness is based on very few roots, so that, with a peculiar kind of regularity and an almost childlike art of expression, they create a new concept by a minute change of the stem, thus combining complexity

---

*The learned man is engaged in such a work on a comprehensive scale.

and poverty, then observe the southern rim of Asia from India to Syria, Arabia, and Ethiopia. The language of Bengal has seven hundred roots, the elements of reason, so to speak, from which it forms verbs, nouns, and all other parts of speech. Hebrew and the languages related to it, as very different in kind as they are, excite astonishment when their structure is considered in even the most ancient writings. All their words may be traced back to roots of three letters, which at first also were probably monosyllables, but afterward, though still at an early stage, in all likelihood through their particular alphabet, were brought into this form, and in this form they shaped the entire language by means of very simple additions and inflections. An inestimable wealth of concepts, for example, is generated by the mature Arabian language on the basis of very few roots, so that the patchwork quality of most European languages, with their useless auxiliary words and their tedious inflections, is never more fully revealed than when they are compared with the languages of Asia. Hence, too, the more ancient these languages are, the more difficult they are for the European to learn; for he must relinquish the useless riches of his own tongue, and he encounters them as if they were a finely conceived, subtly structured hieroglyphics of the invisible language of thought.

The most certain mark of the cultural level of a language is its written form. The more ancient it was, and the more art and reflection it displayed, the more highly developed the language turned out to be. Now, if we except the Scythians, who were also an Asiatic people, no European nation can boast of the invention of an alphabet; in this respect the peoples of Europe stand as barbarians, along with the Negroes and Americans. Asia alone had writing, and this in the most ancient of times. The first civilized nation of Europe, the Greeks, received its alphabet from an inhabitant of the Morn, and *Büttner's* tables demonstrate that all other European letters of the alphabet were derived from, or are distortions of, the Greek.* The most ancient literal writing of the Egyptians, as it appears on their mummies, also is Phoenician, in like manner as the Coptic alphabet is a corrupt Greek. Among the Negroes and the Americans, nothing like an originally invented script is to be supposed, for among the latter the Mexicans never rose beyond their rude hieroglyphics nor the Peruvians beyond their knotted cords. Asia, on the other hand, has in a way exhausted the art of writing in letters and artful hieroglyphs, so that almost all modes of writing which have been invented to capture human speech may be found among them. The Bengal language has fifty letters and twelve vowels; the Chinese has

---

*See Büttner's *Vergleichungstafeln der Schriftarten verschiedner Völker* (Göttingen: 1771).[8]

chosen from its forest of characters designating sound no fewer than one hundred and twelve vowels and thirty-six consonants. So it is with the Tibetan, the Singhalese, the Marathan, and the Manchu alphabets, though the directions of the strokes that form their characters vary. Some of the Asiatic modes of writing are evidently so ancient that they reveal how the language itself grew with them and to them; and the simple and beautiful writing of the ruins of Persepolis is still altogether unintelligible to us.

If we proceed from the instruments of civilization to civilization itself, where did it appear earlier, or where could it appear earlier, than in Asia, from which it dispersed broadly along paths known to us? The dominance over animals was one of the first steps to this end, and it rises on this continent beyond all the revolutions of history. It is not only, as we have seen, that these primeval mountains of the world were the home of the greatest number of and the most readily domesticated animals; but the society of humans tamed them so early that our most useful species of animals, the sheep, dogs, and goats, actually came into being through this domestication, and actually represent new species of animals produced by Asiatic skills. If one wished to stand in the center of the distribution of domesticated animals, one should step upon the heights of Asia; the more distant from these, reckoning on the grand scale of nature, the fewer domesticated animals are to be found. In Asia, all the way down to its southern islands, they abound everywhere; in New Guinea and New Zealand, we find only the dog and the pig; in New Caledonia, the dog alone; and through the whole extent of America, the only domesticated animals are the guanaco and llama. Moreover, the handsomest and finest of these species are found in Asia and Africa. The Asian mule and the Arab horse, the wild and the domesticated donkey, the argali and the sheep, the mountain goat and the angora goat are the pride of their species; the wisest elephant was managed with the greatest art from the earliest times in Asia, and the camel was indispensable to this continent. With respect to the beauty of some of these animals, Africa comes next after Asia; but in the management of them it still is far behind. Europe owes all its domesticated animals to Asia; Europe is able to reckon as its own only fifteen or sixteen wild species, chiefly mice or bats.*

It was no different with the cultivation of the soil and its plants, since a large part of Europe was still forest until very late in time, and since its inhabitants, if they were to sustain themselves on a vegetarian diet, could do no other than to live off roots and wild herbs, acorns and crab apples. In some of the regions of Asia of which we have spoken, grain grows wild and

---

*See Zimmermann's *Geographische Geschichte der Menschen,* vol. 3, p. 183.

husbandry dates from time immemorial. The finest fruits of the earth—the grape and the olive, the lemon and the fig, the pomegranate and all our tree fruits, chestnuts, almonds, nuts, and so on—were first brought from Asia into Africa and Greece, and from there were distributed farther. A few other vegetables we have derived from America, and we know the places from which most of these were procured and the times when they were introduced. Thus, these gifts of nature were conferred upon humankind by way of tradition. America did not cultivate vineyards, and vineyards have been planted in Africa only by the hands of Europeans.

That the sciences and the arts were first cultivated in Asia, and in the adjacent country of Egypt, requires no elaborate proof; ancient monuments and the history of peoples affirm it; and the testimony of *Goguet** is in every hand. In this part of the world, both the useful and the fine arts have been pursued very early, in some place or other, but everywhere in the distinct Asiatic taste, as is sufficiently proved by the ruins of Persepolis, the Hindu temples, the pyramids of Egypt, and many other works of which there are still remains or of which accounts are handed down to us; almost all of these transcend European culture by far, and they have no equals in Africa or America. The lofty poetry of several peoples of South Asia is known worldwide**; and the more ancient it is, the more it gains in dignity and simplicity, which by itself deserves to be called divine. What penetrating thought, yes, I would like to say, what poetic hypothesis has ever entered the soul of a modern inhabitant of the West, whose germ cell is not found in an earlier expression or phrasing by a precursor inhabiting the Morn, as long as the impetus for it fell into his range of vision? The commerce of the Asians is the most ancient upon earth, and the most important inventions relative to it are theirs. The same is true of astronomy and historical chronology. Who would not marvel, even without the slightest allusion to *Bailly's* hypotheses, at the early and extensive propagation of many astronomical observations, periods, and practices, to which the most ancient nations of Asia have a claim not easily to be disputed?*** It is as if their ancient philosophers were preeminently the philosophers of the heavens, the observers of silently progressing time; even to this day, at a time of deep decadence of some of these nations, this calculating, enumerating spirit manifests itself to this effect.† The Brahmin calculates immense sums

---

Vom Ursprung der Gesetze, Künste und Wissenschaften (Lemgo: 1770), p. 4.[9]

**See Jones, *Poeseos Asiaticae commentatorium,* Eichhorn edition (Leipzig: 1777).[10]

***See Bailly's *Geschichte der Sternkunde des Alterthums* (Leipzig: 1777).[11]

†See le Gentil's *Reisen* in Ebeling's *Sammlung,*[12] vol. 2, p. 406; and also Walther's *Doctrina temporum Indica,* appended to Bayer's *Historia regni Graecorum Bactriani* (Petropolis, 1738), etc.

by memory; the divisions of time, from the smallest measure to the greatest revolutions of the heavens, are familiar to his mind, and he makes few mistakes in them, though he has none of the European calculating tools. Antiquity has left to him the formulas which he now does nothing but apply; for even our division of the year is Asiatic; our arithmetical figures and the constellations of our astronomers are of Egyptian or Indian origin.

Lastly, if forms of government are the most difficult of the arts of civilization, where do we find the oldest and greatest monarchies? Where have the empires of the world found their firmest establishment? China has maintained its ancient constitution for some thousands of years; and though this unwarlike country has been overrun several times by Tartar hordes, the conquered yet have always tamed the conquerors and restrained them with the chains of their ancient constitution. What form of government in Europe can make a similar boast? The most ancient hierarchy upon earth reigns in the mountains of Tibet; and the castes of the Hindus betray their primeval establishment from the deep-rooted power that has for millennia been second nature to the gentlest of people. Warlike or peaceable monarchies, already established in the most ancient times in the region of the Euphrates and Tigris, as well as along the Nile and in the Median mountains, have interfered ever since in the history of the western peoples; and even on the heights of Tartary, the unrestricted liberty of the hordes was interwoven with the despotism of the khans, which formed the foundation of many a European form of government. From every corner of the world, the nearer we approach Asia, the closer we come to the firmly established empires, the unlimited power of which has impressed itself for millennia upon the mentality of the peoples, to the point that the king of Siam could ridicule a kingless nation as a headless monstrosity. In Africa, the most firmly established despotisms are located nearest Asia; the greater the distance, the ruder the state of tyranny, until at last, under the Kaffirs, it loses itself in the patriarchal condition of the shepherd. In the South Seas, the closer to Asia, the longer the arts and crafts, splendor and the spouse of splendor, royal despotism, are flourishing; the further from Asia, on the remote islands, in America, or even at the meager fringe of the southern hemisphere, the more the cruder constitution of humankind, the freedom of tribes and families, comes to the fore; for that reason, some historians have traced the two monarchies of America, Peru and Mexico, to the proximity of despotic empires of Asia. The entire image of the continent thus reveals, especially in the vicinity of the mountains, the most ancient human habitation; and the traditions of these peoples with their chronologies and religions are rooted, as is known, in the primeval millennia. All the mythologies of the Europeans and the Africans (from whom I always exclude the Egyptians), and

208 HUMANKIND AND THE BEGINNING OF HISTORY

even more of the Americans and the western South Sea islanders, are nothing but lost fragments of modern fables compared to the gigantic edifices of the ancient cosmogonies of India, Tibet, ancient Chaldea, and even lower Egypt; dispersed sounds of the lost Echo[13] losing herself in the fable, compared to the voice of the primeval Asiatic world.

What then if we were to follow this voice and, as humankind has no means of being formed but tradition, endeavor to trace it to the original source? This is indeed a treacherous path, as if one were to pursue the rainbow or Echo's voice; for as little as a child is able to give an account of its birth, though present at it, as little may we hope that the human species may provide us with historically rigorous reports of its creation, of the earliest teachings, of the invention of language, and of its first habitation. Yet a child, after all, remembers at least a few impressions of its later youth, and if several children who were raised together and later separated were to relate the same thing or something similar, why should they not be heard? Why should we not reflect upon what they say or dream of the past, especially if no other documents are available? And since it is the undeniable design of providence to instruct humans through humans—that is through progressive tradition—so let us not doubt that in this case too she will have granted us as much as we need to have.

4. Asiatic Traditions Concerning the Creation of the Earth and the Origin of Humankind

But where in this wild forest, where so many deceiving voices and flitting lights beckon and draw us to and fro, shall we begin? I have no inclination to add one syllable to the library of dreams on this subject that presses upon human memory; therefore, I thus differentiate as much as I can between the conjectures of the peoples or the hypotheses of their philosophers and the facts of tradition, and in regard to the latter the degree of their certainty and their chronology. The rémotest people of Asia, who boast of the greatest antiquity, the Chinese, have no authentic history prior to the year 722 before our era. The reigns of Fu-hsi[14] and Hoang-ti[15] are mythological, and what precedes Fu-hsi, the age of spirits, of the elements personified, is considered allegorical fiction by the Chinese themselves. Their most ancient book* which was recovered, or rather restored, from two copies saved out of the general book burning in the year 176 before the birth of Christ, contains neither a cosmogony nor the origin of the nation. In it we find Yao[17] reigning with the mountains of his empire, the grandees; he had but to issue

---

Le Chou-king, un des livres sacrés des Chinois (Paris: 1770).[16]

the command and stars were observed, aqueducts were constructed, and divisions of time were established; sacrifices and matters of business were already in fixed order. Thus we have nothing left but the Chinese metaphysics of the great first Y,* how four and eight arose from one and two; how, after the opening of the heavens, P'an-ku and the three Hoangs[18] reigned in miraculous shapes, until the human phase of history began with the first lawgiver, Gin-Hoang, who was born on the mountain Hingma and who divided the land and the water into nine parts. And yet this sort of mythology proceeds down through several generations, so that nothing can be built upon it, except perhaps the seat on which they place these kings and their miraculous manifestations as the high mountains of Asia, which they deem sacred and revere in all their most ancient fables. A great mountain in the center of the earth is highly celebrated, even among the names of these ancient fabulous beings, whom they style kings.

If we ascend to Tibet, we find the notion of the earth surrounding a lofty central mountain still more conspicuous, for the whole mythology of this ecclesiastical empire is founded on it. The notion depicts the elevation and extent of this empire in awesome terms. Monsters and giants are its guardians; seven seas and seven mountains of gold surround it. The lahs dwell on its summit, and other beings on various lower levels. Over the course of eons, those contemplators of the heavens descended into ever-coarser bodies, until they arrived at the human form, in which a repulsive pair of apes were their parents; the origin of the animals likewise is explained on the basis of lahs forced to descend from the heights.** This is a severe mythology, which constructs the world as descending into the sea; surrounding it with monsters; and surrendering the entire system at last to the open jaws of a monster, eternal necessity. But even this degrading tradition, which derives the human being from the ape, is so interwoven with its later manifestations that it would be asking much to consider it an original myth of the primeval world.

It would be of estimable advantage to possess knowledge of the most ancient tradition of the old Hindu people. But, aside from the fact that the first Brahmin sect was long ago extinguished by the followers of Vishnu and Shiva, in what hitherto has been learned by Europeans of their mysteries we have evidently only myths of recent origin, which were either myths for the people or exegetic systems of their philosophers. Moreover, they differ from province to province, so that we probably have long to wait for

---

*See *Recherches sur les tems anterieurs à ceux dont parle le Chou-king* by Premare, prefixed to the edition of the I Ching by de Guignes.
**Georgii alphabetum Tibetanum.* Rome 1762, p. 181 and elsewhere.

the original Sanskrit language as well as for the true vedas of the Indians; and even in them we can expect little of their most ancient tradition, as they themselves deem the first part of the Vedas to be lost. And yet many a later fable reveals a golden kernel of primeval history. The Ganges, for example, is sacred through all India, and it flows immediately from the sacred mountains, the feet of Brahma, the creator of the world. Vishnu appeared in his eighth metamorphosis as Prassarama; the water still covered all the land to the Ghat mountains; he entreated the God of the Sea to give him room, and to withdraw the flood as far as he could shoot an arrow. The god promised, Prassarama shot, and the land dried as far as the arrow flew, the coast of Malabar. This narrative evidently instructs us, as *Sonnerat*[19] observes, that the sea once extended to the Ghat mountains, and that the coast of Malabar is a recent land formation. Other myths of Indian peoples relate the origins of the earth out of water in other ways. Vishnu drifted on a leaf; the first human being came to be out of him as a flower. Or, an egg floated on the surface of the waves, which was hatched by Brahma; from the covering of the egg the air and the heavens were formed, and from its contents the creatures of the earth, animals, and human beings. But the reader should read these tales himself, in the fairytale manner of the childlike Indians.*

The system of Zoroaster** is evidently already a philosophical system, which, even if it were not intermingled with the myths of other sects, could hardly be taken for a primeval tradition; however, traces of such a tradition are recognizable in it. The great mountain Albordi appears again in the center of the earth and surrounds it with its subsidiary ranges. The sun revolves around it; the rivers flow from it, and the seas and the lands are distributed. The shape of things exists first in primeval images, in germ cells; and, as all mythologies of higher Asia abound with monsters of the primeval world, this one too has the great bull Cayamort, from whose carcass all the creatures of the earth came to be. On the summit of this mountain, as on that of the lahs, is paradise, the seat of the blessed spirits and transfigured humans, as well as the original spring of all the streams, the water of life. Moreover, the light that divides, dissipates, and overcomes darkness, that makes the earth fruitful and animates all creatures, is evidently the first principle of the whole fire worship of the Parsees; the simple idea of which they have applied theologically, morally, and politically in a thousand ways.

The farther west we wander down from the mountains of Asia, the briefer we find the epochs and myths of the primeval world to be. We

---

*See *Sonnerat, Baldeus, Dow, Holwell*, etc.[20]
**Zend Avesta* (Riga: 1776–78).

perceive in them all a later origin and the application of alien traditions derived from more elevated regions of the earth and brought to lower-lying countries. Their characterizations of local conditions become ever more inappropriate, but on this account the system itself gains in completeness and clarity, as only a few fragments of the ancient fable occasionally surface, and these too are everywhere clad in a more recent national garb. I am astonished, therefore, how Sanchoniathon[21] has been represented on the one hand as a complete impostor, and on the other as the first prophet of the primeval world, since the very location of his country denied him access to this world. That the beginning of all of this was an atmosphere devoid of light, a dark and murky chaos, and that this chaos, without limits and without form, floated since times immemorial in the emptiness of space, until the moving spirit fell in love with its own principles and out of this union the onset of creation came to be—this is a mythology so ancient and so common an image to the most varied of peoples that little was left here for the Phoenician to invent. Almost every people of Asia, including the Egyptians and the Greeks, related in its own way the tradition of chaos or of the fecundated egg; why then should written traditions of this sort not also be found in a Phoenician temple? That the first seeds of creatures lay embedded in mud and that the earliest beings endowed with reason were a kind of miraculous beings, mirrors of the heavens (zophesamin[22]), who, later roused by the sound of thunder, awoke and gave birth out of their miraculous shape to the variety of creatures, is likewise a widely accepted myth, here shortened, that spread in different garbs over the mountains of Media[23] and Tibet to India and China, and also down to Phrygia[24] and Thrace;[25] for, even in the mythologies of Orpheus and Hesiod, traces of it are found. Now, when we read long genealogies of the wind Colpias, that is, the voice of the breath of God, and his wife *Night,* and of their sons *Firstborn* and *Eon,* their grandchildren *Genus* and *Species,* of their great-grandchildren *Light, Fire,* and *Flame,* and of their great-great-grandchildren, the *Mount Cassius, Mount Libanus,* and *Mount Antilibanus,* and so on, and find human inventions ascribed to these allegorical names, a very indulgent prejudice is needed to discern a philosophy of the world and a most ancient history of humankind in this misconceived confusion of ancient traditions, which the compiler probably encountered as proper names, and which he transformed into people.

We will not take the trouble to search further down into black Egypt for traditions of the primeval world. In the names of its ancient deities are unquestionable remains of a sister tradition to that of the Phoenicians; for ancient Night, the Spirit, the Creator of the world, the mud wherein lay the seeds of things, here occur once more. But as all we know of the most ancient mythology of Egypt is late in origin, uncertain, and obscure, and since moreover every mythological image of this country is entirely tied to the climate, it would not answer our purpose to dig among these evocations of idols or deeper among the tales of Negroes for the myths of the primeval world, to build upon them the foundation of a philosophy of the most ancient history of humankind.

Thus, even in terms of history, there remains nothing for us upon the broad extent of the earth but the *written tradition,* which we commonly call the Mosaic. Laying aside all prejudice, and thus also without the slightest conviction as to its origin, we know that it is more than three thousand years old, and that it is indeed the oldest book possessed by our young species of humankind. A look at its short and simple pages will acquaint us with their design and value, considering them not as history, but as a tradition or as an ancient *philosophy of the history of humankind,* which I will therefore also promptly strip of its poetic ornaments of the Morn.

5. The Most Ancient Written Tradition Regarding the Origins of the History of Humankind

When once upon a time the creation of our earth and of our heaven began, this myth says, *the earth was at first a void, shapeless mass, upon which a dark sea flooded, and a living, life-giving power moved upon these waters.*—Were we, taking account of all the more recent experiences, to describe the most ancient condition of the earth, as the searching mind may describe it without the high-flying benefit of unprovable hypotheses, we would once more encounter exactly this ancient description. An enormous rock of granite, mostly covered by water, above it natural powers pregnant with life, this is what we know and nothing more. That this rock was ejected glowing from the sun is a monumental idea, but founded neither on the analogy of nature nor on the progressive development of our earth, for how did the waters come to be upon this glowing mass? Whence did it acquire its global shape, whence its revolution and its poles, since magnetic power is destroyed by fire? It is much more probable that this wondrous primeval rock formed itself by its inherent powers, that is to say, that congealing into sediment it gathered substance from the pregnant chaos out of which our earth was to come to be. Yet the Mosaic tradition eliminates this chaos also, and proceeds immediately to portray the rock; with that, the chaotic monsters and wondrous figures of the older tradition disappear into the abyss. The only element that this philosophical piece may have in common with those myths are perhaps the Elohim,[26] perhaps the lahs, the zophesamin, and so on, but here exalted to the idea of an active oneness; they are not creatures, but the creator.

The creation of things begins with light; through it the ancient night is torn asunder, through it the elements are set apart; and what other principle of nature that is both separating and animating do we know on the basis of both ancient and modern experiences, but that of light, or, if you will, elementary fire? It is universally diffused throughout nature, though unequally distributed depending on the affinities of bodies. In constant motion and activity, fluid and active of itself, it is the cause of all fluidity, warmth, and motion. Even the electric principle seems only a modification of it; and as all life throughout nature is unfolded solely by warmth, and manifests itself through the motion of fluids; as the semen of animals with its expansive, stimulating, and animating force not only works in a manner similar to light, but light and electricity have also been observed in the insemination of plants; so it is that in this ancient philosophical cosmogony nothing but light acts as the first cause. And, indeed, not light proceeding from the sun, but a light springing from the interior of this organic mass, once more corresponding to experience. It is not from the sun that all creatures derive life and nourishment; everything is pregnant with internal warmth; even the rock and cold iron contain it; indeed, it is only in proportion to this genetic fire, and its more delicate effect through the powerful circulation of internal movement, that a creature is alive, perceptive, and acting. It is here, then, that the first elemental flame was fanned, not a volcanic eruption, not a flaming terrestrial body, but the separating power, the warming, sustaining balm of nature, which gradually set everything in motion. How much more removed from the truth and how much coarser are the expressions of the Phoenician tradition, which awakens the powers of nature as sleeping animals through thunder and lightning; in this more refined system, which experience will certainly further confirm from time to time, light is the agent of creation.

To remove the false notion of the days of creation from the following exposition, let me here point out what is obvious to everyone on bare inspection,* that the whole system of the representation of a self-fulfilling creation rests on a comparison, by means of which the parts do not separate physically, but only symbolically. Since, after all, our eye cannot encompass at once the entirety of creation and its interlocking effects, classes had to be invented, and it was most natural to set up one against the other, heaven and earth, and on the latter the sea and the land, though in nature they remain a connected realm of acting and enduring beings. Thus, this ancient document is the first simple *table of a natural order,* in which the designation of the days of creation, in keeping with another purpose of the

---

Aelteste Urkunde des Menschengeschlechts, part 1.[27]

author, serves merely as a *nominal scale* for the division. As soon as light was present as the agent of creation, it had to activate heaven and earth at one and the same point in time. There it purified the air which, as a thinner water and, according to innumerable modern experiments, as the all-connecting vehicle of creation, serves the light as well as the powers of aquatic and terrestrial beings in a thousand combinations; it could be purified, or brought to its elastic fluidity, by no other known principle of nature than light, or the elemental fire. But how could this purification be effected, unless by the gradual sinking of all the coarser materials in various sedimentations and revolutions, until the water and the land, as well as water and air, eventually became distinct regions? The second and third manifestations thus worked through one another, though in the symbolism of the cosmogony they are set against one another, incarnations of the first principle, the separating light of creation. Without doubt, these developments extended over millennia, as the formation of mountains and terrestrial strata, the excavation of valleys to the beds of rivers, incontestably show. Three powerful agents were at work during these great spans of time, water, air, and fire; the first two in that they formed sediments, washed away, and precipitated, the latter organically operating in them both and in the self-generating earth, wherever it could so operate.

Once more, a grand vision of this most ancient of natural philosophers, whom many are unable to comprehend even in our own day! For the internal history of the earth reveals that in its formation the organic powers of nature were immediately everywhere active, and that wherever one of them was able to manifest itself, it did so promptly. The earth vegetated as soon as it was capable of vegetation, even though entire realms of vegetation were doomed to be extinguished by interruptions in the supply of air and water. The sea teemed with living beings as soon as it was sufficiently purified, even though in the course of floods millions of these beings found their graves thereby serving other organisms as the stuff of life. Yet, in each period of these unfolding purifications, not every creature of every element could survive; the different species of creation followed one upon the other, as they were able to come to be in keeping with their nature and medium. And behold, all this was summed up by our natural philosopher in the one voice of the world creator that, in calling up the light, thereby commanded the air to purify itself, the sea to settle down, and the earth to gradually arise; that is to say, set in motion all the active powers of the natural cycle; by the same token, the earth, the water, and the dust were commanded that *each of them produce organic beings after its own kind, and that creation thus animate itself by its own organic powers implanted in these elements.* Thus spoke this philosopher, not dreading the sight of nature, still perceived

by us wherever organic powers unfold themselves to life in keeping with
their elemental makeup. However, since separation had to take place, he set
the realms of nature separately against one another, as the natural scientist
separates them, although he well knows that they do not exist separated by
fences. Vegetation precedes; and as modern physics has shown how much
plants in particular live through light, a few weather-beaten rocks, a little
washed-up mud, under the powerful warmth of brooding creation, sufficed
to render vegetation possible. The fertile womb of the sea followed with its
emanations and promoted other forms of vegetation. The earth, rendered
pregnant by those sediments and by light, air, and water, hastened to catch
up, and proceeded, but certainly not to give birth to all species at once; for
as little as the carnivorous animals can live without animal food, it is as
certain that their origin presumes the demise of other kinds of animals,
which the natural history of the earth confirms. We find marine and grami-
nivorous animals in the lower strata of the earth as the deposits of the
earliest eons, carnivorous animals never, or rarely. Thus creation matured in
stages of ever more refined organizations, until at last the human being
appears, the finest evocation of the Elohim, the crown that consummates
creation.

But before we approach this crown, let us consider a few more masterful
designs woven by the ancient sage into the fabric of his portrait. *Firstly,* he
does not bring the sun and the stars as weavers into his expanding wheel of
creation. He makes them the center of his symbol, for they do indeed
sustain the movement of our earth and all its organic emanations, and are
thus, as he says, the monarchs of time; however, they do not impart the
organic powers themselves, nor do they transmit them down to earth. The
sun still shines as it did in the beginning of creation; but it does not arouse
and give shape to new species[28]; for even in putrefaction heat would not
develop the minutest living creature if the power at the root of its creation
were not to lie there at the ready for the next transition. The sun and the
stars thus appear in this portrait of nature as soon as they are able to appear,
that is, when the air has been purified and the earth constructed; but only as
witnesses of creation, as the rulers of a sphere organic in itself.

Secondly, the moon appears from the beginning of the world, for me a
beautiful testimony to this ancient portrait of nature. The opinion of those
who deem it a younger neighbor of the earth, and ascribe all the disorders in
and upon the globe to its arrival, is not persuasive to me. It is destitute of all
physical proof, since every apparent disorder of our planet is not only
explicable without this hypothesis, but, on the basis of this better explanation, ceases to be disorder. For it is evident that our earth, with the elements
contained within the shell of its becoming, could not be formed otherwise

than by revolutions, and even by these hardly other than in the vicinity of the moon. The moon gravitates to the earth, as the earth gravitates to itself and to the sun; the movement of the sea, as well as the process of vegetation, is, as far as we can tell from the knowledge of the clockwork of our celestial and terrestrial powers, tied to the moon's circuit.

Thirdly, with equal truth and refinement this natural philosopher places the creatures of the air and the water in one class; and comparative anatomy has shown a marvelous similarity in the inner structure, especially of the brain, as the true indicator of the ladder of creation. For the difference in development is everywhere related to the medium for which the creatures are destined; thus, in reference to the two classes of aerial and aquatic animals, the internal structure must bear the same analogy as exists between air and water. In general, this entire living wheel of the history of creation tends to show that each element produced what it was capable of producing, and that all elements belong to the whole of one work, and thus that only *one organic formation could have become visible on our planet,* which commences in the lowest of living beings, and is completed in the ultimate and most noble evocation of the Elohim.

With joy and wonder I thus approach the rich description of the creation of humankind, for it is the subject of my book and happily its seal. *The Elohim took counsel together,* and impressed this counsel upon the image of the becoming human being; reason and reflectiveness thus are its distinguishing characteristics. *They shape the human being in their likeness,* and all the peoples of the Morn accord these characteristics preeminently to the upright posture of the body. *On it was stamped the character of dominion over the earth;* to the human species thus was given the organic advantage to carry out this dominion everywhere, and to dwell as the most fruitful creature among the nobler animals of creation in all climates as the representative of the Elohim, as visible Providence, as acting God. Behold the most ancient philosophy of the history of humankind.

And now, as the wheel of becoming was completed to the last of the governing springs, *the Elohim rested and created no more;* yes, upon the stage of creation the Elohim are so concealed that it appears as if everything had come to be of itself and thus had been eternally so in necessary generations. The ultimate, however, does not take place, since the structure of the earth and the mutually dependent organization of the creatures prove sufficiently that everything terrestrial had its beginning as an artful formation and rose from the lower to the higher; but now, what about the first? Why did the workshop of creation close, and neither the sea nor the earth give rise to new species of living beings, so that it appears that the creative power is resting and that it seems to work only through the organs of established orders and species? On these points, our natural philosopher gives us a physical explanation in the acting being which he makes into the wellspring of the entire creation. If it was light or the elementary fire that separated the mass, raised the heavens, rendered the air elastic, and prepared the earth for vegetation, so it formed the seeds of things and organized itself from the most primitive to the most refined stage of life; thus creation was completed as, according to the word of the Eternal, that is, according to his ordaining wisdom, *these vital powers were distributed, and had assumed all forms that could and should sustain themselves on our planet.* The animating warmth with which the brooding spirit of creation hovered over the waters, and which had already manifested itself in the earlier subterranean stages, and that with a copiousness and energy with which neither the sea nor the earth is now capable of producing anything, this primal warmth of creation, I say, without which it was then impossible for anything to be organized, as it is now impossible for anything to organize itself without genetic warmth, this primal warmth had informed all emanations that became real, and is still the wellspring of their being. What an infinite measure of roaring fire, for example, did the rocky mass of our earth absorb, that still rests within it, or acts, as is demonstrated by all volcanoes, all combustible minerals, yes, by each tiny pebble that is struck! That combustible matter pervades all vegetation, and that animal life is wholly occupied with the consumption of this combustible matter, has been proved by a number of recent experiments and experiences, so that the entire cycle of creation appears to be that fluids become solid and solids become fluid, that fire erupts and the flame is contained, and that vital powers are contained within organisms and unchained again. Now since the mass destined for the formation of our earth had its number, measure, and weight,[29] so it was that the inner wellspring pervading it also had to find its cycle. All of creation now feeds on itself; the wheel of created beings revolves without the addition of new ones; it destroys and constructs within the genetic limits within which it was placed by the first creative period. Nature, so to speak, through the power of the creator, became consummate art, and the force of the elements was bound in the cycle of fixed organizations, from which it cannot deviate because the shaping spirit has pervaded all it could pervade. But that such a work of art cannot eternally subsist, that the cycle which had a beginning necessarily has to have an end, arises from the nature of things. Beautiful creation, as it produced itself from a chaos, is working itself to a chaos again; its forms wear out; every organism refines itself and ages. Even the grand organism of the earth thus must find its grave from which, in due time, it will arise in a new form.

6. Continuation of the Most Ancient Written Tradition Concerning the Beginning of the History of Humankind

If my reader is pleased by the pure ideas of this ancient tradition, which I have presented without embellishment and free from any hypothesis, let us pursue it further after having cast a single glance at the whole of this portrait of creation. How does it so singularly distinguish itself above all the fables and traditions of the more advanced Asians? By means of cohesion, simplicity, and truth. However numerous the kernels of physics and history those others may contain, everything lies in wild confusion, as it had to lie, owing to the transmission of the unwritten or poetic priestly or popular traditions, a fabulous chaos as at the beginning of creation. This natural philosopher has overcome chaos, and he represents for us a structure that imitates the rich order of nature itself in its simplicity and cohesion. How did he come to this order and simplicity? We need only to compare him to the fables of other peoples to see the foundation of his purer philosophy of the history of the earth and humankind.

Firstly, he excluded everything incomprehensible to human beings and transcending their range of vision, confining himself to that which we can see with our eyes and encompass with our minds. What question, for example, has given rise to more controversy than that concerning the age of the world, the duration of the earth and of humankind? The Asiatic peoples with their infinite computations of time have been deemed infinitely wise, and the tradition of which we are speaking has been considered infinitely childish, because, contrary to all reason, yes, contrary to the evident testimony of the structure of the earth, it hastens over creation as if it were a small matter, rendering humankind so very young. In my opinion this is palpable injustice. Had Moses been nothing more than the collector of these ancient traditions, he, the learned Egyptian, could not have been ignorant of those eons of gods and semigods with which the Egyptians, as did all the nations of Asia, began the history of the world. Why then did he not weave them into his reports; why then did he, in a way to spite and demean them, compress the creation of the world into the symbol of the smallest portion of time? Evidently, he did so because he wanted to eliminate them from the memory of humankind as useless fables. It seems to me that therein he acted wisely, for previous to the completion of our earth, that is, before the origin of humankind and its coherent history, there is for us no chronology deserving that name. Let Buffon[30] assign numbers as great as he pleases to his first six epochs of nature, of twenty-six, thirty-five, fifteen, ten thousand years; the human intellect, conscious of its limitations, laughs at these numbers of the imagination, even if it admits the truth of the development of the epochs themselves; and still less does the historical memory wish to be burdened with them. Now the most ancient, enormous chronologies of peoples are evidently of the same sort as Buffon's; for they run back to those ages in which the powers of the gods and of the world held sway, thus into the ages of the formation of the earth, as they were constructed by nations extremely fond of enormous numbers, either on the basis of the revolutions of the skies or from half-understood symbols of the most ancient pictorial traditions. Thus, among the Egyptians, Vulcan, the creator of the world, reigned an infinite time; the sun, his child and successor, thirty thousand years; and then Saturn, and the other twelve gods, three thousand, nine hundred and eighty-four, before the demigods and their later successors, humans. It is the same with the more advanced Asian traditions of creation and chronology. According to the Parsees, the heavenly host of light reigned for three thousand years without an enemy; there followed another three thousand years before the wondrous figure of the bull appeared, from whose seed the creatures first sprung, and last of all Meschia and Meschiana, man and woman. The first epoch of the Tibetans, when the lahs reigned, is infinite; the second, eighty thousand years; the third, forty thousand; the fourth, twenty thousand; from here the epochs gradually descend to the tenth year, to rise gradually from there once again to the epoch of eighty thousand years. The periods of the Indians, abounding with the metamorphoses of their gods, and those of the Chinese, as abundant in metamorphoses of their most ancient kings, ascend still higher; infinities with which nothing could be done except to discard them, as Moses did, since, from the accounts of the traditions themselves, they belong to the creation of the earth, but not to the history of humankind.

Secondly, if it is disputed whether the world is young or old, both disputants have right on their side. The rock of our earth is very ancient, and its covering has required long revolutions; of that there can be no doubt. Here Moses leaves everyone at liberty to frame epochs as he pleases, and, with the Chaldeans, to let king *Alorus,* or light, *Uranus,* heaven, *Gaia,* the earth, *Helios,* the sun, and so on, reign as long as is desired. He does not reckon any epochs of this kind and, to obviate them, has represented his interlocking, systematic depiction precisely within the plainest cycle of a terrestrial revolution. But, the older these revolutions are and the longer their duration, the younger the human species must necessarily be, which, according to all traditions and to the nature of the thing itself, was the last production of the completed earth. Thus I thank the natural philosopher for his bold amputation of the monstrous ancient fable; for nature as it now is, and humankind as it presently exists, are sufficient for the range of my comprehension.

With regard to the creation of the human being, too, the tale repeats[*] that it took place as soon as it naturally could. "While there was neither plant nor tree upon the earth," it proceeds, "man, destined by nature to cultivate it, could not live: no rain yet descended, but mists arose, and from such an earth moistened with dew he was formed, and, animated with the breath of life, became a living being." It seems to me that the simple narrative says all that human beings, even after all explorations of physiology, are capable of knowing of their organization. In death our synthetic frame dissolves into earth, water, and air, which are now organically united in it; but the internal economy of animal life depends on the hidden stimulus, or balm, within the element of the air, which sets in motion the more perfect circulation of the blood, yes, the whole of the internal dialectic of the vital powers of our machine; and it is thus that the human being really becomes an active soul through the breath of life. Through it the human sustains and exerts the power to generate vital warmth, and to act as a self-moving, sentient, and thinking being. In this the most ancient philosophy is consistent with the most modern experiments.

The first abode of man was a garden[31]; and this feature of tradition, too, is as philosophy alone could invent. Life in the garden is the most appropriate for the newborn human species; for every other way of life, in particular that of agriculture, already demands a diversity of experiences and arts. Moreover, this feature of tradition also demonstrates what the whole disposition of our nature confirms, that the human being was not created to savagery, but to the gentle life, and thus, as the creator best knew the destination of his creature, the human being, like all other beings, was created as it were in his element, in the realm of living for which he was intended. Every form of savagery among the human tribes is degeneracy, to which the human being was impelled by necessity, climate, or a habit of passion; wherever this coercion ceases, the human being everywhere on earth lives a more gentle life, as is demonstrated by the history of nations. It was only the blood of animals that made the human being savage; the hunt, warfare, and also, unfortunately, the diverse vicissitudes of civil life. The most ancient tradition of the earliest peoples of the world knows nothing of those monsters of the forest, who as natural incarnations of the inhuman roamed about for millennia and are said thereby to have fulfilled their original destination. These savage tales first begin in remote, coarser regions, following upon far-flung dispersions of humankind; later poets willingly embellished them, followed at last by the compiling historian, and then again the abstracting philosopher; but abstractions provide as little a true original history of humankind as do the depictions of poets.

---

*Genesis 2:5–7.

Where then lay the garden in which the creator placed his gentle, defenseless creature? As this tradition is from the west of Asia, it places it eastward, farther up toward the Morn, on a hill, from which broke forth a stream, which from here divided into four great rivers.* No tradition can be more impartial; for, since every ancient nation is fond of representing itself as the firstborn, and considers its land as the birthplace of humankind, so it removes the primal land ever farther up to the highest spine of the inhabited earth. And where is this height of the earth? Where do the four named rivers originate in a spring or a stream, as the original scripture clearly indicates? Nowhere in our geography; and it is in vain that one exposes the names of the rivers to thousandfold torture, since an impartial look at the map of the world teaches us that nowhere on earth does the Euphrates, together with three other rivers, spring from one source or stream. But if we recollect the traditions of all the other more advanced peoples of Asia, we encounter this paradise of the highest earthly summit with its living primal spring, with its streams fructifying the world, in all of them. The Chinese and the Tibetans, the Indians and the Persians, speak of this primal mountain of creation, around which the lands, the seas, and the islands are situated, and from the heavenly summit of which the earth received its streams. This tale is not by any means devoid of physical principles; for without mountains our earth could not have running waters, and that all the streams of Asia flow from this summit is demonstrated by the map. Moreover, the tale elucidated here bypasses everything fabulous respecting the rivers of Paradise, and names the four most widely known in the world that flow from the mountains of Asia. It is true, they do not flow from one stream; but to the later collector of these traditions they must have been sufficient to place the primal seat of humankind in an eastern world remote to him.

And there can be no doubt for him that this primal seat should be a region between the Indian mountains. The land he describes, abounding in gold and precious stones, can hardly be any other than India, which has been known from the days of yore for these treasures. The river that flows round it is the twisting, sacred Ganges**; all of India recognizes it as the stream of paradise. That Gihon is the Oxus cannot be discounted; the Arabs still give it this name, and traces of the country it was said to water may be perceived in several adjacent Indian geographical terms.*** The two re-

---

*Genesis 2:10–14.

**The word Pison signifies a fructifying, inundating stream, and seems a translation of the name Ganges; thus, an ancient Greek translation already designates it as the Ganges, while the Arabs render it the Nile, and the country through which it flows India, which otherwise had no rhyme nor reason.[32]

***Cashgar, Kashmir, the Cathian Mountains, Caucasus, Cathay, etc.

maining rivers, the Tigris and the Euphrates, flow far to the west, it is true; but as the collector of these traditions lived at the western edge of Asia, these regions were necessarily lost to him in the remote distance, and it is possible that the third river that he named was meant to designate a more easterly Tigris, the Indus.* For it was the custom of the ancient peoples, when they migrated, to appropriate the myths of the mountains of the primal world to the mountains and rivers of their new country, and to nationalize them by means of a local mythology, as may be demonstrated from the Median Mountains to Olympus and Ida. In keeping with his own location, the collector of this tradition could do no other but indicate the broadest possible region presented to him by the tale. The Indians on the Paropamisus,[34] the Persians on the Imaaus,[35] and the Iberians[36] on the Caucasus were included here, and each was in the habit of placing his paradise in that part of the mountain range to which his tradition pointed. But our tale actually hints at the oldest of the traditions, for it places paradise above India, and gives the others merely as complements. What now? With a felicitous valley such as Kashmir, situated almost at the center of these rivers, surrounded by walls of mountains, famed both because of its healthful and refreshing water and its rich fertility and freedom from wild beasts, yes, praised to this day because of the beauty of its inhabitants, as the paradise of all paradises; may not this have been the primal seat of our species? But it will be shown in the following that all researches of this kind on our present earth are in vain; we will therefore consider the region as indeterminate as it is designated by the tradition, and continue to follow the thread of the narrative.

Of all the miraculous things and the adventurous figures with which the mythology of all of Asia richly populated its paradise of the primal world, this tradition retains only two miraculous trees, a speaking serpent, and a cherub; the philosopher has sorted out the innumerable multitude of others, and he has garbed those that he kept in a meaningful tale. In paradise there is one single forbidden tree, and this tree, according to the persuasion of the serpent, bears the fruit of divine knowledge, for which the human being longs. Could he long for anything more sublime? Could he be more enno-

---

Hidekel is the name of the third river and, according to *Otter,*[33] the Indus is still called by the Arabs *Eteck,* by the ancient Indians *Enider.* Even the ending of the word appears to be Indian: dewerkel, as they call their semigods, is the plural of dewin. It is probable, however, that the collector of the tradition took it for the Tigris, since he located it farther to the east, beyond Assyria. The more distant countries appeared to him to be too remote. The Phrathes too was probably another river, here translated in a generic way, or designated the most celebrated river of the east.

bled even in his fall? Compare this narrative, even if considered merely as an allegory, with the tales of other nations; it is the most refined and beautiful of all, a symbolical representation of what has always been the cause of human happiness and misery. Our ambiguous striving after knowledge not suited to us, the wanton use and abuse of our freedom, the restless extension and transgression of the limits within which it is necessary to confine a creature so feeble, who yet has to learn to govern himself, form the fiery wheel under which we groan, and which still constitutes nearly the entire circle of our life. The ancient philosopher of the history of humankind knew this as well as we know it, and he reveals its knot to us in a children's tale, which ties together all the ends of humankind. Even though the Indian tells of giants digging for the fruit of immortality, even though the Tibetan speaks of his lahs, degraded by misdeeds, nothing, it seems to me, equals the unsullied profundity, the childlike simplicity, of this tale, which retains only as much of the miraculous as serves for the identification of its time and region. All the dragons and wondrous figures of the ancient fairyland stretching over the Asiatic mountains, the simurgh[37] and soham, lahs, dewetas, jinns, deeves, and peries,[38] a mythology of this quarter of the globe widely spread in a thousand tales of Jinnistan,[39] Righiel, Meru, Albordi, and so on, disappear in the most ancient written tradition, and only a cherub keeps watch at the gate of paradise.

On the other hand, this instructive story informs us that the first-created humans held discourse with the instructing Elohim; that, under their guidance, through the knowledge of the animals, humans acquired language and sovereign reason; that, as humans were desirous in forbidden ways of resembling them also in the knowledge of evil, this knowledge was acquired to their misfortune, and humans thenceforward occupied another place and began a more artificial way of life: all of these are plain traits of the tradition that conceals behind the veil of a fabulous narrative more human truth than the grand system of the natural state of the autochthons. If, as we have seen, the superior qualities of humankind are inborn only as capacities, but are actually acquired and passed on through education, language, tradition, and art, not only must the threads of this humanity formed from all nations and corners of the world be derived from one source, but these threads must have been artfully tied together from the beginning, if humankind was to become what it was meant to be. As little as it is possible for a child to be abandoned and left to itself for years without perishing or becoming degenerate, so little could the human species be left to itself in its first germinating sprout. Humans, once accustomed to live like orangutans, would never of themselves act in spite of themselves and learn to transform from a speechless, hardened animality into humanity. If the deity thus willed that the human being exercise reason and foresight, it also had to care for humans with reason and foresight. Education, art, and culture were indispensable to humankind from the first moment of its existence; and thus the specific character of humankind of itself is a testimony to the intrinsic truth of this most ancient philosophy of our history.*

7. Conclusion of the Most Ancient Written Tradition Concerning the Beginning of Human History

The rest of what this ancient tale of names, years, the invention of arts, revolutions, etc., has preserved for us is in everything the echo of a national narrative. We do not know the name of the first human being, or the language he spoke. For Adam signifies a man of earth, Eve a living being,[40] in the language of *this* people; their names are symbols of their history, and every other people gives them other significant names. The inventions considered here are only those that suit a pastoral and agricultural people of western Asia, and even of them the tradition knows nothing but names. The enduring tribe, it says, endured; the possessor possessed; he who was mourned had been murdered; in such verbal hieroglyphics is drawn the genealogical tree of two modes of living, the pastoral and that of the agriculturalists or cave dwellers. The history of the Sethites and the Kenites[41] is at bottom nothing more than the account of the followers of the two most ancient modes of life, called in the Arabic Bedouins and Kabyles,** who still remain distinct from and at enmity with each other, in the east. The genealogical narrative of a pastoral people of this region intended to do nothing but take note of these tribal characteristics.

The same goes for the so-called Great Flood. For certain as it appears from natural history that the habitable earth was ravaged by an inundation, and that Asia bears incontestable marks of this deluge, what is delivered to us in this tale is nothing more nor less than a national narrative. With great care, the compiler has brought together several traditions,*** and he even provides his tribe's daily chronicle of this terrible revolution; the tone of this narrative is also so fully evocative of the mentality of this tribe that it

---

*But how did the Elohim now deal with humankind; that is, how did they teach, caution, and instruct them? If it be not equally bold to ask this question as to answer it, the tradition itself will give us an answer in another place.

**Cain* is called by the Arabs *Kabyle;*[42] the castes of the Kabyles are called Kabeil; the Bedouins, even according to the signification of their name, are lost shepherds, *inhabitants of the desert.* Thus it is with the names *Cain, Enoch, Nod, Jabal-* and *Jubal-,* or *Tubal-Cain,*[43] each expressive of a tribe and a way of life.

***Genesis 6–8. See *Eichhorn's* introduction to the Old Testament, vol. 2, p. 370.

would amount to abuse to remove it from the limits within which, after all, it finds its credibility. As one family of *this* people, with a richly endowed household, saved itself, so other families among other peoples could also have escaped, as their traditions demonstrate; thus in Chaldea, Xisuthrus[44] escaped with his clan and a number of animals (without which humans were then unable to sustain themselves) in almost identical manner, and in India, Vishnu himself was the rudder of the ship that conveyed the distressed people to land. Similar tales exist among all the nations of this part of the world, each adapted to its tradition and region, and, as persuasive as they are that the deluge of which they speak was general in Asia, they help us at once out of the strait in which we unnecessarily confined ourselves when we took every circumstance of a family history exclusively for the history of the world, thereby depriving this history itself of its well-founded credibility.

It is no different with the genealogical table of these tribes after the deluge; it confines itself to the limits of its ethnology and its geographical region, not roaming beyond it to India, China, eastern Tartary, and so on. The three principal tribes of those who were saved are evidently the people on either side of the western Asiatic mountains, including the eastern coast of Europe and the northern coast of Africa, as far as they were known to the collector of the tradition.[*] He traces them as well as he can, and endeavors to connect them with his genealogical table; but he does not give us a general map of the world or a genealogy of all peoples. The pains that have been taken to make all the peoples of the earth, according to this genealogy, descendants of the Hebrews and half-brothers of the Jews, are contradictory not only to chronology and universal history, but to the point of view of the narrative itself, which was almost totally deprived of its credibility by these kinds of exaggerations. On all the primal mountains of the world, peoples, languages, and states form themselves after the deluge without waiting for the legation of a Chaldean family; and in ancient Asia, the primal seat of humanity and also the most heavily settled part of the world, there evidently exist to this day the most ancient institutions, the most ancient customs and languages, of which this western branch of a later people knew nothing, and

---

[*]*Japhet's* name, as well as his blessing, *was widely known;* the same is true for the way of life, and in part even for the name, of the peoples north of the mountains. *Shem* comprised tribes with whom the name, that is, the ancient tradition of religion, scripture, and culture was preeminently associated, and who therefore claimed for themselves over others, especially the Hamites, the advantage of civilization. *Ham* derived his name from heat, and he belongs to the torrid zone.[45] In the three sons of Noah, therefore, we find nothing but the three continents of Europe, Asia, and Africa, as far as they lay within the sphere of this tradition.

could know nothing. It would be as strange to ask whether the Chinese descended from Cain or Abel, that is, from a tribe of troglodytes,[46] shepherds, or husbandmen, as it would be to ask whether the American sloth once hung from a beam in Noah's Ark. But I ought to enlarge here on this subject; yes, even the examination of an issue as important for our history as the shortening of the human lifespan and the above-mentioned great deluge itself must await discussion at another place. Suffice it to say, that the center of the largest continent, the primal mountains of Asia, has provided for humankind its first dwelling, and has maintained itself through every revolution of the earth. Not first raised through the great deluge from the bottom of the sea, but, according to both natural history and the most ancient tradition, the primal seat of humanity, it became the first great theater of the nations, the instructive inspection of which we shall now pursue.

Part IV

Reflections on World History

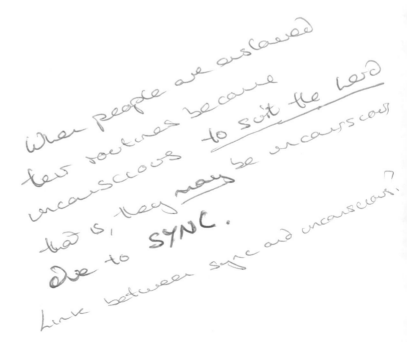

When people are enslaved few routines become unconscious to suit the herd that is, they *may* be unconscious due to SYNC.

Link between sync and unconscious?

~ 25 ~

China

The following three chapters are representative parts (three out of five) of Herder's East Asian account in his *Reflections on the Philosophy of History of Humankind.* The reflections on the Far East constitute a separate section (Book Eleven) within the third part of the *Reflections,* while the following three books are dedicated to other regions: Book Twelve to the Near East, Book Thirteen to Greece, and Book Fourteen to Italy. All these books follow the same pattern by opening with facts from geography, demography, and culture. In a concluding chapter, Herder then tries to point out commonalities that provide evidence for the existence of globally valid laws of history. However, he is not simply the impartial observer of world history and the provider of historical knowledge, nor is he satisfied with reflecting the facts, as if in a mirror. Although one of Herder's principles as a historian and a philosopher of history is to derive hypotheses not out of mere speculation but out of the accessible facts at his time, every now and then he presents harsh criticism of distant cultures, as is the case with this chapter on China. Herder assumed that Europe would play a leading role in the history of the coming nineteenth century. Seen from the historical angle of Herder's historiography, his criticism cannot be ruled out as a result of a narrow-minded modern "Eurocentrism." He does not pursue history from a merely subjective perspective, but asks for the relevant contributions within the process of history: "Which country or culture contributes in a decisive way to the course of world history?"

In the eastern corner of Asia, at the feet of the mountains, lies a country which calls itself, in terms of age and culture, the first of all countries, the central flower of the world; and certainly China is one of the most ancient and the most remarkable. Smaller than Europe, it boasts a proportionally greater number of inhabitants than this densely populated continent, for it counts in excess of twenty-five million tax-paying husbandmen, one thousand, five hundred and seventy-two towns large and small, one thousand, one hundred and ninety-three castles, three thousand, one hundred and fifty-eight stone bridges, two thousand seven hundred and ninety-six temples, two thousand, six hundred and six monasteries, ten thousand, eight hundred and nine ancient edifices, and so on[*]; all of these, including mountains and rivers, warriors and scholars, products and commercial goods, are annually entered in long catalogs by the governments of the eighteen provinces into which the country is divided. Various travelers agree that, except for Europe and perhaps ancient Egypt, there is no country where so much industry has been employed on roads and rivers, bridges and canals, and even the terracing of mountains and rock, as China; all of these, together with the Great Wall, give testimony to the patient diligence of human hands. From Canton, one can go by ship almost all the way to Peking, and so the entire empire, cut through by mountains and deserts, has been laboriously connected by highways, canals, and rivers; villages and towns float on the waters, and the domestic trade between the provinces is brisk and lively. Agriculture is the main pillar of China's economic constitution; we are told of luxuriant fields of grain and rice, of irrigated deserts, of barren mountains rendered fertile; every plant and herb is cultivated and used; the same is true for metals and minerals, except for gold, which is not mined. The country is rich in animals; lakes and rivers teem with fish; the silkworm alone supports thousands of diligent people. All classes of people, regardless of age, even the infirm, the blind, and the deaf, are obliged to engage in productive labor and crafts. Gentleness and flexibility, courteous civility and affable conduct, are the basic lessons learned by the Chinese from childhood on and practiced by them incessantly throughout life. Their government and laws are marked by regularity and exactly fixed order. The entire system of the state, in all the relations and duties of the estates to one another, is based on the respect owed by the son to the father, and by the subject to the father of the country, who governs and protects them like children through the chain of command of the authorities; can there be a nobler principle for the governance of human beings? No hereditary nobility, but only the nobility of merit prevails in all estates; men of proven worth are destined to positions of honor, and this honor alone confers dignity. The subject is not compelled to abide by any religion, and no religion is persecuted unless it opposes the state; the followers of the teachings of Confucius, of Lao-tzu, and Fo[2] and even Jews and Jesuits, once admitted to the state, live peace-

---

[*]Leontiew's excerpts of the *Sinesischen Reichsgeographie,* in Büsching's *Historisches und geographisches Magazin,* part 14, pp. 411 f. In Hermann's *Beiträge zur Physik* (Berlin: 1786), part 1,[1] the size of the empire is estimated as one hundred and ten thousand German square miles, and the population as one hundred and four million sixty-nine thousand, two hundred and fifty-four, with nine persons per family.

fully side by side. Their laws are unalterably founded on moral teachings, their moral teachings on the sacred books of the ancestors; the emperor is their sovereign pontiff, the son of heaven, the guardian of ancient customs, the soul of the body politic pervading all its members. If each of these conditions were to prove effective and these principles be carried into actual practice, could one conceive of a more perfect political constitution? The entire empire would be the home of virtuous, well-bred, diligent, modest, and happy children and brothers.

Everyone knows the superior image of the Chinese government sent to Europe, especially by missionaries, to be admired there not only by speculative philosophers, but even by statesmen, as a political ideal; until at last, since the current of human opinions refracts at opposite angles, incredulity awakened to deny them their high culture, and even their remarkable particularity. Some of these European objections have had the good fortune to be answered in China itself, though rather in the Chinese vein,[*] and as most of the books that form the foundation of their laws and moral teachings, including the extensive history of their empire, and other undeniably impartial reports, lie before us[**]; so it would be regrettable if we could not find a middle way between the exaggerated praise and blame, which would thus probably point the correct path to truth. The question of the chronological age of the empire may thereby be placed entirely aside; for, as the origin of all empires on earth is wrapped in darkness, it may be irrelevant to the explorer of human history whether this remarkable people needed a few more millennia or not for its development; it is sufficient that this development took place, and that we are able to discern the obstacles in its gradual course that prevented it from going farther.

Now these obstacles are clearly evident to our eyes in the character of this people, the place of its abode, and its history. That the nation is of Mongol origin is demonstrated by their features, by their gross or odd taste, yes, even by their clever artfulness, and by the earliest seat of their culture. It was in the north of China that their first kings ruled; it was here that the foundations were laid for the semi-Tatar despotism that afterward, gilded

---

[*]*Memoires concernant l'histoire, les sciences, les arts, les moeurs, les usages . . . des Chinois,* part 2, pp. 365 ff.[3]

[**]Aside from the older editions of a few of the Chinese classics by Father Noel, Couplet, et al., the edition of the I Ching by de Guignes, the *Histoire générale de Chine* by Mailla, the above-mentioned *Mémoires concernant les Chinois* in ten volumes quarto, in which translations of some original works of the Chinese are inserted, etc., afford materials sufficient for giving correct ideas regarding this people. Among the many accounts by missionaries, the one by Father le Comte is especially to be esteemed, because of the soundness of his judgment. *Nouveaux Mémoires sur l'état présent de la Chine,* 3 vols., 8° (Paris: 1697).[4]

with moral maxims, extended its sway through various revolutions down to the South Sea. A feudal Tatar constitution was for centuries the bond that tied the vassals to the ruler, and the many wars of these vassals against one another, the frequent overthrows of the throne at their hands, yes, even the entire conduct of the emperor's court, his governance through mandarins— an ancient institution, not first introduced to China by the successors of Genghis Khan or the Manchus[5]—all of these show what kind of nation it is and evince its genetic character; this uniquely shaped character is not easily lost to the eyes of the beholder of the whole and its parts, including their dress, food, customs, domestic way of life, and the varieties of their arts as well as their amusements. Now, as little as an individual person can alter his genius, that is, his innate character and complexion, so little could this northeastern Mongol people deny its natural makeup by means of its acquired institutions, though they endured for millennia. It was planted upon this spot on the globe, and as the compass needle in China does not have the European deviation, this branch of humankind, in this region, could never turn into Greeks and Romans. They were and remained Chinese, a people endowed by nature with small eyes, snub noses, flat foreheads, scant beards, large ears, and protruding bellies; whatever could be achieved by such a people was indeed achieved; nothing else could be demanded of it.[*]

All accounts agree that the Mongol nations of the northeastern heights of Asia are distinguished by an acuteness of hearing, as readily accounted for among them as it would be vain to seek in other nations; the language of the Chinese bears testimony to this delicacy of the ear. Only the auditory organs of a Mongol could come to the point of forming a language out of three hundred and thirty syllables, differentiating each word by five or more accents, so that the lord would not be called beast, and the most ridiculous confusions liable to occur at any given moment would be avoided; it stands to reason that a European ear and European organs of speech will hardly ever, if at all, accommodate to this coerced syllabic music. What want of inventiveness in matters large, and what unfortunate excessive refinement in trifles was required to find for this language from a few raw hieroglyphics the infinite number of eighty thousand compound characters, resulting in the six or more modes of writing with which the Chinese nation distinguishes itself among all the peoples on earth. It took a basic Mongol makeup for the Chinese to become used, in matters of the imagination, to dragons and monsters; in the art of drawing, to that careful minuteness of irregular figures; in the pleasures of the eye, to the formless jumble of their gardens; in respect to their edifices, to vast size or punctilious smallness; in

---

[*]See Chapter 19 of this volume.

their parades, dress, and amusements, to that vain splendor, to those lantern festivals and fireworks, to excessively long fingernails, to compressed and misshapen feet, and to a barbaric train of attendants, genuflections, ceremonies, distinctions, and courtesies. In all these, there is so little evidence of an appreciation of genuine natural proportionality, so little feeling for inner calm, beauty, and dignity, that only a deranged sensibility could arrive at this course of political culture and let itself be so completely shaped by it. As the Chinese are excessively fond of gilded paper and varnish, the neatly painted lines of their intricate characters, and the jingle of their well-constructed sentences, the cast of their minds thoroughly resembles this gilded paper and varnish, these characters, and this jingling of their syllables. Nature seems to have denied to them, as well as to several other nations of this corner of the world, the gift of grand and free invention in the sciences; while, on the other hand, she has bountifully endowed their little eyes with that adroitness, that clever industriousness and refinement, that artistic talent for imitating whatever their cupidity found useful. Eternally in motion, eternally industrious, they come and go for the sake of gain and service, so that one still may take them, even in their highest political manifestation, for wandering Mongols; for notwithstanding all their innumerable regulations, they have not yet learned the rule that pairs acquisitiveness with rest in such a way that each occupation will find everyone in his place. Their pharmaceutical art, like their commerce, amounts to a delicate and deceptive feeling of the pulse, reflective of their entire character with its sensuous refinement and uninventive ignorance. The makeup of the people represents a remarkable uniqueness in history, because it reveals what a Mongol people, unmixed with other nations, could become or fail to become by means of a highly developed political culture; that the Chinese in their corner of the world, like the Jews, have kept free from mixing with other peoples is demonstrated by their vain pride, if by nothing else. Let them have acquired particular branches of knowledge wherever they will; the entire structure of their language and constitution, their institutions, and their way of thought are peculiarly their own. Just as they are averse to the grafting of trees, so they themselves, notwithstanding their various encounters with other peoples, to this day have remained unmixed, a Mongol tribe, in one corner of the world, degraded to the Chinese mode of slave culture.

All human cultural formation takes place through education; the mode of Chinese education, together with the national character, contributed to the fact that the Chinese are what they are and have not progressed any further. Since, according to the Mongol nomad custom, childlike obedience was the foundation of all virtues, not only in the family but now also in the state, it was inevitable that over the course of time that specious modesty and that complaisant courtesy had to develop, that are celebrated as characteristic features of the Chinese even by hostile tongues. But as beneficial as this principle may be for nomads, what would be its consequences in a large state? In such a state, in which filial obedience finds no limits; in which the grown man who has children of his own, and conducts an adult's business, is burdened with the same duties that are appropriate only to the uneducated child; in such a state, in which these duties were also imposed by any kind of autonomous authority that after all is only figuratively called patriarchal, out of coercion and necessity, not because of the sweetness of natural inclination; in such a state, what else could result, yes, had to result from this unnatural quest for a new human heart but the accommodation of the genuine human heart to deceitfulness? If the mature man is forced to follow the obedience of the child, he must surrender the strength of autonomy that nature has made the duty of his years; empty ceremonies take the place of heartfelt integrity, and the son who drifted along in childish devotion to his mother during his father's life will neglect her after his death, if the law but terms her a concubine. It is the same with the filial duties toward the mandarins; they are not the product of nature, but of authority; they are customs, and as soon as they run counter to nature, they become debilitating, false customs. Hence the discrepancy between the Chinese legal and moral teaching and the actual history of China. How often have the empire's heirs deposed the father from the throne! How often have the fathers raged against their children! Covetous mandarins cause the starvation of thousands, and when their misdeeds come before the sovereign father, they are caned, without effect, like little boys. Hence the want of masculine strength and honor, which is reflected even in the visual representations of their heroes and grandees; honor has become a childish duty; strength has been degraded to modish obedience to the state; service is rendered not by a noble stallion, but by a tamed mule often conditioned to play the role of the fox from morning to nightfall.

   This childish confinement of human reason, strength, and sensibility necessarily exerted a debilitating influence upon the entire structure of the state. When once education is nothing but affectation, when affects and manners not only bind but overwhelm all the relations of life, what treasures of effectiveness does the state lose, particularly the noblest effectiveness of the human heart and spirit. Who is not astonished, upon observing in the history of the Chinese the course and management of their affairs, with how much effort nothing is accomplished? Here a collegium is employed on what, to be well done, should be done by one person; here inquiry is made, though the answer is clearly evident; they come and go, put off and avoid, merely so that the ceremonial of childish respect for the state will not be infringed. The martial as well as the reflective spirit must be absent from a nation bedded on warm stove tiles, drinking warm water from morning till night. In China, royal favor is open only to virtues such as regularity in a beaten track, acuteness in the pursuit of personal gain and a thousand clever tricks, and the childish preoccupation with multiple tasks that lacks the mature reflectiveness that asks whether this or that action need be undertaken at all, and whether it might not be done better. The emperor himself is harnessed to this yoke; he must set a good example and exaggerate each movement like the pivotal man in a military drill. He not only makes sacrifices in the hall of his ancestors on days of special observance, but is compelled to do so in carrying out any business, at any moment of his life, and any praise or blame coming his way may be equally undeserved.*

Is it to be wondered at that a nation of this kind should have invented little in the sciences according to the European standard, or that it has remained at the same point for some thousands of years? Even Chinese books of law and morality continually follow the same circle, and carefully and precisely say the same things about childish duties, in a hundred different ways, with systematic hypocrisy. Among these people, astronomy and music, poetry and the art of war, painting and architecture, are what they were centuries ago, children of their eternal laws and of their unalterably childish institutions. The empire is an embalmed mummy, painted with hieroglyphics and wrapped in silk; its internal life is like that of animals in hibernation. Therefore the seclusion from, the spying upon, and the placing of restrictions on all that is foreign; therefore the pride of the nation that focuses only on itself and neither knows nor cares for anything outside itself. It is a nation thrust into a corner of the earth, placed by fate outside the connectedness of nations, and to that end entrenched behind mountains, deserts, and a sea virtually devoid of the shelter of bays. Without this geographical situation, it would hardly have remained what it is; for the fact that its constitution has held up under the Manchus proves nothing but that it is founded within itself, and that the even coarser conquerors found such childish slavery quite a convenient seat for their dominion. They needed to change nothing in it and placed themselves upon it and reigned. The nation, in the meanwhile, serves as slavishly in every joint of its self-made engine of state as if it had been specifically invented to serve such slavery.

---

*Even the much praised Ch'ien-lung emperor was deemed the most extreme tyrant in the provinces; and in such an extensive empire, with such a constitution, this must be the case, let the emperor's way of thinking be what it will.

All accounts of the language of the Chinese agree that with its artificial way of thinking it contributed immeasurably to the makeup of this people; for is not the language of every country the vessel in which the ideas of the people are formed, sustained, and passed on, particularly when a nation is tied to its language as firmly as this one, and draws all its culture from it? The language of the Chinese is a dictionary of morals, that is, of courtesy and good manners; it differs not only according to provinces and cities, but also by estates and in individual written works, so that the largest part of the people's learned diligence concentrates upon language as a tool, without accomplishing anything with that tool. In this language everything depends on the regularity of trifles; with few sounds it says much, in order to convey with many strokes one and the same sound, and with many books one and the same thing. What wretched diligence is needed for the penciling and printing of their writings! And it is precisely this diligence that is their passion and their art, as they take greater pleasure in beautiful lettering than in the most enchanting painting, and they esteem the monotonous jingling of their moral maxims and compliments as the pinnacle of elegance and wisdom. Nothing but an empire as extensive as the Chinese, and the Chinese fondness for industry, could have produced, for example, forty books, painted in eight large volumes, on the single town of K'ai-feng,* and to distribute this product of toilsome exactitude far and wide at any command and word of praise by the emperor. The monument of the emigration of the Torguts[6] is an immense book of stones,** and the whole of the learning of the Chinese is exhausted in artificial and political hieroglyphics. The impact which this mode of writing alone leaves upon the soul that thinks in it must be incredible. It reduces thoughts to pictorial symbols and turns the entire way of thought of the nation into arbitrary characters that are painted or written in the air.

This exhibition of Chinese peculiarities is not by any means based on hostile contempt, for it is drawn, feature by feature, from the accounts of their warmest advocates, and it may be supported by a hundred proofs from every aspect of their institutions. This exhibition is nothing more than a reflection of the nature of the case, that is, the representation of a people formed from remote antiquity in such a geographical location, with such a makeup, governed by such principles, with such resources, and under such circumstances, a people which, contrary to the usual course of fate among other peoples, preserved its way of thought for so long a time. If ancient Egypt were still before our eyes, we would observe, without being allowed

---

*Mémoires concernant les Chinois, vol. 2, p. 375.
**Ibid., vol. 1, p. 329.

to think of reciprocal influence, in many aspects a similarity,[7] which according to the inherited traditions could only have been modified by reason of geography. It was the same with several other peoples who were once at the same stage of cultural development; but these have moved on or have perished and mingled with others; ancient China, at the edge of the world, with its semi-Mongolian institutions, remains standing like a ruin of primeval time. It would be difficult to prove that the basic outlines of its culture were brought by Greeks from Bactria,[8] or by Tatars from Balkh; the fabric of its constitution is certainly indigenous, and the slight influence of foreign peoples upon it are readily recognized and singled out. I honor the Chings,[9] as a Chinese would, for their superior principles, and the name of Confucius is a great one to me, though I do not overlook the fetters that bound him too, and which he imposed for eternity, with the best of intentions, upon the superstitious mob and the whole Chinese institution of state by means of his political morality. Because of this political morality, this people, like various other nations of that latitude, has remained mired in its development, in its childhood as it were, because this mechanical drive train of moral teaching permanently retarded the free progress of the spirit and a second Confucius did not arise in the despotic empire. When the time comes that the enormous state either divides itself, or more enlightened Ch'ien-lungs take the paternal resolution to send forth as colonists those whom they cannot feed, and to ease the yoke of customs, thereby introducing, and not without considerable peril, a freer autonomy of spirit and heart; thereupon—but even then Chinese will remain Chinese, just as Germans remain Germans, and just as there are no ancient Greeks born at the eastern extension of Asia. It is the evident purpose of nature that everything will thrive on earth that is capable of thriving, and that this very variety of creations give praise to the creator. The body of laws and morality erected as a childhood experiment by human reason in China is found nowhere else on earth in such stability; let it remain in its place, without ever giving rise in Europe to a secluded China filled with childish piety toward its despots. This nation will retain to its end the fame of its diligence, of its sensual acuity, of its refined artfulness in a thousand practical things. Porcelain and silk, gunpowder and lead, the mariner's compass perhaps, the art of printing, bridge building and navigation, aside from many other refined manufactures and arts, were known to the Chinese before they were known to Europe, except that in almost all the arts they lacked spiritual progress and the drive to improve. For the rest, that China secludes itself from our European nations and that it places extreme restrictions upon the Dutch as well as Russians and Jesuits, is not only consistent with its entire way of thinking, but certainly also politically acceptable, as long as the Chinese see all around themselves the conduct of the Europeans in East India and on the islands, in northern Asia and in their own country. Dizzied by Tatar pride, the Chinese despise the merchant who leaves his own country, and they exchange goods of deceptive value for what appears to them to be the most solid merchandise; they take his silver and give in exchange millions of pounds of debilitating tea to the perdition of Europe.

~ 26 ~

India

Even though the teaching of the Brahmins is no more than a branch of a widely dispersed religion, which has formed autonomous sects from Tibet to Japan, it nevertheless merits particular attention in the land of its birth, because it formed there the most singular and perhaps the most enduring governance of the world—that is, the division of the Indian nation into four or more castes, over which the Brahmins rule as the first caste. It is improbable that they attained this dominion by means of physical subjection, for they are not the military caste of the people; this, including the ruler himself, is the next highest caste in line; moreover, they do not base their renown on any such martial means, even in their mythology. Their dominion over people is based on their origin, according to which they deem themselves to have sprung from the head of the Brahma, as the warriors claim to have sprung from his breast, and the other castes from the other members of his body. It is upon this origin that the laws and all the institutions of the nation are founded, according to which the Brahmins, as an indigenous caste, as the head, are part of the body of the nation. Divisions of this kind according to caste have also marked the simplest organization of human society in other regions, in imitation of nature, which divides trees into branches, and people into castes and families. Such was the system in Egypt, which was structured like India with its hereditary crafts and arts; and we see even more frequently in other nations that the caste of the sages and priests elevated itself to the highest level. It seems to me that, at this stage of cultural development, such a system was rooted in the nature of things, since wisdom is superior to strength, and since the caste of priests in ancient times appropriated almost all political wisdom for itself. The renown of the priests declines only with the diffusion of enlightenment through all estates, and it is for this reason that priests have so frequently opposed a more general enlightenment.

The history of India, of which we unfortunately still know little, affords us a clear hint respecting the origin of the Brahmins.* It makes Brahma, a wise and learned man, the inventor of many arts, in particular that of writing, the vizier of one of their ancient kings, Krishna, whose son is said to have legislated the division of his people into the four well-known castes. He placed the son of the Brahma at the head of the first caste, which included astrologers, physicians, and priests; others of noble descent were named the hereditary governors of provinces, which resulted in the second order of the Indian ranks. The third class was assigned to agriculture, and the fourth to the arts and crafts, and this establishment was to continue forever. He built the city of Bahar to house the philosophers, and since the capital of his empire and the most ancient schools of the Brahmins were principally located at the Ganges river, this explains why the Greeks and the Romans took so little note of them. For they were not familiar with these deeper regions of India, as Herodotus describes only the peoples along the Indus river and along the northern route of the gold trade, and Alexander advanced no farther than the river Hydaspes. One should not be surprised, therefore, that at first the Greeks and the Romans obtained only general accounts of the Brahmins, that is, the solitary philosophers, who lived in the manner of the talapoins[2]; however, they later also heard vague rumors of the Samanaeans and Germans at the Ganges, of the division of the people into castes, and of their doctrine respecting the migration of souls. Even these mutilated myths, however, show that the institution of the Brahmins is an ancient one and that it is indigenous to the land of the Ganges, a fact that is confirmed by the very ancient monuments of Jagannath,[3,**] Bombay, and in other regions of the western part of the peninsula. Both these idols and the entire institutions of the temples devoted to them are in keeping with the way of thought and the mythology of the Brahmins, spreading from their sacred Ganges throughout all India and farther south, and receiving veneration that increased proportionally with the ignorance of the people. The sacred Ganges, as the Brahmins' place of birth, remained the preeminent seat of their sacred idols, even though as Brahmins they are not only a religious caste, but actually a political caste that—like the orders of the Lamas, the Levites, the Egyptian priesthood, and others—were everywhere considered part of the very ancient Indian imperial constitution.

---

*Dow's *History of Hindostan,* vol. 1, pp. 10, 11.[1]

**Zend-Avesta, by d'Anquetil, vol. 1, pp. 81 f; Niebuhr's *Reisebeschreibung,* vol. 2, pp. 31 f.[4]

For thousands of years, the influence of this order upon the minds of the people has been singularly profound; for, in spite of the Mongol yoke, which they have borne for so long, its renown and doctrine not only remain yet unshaken but also exert upon the governance of the Hindus a power hardly shown by any other religion.* The character, the way of life, and the customs of the people, to the most minute functions, even to their thoughts and words, are the result of their influence; and though many aspects of the Brahmin religion are extremely oppressive and burdensome, the religion itself remains as sacred as the natural laws of God even to the lowest of the castes. Such of them as embrace a foreign religion are for the most part malefactors and outcasts, or poor deserted children. The sense of superiority, too, with which the Indian, even under the pressure of extreme want, contemplates the European whom he serves is a sufficient guarantee that this people, while it exists, will never mix with any other. No doubt the character of the nation and the climate are the basic cause of this unparalleled effect, for no people exceeds them in patience or in gentler submissiveness of soul. However, that the Indian does not follow any foreigner in doctrine and customs is evidently due to the fact that the institution of the Brahmins has so completely taken hold of his soul and of his entire life as to leave no room for any other. This explains the many customs and festivals, the many gods and tales, the many sacred places and good works, so that from childhood on the imaginative faculty of the Indian is occupied and he is reminded at almost every moment of his life of what he is. In the face of this dominion over the soul, which will endure, as far as I can see, as long as an Indian shall exist, all European institutions touch only the surface.

The question whether something is beneficial or evil is necessarily complicated in respect to all human institutions. Undoubtedly the institution of the Brahmins, when first established, was beneficial; otherwise it could not have spread as widely, penetrated as deeply, and endured as long as it did. The human heart shakes off what is pernicious to it as soon as it can, and though the Indian is capable of enduring more than any other, even he would not welcome poison. It is also incontestable that the Brahmins formed their people to such a degree of gentleness, courtesy, temperance, and chastity, or at least have so confirmed them in these virtues, that Europeans, compared with them, frequently appear as impure, inebriated, and deranged. Their manners and language are of free and easy delicacy, their discourse is peaceful, their bodies are clean, and their way of life is simple

---

*See, on this subject, *Dow, Holwell, Sonnerat, Alexander Ross, Mackintosh*, the Missionary Reports of Halle, the *Lettres édifiantes*, and any other description of Indian religion and ethnology.[5]

and nonviolent. Their children are raised without severity, yet they are not destitute of knowledge, and still less of quiet diligence and refined imitative art; even the lowest castes learn to read, to write, and to practice arithmetic. As teachers of the young, the Brahmins cannot be denied the merit of having been benefactors of humankind for some thousands of years. Let the reader observe the accounts in the Missionary Reports of Halle of the common sense and benign disposition of the Brahmins and the Malabars in their observations, questions, and answers, as in their entire conduct, and he will rarely find himself on the side of those who would convert them. The leading idea the Brahmins entertain of God is so grand and beautiful, their morality so pure and sublime, and even their fables when pervaded by reason are so refined and charming, that I cannot altogether ascribe to their inventors that reputation of absurdity, even in the monstrous and adventurous, which they probably gained over the course of time by passing through the mouths of the common people. It is in itself not without value that, despite all the oppression of the Mohammedans and Christians, the order of Brahmins has preserved its artful and beautiful language,* and with it some of the relics of ancient astronomy and chronology, jurisprudence, and medicine**; for the mechanical manner in which they exercise these sciences is sufficient for their sphere of life, and whatever is lacking in the deepening of their sciences is made up for by the intensity of their impact and by their duration. Moreover, the Hindus do not persecute others, they leave each and all to their religion, way of life, and wisdom; why should they not be left to their own, and be left to the errors of their inherited tradition, and thus be considered deceived for good cause? Compared to all the sects of the Fu that pervade the world of eastern Asia, this is the flower, more learned, more humane, more useful, more noble, than all the bonzes, lamas, and talapoins.

This said, it must not be concealed, that in this, as in all other human institutions, there is much that is oppressive. Not to mention the endless coercion, which the confinement of the different ways of life to hereditary castes necessarily involves, as it all but completely precludes all free improvement and perfecting of the arts, there is the contempt with which the lowest of the castes, the pariahs, are treated. They are not only condemned to carry out the most menial of tasks, and eternally secluded from contact with all the other castes, but they are even deprived of human rights and religion, for no one may touch a pariah, and the very sight of one profanes a

*See Halhed's *Grammar of the Bengal Language,* printed at Hoogly in Bengal (1788).
**See le Gentil, *Voyage dans les mers de l'Inde,* vol. 1; Halhed's *Code of Gentoo Laws;* et al.[6]

Brahmin. Though this debasement is attributed to many reasons, among others that the pariahs may be a subjugated nation, none of them is sufficiently verified by history; in their makeup, at least, they do not differ from the other Indians. Thus here, as in so many other matters of ancient origin, one must recur to the earliest merciless initiative, according to which perhaps the very poor, or the malefactors and despised, were destined to a form of debasement, to which their innocent and numerous descendants continue, incredibly, to submit. The flaw here lies solely in the classification by families, according to which the lowest lot of life must fall to some, and the purity arrogated by the other castes over the course of time was bound to increase the burden that rested upon them. Now what would be more natural than eventually to consider it a punishment from heaven to be born a pariah, and, according to the doctrine of the transmigration of souls, to have earned this station in life by fate, because of misdeeds committed in a previous life? This doctrine of the transmigration of souls, as great as its hypothesis was in the mind of its first inventors, and as beneficial as it may have been for the advancement of the humane, must necessarily have occasioned much evil also, as does every other delusion that reaches beyond humankind. In that it indeed aroused a false compassion for all that lives, it thereby diminished genuine compassion for the misery of our own kind, the unfortunate of which were presumed to be malefactors burdened by past crimes, or as people tested by the hand of fate whose virtue would be rewarded in a future state of existence. Accordingly, a lack of compassion is observed even in the gentler Hindus, which is probably the consequence of their basic makeup, but even more of their profound surrender to eternal fate, a faith that plunges the human being into an abyss and blunts his active sensibility. The burning of widows on the funeral pyres of their husbands may be reckoned among the barbarous consequences of this doctrine; for whatever the causes of its initial introduction, whether it became customary in emulation of great souls or as a form of punishment, the doctrine of the Brahmins has incontestably ennobled the unnatural customs of that world, and given the unfortunate victims of the slaughter reasons to welcome death for the sake of the future state of existence. No doubt this cruel custom renders the life of the husband more dear to the wife, as she becomes inseparable from him even in death, and cannot remain behind without disgrace, but is this worth the sacrifice, when tacit custom alone gives it the force of law? Lastly, I pass over the manifold deception and superstition inevitable in the Brahminical system by the very nature of astronomy and chronology, medicine and religion, propagated as they were by oral tradition, and turned into the secret science of one caste; the pernicious consequence for the entire country was this, that any government of Brahmins will sooner or later render a people ripe for subjugation. The warrior caste soon had to become unwarlike, since its assigned functions ran counter to the principles of the religion, and since it was subordinate to another, nobler caste which abhorred all shedding of blood. It would have been fortunate for such a peaceful people to have dwelt on a solitary island, remote from all conquerors; but at the foot of the mountains inhabited by those human beasts of prey, the bellicose Mongols, and near those coasts abounding with bays to receive covetous and cunning Europeans, unfortunate Hindus with their peaceful institutions were bound sooner or later to perdition. Thus it was with the political constitution of India; it succumbed to internal strife and foreign wars, until at last the maritime power of Europe subjected it to a yoke under which it languishes with expiring power.

Hard course of the fate of peoples! Yet it is nothing more than the order of nature. In the most beautiful and fertile region of the earth, the human being needed early on to attain refined concepts, an imagination broadly expatiating on nature, gentle manners, and regular institutions; but in this region he soon had to part with toilsome activity and thus become the prey of every robber who visited this happy land. From ancient times, the trade to the Indies was a very lucrative branch of commerce; from their treasures, the industrious and contented people gave to other nations an abundance of precious articles by sea and land, and, in consequence of their remote location, remained in tolerable peace and tranquility, until at length Europeans, for whom nothing is remote, came and established empires of their own among them. All the reports and all the goods these Europeans brought us from there do not compensate for the evil they have imposed upon a people who had never offended them. Yet in this the chain of destiny has been forged, and fate will either loose the chain or extend its links.

27

General Reflections on the History of the Asian States

Up to this point, we have been considering the political constitutions of Asia, which boast the greatest antiquity as well as the most solid duration; now, what have they attained in the history of humankind? What does the philosopher of human history learn from them?

1. History presumes a beginning, the history of a state and of a culture, a commencement. But how obscure is this commencement among all the peoples we have so far contemplated! Were my voice here of any weight, I would employ it in exhorting every astute and discrete investigator of history to study the origins of culture in Asia among its most celebrated empires and peoples, laying aside all hypotheses and throwing off the shackles of preconceived opinion. A close comparison of the surviving accounts as well as of the monuments of these nations, in particular of their script and language, of their most ancient works of art and their mythologies, or of the principles and practices that still govern their few sciences, taking into account in all this the place where they lived and the contact they could have had with others, would certainly reveal a trail of their enlightenment that probably would find the first instance of this culture neither in Selenginsk[1] nor in Greek Bactria. The diligent attempts of *de Guignes, Bayer, Gatterer,* and others, the more daring hypotheses of *Bailly, Pauw, Delisle,* and so on,[2] the useful endeavors that have been made toward collecting and disseminating Asian languages and writings, are preparatory steps to an edifice, the first solid cornerstone of which I desire to see in place. Perhaps it may be found in the ruins of a temple of a Protogaea,[3] which displays itself to our view in so many natural monuments.

2. The term "civilization of a people" is difficult to express; but it is even more difficult to conceive and to bring into being. That a stranger arriving in a country should enlighten an entire nation, or that a king should enjoin the civilization of a people by law, can be possible only through a coincidence of various ancillary circumstances; for humans are formed only by education, instruction, and lasting example. Thus it came about that all peoples soon fell upon the method of admitting into the body politic a class of men appointed to instruct, educate, and enlighten the rest, setting them above or inserting them in between the other classes. Let this be a stage in the development of a yet very imperfect culture, it is nevertheless a very necessary stage in the childhood of humankind; for wherever such teachers of the people were wanting, these peoples remained eternally mired in their ignorance and indolence. Consequently some sort of Brahmins, mandarins, talapoins, lamas, or the like, have been necessary to every nation in its political youth; and indeed we see that this order of humans has by itself widely distributed the seeds of refined culture in Asia. If there are such, the emperor Yao may say to his servants Hi and Ho,[*] "Go and observe the stars, take note of the sun and divide the year." If Hi and Ho are not astronomers, his imperial command is of no effect.

3. There is a difference between the culture of the men of learning and the culture of the people. The scholar must have mastery of sciences, the application of which is enjoined upon him for the benefit of the state; he preserves these, and he entrusts them to those of his own class, not to the people. The same is true for us with respect to higher mathematics and many other branches of knowledge which are not suitable for common use, and therefore are not for the people. These were the occult sciences, as they were called, of the ancient political constitutions, which the priest or the Brahmin preserved for members of his caste only, because it was appointed for their exercise, and every other class in the state had another occupation. So it is that algebra to this day is an occult science, for few in Europe understand it, though learning it is prohibited to none. Now we have indeed, in a useless and damaging manner, in many respects confused the spheres of learned and popular culture, thereby extending the range of the latter almost to that of the former; the ancient founders of states, who thought in more human terms, thought more wisely on this subject also. They rooted the culture of the people in sound morals and useful arts; they deemed the people neither qualified nor likely to benefit from grand theories, even in philosophy and religion. Hence the ancient mode of teaching by fables and

---

[*]Beginning of the I Ching, p. 6, in the edition of *de Guignes.*

allegories, such as the Brahmins present to this day to the unlearned castes; hence in China the difference in general concepts in line with almost every class of the people, fixed by the government and not unwisely maintained by it. If we would, then, compare an East Asian nation with ours in respect to culture, it is necessary first to know what each deems culture to consist of, and of what class of people we speak. If a nation, or a class of its people, possesses good morals and arts, if it has such ideas and such virtues as suffice for its labors and a happy and contented life, it is sufficiently enlightened for its needs, even if it is unable to account for an eclipse otherwise than by the well-known tale of the dragon. This tale was perhaps told it by its teachers precisely so that no one might grow gray in the study of the orbits of the sun and the stars. It is impossible for me to imagine that all nations, in their individual members, are on earth in order to attain a metaphysical concept of God, as if, without this metaphysics, which in the end is based perhaps on a single word, they were doomed to be superstitious and barbarous monsters. If the Japanese is a wise, resolute, dexterous, and useful human being, then he is cultured, let him think as he will of his Buddha and Amida. If he relates fabulous stories to you concerning these, tell him other fables in return, and you will balance the account.

4. Even a perpetual progress in the culture of learning is not essential to a state, at least not according to the concept prevailing in the ancient eastern empires. In Europe, all the men of learning form a state of their own, erected on the previous labors of many centuries, sustained artificially by shared auxiliary disciplines as well as the competition of realms; but the general course of nature is not served by the pinnacle of science after which we strive. All of Europe is a learned empire which, partly by internal competition, and partly—during the more recent centuries—by means of resources procured from all around the globe, has attained an ideal shape that is penetrated only by the scholar and utilized by the statesman. Once entered on this course, we cannot stand still; we pursue the magic image of a sublime science and universal knowledge, which it is true we shall never attain, but which will hold us in pursuit as long as the constitution of Europe shall endure. It is not so with the empires that have never engaged in this contest. Behind its mountains, orbicular China is a uniform and secluded empire; all its provinces, however different its peoples, governed by the principles of an ancient constitution, are in a state not of rivalry with one another, but of the profoundest obedience. Japan is an island; like ancient Britain an enemy to every stranger, it stands among the rocks of its stormy sea as if it were a world by itself. It is the same with Tibet, surrounded by mountains and barbarous peoples; the same with the constitu-

tion of the Brahmins which has groaned for centuries under the yoke. How could the sprouts of progressive science that break through the walls of rocks in Europe come forth in realms such as these? How could they even accept the fruits of this tree from the threatening hands of the Europeans who deprive them of what is around them, political security and their very land itself? Hence, after a few attempts, every snail has retreated within its shell, and despised even the most beautiful rose brought to it by a serpent. The science of their pretentious scholars is calculated to meet the needs of their country, and even from the servile Jesuits, China accepted no more than what it deemed it could not do without. Were it to come under circumstances of need, perhaps it would accept more; however, since most of the people, and even more the great bodies politic itself, are very hard, unyielding animals, they would have to be approached closely by danger before they might change their habitual ways; everything, without signs and wonders, will remain as it is, though the nations may be by no means deficient in their capacity for science. It wants nothing but motivating forces, for the ancient habit runs counter to every new impulse. How slow was Europe herself in acquiring her finest arts!

5. The state of a realm may be estimated either in itself or in comparison with others; Europe is under the necessity of employing both standards; the Asiatic realms have only one. None of these has visited other worlds, to employ them as the pedestals of their own greatness, or to poison themselves by indulging in their affluence; each of them utilizes what it has and is satisfied with its own. China has even refrained from working her own mines of gold, from a consciousness of her weakness not venturing to use them; and the foreign trade of China is carried on without the subjugation of other peoples. Under this parsimonious prudence, all of these countries have acquired for themselves the undeniable advantage of being compelled to make more use of their internal resources, as they made less use of foreign trade. We Europeans, to the contrary, wander over the whole world as merchants or as brigands, thereby neglecting what is our own; even the British Isles are not as far developed as Japan and China. Our bodies politic thus are animals which insatiably devour the foreign, good and bad, spices and poison, coffee and tea, silver and gold, feverishly displaying a great deal of strenuous vivacity; those countries rely only on their internal circulation. Theirs is a slow-paced life, like that of the woodchuck, but a life which for that reason has long endured, and will endure still longer, unless external circumstances kill the sleeping animal. Now it is well known that in all things the ancients reckoned on the longer term, in their monuments as well as in their political systems; we work at a lively pace

and run perhaps so much the more speedily through the brief lifespans allotted us by fate.

6. Lastly, as everything earthly and human depends on time and place, so does everything in the life of nations depend on their characters, without which they are unable to do anything. Were East Asia located next to Europe, it would long have ceased to be what it has become. Were Japan not the island that it is, it would long have ceased to be what it has become. Were all these empires to be formed now, they would hardly become what they did three or four thousand years ago; the entire beast called earth, upon whose back we dwell, is now some thousands of years older. It is indeed a wonderful and curious thing, what we call the genetic spirit and character of a people. It is inexplicable and ineradicable, ancient as the nation, ancient as the country it inhabits. The Brahmin is part of his region of the world; no other region is worthy of his holy nature. It is the same with the Chinese and the Japanese; anywhere outside their country, they are nothing but wilted shrubs, untimely planted. What the Indian hermit thinks of his god, and the Chinese thinks of his emperor, we do not think; what among us is deemed effectiveness and freedom of thought, or manly honor and female beauty, is seen quite differently by them. To them the confinement of Indian women is not insufferable; to any other but to himself, the empty pomp of a mandarin will be an insipid farce. It is the same with all the habits of the many-sided human figure, yes, with all else that appears on earth. If our species is destined to approach, in the eternal path of an asymptote, a point of perfection which it does not know, and which with all the labors of a Tantalus it can never touch, you Chinese and Japanese, you lamas and Brahmins, are traveling on this pilgrimage in a rather quiet corner of the vessel. You do not trouble yourselves about the unattainable point, and remain what you were thousands of years ago.

7. It is consoling for the researcher into human affairs to observe that Nature, with all the evils she has assigned to humankind, has not forgotten in any of her organizations the balm that at least mitigates their wounds. Asiatic despotism, this oppressive burden of humankind, is found only among nations who are willing to bear it, that is, who feel its heavy weight to a lesser degree. The Indian awaits his fate with resignation, when during the worst famine his emaciated body is pursued by the dog that will eat it when he falls by the wayside; he props himself up that he may die erect, while the dog, patiently waiting, looks upon his pale face, a mask of death. It is a resignation of which we have no idea, yet it frequently alternates with the most violent gusts of passion. This resignation, alongside various other kinds of relief provided by their way of life and climate, is the mitigating

antidote to the many evils of those political constitutions, which appear insufferable to us. If we lived there, we would not need to endure these evils, because we would have sufficient sense and courage to amend the evil constitution; or we too would grow weak and would patiently bear these evils as the Indians do. Great Mother Nature, to what trifles have you tied the fate of our kind! With a change in the form of the human skull and brain, with one tiny alteration in the structure of our organism and nervous system, conditioned by climate, descent, and habit, the fate of the world, the entire sum of what humankind does and suffers throughout the earth, is also changed.

28

Babylonia, Assyria, and Chaldea

The following four chapters are representative selections (three of six) from Herder's account of the Near East in his *Reflections on the Philosophy of History of Humankind*. As with his reflections on the Far East (Chapters 25, 26, and 27), the Near East section forms a book of its own (Book Twelve). In this part, Herder prepares the ground for an explanation and historical assessment of Greek culture via an understanding of the cultures of Asia Minor and the Mediterranean. The chapter on the Hebrews is particularly complex in that it displays a blend of praise (which dominates throughout Herder's work wherever he mentions the Hebrews), description, and criticism. As Herder always did, here too he holds to the idea that history is driven by the dynamics of different cultures. His criticism is directed toward "scleroticizing" forces in history—that is, those forces that cling to mere formal ("dead") traditions and customs. Much as twentieth-century allusions may impose themselves upon the reader, in order to do justice to these texts, they should be read with an awareness of the historical context in which they were written.

In the vast nomad stretches of Asia Minor, the fertile and pleasant banks of the Euphrates and the Tigris soon had to attract a number of pastoral hordes; and as these banks resemble a paradise, located as they are between mountains on the one side and deserts on the other, they must have been a welcome dwelling for these hordes. Although this region now has lost much of its attractiveness, since it was deprived almost entirely of all cultivation, and has been subject for centuries to pillage by roaming hordes, particular districts still confirm the general testimony of the ancient writers whose praise of it knew no bounds.* Thus, here one finds the fatherland of the

---

*See Büsching's *Erdbeschreibung*, vol. 5, part 1.[1]

earliest monarchies of our world history, and at the same time an early workshop of useful arts.

Indeed, in the life of wandering nomads, nothing was more natural than for some ambitious sheikh to conceive the plan of appropriating for himself the delightful banks of the Euphrates, and of uniting a few hordes to maintain possession of them. The Hebrew chronicle gives this sheikh the name of Nimrod,[2] who founded his kingdom with the towns of Babylon, Edessa, Nisibis, and Ctesiphon; and it places another in the vicinity, the Assyrian empire, with the cities of Rezin, Nineveh, Adiabene, and Calah. The location of these empires, together with their origin and makeup, ties up the thread of fate that later unwinds to the time of their fall. For, having been founded by diverse tribes, and bordering too closely on each other, what could follow from the quarrelsome spirit common to the hordes of these regions but mutual hostility, repeated subjugation under the dominion of one power, and partitions of various sorts under the pressure of northern mountain peoples? This is the brief history of the states along the Tigris and the Euphrates, a history which, coming from such distant periods and from the tongues of several peoples, cannot have been handed down to us without confusion. However, both history and fable agree with respect to the origins, spirit, and constitutions of these states. They sprang from the small beginnings of nomadic peoples, and they always retained the character of predatory hordes. Even the despotism that arose in them, and the various artistic skills for which Babylon was particularly famous, are perfectly consistent with the spirit of the region and the national character of its inhabitants.

For what were these earliest cities, founded by these fabled world rulers? Great, fortified hordes; the fixed encampment of a tribe enjoying these fertile regions and bent upon excursions to plunder others. Hence the vast circumference of Babylon, so soon after it was founded, on either side of the river; hence its huge walls and towers. The walls were lofty, thick ramparts of baked clay, designed to protect an extensive military encampment of nomads; the towers were watchtowers; the entire city, interspersed with gardens, was, according to the expression of Aristotle, a Peloponnesus. The countryside furnished an abundance of materials for this sort of nomad architecture: clay, to produce bricks, and bitumen, with which they learned to cement them. Thus, nature facilitated the labors of the people, and, the foundations once being laid in the nomad fashion, it was easy to enrich and beautify them, when the horde had made excursions and returned with booty.

And what were the famous conquests of a Ninus,[3] a Semiramis, and the rest, other than predatory expeditions, like those conducted to this day by the Arabs, Kurds, and Turkomans? By their very tribal makeup, the Assyrians were predatory mountain people whose character has been passed on to posterity as one marked by nothing but conquest and plunder. From the earliest times, the Arabs are particularly named as serving these world conquerors, and the unchanging way of life of these people will endure as long as the deserts of Arabia exist. At a later time, the Chaldeans appear on the stage; according to their descent and their earliest habitat, they were predatory Kurds.[*] In world history they have distinguished themselves by nothing but devastation; for the name given to them by researchers is probably no more than an honorary title which they gained as part of their booty in the conquest of the Kingdom of Babylon. Thus we may consider the fine country bounded by these streams as a gathering place, in ancient and in more recent times, of wandering nomads or predatory peoples, who brought together their booty here in fortified places; these peoples themselves eventually succumbed to the voluptuous warmth of this region of the compass and, debilitated by opulence, became prey to others.

The celebrated works of art of a Semiramis, of even a Nebuchadnezzar hardly say anything different. The earliest expeditions of the Assyrians went toward Egypt; the works of art of this peaceful and civilized nation probably became the first model for the beautification of Babylon. The famous colossal stelae of Belus[5] and the images baked into the brick walls of the great city appear to be entirely in the Egyptian style, and the assertion that the fabulous queen repaired to the mountain Bagisthan,[6] to imprint her image on its back, plainly indicates an imitation of Egypt. She needed to undertake this journey because the south did not offer her the granite rocks, suitable for eternal monuments, that are found in Egypt. Nebuchadnezzar, too, produced nothing but colossi, brick palaces, and hanging gardens. What was wanting in art and materials was to be made up for by size, and the pleasant gardens at least gave the inferior monuments a Babylonian character. I do not much regret, therefore, the downfall of these enormous piles of clay, as they probably were far from ranking high as works of art; what I wish is that one would seek among their ruins for tablets with Chaldaic writing, which are certainly to be found there, according to the testimony of several travelers.[**]

Not properly Egyptian art, but the art of nomads and, later, mercantile arts were the hallmark of this region, as dictated by its natural location. The Euphrates was subject to flooding, and consequently required canals to draw off its waters, so that a larger area of land might be fertilized; thus the

---

[*]See *Schlözer* on the Chaldeans in the *Repertorium für die morgenländische Literatur*, vol. 8, p. 113.[4]

[**]See *Della Valle* on the ruins at Ardesh; *Niebuhr* on the heaps of ruins at Hella; etc.[7]

invention of waterwheels and pumps, unless they too were built after Egyptian models. The area at some remove from these streams, once populated and fertile, now suffers want because it is not worked by diligent hands. Here it was an easy step from raising livestock to taking up agriculture, since nature itself invited the settled inhabitant to do so. The fine fruits of garden and field, which spontaneously shoot forth on riverbanks, richly rewarding the small effort that goes into their care, turned the shepherd into an agriculturalist and a gardener almost without his being conscious of it. A forest of beautiful date palms provided him with lumber for a permanent dwelling instead of the insecurity of the tent, and with fruit for his nourishment; the readily baked clay contributed to construction, so that the tent dweller found himself, before he knew it, in a superior dwelling, though embedded in clay. That very clay gave him vessels, and with them a hundred conveniences of domestic life. He learned to bake bread and to prepare meals, leading at last, with the assistance of trade, to those opulent banquets and feasts for which the Babylonians were famous in very ancient times. As they learned to create small idols, teraphim, from baked clay, so they soon also learned to form and bake colossal statues, the models of which readily served in the creation of molds for the casting of metals. As they learned to impart to the soft clay images and written symbols that were hardened by fire, they learned accidentally to retain on baked bricks the knowledge of a previous world, and thereby to extend the observations of ancient times. Even astronomy was a fortunate nomad invention of this region. Sitting on the broad and pleasant plain, the pastoral nomad observed in quiet leisure the rising and setting of the brilliant stars in his vast and clear horizon. He named them as he named his sheep, and committed the changes in the sky to his memory. These observations were continued on the flat roofs of the houses of Babylon, on which people rested after the heat of the day, until at length a specific order of men was established, devoted to this exciting and at the same time indispensable science, that was to carry on these annals of the heavens for ages to come. So it was that nature herself incited humankind to the acquisition of knowledge and science, so that even these gifts of hers are as much local productions as any other products on earth. At the foot of the Caucasus, her fountains of naphtha put fire into the hands of humans, so that there is no doubt that the fable of Prometheus originated there; in the pleasant date palm groves of the Euphrates, nature gently molded the roaming shepherds into industrious inhabitants of towns and cities.

A number of other Babylonian arts arose from the circumstance of this region's central location in the trade between east and west, from the most ancient times and for all times to come. No well-known state was founded in the center of Persia because no river emptied from there into the sea; but how much more quickened by life were those areas along the Indus, on the Ganges, and here between Euphrates and Tigris! Here, the Persian Gulf was near, where an early port of entry for Indian goods also enriched Babylon, making her a parent of mercantile industry. The Babylonian splendor of linen, carpets, embroidery, and sundry apparel is well known; such wealth created luxury; luxury and industry brought the sexes closer to each other than is customary in other regions of Asia, a state of affairs to which the reigns of several queens probably made no small contribution. In short, the formation of this people proceeded so entirely from their location and way of life that it would have been a subject of wonder if nothing extraordinary had been produced from such circumstances, in such a part of the world. Nature has her favorite spots on the earth, which are located particularly along the banks of rivers and on selected shores of the sea, stimulating and rewarding human activity. As Egypt arose along the Nile, and India on the Ganges, so it was that here a Nineveh and a Babylon and, in more recent times, a Seleucia and a Palmyra were created. Yes, had Alexander fulfilled his wish to rule the world from Babylon, how different a shape this delightful region would have received for centuries to come!

The Assyrians and the Babylonians also shared in alphabetical writing, the possession of which the nomadic tribes of Asia Minor have counted among their advantages since time immemorial. I shall not enter here into the question of which people properly deserve credit for this splendid invention; suffice it to say that all Aramaic tribes boasted of this gift of the earlier world, and held hieroglyphics in a sort of religious abomination. I cannot persuade myself, therefore, that hieroglyphics were employed by the Babylonians; their magi interpreted stars, events, accidents, the visions of dreams, and secret written symbols, but not hieroglyphics. Even the handwriting of fate that appeared to the reveling Belshazzar** consisted of syllables that, in the manner of the art of writing prevalent in the Morn, appeared to him in an intricate script but not in pictorial images. Even the paintings that Semiramis placed on the brick walls, the Syrian letters that she directed to be cut next to her image, confirm the use of alphabetic letters without hieroglyphics among these peoples in the most ancient times. These letters alone made it possible for the Babylonians so early to have written contracts, chronicles of their empire, and a continued series of celestial observations; by these alone they have transmitted themselves to posterity as a civilized people. It is true, neither their astronomical catalogs nor any of

---

*Eichhorn's *Geschichte des Ost-Indischen Handels,* p. 12; Gatterer's *Einleitung zur synchronistischen Universal-Historie,* p. 77.[8]

**Daniel 5:5–25.

their writings have come to us, though they were sent to Aristotle; yet the fact that this people once had such things is itself a basis for their fame.

By the way, when we talk of the learning of the Chaldeans, we must not do so in terms of our own knowledge. The sciences possessed by Babylon were entrusted to a closed order of learned men—an order which, at the time of the decay of the nation, ultimately turned into a group of odious impostors. They were probably called Chaldeans from the time that Chaldeans ruled over Babylon; for, as the literati had been a creation of the rulers and an order of the state since the times of Belus, so it is probable that they pleased their new rulers by assuming the name of their nation. They were court philosophers, and as such, they also lowered themselves to all the deceptions and idle arts of court philosophy. It is probable that during these times they enriched their ancient science as little as the Chinese tribunal enriched the learning of China.

It was both fortunate and unfortunate for this pleasant stretch of the earth that it was proximate to a ridge of mountains, from which so many savage mountain peoples pressed down. The Assyrian and Babylonian empires were overcome by the Chaldeans and the Medes, who in turn were overcome by the Persians, until everything was at last a subjugated desert, and the seat of the empire was shifted to the northern regions. Thus we do not have much to learn from these empires, either in war or in politics. Their mode of attack was brutal, their conquests were merely excursions, their political constitution was that miserable form of government by satraps that has almost always prevailed in these parts among the countries of the Morn. Hence the impermanent structure of these monarchies, hence the frequent revolts against them and their total overthrow by the capture of one city, or by one or two major defeats. It is true that, soon after the first downfall of the empire, Arbaces endeavored to establish an aristocracy of allied satraps; but he did not succeed, because all the Median and Aramaean tribes knew no other form of government than the despotic. They had proceeded from nomadic life; the image of the king as patriarch and sheikh shaped their concepts and left no room for political liberty or the joint rule by more than one. As one sun radiates in the sky, so there should also be one ruler on earth, and he soon assumed all the splendor of the sun, yes, the brilliance of an earthly divinity. Everything flowed from his favor, everything depended on his person, the state lived in him, and usually it terminated with him. A harem was the court of the prince; he knew nothing but silver and gold, manservants and maidservants, lands that he possessed as fields of pasture, and herds of men whom he drove wherever he pleased, if indeed he did not strangle them. A barbaric nomad government, although it found in rare good princes true shepherds and fathers of the people.

~ 29 ~

The Hebrews

The Hebrews cut a very small figure when they are considered immediately after the Persians[1]; their country was small, and poor the role they played in and outside their country on the world stage, a stage on which they almost never were conquerors. Yet through the will of fate and a series of initiatives, the causes of which are readily ascertained, they have had a greater impact on other peoples than any Asian nation; yes, to a certain extent, they have become, through Christianity as well as Mohammedanism, a source for the greatest proportion of the enlightenment of the world.

A remarkable distinction is already found in that the Hebrews have written chronicles of their undertakings, dating from times in which most of the now enlightened nations were still unable to write, by which token they venture to trace their accounts back to the origin of the world. But they are even more advantageously distinguished by the fact that these accounts were not derived from hieroglyphics, or obscured by them, but rather derived from genealogies and were interwoven with historical tales and songs; this simple form evidently enhances their historical value. Finally, these narratives derive singular weight from the fact that, representing a divinely inspired tribal prerogative of this nation, they have been preserved *almost* with superstitious exactitude for thousands of years, and through Christianity were delivered into the hands of nations that examined and contested, elucidated and used them with a freer spirit than the Jewish one. It is indeed remarkable that the accounts of this people by other nations, especially that by Manetho the Egyptian,[2] should differ so widely from the history of the Hebrews themselves; yet, if the latter is impartially considered, it certainly deserves more credit than the slanders of foreign enemies who despised the Jews. I am not ashamed, therefore, to take for my groundwork the history of the Hebrews as related by themselves; but I wish, nevertheless, that the tales of their enemies too will be not merely despised, but also used.

Thus, according to the most ancient national myths of the Hebrews, their patriarch passed the Euphrates as the sheikh of a nomad trek and at last arrived in Palestine. Life here pleased him, because he found unimpeded space to carry on the way of life of his pastoral ancestors, and to serve the god of his fathers in the manner of the tribe. In the third generation, his descendants were led into Egypt by the singular good fortune of one of their family, and there continued to follow the pastoral life without mixing with the inhabitants of the country; until, it is not exactly known in which generation, they were liberated by their future lawgiver from the contemptuous oppression under which they, as shepherds, had to live among these people, and conducted into Arabia. Here now the great man, the greatest this people ever had,[3] completed his work and gave them a constitution which, though based on the religion and the way of life of their tribe, was so interwoven with Egyptian political wisdom that on the one hand the people was raised from a nomadic horde to the level of a civilized nation, but on the other hand it was weaned so completely away from Egypt that it would never again be incited to tread upon Egypt's swarthy soil. All the laws of Moses are based on marvelous reflection; they extend from the greatest to the smallest things, to sway the spirit of the nation in all circumstances of life and to become, as Moses so frequently exclaims, an eternal body of laws. Moreover, this thoroughly deliberated system of laws was not the work of a moment; the lawgiver added to it as circumstances required, and before his death he bound the entire nation to its future political constitution. For forty years he exacted strict obedience to his laws, and perhaps this was why the

people had to remain for so long in the Arabian desert, until, with the passing of the first stubborn generation, a new people raised in these customs could fully establish itself in keeping with them, in the land of their fathers. But the patriot's wish was not fulfilled. The aged Moses died at the border of the land he had sought, and as his successor entered it, he did not enjoy sufficient authority and respect to follow the lawgiver's plan completely. The conquest was not carried out as far as it should have been; the tribes divided the land and rested too soon. The most powerful tribes grabbed the largest portion for themselves, so that the weaker brethren hardly had room to settle, and one of the tribes actually had to be split up.[*] Besides this, many small nations remained in the country, so that Israel retained its bitterest hereditary enemies within its borders, and the country

---

[*]The tribe of Dan received a corner at the top and on the left of the country. See *The Spirit of Hebrew Poetry*, vol. 2.[4]

thus lacked the full internal and external stability that its prescribed borders alone could provide. What else could follow from this incomplete structure but those succeeding insecure times that almost never allowed the people who had entered the country to come to rest. The military chiefs raised by necessity were for the most part merely roving battlers; and when the people came to be governed by kings at last, they were so preoccupied with their own country, divided as it was into tribal territories, that the third king at the same time was the last of the whole disjointed country. Five-sixths of the country fell away from his successor, and what could now become of two such monarchies, so feeble, living in the vicinity of powerful enemies and incessantly waging war against each other? The kingdom of Israel did not actually have a lawful constitution; it therefore adhered to the gods of foreign countries, to avoid reunion with its rival, which worshipped the ancient and legitimate God of the country. It is clear therefore that in terms of the language of this people no God-fearing man was king of Israel at the time; for otherwise his people would have moved to Jerusalem and the interrupted regency would have been restored. Thus, one carried on insecurely, in the most unholy imitation of foreign mores and customs, until the King of Assyria came into the country and plundered the little land like a bird's nest discovered. The other kingdom, which at least was based on the ancient constitution of two powerful kings and a fortified capital city, lasted a little longer, but only until an even stronger conqueror decided to obtain it by force. Nebuchadnezzar, the scourge of the land, came and at first made the weak kings of the country into tributaries; ultimately, after they revolted, he made them slaves; the land was devastated, the capital was razed, and the people of Judea were led to Babylon, into a captivity as disgraceful as that of Israel in Media. Considered as a state, hardly any people has cut a more miserable figure in its history than this one, the reigns of two of its kings excepted.

What was the cause of this? In my opinion, the course of the narrative itself clarifies the cause; for a country endowed with so poor a constitution internally and externally had no possibility to thrive in this area of the world. If David overran the desert as far as the banks of the Euphrates, and thereby only stirred a greater power against his successors, could he thereby give his country the stability it lacked, especially since the seat of his power was located at the southern extremity of the kingdom? His son brought foreign wives, trade, and luxury into the country—into a country that, like the Swiss Confederation, was able to support only shepherds and agriculturalists, and actually had such in great multitudes to support. Besides, since he carried on his trade, for the most part, not through members of his own nation, but through the subjugated Edomites, luxury was pernicious to his kingdom. For the rest, since the time of Moses no second legislator was found among this people, who would have been able to restore the state, unsettled from the outset, to a basic system of laws suitable to the times. The learned class soon disintegrated; those zealous for the laws of the land had voices, but not the arm of power; and the kings for the most part were weaklings or creatures of the priests. The refined nomocracy aspired to by Moses, and the kind of theocratic monarchy prevalent among all the peoples of this despotic region, were two systems so opposite to each other that the law of Moses had to become a law of bondage to a people for whom it was intended to have been a law of freedom.

In the course of time, things changed, but not for the better. When the Jews, freed by Cyrus, returned from captivity, diminished in numbers, they had learned much else, but not how to live under a genuine political constitution; how, indeed, was the knowledge of such a constitution to have been acquired in Assyria or Chaldea? Their sentiments fluctuated between princely and sacerdotal government; they built a temple, as if this would have revived the times of Moses and Solomon; their religion now became pharisaical, their learnedness a pondering cleverness concerned with syllables, and this confined to a single book, and their patriotism a servile loyalty to the misunderstood ancient law, so that they appeared contemptible or ridiculous to all neighboring nations. Their only solace and their hope was built upon ancient prophecies which, equally misunderstood, were to secure for them the vainest kind of world dominion. So they lived and suffered under the Syrian Greeks, the Idumaeans, and the Romans, until ultimately, through an animosity to which history hardly finds a parallel, the land as well as the capital succumbed in a manner that pained the humane conqueror himself. And now they were dispersed over all the lands of the Roman world, and it was with this dispersal that there commenced an influence of the Jews upon humankind which could hardly have been imagined from a land so confined; for in their entire history these people had not distinguished themselves as skilled in politics and warfare, least of all as inventive in science and art.

But, shortly before the downfall of the Jewish state, Christianity arose in the heart of it, and Christianity initially not only failed to separate from Judaism, adopting the sacred writings of the Jews, but also and especially based upon these writings the divine mission of its Messiah. Hence, it was through Christendom that the books of the Jews came into the hands of all the nations that embraced the Christian doctrine; and according to the manner in which they have been understood, and the use that has been made of them, they have had good or ill effects on all Christian centuries. Their effect was good, insofar as in them the law of Moses made the doctrine of the one God, creator of the world, the basis of all philosophy and religion, and in so many hymns and precepts throughout these writings spoke of this God with a dignity and loftiness, with a devotion and gratitude, attained by few other human writings. These books ought not to be compared with the I Ching of the Chinese, or with the Sadder[5] and Zend-Avesta of the Persians; but even when they are compared with the much more recent Koran of the Mohammedans, which after all utilized precepts of the Jews and Christians, the superiority of the Hebrew scriptures over all the other ancient religious writings is unmistakable. It was also gratifying to the curiosity of the human mind to find in these books such accessible answers to questions about the age of the world and its creation, the origins of evil, and so on, as could be understood and grasped by everyone, to say nothing of the whole instructive history of the people and the pure moral teaching of several books in this collection. Let the chronology of the Jews be what it may, it constituted a received and general standard, and a thread with which to connect the events of world history. Many other advantages of philology, exegesis, and dialectic may be passed over, as indeed they might have been obtained from other works. In all these ways, the writings of the Hebrews unquestionably have had an advantageous effect on the history of humankind.

With all these advantages, however, it is equally incontestable that the misinterpretation and the abuse of these writings have been detrimental to the human mind in various ways, and the more so as they have operated upon it under the aspect of divinity. How many foolish cosmogonies have been spun from the simple and sublime Mosaic story of creation, how many rigid doctrines and unsatisfactory hypotheses from his apple and the serpent's temptation! For centuries, the forty days of the deluge have formed the peg on which natural scientists have deemed it indispensable to hang all the phenomena of the formation of the earth, and, for an equally long time, the historians of humankind have chained all the peoples of the earth to the people of God, and to the misunderstood prophetic vision of four monarchies.[6] Many a history has been mutilated so that it might be elucidated by means of a Hebrew name; the entire human, terrestrial, and solar system has been narrowed for the purpose of vindicating the sun of Joshua[7] and a date in the chronology of the world, the fixation of which was never meant to be the purpose of these writings. How many great men, among whom even a Newton himself is to be counted, have the Jewish chronology and apocalypse robbed of time that might have been employed in more useful inquiries! Yes, even with respect to the teachings of morality and political institutions, the Hebrew scriptures, through misunderstanding and ill application, have placed real fetters upon the nations that accepted them. For want of making a distinction between the times and the stages of development, it was believed that there was in the intolerance of the Jewish religion a model that could also be followed by Christians; passages of the Old Testament have been adduced to justify the contradictory design that was to turn Christianity, which is voluntary and exclusively a moral system, into a Judaic religion of state. In like manner, it is undeniable that the ceremonies of the temple and even the language of Hebrew worship have influenced the spiritual oratory, hymns, and litanies of all Christian nations, often turning their worship into the idiom of the Morn. The laws of Moses were to be applicable in every region of the compass, even among people with entirely different constitutions; hence, there is not one Christian nation that has formed for itself its system of laws and political constitution from the bottom up. So it is that the most sublime good, because of often false application, borders on various evils; for is it not true that even the most sacred elements of nature may turn to destructiveness, and the most effective remedies into creeping poison?

According to the use that has been made of it, the Jewish nation itself, since its dispersal, has by its presence done service and injury to the peoples of the earth. In the early ages, Christians were considered to be Jews, and were despised and oppressed in common with them, because the Christians too burdened themselves with many of the reproaches of Jewish pride, superstition, and hatred of other peoples. Later, when the Christians themselves oppressed the Jews, they almost everywhere gave them the opportunity to take control of internal trade, particularly the money trade; thus, the less refined nations of Europe voluntarily became the slaves of the usury of Jews. Although the Jews did not invent the trade in bills of exchange, it is true, they soon brought it to perfection, because it was their very insecurity in the realms of the Mohammedans and the Christians that made this invention necessary. Thus, it is undeniable that this extensive republic of clever usurers long restrained many a nation of Europe from exercising and utilizing its own industry and trade; for these nations deemed themselves too big to follow a Jewish trade, and they were as little inclined to learn this kind of rational and refined industry from the servile treasurers of the holy Roman world, as were the Spartans to be taught agriculture by their helots. Should anyone collect a history of the Jews from all the countries into which they have been dispersed, there would be exhibited a picture of humankind, equally remarkable as a natural and a political manifestation. For no other people upon earth have spread abroad like these; no other people upon earth have remained so distinguishable and vigorous in all climates.

Let no one, however, superstitiously infer from this a revolution, to be wrought by these people at some future time on all the nations of the earth. All that was intended to be wrought has probably been accomplished; and neither in the people themselves nor in historical analogy can we discover the slightest disposition to such a revolution. The continued existence of the Jews is as naturally to be explained as that of the Brahmins, the Parsees, and the Gypsies.

No one, in the meanwhile, will deny to a people that has been such an active instrument in the hand of fate those great qualities which are conspicuous in its entire history. Ingenious, crafty, and industrious, the Jews have at all times borne up even under the most extreme oppression by other peoples, such as for more than forty years in the deserts of Arabia. Nor have they lacked warlike courage as well, as shown by the times of David and of the Macabees, and still more by the ultimate and most dreadful downfall of their state. In their own country, they were once an industrious and diligent people who, like the Japanese, knew how to cultivate their naked mountains by means of artificial terraces, thus supporting an incredible number of people in a narrowly confined region, not nearly the most fertile in the world. In the arts, it is true, the Jewish nation remained always unpracticed, although their country was situated between the Egyptians and Phoenicians; for even their temple of Solomon had to be built by foreign laborers. In like manner, although they possessed for some time the ports of the Red Sea, and dwelt so near the shores of the Mediterranean, they never became a seafaring people, notwithstanding this most fortuitous location with respect to trade with the world and the fact that the size of their population was a heavy burden upon the country. Like the Egyptians, they dreaded the sea, and from times immemorial preferred to live among other nations, a feature of their national character against which Moses strenuously fought. In short, they are a people spoiled in their education, because they never attained political maturity on their own soil, and consequently never attained a genuine awareness of honor and freedom. In the sciences pursued by their most outstanding minds, there was manifested at all times more of a legalistic exactitude and order than a fruitful freedom of the spirit, and almost from the outset their condition deprived them of the virtue of the patriot. The people of God, whose country was once given them by heaven itself, have been for thousands of years, yes, virtually from their inception, a parasitical plant[8] upon the trunks of other nations; a tribe of cunning brokers throughout almost the whole world who, in spite of all oppression, nowhere long for their own honor and habitation, for a country of their own.

～ 30 ～

Egypt

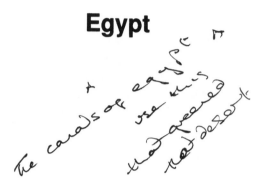

We now come to the country which, owing to its antiquity, its arts, and its political institutions, stands like an enigma of the primeval world, and which has also copiously exercised the conjectural skill of the inquirer. This is Egypt. The most authentic information we have respecting it is derived from its antiquities, those enormous pyramids, obelisks, and catacombs, those ruins of canals, cities, columns, and temples which, with their hieroglyphics, are still the astonishment of travelers, as they were the wonder of the ancient world. What an immense population, what art and government, but even more, what a singular way of thinking was required to hollow out these rocks and to pile them one upon another; not only to delineate and carve out the images of animals, but also to bury them as sacred relics; to transform a wilderness of rocks into an abode for the dead, and in such multifarious ways to render the spirit of an Egyptian priesthood eternal in stone! All of these relics stand or lie about like a sacred sphinx, like a grand problem, demanding explication.

Some of these works, of obvious utility or even indispensable to the country, explain themselves; such are the amazing canals, dikes, and catacombs. The canals served to convey the Nile to even the remotest parts of Egypt, which now, owing to the deterioration of the canals, have become a silent desert. The dikes facilitated the establishment of cities in the fertile valley flooded by the Nile, which, truly the heart of Egypt, nourishes the entire country. Setting aside the religious ideas linked to them by the Egyptians, the catacombs also undeniably contributed to the healthy quality of the air and the prevention of diseases that otherwise are usually the plague of hot, humid regions. But why the vastness of these caves? Whence and why the labyrinths, the obelisks, the pyramids? Whence came the wonderful artistic inclination with which they so laboriously conferred immortality upon the sphinxes and colossi? Did the Egyptians arise from the mud of their Nile as the original nation of the world? Or, if they came from elsewhere, what were the circumstances and motives that rendered them so different from all the peoples dwelling around them?

That the Egyptians are not an indigenous primeval people is demonstrated, it seems to me, by the natural history of the country; for not only ancient tradition, but every rational study of the earth clearly demonstrates that Upper Egypt was inhabited earlier, and that the lower part was wrested from the mud of the Nile only by the skillful industry of the people. The most ancient Egypt therefore was located on the Thebaid,[1] where also was located the residence of its ancient kings; for if the settlement of the country had proceeded by way of Suez, it would remain inexplicable why the primeval rulers of Egypt chose the Thebaid desert as their habitation. If, on the other hand, we follow the settlement of Egypt as it appears before our eyes, we immediately see the reason why its inhabitants could become so singularly excellent a people in terms of culture as well. For they were no amiable Circassians,[2] but probably a people of South Asia, who came westward across the Red Sea, or from even further away, and spread gradually through Egypt from Ethiopia. Since they found the country bounded, as it were, by the inundations and marshes of the Nile, is it cause for wonder that they initially established themselves upon these rocks as troglodytes,[3] and afterward gradually gained the whole of Egypt by their industry, improving themselves as they improved the country? The account Diodorus[4] gives of their southern descent, though intermingled with various fables of his Ethiopia, is not only probable in the highest degree, but also the only key to an explanation of this people, and its astounding conformity with some distant East Asian peoples.

Since I could but very imperfectly work out this hypothesis here, it must be deferred to another place; of use here are only a few of its obvious consequences with regard to this people's role in the history of humankind. The Egyptians were a quiet, industrious, well-intended people, as their entire constitution, their arts, and their religion demonstrate. No temple, no column of Egypt, has a joyful, airy, Grecian appearance; of this design of art they had neither a concept nor the intention to pursue it. The mummies reveal that the figure of the Egyptians was not beautiful; and as the human form appeared to them, such would necessarily be their imitations of it. Wrapped up in their own land, as in their religion and their constitution, they did not care for the foreign; and since, in keeping with their character, fidelity and precision were their principal objects in the imitative arts, and since all of their art was handicraft, the religious craft of a particular class, resting therefore largely upon religious concepts, inconceivable are any deviations into that realm of beautiful ideals, which in any event without a natural prototype remains a mere phantom. In recompense, they turned their attention more to the solid, the enduring, and the monumental, or to a perfection based on the most exact and artful industry. In their rocky region of the world, their temples were conceived in terms of enormous caverns. Hence in their architecture they were bound to be fond of majestic immensity. Their statues were derived from mummies; therefore, they were marked by the closely paralleled position of the feet and the hands, a posture tending in itself to durability. To support caverns, to set apart tombs, that is the purpose of pillars; and since the art of architecture of the Egyptians proceeded from rocky caverns, and since in their construction they had not yet mastered our art of vaulting, the pillar, often with colossal dimensions, became indispensable. The desert around them, the realm of the dead that hovered about them because of their religious ideas, also turned their pictorial images into representations of mummies, characterized not by action, but by eternal rest, on which their art was fixed.

It seems to me that one need marvel even less over the pyramids and the obelisks of the Egyptians. In all parts of the world, even in Tahiti, pyramids are erected over tombs, not so much as emblems of the immortality of the soul, but as memorials enduring beyond the grave. Their origin on these graves may be traced to those heaps of rock piled together as memorials to worthwhile causes by several nations in very remote antiquity; to rest securely, the heap of rocks forms itself into a pyramid. When human art applied itself to this general custom, as no occasion for a memorial is so dear to the human being as the interment of the revered dead, the heap of rocks, perhaps also designed at first to protect the corpse from the fangs of wild beasts, was naturally transformed into a pyramid or commemorative column, erected with more or less artistic skill. That the Egyptians eventually exceeded other peoples in this form of construction has the same basis as the more durable construction of their temples and catacombs. They had ample stone for these memorials, since most of Egypt actually is composed of rock. They also had sufficient hands for their construction, since in their fertile and densely populated country the Nile enriches the earth and the tilling of the soil costs little effort. Moreover, the Egyptians lived with great temperance. Thousands of people who worked like slaves on these monuments for centuries were so easily maintained that it depended merely on the will of the king to erect these pointless, massive memorials. Individual lives in those times were valued differently than today, since names were reckoned only in terms of occupational groups and geographical regions. The useless labor of many individuals was then more readily sacrificed to the notion of a ruler who wished to secure immortality through such a mass of stones, and to retain the departed soul in the embalmed corpse, in conformity with his religious delusion. Over the course of time, as with many another useless art, this turned into a competition. One king imitated the other, or attempted to outdo him, while the pliant people were compelled to waste their days in the construction of these monuments. Thus, in all likelihood, arose the pyramids and obelisks of Egypt; they were built only in the most remote times, for later times and nations, disposed to learn more useful trades, no longer erected pyramids. Thus, far from being a token of the happiness and enlightenment of the ancient Egyptians, the pyramids are incontrovertible testimonies to the superstition and thoughtlessness both of the poor who built them, and of the ambitious who commanded their erection. In vain do you seek secrets within these pyramids or concealed wisdom from the obelisks; for even if the hieroglyphs of the latter could be deciphered, what would, what could one possibly read on them, other than, perhaps, a chronicle of forgotten events or a symbolic apotheosis of their builders? And then, what are these masses to a mountain range of nature's construction?

Moreover, there is so little that may be inferred from the hieroglyphs regarding the profundity of Egyptian wisdom, that the opposite impression is more likely to be deduced from them. Hieroglyphs represent the earliest untaught attempt of the human mind in its infancy seeking symbols to express its thoughts; the most primitive savages of America had hieroglyphs sufficient for their needs. For could not the Mexicans report in hieroglyphs even the most unheard-of event, the arrival of the Spaniards? But what poverty of ideas, what stagnation of mind was displayed by the Egyptians in retaining for so long this imperfect mode of writing, and for centuries painting it with enormous effort upon rocks and walls! How restricted must have been the range of knowledge of a nation, and its extensive learned class, who could content themselves for some thousands of years with these birds and strokes! For their second Hermes who invented letters came very late, and he was not an Egyptian. The alphabetical writing of the mummies is nothing but the foreign Phoenician writing intermingled with hieroglyphic symbols, which also in all probability were learned from the mercantile Phoenicians. The Chinese themselves advanced further than the Egyptians, developing from similar hieroglyphs real conceptual characters, to which the latter, as it appears, never attained. Need we wonder, therefore, that a people so poor in writing, and yet not unskilled, excelled in mechanical arts? The path to scientific literature was obstructed by hieroglyphics, so their attention was drawn toward sensory objects. The fertile valley of the Nile made their agriculture easy; they learned to measure and calculate those periodic inundations on which their welfare depended. The year and the seasons had to become familiar in the end to a nation whose life and well-being depended on one single natural change that, annually recurring, created for them an eternal calendar of the land.

Thus, all the familiarity with the course of nature and the heavens too, for which this people is famous, was an equally natural result of their country and their climate. Enclosed among mountains, seas, and deserts, in a narrow fertile valley, where everything depended on one natural event and was connected to that event, where seasons and harvest, diseases and winds, insects and birds were governed by one and the same revolution, the over-flowing of the Nile, how could the grave Egyptian and his extensive, idle order of priests fail to collect a sort of history of nature and the heavens? From all quarters of the world it is known that confined, sense-oriented peoples display the richest and most living knowledge of their country, though they did not gather it from books. What the Egyptians added to that with hieroglyphics was harmful to science, not useful. The observation drawn from life became with them not only an obscure but also a dead image, which in fact retarded, rather than advancing, the progress of the human mind. There has been much discussion of whether the hieroglyphics concealed sacerdotal mysteries. It seems to me that each hieroglyph by its nature contains a secret, and a series of these, preserved by an exclusive guild, must necessarily become a mystery to the many, even if it is assumed that this writing is put before them at every turn. The many cannot be initiated into its study, for this is not their task, and they will not find its meaning of themselves. Hence the inescapable lack of broadly based en-lightenment in every country, in every guild of men possessed of hiero-glyphic wisdom, as it is called, whether taught by priests or laymen. They cannot and will not decipher their symbols to everyone, and whatever can-not be learned of itself, by its nature will retain the air of mystery. Thus, all hieroglyphical wisdom of modern times represents a single-minded obstacle to any kind of broader enlightenment, because even in more ancient times hieroglyphics always was the most imperfect mode of writing. It would be unreasonable to insist upon understanding in and of itself something that might be interpreted in a thousand different ways, and deadly would be the effort expended upon arbitrary symbols as if they were necessary and eter-nal matters. Hence Egypt has always remained a child in knowledge, be-cause it always expressed its knowledge as a child, and these childlike ideas are probably forever lost to us.

Therefore, respecting the religion and political wisdom of the Egyptians, we can do little more than think of a stage of development observed earlier in several peoples of high antiquity, and still partially observable to this day among the nations of East Asia. Indeed, if it could be shown to be probable that a good part of the knowledge possessed by the Egyptians could hardly have been invented in their country, and that, rather, they continued what others began and adapted it to their country like so many given formulas and premises, their infantile state in all these sciences would become so much more apparent. Hence, in all likelihood, their long registers of kings and of the ages of the world; hence their much-interpreted stories of Osiris, Isis, Horus, Typhon, and others[5]; hence the great number of their religious fables. They have the principal ideas of their religion in common with several countries of Upper Asia; only here they were disguised in hieroglyphics, adapted to the natural history of the country and the character of the people. The basic features of their political constitution are not foreign to other peoples at the same stage of cultural development, except that here, in the beautiful valley of the Nile, an enclosed people thoroughly worked them out and utilized them in its own fashion. Egypt would hardly have attained its high reputation for wisdom, except for its proximity to us, the ruins of its antiquities, and, above all, the impact of the Greek fables.

And it is this very location that demonstrates the place it holds in the rank order of peoples. Few nations sprang from Egypt, or were civilized by it: of the former I know only the Phoenicians, of the latter only the Jews and Greeks; it is not known how far their influence spread into inner Africa. Poor Egypt, how much have you changed now! Once industrious and endowed with patient diligence, a thousand years of despair have reduced you to indolence and wretchedness. At the nod of their Pharaohs, the Egyptians spun and wove, carried stones and excavated in the mountains, pursued the arts and tilled the land. Patiently they suffered themselves to be shut off from the world and to be assigned their lot of labor; they were prolific and raised their children frugally, shied away from strangers and enjoyed the confinement of their land. Ever since they gained entry to this country, or rather, since Cambyses[6] opened the way into it for himself, it became for thousands of years the prey of people after people. Persians and Greeks, Romans, Byzantines, Arabs, Fatimids, Kurds, Mamlucks, and Turks plagued it in succession, and, to this day, this beautiful region of the world is a miserable meeting ground of Arab strife and Turkish barbarities.

～ 31 ～

Further Reflections on the Philosophy of the History of Humankind

Having now gone over a wide range of human events and institutions, from the Euphrates to the Nile, from Persepolis to Carthage, let us sit down and take a retrospective view of our journey.

What is the principal law that we have observed in all the great occurrences of history? In my opinion, it is this: *Everywhere on our earth, that which can be will come to be, partly in keeping with the location and needs of the place, partly according to the circumstances and opportunities of the time, partly in line with the innate or developing character of the peoples.* Once active human powers are unleashed on earth under certain conditions of place and time on earth, all the transformations of human history will take place. Here empires and states crystallize into shape, there they dissolve and assume other forms. Here from a nomad horde rises a Babylon, there from the straitened inhabitants of a coast springs up a Tyre; here, in Africa, an Egypt is formed; there, in the deserts of Arabia, a Jewish state. And all of that in one region of the world, in neighborly proximity to one another. Time, place, and national character alone—in short, the complete collaboration of active powers in their most determinate individuality—determine both all the productions of nature and all the events in the human realm. Let us put this governing law of creation into the light it deserves.

1. *Active human powers are the wellspring of human history,* and since the human being derives his origin from and within one species, his makeup, education, and mentality are thereby already rendered genetic. Hence those singular national characters, which, so deeply imprinted upon

the most ancient of peoples, unmistakably manifest themselves in all of their effects upon earth. As a mineral spring draws its components, healing powers and taste, from the soil within which it came to be, so the ancient character of the peoples sprang from the features of the race, the climate, the way of life and education, from the early endeavors and attainments that became peculiar to this people. The customs of the fathers were deeply rooted, and they became the guiding light of the race. An example of this may be found in the mentality of the Jews, which is known to us most intimately on the basis of both their scriptures and actions; in the land of their fathers as well as amidst other nations, they remained what they were, and even when intermingled with other peoples, they are discernible for several generations. It was and remains the same with all the peoples of antiquity, Egyptians, Chinese, Arabs, Hindus, and so on. The more enclosed their lives, yes, the more they were oppressed, the more their character was confirmed so that, had each of these nations remained in its location, the earth might be regarded as a garden, where here the one and there the other human national plant flowered in keeping with its own formation and nature, where here the one and there the other animal species, each according to its own instinct and character, pursued its course.

But as humans are not firmly rooted plants, the calamities of hunger, earthquakes, war, etc., over the course of time often compelled them to change their location and to settle in another region in a more or less different manner. For even though they might adhere to the customs of their fathers with an obstinacy almost equal to the instinct of animals, and even though they named their new mountains, rivers, cities, and institutions after those of their original country, the great change in the climate and soil made eternal sameness in everything impossible. At this point, then, it occurred to the transplanted people to construct for itself a wasp's nest or an anthill after its own fashion. The construction would be a compound of the ideas of the original country and those of their new home, and this stage of development is usually described as the youthful flowering of the peoples. Thus did the Phoenicians, removed from the Red Sea to the shore of the Mediterranean; thus Moses endeavored to form the Israelites; so it was with several peoples of Asia; for every nation on earth, sooner or later, for a long or a short time, has migrated at least once. It is readily apparent that much depended on when the migration took place, the circumstances by which it was occasioned, the length of the journey, the previous state of civilization of the people, the agreeable or disagreeable conditions they met in their new country, and so on. Thus, even in unmixed peoples, the historical account, merely in terms of geographical and political causes, is so complex that a mind free of preconceived hypotheses is called for lest the thread be lost.

The thread is lost most readily if any one tribe of the peoples is chosen as the favorite and contempt is felt for what is not like it. The historian of humankind must be impartial like the creator of our race or the genius of our earth, and he must judge dispassionately. To the naturalist who will come to know and order all the species of his realm, the rose and the thistle, the skunk and the sloth and the elephant are all equally dear; he most examines that, from which most is to be learned. Now Nature has given the whole earth to humankind, her children; and she has allowed the earth to let spring forth whatever, according to place, time, and inherent power, could do so. Everything that can exist, does exist; everything that can come to be, will come to be, if not today, then tomorrow. Nature's year is long, and the blossoms of her plants are as multifarious as the plants themselves and the elements that nourish them. That which happened in India, Egypt, and China, can never and nowhere on earth happen again; the same is true for Canaan, Greece, Rome, and Carthage. The law of necessity and convenience, composed of inherent powers, place, and time, everywhere brings forth different fruits.

2. If, then, it principally matters *at which time and in which region an empire arose, of what components it consisted, and what external circumstances surrounded it,* we see that a large part of the empire's fate also rests on these features. A monarchy founded by nomads who continue their way of life also in the realm of politics, will hardly endure for long; it destroys and subjugates, until it is destroyed in turn; only the seizure of the capital and often the death of a king put an end to the entire scene of brigandage. So it was with Babylon and Nineveh, with Persepolis and Ecbatana; so it is in Persia to this day. The empire of the Moguls in India has almost come to an end, and the empire of the Turks will suffer the same fate, as long as they remain Chaldeans, which is to say foreign conquerors, and they do not establish a more moral foundation for their regime. The tree may reach to the heavens and overshadow entire regions of the world, but if it has no roots in the earth, it will suffer the fate of a castle in the sky. The tree will fall through the cunning of a single disloyal slave or through the ax of a daring satrap. The ancient and modern history of Asia is full of these revolutions; therefore, little is learned from them by political philosophy. Despots are flung from the throne, and other despots are raised to it. The empire depends on the person of the monarch, on his tent, on his crown; whoever controls these is the new father of the people, that is, the leader of a horde made up mostly of brigands. A Nebuchadnezzar was a terror to all Asia Minor, and under the heir of the second generation the unstable empire was turned to dust. Three victorious battles of Alexander put a complete end to the enormous Persian Empire.

It is a different matter with states that grow from their own roots and rest within themselves; they may be subdued, but the nation endures. So it is with China; it is known how much effort it has cost the conquerors to introduce a mere custom, the Mongol manner of shearing their hair. So it was with the Brahmins and the Israelites, who are eternally set apart from all other people merely by their ceremonial system. Thus Egypt long withstood any intermixture with other peoples, and how difficult it was to extirpate the Phoenicians, merely because they were a people rooted where they lived. Had Cyrus succeeded in founding an empire like those of Yao, Krishna, and Moses, it would still, though mutilated, survive in all its members.

Hence we may infer why ancient political constitutions laid so much stress on the formation of customs through education, as their internal strength depended entirely on this wellspring. Modern empires are founded upon money or the mechanics of politics; the ancient ones were founded on the entire way of thought of a nation since its childhood, and, as there is in the time of childhood no more effective wellspring than religion, most of the ancient states, especially those of Asia, were more or less theocratic. I know the hatred with which this word is regarded, as all the evil that has ever oppressed humankind is ascribed to it; nor do I wish to speak on behalf of any of its abuses. But it is equally true that this form of government was for the childhood of our species not only appropriate, but also necessary; otherwise, it would not have been retained and preserved for so long. From Egypt to China, yes, in almost all countries, it has predominated, so that Greece was the first country to gradually separate its legislation from its religion. And since every religion is politically more effective the more indigenous are the objects of its devotion, its gods and heroes with all their attainments, so we see that every ancient, firmly rooted nation adapted even its cosmogony and mythology to the land it inhabited. The Israelites alone distinguish themselves from all their neighbors in that they attribute neither the creation of the world nor that of humankind to their country. Their lawgiver was an enlightened foreigner who did not in his lifetime reach the land that was to be their future possession; their ancestors had lived elsewhere, their laws had been given to them outside their borders. This probably contributed later to the fact that the Jews, unlike almost all others of the ancient nations, prospered well outside the borders of their own country. The Brahmin and the Chinese cannot live outside their country; and since the Mosaic Jew actually is only a creature of Palestine, outside Palestine there ought not to be any Jews.

3. Finally, from the whole region of the earth over which we have wandered, we perceive how *transitory all human attainments are, yes, how oppressive even the best of institutions come to be within a few generations.*

The plant flowers and fades; your fathers died and decayed; your temple deteriorates; your tabernacle, your tables of laws are no more; language itself, the eternal bond of humankind, becomes antiquated; and can, or should a human constitution, a political or religious institution, which after all can only have been founded upon these, endure forever? If so, the wings of time would be enchained and the revolving globe hang suspended, an idle ice floe over the abyss. How would we feel if we could see King Solomon sacrifice twenty thousand oxen and one hundred and twenty thousand sheep at a single feast, or the Queen of Sheba tax him with riddles at a banquet? What would we say about all the wisdom of the Egyptians if we were shown the bull Apis, the sacred cat, and the revered billy goat in the most splendid of temples? It is the same with the oppressive customs of the Brahmins, the superstitions of the Parsees, the empty presumptions of the Jews, the rhymeless pride of the Chinese, and whatever else may be based on antiquated human institutions of three thousand years' date. Zoroaster's teaching may have been a praiseworthy effort to account for the evil of the world, and to animate his countrymen to all the deeds of light; but what is his theodicy now, even in the eyes of a Mohammedan? The metempsychosis of the Brahmins may be valid as a juvenile dream of the human power of imagination attempting to care for immortal souls in the realm of the visible, and tying moral concepts to this well-intentioned delusion; but what has it come to be but an irrational sacred law, with its thousand appendices of customs and precepts? Tradition in itself is an excellent institution of nature, indispensable to our species; however, as soon as it fetters all power of thought both in practical politics and in education, and impedes all progress of human reason and all the improvements demanded by new circumstances and times, it is the true opium of the spirit for states as well as sects and individual human beings. Magnificent Asia, the mother of all enlightenment of our inhabited earth, has tasted much of this sweet poison and passed it on to others to taste. Great states and sects slumber within Asia, as, according to the fable, St. John sleeps in his grave; he breathes softly, though he died two thousand years ago, and waits slumbering until his awakener shall come.

～ 32 ～

The Language, Mythology, and Poetry of Greece

The following three chapters are representative selections (three out of seven) from Herder's account of Greece in his *Reflections on the Philosophy of History of Humankind.* Ancient Greece, with its geographical situation, its climate, and other favorable circumstances, represents for Herder—and most of the best minds in Germany were in enthusiastic accord with him—a moment in history when the greatest possible development of the power of humanity took place. But unlike many of his contemporaries, Herder does not stylize Greece by dehistoricizing it—as did, for instance, Johann Joachim Winckelmann, the founder of art history. "The genius of those times is gone by," Herder states as historian and philosopher of history. Greek antiquity and classicism are nonetheless a history that shows the quality of cultural achievement that humankind is capable of. Herder suggests not that we imitate the Greeks, but rather that we study the constellation of factors that created their outstanding result, in order to discover how the present age might best bring about a comparable development.

We now come to subjects that have been for some thousands of years the delight of the finer part of humankind, and I hope will ever continue to be so. The Greek language is the most refined of any in the world; Greek mythology the richest and the most beautiful on earth; Greek poetry, at last, considered with respect to time and place, perhaps the most perfect of its kind. Who now gave these once-coarse tribes such a language, such poetry, and such evocative wisdom? These gifts were given to them by the genius of Nature, their country, their way of life, the time in which they lived, and their tribal character.

The Greek language sprang from coarse beginnings; but these beginnings already contained seeds of what it was to become. It was not a hieroglyphic patchwork, not a series of singly ejected syllables, as were the languages beyond the Mongolian mountains. More flexible, more delicate speech organs led to lighter modulation among the peoples of the Caucasus, which could soon be reduced to form by the social propensity for music. The words were linked more gently, the tones modulated into rhythm; thus the language flowed in a fuller current, its images in pleasing harmony; it raised itself to the melody of a dance. And so that unique character of the Greek language came to be, unforced by empty laws, a character which, like a living emanation of nature, developed through music and dance, through song and history, finally through the free and casual discourse of many tribes and colonies. The northern tribes of Europe were not as fortunate in their development. Since foreign customs were imparted to them by foreign laws and a religion devoid of song, their language was also subdued. The German language, for example, has unquestionably lost much of its intrinsic flexibility, much of its more precise expression in the inflecting of words, and still more of that vibrant sound that in a more favorable climate it once possessed. Once it was a close sister of the Greek language, but how far from this it has now developed. No language beyond the Ganges has the flexibility and the smooth flow of the Greek idiom; no Aramaic dialect on this side of the Euphrates in its ancient form had these qualities. The Greek language alone appears as if derived from song; for song and poetry, and an early enjoyment of freedom, fashioned it as the universal language of the muses. Improbable as it is that those conditions of Greek civilization can now gather momentum once more, that humankind can return to its infancy and bring back from the dead, with all that came with them, an Orpheus, a Musaeus, a Linus,[1] a Homer, or a Hesiod, so little would the genesis of a Greek language be possible in our day, even in those regions.

The mythology of the Greeks flowed from the fables of various regions, fables that reflected the belief of the people, narratives of the tribes drawn from their progenitors, or the earliest efforts of reflective minds to explain for themselves the wonders of the world and to give shape to human society.[*] No matter how spurious and newly modified our hymns of the ancient Orpheus may be, they nevertheless are still imitations of those active devotions and salutations to nature to which all nations in the first stage of civilization are prone. The coarse hunter addresses his dreaded bear,[**] the Negro his sacred fetish, the Parsee Mobed[2] his natural spirits and elements,

---

[*]See Heyne, *de fontibus et caussis errorum in historia Mythica; de caussis fabularum physicis; de origine et caussis fabularum Homericarum; de Theogonia ab Hesiodo condita;* etc.[3]

[**]See Georgi, *Abbildungen der Völker des Russischen Reiches,* vol. 1.[4]

almost in Orphic fashion; but how refined and ennobled is the Orphic hymn to nature, merely by the Greek words and images. And how pleasantly accessible did Greek mythology become, as, over time, even in the hymns themselves, it threw off the fetters of mere epithet and instead recited fables of the gods, as in the Homeric songs. In the cosmogonies, too, with the passage of time, the ancient, hard primeval fables were constricted, and human heroes and tribal patriarchs were celebrated, closely tied to the ancient fables and to the figures of the gods. Fortunately, the ancient narrators of the theogonies had brought such fitting and beautiful allegories into the genealogies of the gods and heroes, often by merely injecting one word of their sublime language, that a new and beautiful cloth emerged when later philosophers merely endeavored to spin out their meaning and to link their own finer ideas to them. Thus, in time, even the epic bards laid aside their often-repeated fables of the creation of the gods, the storming of the heavens, the deeds of Hercules, and the like, and sang more human themes for the use of humankind.

Of these, Homer, the father of all Greek poets and philosophers who succeeded him, is the most celebrated. Owing to a fortunate destiny, his scattered songs were collected in time[5] and brought together in a twofold whole that even after millennia stands in splendor like an indestructible palace of the gods and heroes. As there have been endeavors to explain the wonders of nature, so efforts are made to explain the unfolding of Homer,[*] who after all was nothing but a child of nature, a happy bard of the Ionian shore. Many of his kind may have disappeared, who might have been competitors for part of the fame he alone enjoys. Temples have been erected in his honor, and he has been revered like a human god; the greatest reverence, however, is found in the lasting impact he had upon his nation, and still has on all those who are capable of appreciating him. The subjects of his songs, it is true, are trifles in our eyes; his gods and heroes with their customs and passions are none other than those given to him by the fables of his time and the ages before; by the same token, his knowledge of nature and the earth, his understanding of morals and politics, are equally confined. But the truth and wisdom with which he has molded all the objects of his world into a living whole; the firm outline of every feature in every person of his immortal paintings; the unlabored, gentle manner in which he, free as a god, sees all characters, relates their vices and virtues, their fortunes and misfortunes; the music, at last, that unceasingly flows from his lips in such varied and grand poems, imparted to each image, to each sound of his

---

[*]Blackwell's *Enquiry into the Life and Writings of Homer* (1736); Wood's *Essay on the original Genius of Homer* (1769).[6]

words, living eternally at once with his songs—these are what made Homer
unique in the whole history of humanity and make him worthy of immortality, if anything on earth can be immortal.

Necessarily, Homer had a different effect on the Greeks from what he
can have upon us, from whom he so often obtains a forced and frigid
admiration, or indeed cold contempt. Not so with the Greeks. To them he
sang in a living language, at that time still completely unfettered by what
were subsequently termed dialects; to them he sung with patriotic feeling
the exploits of their ancestors against foreigners, and thereby chanted of
families, tribes, constitutions, and regions, which were partly before their
eyes as their own possessions, and lived partly in the memory of their
ancestral pride. Thus to them Homer was in many respects the divine herald
of national fame, a source of the most diversified wisdom. The later poets
followed him; the tragedians drew fables from him, the didactic poets allegories, examples, and sentences; everyone who undertook to write first in a
new genre took from Homer's artistic edifice the model of his own, so that
Homer was soon the paragon of Greek taste, and with weaker minds the
standard of all human wisdom. He also influenced the Roman poets, and
but for him the *Aeneid* would never have existed. Still more has he contributed to reclaiming the modern nations of Europe from barbarism; many a
youth was formed through being delighted by him, and both the active and
the contemplative man drew from him the rules of taste and of human
nature. Yet it is equally undeniable that, as every great man has been the
cause of abuses from an inordinate admiration of his talents, so has the
good Homer, so much so that no one would be more amazed than he, if he
were to rise from the dead and see what has been extracted from him at
various times. Among the Greeks, he maintained the fable longer and more
firmly than it probably would have been maintained without him; rhapso-
dists sang his lines casually, frigid poetasters imitated him; and at length the
enthusiasm among the Greeks for Homer became so barren, insipid, and
overly pointed an art as scarcely has been paralleled for any poet by any
other people. The innumerable commentaries of the grammarians upon him
are for the most part lost; otherwise, we would see in them too the miserable toil God imposes upon the succeeding generations of every preponderat-
ing genius. For are not sufficient examples extant of the erroneous study
and misapplication of Homer in modern times? This much, however, is
certain, that a spirit like his, in the period in which he lived, and for the
nation by which his works were collected, was such an instrument of improvement as scarcely any other people can boast. No people of the Morn
possess a Homer; no poet like him has appeared, at the proper season, in the
bloom of youth, to any people of Europe. Even Ossian[7] was not the same

for his Scots; and to the question whether fate will ever cast a second felicitous lot, to give to the new Grecian archipelago, the Friendly Islands, a Homer, who will lead them to as high a place as his elder twin led Greece, let fate provide the answer.

As Greek civilization thus proceeded from mythology, poetry, and music, we need hardly wonder that a taste for them remained a leading feature of their character, as evinced by their most serious writings and institutions. To our mores, it appears incongruous that the Greeks should speak of music as the principal component of education, that they treat it as a great tool of the state, and that they ascribe the most important consequences to its decline. Still more singular appear to us the animated and almost rapturous praises they bestow on dancing, pantomime, and the dramatic arts, as the natural sisters of poetry and wisdom. Many who read these panegyrics believed that the music of the Greeks was also a wonder of the world in its systematic perfection, because its celebrated effects remained so totally foreign to us. But that which mattered primarily to the Greeks was not the scientific perfection of music, as demonstrated by the use they made of it, for they did not treat it as a distinct art, but employed it subserviently to poetry, the dance, pantomime, and the drama. Thus it is in this connection, and in the entire course of Greek culture, that the major impact of its notes is found. The poetry of the Greeks, which had proceeded from music, was prone to return to it; sublime tragedy itself originated from the chorus; by the same token, the Greeks' ancient comedy, public entertainments, marches into battle, and domestic rejoicing at the feast were rarely unaccompanied by music and song, and most of their games included dance. In these, indeed, as Greece consisted of many states and tribes, one province differed greatly from the other; the times, the various stages of civilization and luxury induced still greater variation; yet, on the whole, it remains perfectly true that the Greeks considered the joint refinement of these arts the summit of human attainments, and attached to that refinement the highest value. It may after all be conceded that neither pantomime nor the drama, neither the dance nor poetry and music, are with us what they were among the Greeks. With them, these arts were but one creation, one flowering of the human spirit, the rough seed that we observe in all savage nations, as long as they are of an amicable and lighthearted disposition and dwell in a felicitous climate. Absurd as it would be to try to transport ourselves back to this period of youthful lightness, since it is gone once and for all, and to skip as a hobbling graybeard among boys, why should this graybeard resent youth for dancing and being lively? The civilization of the Greeks fell upon this period of youthful exuberance, and they made of its arts all that could be made of them; thus they necessarily attained an effect whose possibility we can hardly discern in our diseases and excesses. For I doubt whether there is a greater moment in the delicate shaping of the human sensibility than the fully developed high point of the conjunction of these arts, especially among sentient beings raised and educated to live in a vibrant world of such impressions. So then, let us rejoice at least, if we cannot be Greeks ourselves, that there once were Greeks, and that this blossom of human thought, like any other, found the proper place and time for its most beautiful unfolding.

From what has been said, it may be conjectured that many species of Greek composition which aim at animated representation by means of music, dance, and pantomime, appear to us as phantasmagoria, and may perhaps mislead us, even with the most careful explanation. The theater of Aeschylus, Sophocles, Aristophanes, and Euripides was not our theater; the actual drama of the Greeks is no more to be seen among any people, however excellent may be the pieces of this kind produced by other nations. Without song, without the ceremonial solemnity of the Greeks and their exalted expectations of their plays, Pindar's odes must appear to us as outbursts of intoxication, just as even in the dialogues of Plato, abounding in melody of language and beautiful composition of images and words, those very passages that were expressive of the highest art have been subject to most of the criticism. Youth, therefore, must learn to read the Greeks, since the aged are rarely inclined to look at them or to appropriate their beauties to themselves. Granting that their imagination often transcends the understanding, and that the refined sensuality in which they locate the essence of higher culture often oversteps the bounds of common sense and virtue, let us learn to appreciate them without becoming Greeks ourselves. From their rendering of the subject, from the fine proportion and outline of their thoughts, from that resounding rhythm of their language, which never and nowhere has found its equal, we still have much to learn.

~ 33 ~

Greek Arts

A people endowed with such sensibility also had to ascend from the necessary to the beautiful and pleasing in all the arts of life; the Greeks attained to almost the point of highest perfection in everything they encountered. Their religion required images and temples; their political constitutions demanded monuments and public buildings; their climate and way of life, their industriousness, opulence, vanity, and so on, rendered various works of art indispensable. The genius of the beautiful thus presented them with these tasks, and assisted them—alone in the history of humankind—to complete them; for though the greatest wonders of this art have long been destroyed, we still admire and cherish their ruins and fragments.

1. As we see from the catalogs of their artworks in Pausanias, Pliny,[1] or any of the collections that speak of their remains, religion greatly promoted the art of the Greeks; and this is consistent with all the histories of individual peoples and of humankind. The desire to see the objects of worship was universal, and where this was not forbidden by the law or by the religion itself, attempts were made to represent or shape the image. Even Negro peoples evoked the presence of their god through a fetish, and it is known that the Greeks' images of their gods originally proceeded from a stone or a carved wooden block. A people as industrious as this could not long remain in such artistic meagerness; the wooden block became a herm or a statue, and since the nation was divided into many small tribes and peoples, it was also natural that each wanted to embellish its domestic and tribal deity in its artistic representation. A few felicitous efforts of the ancient people of Daedalus,[2] and probably the observation of the artwork of neighboring peoples, led to emulation, and soon there were several tribes

and city-states that envisioned their god, their most sacred possession, in a more attractive figure. The art of the most ancient times was primarily inspired by the images of gods, and, in a manner of speaking, it learned to walk through them. *This also explains why all the peoples who were forbidden to create images of their gods never advanced very far in sculpture and painting.

However, since the gods of the Greeks were introduced through song and poetry, and lived in it in splendid figures, what was more natural than that sculpture and painting even in early times should be the daughters of poetry, and that the mother, as it were, sang the splendid figures into the daughters' ear? It was from the poets that the artist had to learn the history of the gods, and with it also the manner of their representation. Therefore, the most ancient art did not reject even the most horrible representations of the gods, because the poet had sung them.** In the course of time, more pleasing representations were created, because poetry itself became more pleasing, and thus it was Homer who became a father of the fine arts of the Greeks, as he was the father of its more refined poetry. He conveyed to Phidias[4] that exalted idea of his Jupiter, which became the model for the other works of this sculptor of the gods. In keeping with the relationships of the gods in the narratives of their poets, more fixed characteristics and even family traits entered their representations, until at last the received tradition of the poets became the codex of the figures of deities in the entire realm of art. Thus, no people of antiquity could have the art of the Greeks unless it also had Greek mythology and poetry, and at the same time achieved its culture in the Greek manner. But such a people is not to be found in history, and consequently the Greeks, with their Homeric art, remain unique.

Thus may be explained the ideal creation of Greek art, which arose neither from a profound philosophy of the artists, nor from an ideal natural formation of the nation, but from causes that have been presented up to this point. Unquestionably it was a fortunate circumstance that the Greeks, considered on the whole, were a finely formed people, though this attribute must not be extended to every individual Greek as a model of ideal beauty. In Greece, as everywhere else, nature, abundant with so many shapes, was not to be impeded in its thousandfold variation of human figures, and, according to Hippocrates, there were, as everywhere, deforming diseases and evils among the handsome Greeks as well. But admitting all this, and taking into account many happy opportunities, when the artist could exalt a

---

*See Winckelmann's *Geschichte der Kunst*, vol. 1, ch. 1. *Heyne*, critique of and additions to this work in the *Deutsche Schriften der Götting. Societät*, vol. 1, pp. 211 f.[3]
**See *Heyne* on the Coffer of Kypselus, etc.[5]

beautiful youth into an Apollo and a Phryne and a Lais[6] into a goddess of love, this would still not explain the received ideal of the artists' gods, which had become the rule. It is probably as little possible that a head of Jupiter should exist in human form as that the Jupiter of Homer actually existed in the world. The great anatomical draftsman *Camper* has clearly shown* the thought that went into the rules on which the Greek artistic ideal rested; but only the imagination of the artists and the intent of sacred reverence could have led to these rules. If, therefore, you would produce a new Greece in divine images, give to a people once more this poetic-mythological superstition, with everything that goes with it, in all its natural simplicity. Travel through Greece and contemplate its temples, its grottoes, and its sacred groves, and you will abandon even the idea of wishing the sublimity of Greek art upon a people that knows absolutely nothing of such a religion—that is, of such a lively superstition that filled every city, every spot, every nook with an innate sacred presence.

2. All the heroic fables of the Greeks, in particular those relating to the progenitors of their tribe, fall under the same consideration; for they too passed through the souls of the poets and in part lived in eternal songs; the artist who shaped them, emulated their stories with a sort of artist's religion, to gratify the pride of his countrymen and their attachment to their ancestors. The most ancient history of the arts, as well as a survey of Greek artworks, confirms this. Tombs, shields, altars, holy places, and temples preserved the remembrance of their forefathers, and these objects also occupied the working artists of several tribes from the most ancient times on. All the warlike peoples of the world painted and embellished their shields; the Greeks went further: they engraved, or cast, and carved upon them memorials of their ancestors. Hence the early works of Vulcan in very ancient poets[7]; hence in Hesiod the shield of Hercules[8] with the deeds of Perseus. Alongside the shields, representations of this kind adorned the altars of heroes and other family memorials, as shown by the coffer of Kypselus, the figures on which were completely in the style of Hesiod's shield. Noble works of this kind had been written as early as the times of Daedalus, and since many temples of the gods were originally tombs,** in them the memories of the ancestors, the heroes, and the gods came so close together that they coalesced almost into one veneration, at least into one wellspring of art. Hence the representation of the ancient heroic stories on

---

*Camper's *Kleinere Schriften,* pp. 18 f.
**As, for example, the temple of Pallas at Larissa was the tomb of Acrisius; that of Minerva Polias at Athens was the tomb of Ericthonius; the throne of Amyclus was the tomb of Hyacinthus; etc.

the gowns of their gods, and on the sides of the altars and the thrones; hence the monuments of the deceased frequently seen in the city's marketplace, or the herms and columns on graves. If we add to these the innumerable works of art presented to the temples of the gods by states, families, or individuals, as memorials or pledges of gratitude, and frequently adorned, according to custom, with representations of tribal and heroic history, what other people can boast such an incentive to the most diversified art? Our galleries of ancestors, with their portraits of forgotten progenitors are nothing in comparison with these, as all Greece was filled with fables and songs, and with sacred places of their gods and heroic ancestors. Everything was linked to the bold idea that the gods were related to them, that superior men and heroes were lesser gods; but this concept was created by the poets.

With regard to family and patriotic fame that promoted art, I also include the Greek games. They were instituted by their heroes, and at the same time were their memorial celebrations, customs serving both divine worship and the promotion of art and poetry in a most advantageous way. It was not only that partly naked youths exercised themselves in various contests, and thus served the artist as living models, but rather that through these exercises their bodies became suitable for such artistic emulation, and that through their youthful victories their spirit was preserved in the homage paid to the glory of their families, ancestors, and heroes. We know from Pindar and from history how highly victories of this kind were esteemed all over Greece, and how passionately they were competed for. The entire city of the winner was thus honored; gods and heroes of bygone ages descended upon the family of the victor. Herein resides the economy of Pindar's odes,[9] works of art which he raised above the level of decorative columns. Here was rooted the honor merited by the victor, conferred by the tomb or statue, which largely idealized him. By this fortunate emulation of his heroic ancestors, the victor had in a way become a god and was exalted above men. Where now are such games possible, equally prized and with equal consequences?

3. The political constitutions of the Greeks likewise promoted the arts, not only because they were free city-states, but because these free city-states used the artists in the attainment of great works. Greece was divided into many states, and whether they were ruled by kings or archons, the arts were fostered. Their kings were also Greeks, and all the requirements for art, whether founded on religious reasons or tribal fables, were the requirements of the kings, who often were even the supreme priests. So it was that from very ancient times the decoration of their palaces was distinguished by precious relics of their tribal or heroic ancestors, as Homer relates. But the republican constitutions, which were introduced all

over Greece in the course of time, gave a wider scope to art. In a common-wealth, buildings were necessary for the assembly of the people, for the public treasury, and for general exercise and amusement; and thus arose in Athens, for example, the magnificent gymnasia, theaters, and galleries, the Odeum and the Prytaneum, the Pnyx,[10] and so on. Since everything in the Greek republics was conducted in the name of the people or the city, nothing that was expended on their patron gods or the glory of their names was too costly, whereas the individual, even the most noble citizen, contented himself with more modest dwellings. This public spirit of doing everything, in appearance at least, for the community, was the soul of the Greek states, as *Winckelmann*[11] no doubt considered when he esteemed the liberty of the Greek republics the golden age of the arts. In them, grandeur and splendor were not distributed as in modern times, but coalesced in whatever pertained to the state. Pericles flattered the people with tributes of this kind, and he did more for the arts than ten Athenian kings would have done. Everything built by him was done in grand style, because it was dedicated to the gods and to the immortal city. And it is certain that few Greek cities and islands would have erected such buildings, and would have promoted such works of art, had they not been free city-states existing apart from one another and competing for glory. Since, moreover, in democratic republics, the leader must please the people, what manner of expenditure would he employ but the one that, in addition to pleasing the patron gods, also caught the eye of the people and afforded sustenance to many of them?

No one can doubt that this expenditure also had consequences that humankind would much rather forget. The severity with which the Athenians oppressed the conquered, even their colonies, the brigandage and warfare in which the Greek states were incessantly engaged, the burdensome services the citizens themselves were obliged to render to the state, and many other things, rendered the Greek states less than desirable abodes; but even these grievances became the subjects of the public arts. The temples of the gods for the most part were sacred also to the enemy. But with the turning of fate, even the temples laid waste by the enemy arose from the ashes more beautiful than before. From the spoils gained from the Persians a more magnificent Athens was built, and after almost all victorious wars, from the part of the spoils belonging to the state, contributions were made to one or the other art. Even in later times, notwithstanding the devastation brought about by the Romans, Athens preserved the glory of its name through statues and edifices, for several emperors, kings, heroes, and wealthy private citizens competed to preserve and beautify a city that they recognized as the mother of all refined taste. Hence we also observe that Greek art did not perish under the Macedonian empire;

it merely changed its seat. Even in distant countries, Greek kings were still Greeks, and they were fond of Greek art. Hence Alexander and many of his successors built splendid cities in Africa and Asia; the Romans and other peoples also learned from the Greeks, as they missed the time for indigenous artistic development in their own country; for, everywhere on earth, there was only one form of Greek art and architecture.

4. Finally, it was also the environment of the Greeks that sustained the arts, not primarily in how it shaped the people, for that depends more on tribal descent than on climate, but because of the convenient location of the materials for the creation of artworks and their erection. Their country afforded them the fine Parian and other marbles; ivory, ores, and whatever else their art called for were provided for them by a system of trade routes that found them in the center. In a way, their trade preceded their art, as it conveyed to them from Asia Minor, Phoenicia, and other countries precious articles that they themselves did not know how to shape at the time. Thus the sprouts of their artistic talent were coaxed forth early, especially also because their proximity to Asia Minor, their colonies in Magna Graecia,[12] and so on, aroused in them a taste for opulence and the good life that could not fail to promote the arts. It was far from the serenity of the Greek character to waste its diligence on useless pyramids; individual cities and states could never lose themselves in this desert of the monstrous. Thus, perhaps with the single exception of the Colossus of Rhodes,[13] even in their works of greatest magnitude they adhered to that beautiful proportion in which the graceful meets the sublime. For this their serene sky gave them ample opportunity. It allowed them those numerous uncovered statues, altars, and temples, and in particular the beautiful column, that pattern of simplicity, correctness, and proportion, whose slender graciousness could replace the inert northern wall.

If all these circumstances are taken together, it is obvious how even in the field of art, that spirit could prevail in Ionia, Greece, and Sicily that characterizes the style of the Greeks in all their works. It cannot be learned through rules alone, but it displays itself in the observation of rules; and, though originally the inspiration of a happy genius, through continuous practice it became a craft. Even the meanest Greek artist is Greek in his manner; we may excel him, but we shall never achieve the whole genetic spirit of Greek art; the genius of those times is gone by.

～ 34 ～

General Reflections on the History of Greece

We have considered the history of this remarkable region from several points of view, as it represents in a way for the philosophy of history a development unique among all the peoples of the earth. The Greeks not only remained free from any intermixture with foreign nations, so that their formation has been entirely their own, but they also lived their historical epochs to the fullest, and from the smallest beginnings journeyed through their entire course in a manner unmatched by any other people in history. The nations of the continent either have stopped at the earliest beginning of civilization, and unnaturally perpetuated it by laws and customs, or have become prey to conquest before they had lived their course; the flower was cut down before it blossomed. Greece, on the contrary, enjoyed the fullness of its time; it developed of itself what it was capable of developing, a perfection to which it was helped once more by the good fortune of its circumstances. On the continent, undoubtedly it would have soon become the prey of a conqueror, like its Asiatic brethren; had Darius and Xerxes attained their purposes in Greece, there would not have been an "Age of Pericles."[1] Or if a despot had reigned over Greece, he would have soon become a conqueror himself, according to the disposition of all despots, and, as Alexander did, would have stained the water of distant rivers with the blood of his Greeks. Foreign peoples would have been mingled into their country, and the Greeks in turn, in gaining their victories, would have been dispersed through foreign countries, and so on. They were now protected from all of this by the modesty of their power, and even by their restricted trade, which never dared reach beyond the limits of the Pillars of Hercules[2] and of fortune. As the botanist cannot completely behold a plant

287

unless he first has gained knowledge of it from seed and sprout to bloom and withering, so is Greek history to us such a plant; it is only to be regretted that, as is usually the case, it is still far from having been studied, like that of Rome. At present it is my place to indicate, from what has been said, a few viewpoints about the entire history of humankind that present themselves immediately to the eye of the beholder; and to this end, I begin by repeating the grand principle:

First: *Whatever can take place in the realm of humankind, within the sphere of given circumstances of time, place, and nation, actually does take place.* Of this Greece affords the most ample and beautiful evidence.

In physical nature we never count on miracles; we observe laws that we find everywhere to be equally effective, unchangeable, and regular; and shall the realm of humankind, with its energies, transformations, and passions, escape from this chain of nature? Place the Chinese in Greece, and our Greece would never have come to be; place our Greeks where Darius led the captured Eretrians[3]; they will not found a Sparta or an Athens. Behold Greece now; you will no longer find the ancient Greeks, yes, often not even their country. If a remnant of their language were not still spoken, if indications of their way of thought, ruins of their art, their cities, or at least their ancient rivers and mountains were not still visible, you could not but believe that ancient Greece had been presented to you as a poetic fantasy, an island of Calypso or the gardens of Alcinous.[4] But as it is only through the course of time, in a given series of causes and effects, that the modern Greeks have become what they are, so too did the ancient ones, and no less so every other nation on earth. The entire history of humankind is the pure natural history of human powers, actions, and propensities, modified by time and place.

As simple as this principle may be, just as luminous and useful does it become in treating of the history of peoples. Every historian agrees with me that a barren wonder and recital do not deserve the name of history; and if this is true, the examining mind must bring all of its acumen to bear on every historical event as on a natural phenomenon. Thus, in the narration of history, the historian will seek the most profound truth, in comprehending and evaluating the most complete connectedness, and never attempt to explain something that is, or happens, by means of one that is not. With this strict principle, all ideals, all phantoms of a magic realm disappear; everywhere one seeks to see only that which is, and as soon as this is seen, the eye sees the reason why it could not be otherwise. As soon as the sentient being has acquired this habit in the pursuit of history, he will have found the way to that more wholesome philosophy which rarely occurs except in natural history and mathematics.

This philosophy will, first and foremost, guard us from attributing the facts that appear in history to the particular purposes of a scheme of things unknown to us, or to the magical influences of invisible demons, whose names one would not dare even to utter in terms of the manifestations of nature. Fate reveals its purposes through the events that occur and the manner of their occurrence; thus the observer of history develops these purposes exclusively from what is here and what reveals itself in its entire extent. Why were the enlightened Greeks in the world? Because they were there, and could, under such circumstances, be none other than enlightened Greeks. Why did Alexander invade India? Because he was Alexander, the son of Philip; and from the dispositions his father had made, and in keeping with the deeds of his nation, his own age and character, his reading of Homer, and so on, he knew of nothing better that he could undertake. But if we attributed his bold resolution to the secret purposes of a higher power, and his heroic achievements to a particular goddess of good fortune, we would run the danger of on the one hand turning Alexander's recklessness into ultimate divine objectives, on the other diminishing his personal courage and military skill, while generally depriving the entire event of its natural form. He who takes with him into natural history the fairy-tale belief that invisible sylphs tinge the rose or moisten its blossoms with silvery dew drops, and who believes that little spirits of light take the body of the glowworm as their cover or dance on the peacock's tail, may be an ingenious poet, but he will never shine as a naturalist or a historian. History is the science of what is, not of what may possibly be according to hidden designs of fate.

Second: *What is true of one people holds also for the connection of several peoples with each other; they are joined as time and place tied them together; they act upon one another as the combination of active powers directs.*

The Greeks have been acted upon by Asians, who have in turn been acted upon by the Greeks. Romans, Goths, Turks, and Christians have overcome the Greeks, and Romans, Goths, and Christians have received various kinds of enlightenment from them; how are these things connected? Through place, time, and the natural operation of active powers. The Phoenicians gave the Greeks the use of letters; they had not invented the letters for the Greeks, but brought them along when they established a colony among the Greeks. So it was with the Hellenes and the Egyptians, so it was when the Greeks moved into Bactria, so it was with all the gifts of the muse we received from the Greeks. Homer sang, but not for us; we have him, and have the chance to learn from him, merely because he came down to us. Had any circumstance in the course of time deprived us of him, as we have been deprived of many other excellent works, who would want to quarrel with the purposes of some secret fate, when the natural causes of the fall are before our eyes? Let someone reflect on the writings that are lost and those that remain, on the works of art that are destroyed and those that are preserved, together with the accounts that are given of their destruction and their preservation, and venture to point out the rule that fate has followed in transmitting these to us, and depriving us of those. The works of Aristotle were preserved in a single copy underground, other writings as waste parchments in chests and cellars, the humorist Aristophanes under the pillow of St. John Chrysostom, who learned to compose homilies from him; and thus all our enlightenment depended completely on the most odd and obscure byways. Now there is no question that our enlightenment is a grand matter in world history; it has caused upheaval among all peoples, and now, with the aid of *Herschel*,[5] it dissects the milky ways of the heavens as if they were strata. And yet it depended on such trifling circumstances, to bring us eyeglasses and some books; so that without these trifles we should still perhaps be wandering about in wagons, with our wives and families, like our elder brothers, the immortal Scythians! Had the sequence of events determined that we receive Mongol letters instead of Greek, we would now write Mongolian instead of Greek, and the earth would nonetheless carry on its grand revolution with its annual calendar and seasons, sustaining all that lives and acts upon her according to the divine laws of nature.

Third: *The civilization of a people is the flower of its existence; it manifests itself in it in a pleasing but transitory way.*

As the human being comes into the world knowing nothing, having to learn all he wants to know, so an untutored people learns through practice, or from interaction with others. But every kind of human knowledge has its own particular sphere, that is, its nature, time, place, and span of life; Greek civilization, for example, grew out of times, places, and circumstances, and declined with them. Certain arts and poetry preceded philosophy; where art and oratory flourished, military skill and patriotic virtue were not necessarily also given to thrive; the orators of Athens showed their greatest enthusiasm as the state declined and its integrity waned.

But all kinds of human enlightenment have in common that each strives toward a point of perfection which, when attained here or there through a concatenation of fortunate circumstances, neither will preserve itself there forever, nor can instantly reappear, but must begin a sequence of decline. For every consummate achievement, insofar as perfection may be expected of humanity, is the most sublime of its kind; following upon it, only imitations or unfortunate attempts to surpass it are possible. When Homer had completed his song, no second Homer was conceivable; he had gathered the blossom of the epic garland, and whoever followed him had to be content with individual leaves. The Greek tragedians, therefore, chose a different career; they ate, as Aeschylus says, at Homer's table, but prepared a different banquet for their age. Their age also went by; the subjects of tragedy were exhausted, and all that the successors of the greatest poets could do was merely to alter them, that is, to present them in inferior form, because the most beautiful form of Greek drama had already been presented in those models. Notwithstanding all his morality, Euripides could not measure up to Sophocles, to say nothing of being able to exceed him in the essence of his art, and the clever Aristophanes therefore chose another career. So it was with all the forms of Greek art, and will remain so among all peoples; yes, that the Greeks in the times of their glory understood this law of nature, and that they did not attempt to surpass the sublime by something still higher, that made their taste so sure and its manifestation so varied. When Phidias had created his omnipotent Jupiter, a superior Jupiter was not within the realm of possibility; but the ideal of his Jupiter could also be applied to other gods of his kind, and so each god was given his particular character, and the entire province of art was given life.

It would be poor and petty of us to prescribe our attachment to any object of human civilization as a rule for all-disposing providence, in order to confer an unnatural eternity on that one moment in which it could have occurred. Such a wish would be nothing less than to annihilate the essence of time and destroy the entire nature of finitude. Our youth comes not again, nor do the faculties of our souls as they were at that time and place. The fact that the flower appeared shows that it will fade; it has drawn to itself the powers of the plant from its very root; and when the flower dies, the death of the plant must follow. It would have been unfortunate if the age that produced a Pericles and a Socrates could have been prolonged a moment beyond the time that the chain of events prescribed for its duration; it was for Athens a perilous and unbearable moment in time. Just as limited would be the notion that the mythology of Homer should endure forever in the human heart, that the Greek gods should rule forever, that their Demosthenes should thunder eternally, and so on. Every plant of nature must fade, but the faded plant scatters its seeds and thereby renews living creation. Shakespeare was no Sophocles, Milton no Homer, Bolingbroke[6] no Pericles; yet they were in their kind and place what those were in theirs. Let everyone, therefore, strive in his place to be what he can be in the course of things; this he will be, and to be anything else is impossible.

Fourth: *The health and duration of a state rest not on the highest point of its civilization, but on a wise and felicitous equilibrium of its active living powers. The deeper its center of gravity lies within this active striving, the firmer and more durable will it be.*

On what did those ancient founders of states rely? Neither on lethargic inactivity nor on the most extreme movement; rather, they relied on order and an appropriate distribution of the never-resting, ever-active powers. The principle of these sages was genuine human wisdom, learned from nature. Whenever a state was driven to its utmost point, though it be by the most brilliant of men and for the most striking of reasons, it ran the danger of destruction, and it recovered its former status only by the successful application of violence. So Greece found itself, in the conflict with the Persians, at a frightening point; so it was when Athens, Lacedaemon,[7] and Thebes contended to the utmost with one another, leading to the loss of liberty for all of Greece. Likewise Alexander, with his brilliant victories, drove his entire state to the pinnacle of danger; it fell and disintegrated. How dangerous Alcibiades[8] and Pericles were to Athens is shown by their history; though it is no less true that episodes of this kind, especially when they are resolved quickly and successfully, will produce effects rarely seen and arouse incredible powers. Everything brilliant in Greece was created by the vigorous activity of many states and vital energies; everything enduring and sound in its taste and in its constitution, on the contrary, was caused by the felicitous equilibrium of its striving powers. In each case, the happy state of its institutions was more noble and permanent in proportion as they were founded on humanity, that is, reason and equity. Here the constitution of Greece affords us an ample field for reflection, in what it contributed by its innovations and institutions both to the happiness of its citizens and to that of all humankind. But it is still too early for this. We must first take a view of many periods and peoples before we can arrive at firm conclusions on these subjects. . . .

∽ 35 ∽

Germanic Peoples

The following two chapters are parts of Book Sixteen of Herder's *Reflections on the Philosophy of History of Humankind,* where he gives a survey of different peoples in Europe at the time of the migration of the nations. With these chapters Herder finishes his large-scale survey of world history up to the beginning of the Middle Ages, an account that is constantly interwoven with philosophical reflections. By scrutinizing different factors that determine historical development, Herder tries to explain why Central Europe became what it was at the end of antiquity. The chapter entitled "Slavic Peoples" became particularly famous in Eastern Europe because of Herder's extraordinarily positive characterization. This idealization, which is buttressed by the contrast with the previous chapter on the belligerent Germanic peoples, is at least partially due to Herder's own experiences in Riga during the 1760s.

We now come to the people who, by their numbers and strength of body, by their enterprising, bold, and persevering spirit in war, by their heroic devotion to service, to following their leaders in the cohort wherever they might go, and to dividing the conquered lands as spoils among them, and thus with their extensive conquests and the establishment everywhere of constitutions in the German manner, have contributed more to the woe and well-being of this continent than any other people. From the Black Sea throughout all of Europe, the arms of the Germans became feared; a Gothic kingdom once extended from the Volga to the Baltic; in Thrace, Moesia, Pannonia, Italy, Gaul, Spain, even in Africa, various Germanic peoples settled and founded kingdoms; by them the Romans, Saracens, Gaels, Cymri, Laps, Finns, Estonians, Slavs, Courlanders, Prus, and even some of their own peoples, were driven from their possessions; by them all the modern kingdoms of Europe were founded, their estates introduced, and their laws established. More than once they defeated Rome, captured the city and plundered it; several times they besieged Constantinople, and even made themselves masters of it; at Jerusalem they founded a Christian monarchy; and to this day, partly through the princes they have seated on every throne of Europe and partly through their own kingdoms, as owners of property or through manufacture and commerce, they essentially exercise dominion over the four quarters of the globe. But since no effect is without cause, there must also have been some cause for this enormous series of effects.

1. *This cause does not lie in the character of the nation alone; their physical as well as their political makeup, indeed, a number of circumstances that do not apply to any other northern people, have contributed to the course of these achievements.* Their large, strong, and well-proportioned bodies, and their fearsome blue eyes, which were animated by a spirit of loyalty and self-denial, obedience to their superiors, boldness in attacking, and perseverance in times of danger, rendered them to other peoples, especially the degenerate Romans, pleasing as friends, fearsome as enemies. Early on, Germans served in the Roman armies, and they were given preference in the selection for the imperial guard; indeed, when the threatened empire was unable to protect itself, German armies served for pay against any enemy of Rome, even their own brethren. Because of this mercenary service, which continued for centuries, many of their peoples not only obtained knowledge of the science of war and military discipline that remained foreign to other barbarians, but they also gradually developed, through the example of the Romans and their awareness of Roman weakness, a taste for conquests and military excursions of their own. If Rome, now so degenerate, had once suppressed peoples and risen to dominion over the world, why should they, without whose arms Rome no longer was capable of vigorous action, not do the same? Accordingly, if the earlier incursions of the Teutons and Cimbri are put aside, and the account is begun with the most enterprising men, Ariovistus, Marbutus, and Arminius,[1] the first thrust against Roman territories came from border peoples or leaders who were acquainted with this empire's way of war, and who had often served in its armies themselves and were thus thoroughly familiar with the weaknesses of Rome and, later, Constantinople. Even then a few of them were Roman auxiliaries, as they came to deem it beneficial to preserve for themselves what they had heretofore saved from others' threats. As a rich and feeble state, dependent on a strong and ambitious neighbor, will come inevitably to be dominated by that neighbor, so in this case the Romans put the sword into the hands of the Germans, who were established

directly before them, and whom they soon admitted from necessity into their state or into their armies.

2. *The long resistance that several peoples of our Germany had to put up against the Romans necessarily strengthened their powers and intensified their hatred of a hereditary enemy, who boasted more of the triumphs over them than any other victories.* Both on the Rhine and on the Danube, the Romans had been a threat to the Germans; as much as the Germans had been inclined to serve the Romans against the Gauls and other peoples, they were not by any means willing to serve them by subjugating themselves. Hence the long wars from the time of Augustus, which, the feebler the Roman Empire became, deteriorated the more into raids and plundering, and could only end with Rome's demise. The *Marcomannic* and *Swabian leagues,* which several peoples formed against the Romans, the *Heerbann,* which covered all the German tribes, even the most remotely located, and which made every man a *warrior,* obliged to fight for the common cause, this and several other institutions gave to the entire nation the name as well as the constitution of *Germans,* or *Alemanni,* that is, of allied peoples under arms, precursors of a system that, centuries later, was to spread to all the nations of Europe.[*]

3. *Given such a permanent military constitution, the Germans were necessarily deficient in various other virtues, which they not unwillingly sacrificed to their leading inclination, or principal necessity, war.* They did not engage in agriculture nearly as diligently, and among several tribes, by the annual reallocation of their acreage, they precluded that pleasure which individuals take in their own possessions, and in the improvement of their lands. Some, especially of the eastern tribes, were and long remained Tatar-like hunters and pastoral peoples. The primitive concept of common pastures and the collective ownership of property was a favorite notion of these nomads, which they brought with them into the countries and kingdoms they conquered. Thus Germany long remained a forest, interspersed with pastures, bogs, and swamps, where the wild ox and the elk, the now extirpated animals of the German heroic age, dwelt among the ancient Germanic heroes. Of science they were ignorant, and the few arts with which they could not dispense were carried on by women and by servants who, for the

---

[*]An extensive description of German constitutions, which differed greatly from one another according to time, tribe, and region, would be pointless here, since their impact on the history of the peoples will soon enough reveal itself. Following the elaborate explanations of Tacitus, and concentrating on his own region, Möser has presented a description of them which, with its harmoniously blended components, conveys an almost ideal system, though in parts it appears to be quite realistic. See Möser's *Osnabrückische Geschichte,* vol. 1, and, here and there, in his *Patriotische Phantasien.*[2]

most part, had been captured. It must have pleased such people to quit their deserted forests in quest of better regions or to serve as mercenaries, whenever prompted by revenge, want, boredom, companionship, or any other incentive. Hence a number of tribes were in a state of unceasing turmoil with and against one another, either as enemies or as allies. No people have so often shifted their quarters as these, if we except among them a few tribes of more settled disposition; and when one tribe departed, several others commonly joined it, so that the cohort grew to an army. Many German peoples, Vandals, Suevi, and others, derive their names from roaming about, wandering; thus it was by land, thus by sea: a rather Tataric existence.

With respect to the most ancient history of the Germans, we must take care not to read into it one favorite aspect of our modern constitution; the ancient Germans do not have a place in our modern constitution; they followed a different stream of peoples. Toward the west they put pressure upon the Belgians and Gauls, until they found themselves in the midst of other tribes; toward the east they advanced to the Baltic Sea, and since they could not find any spoils at sea, nor use it to move further, and could not find sustenance on its sandy shores, it was only natural that they turned south toward deserted lands at the first opportunity. So it is that several nations that entered the Roman Empire had earlier dwelt by the Baltic Sea, but they were merely the more primitive peoples, whose settlement at the Baltic was not of itself the cause for the fall of Rome. This cause was located at a much greater distance, in *Asiatic Mongolia;* for there the western Huns were pressed upon by the Igurians and other peoples; they crossed the Volga and encountered the Alani at the Don, they came upon the great kingdom of the Goths at the Black Sea, and now various southern Germanic peoples began to move, Visigoths and Ostrogoths, Vandals, Alani, and Suevi, followed by the Huns. With the Saxons, Franks, and Burgundians, it was a different matter, as it was with the Heruli, who long served in the Roman armies as heroes who sold their blood for pay.

We must likewise take care not to ascribe similar customs or a similar degree of civilization to all these peoples, as shown by the differences in their conduct toward the nations they conquered. The savage Saxons in Britain and the roaming Alani and Suevi in Spain did not conduct themselves like the Ostrogoths in Italy or the Burgundians in Gaul. The tribes that had long dwelt on the Roman frontiers in the west or the south, near their colonies and commercial centers, were milder and more polished than those who came from the northern forests or the barren seacoasts; hence it would be arrogant for every horde of Germans to ascribe to itself, for instance, the mythology of the Scandian Goths. How far these Goths advanced! And in how many ways was this mythology afterward refined! To the brave original German there is perhaps nothing left but his *Theut* or *Tuisto, Mann, Hertha,* and *Wotan,*[3] that is, a father, a hero, the earth, and a general.

Yet we may at least fraternally enjoy that remote treasure of *Germanic mythology,* which was preserved at the end of the inhabited world, in Iceland, and obviously enriched by the legends of the Normans and Christian scholars: I mean the Nordic *Edda.*[4] As a collection of documents of the language and way of thought of a Germanic tribe, it is indeed most noteworthy to us too. Depending on how the examination is undertaken, a comparison of the mythology of these Nordic peoples with that of Greece may be either instructive or useless; but it would be vain in the extreme to expect a Homer or an Ossian among these skalds.[5] Does the earth produce the same fruits everywhere? And are not the most precious fruits of this kind the consequence of an extraordinary condition of peoples and times, which had been long in ripening? Thus, let us appreciate in these poems and fables what we find in them, a unique spirit of primitive and bold poetry, strong, pure, and faithful sentiments, together with a slightly too artful employment of the core of our language; and thanks be offered to every hand that helps preserve and communicate these national treasures, that has contributed to the more general or better use of them. Among the names of those, who in earlier and modern times made praiseworthy contributions,* I must mention, in our own days, with respect and gratitude, the name of *Suhm.*[7] He has made this beautiful northern light from Iceland shine over us with new splendor; he and others try to introduce it also into the realm of our more formal knowledge, for more appropriate utilization. It is to be regretted that we Germans have little of the ancient treasures of our language to display;** the poems of our bards are lost; the ancient oak tree of our epic language exhibits few blossoms except those of very recent date.

After the Germanic nations had accepted Christianity, they fought for it as they fought for their kings and noblemen; this genuine loyalty of the sword was amply experienced by—aside from their own peoples, the Alemanni, Thuringians, Bavarians, and Saxons—the unfortunate Slavs, Prus, Courlanders, Livonians, and Estonians as well. It is to the glory of the German nations that embraced Christianity that they stood as a living wall against the later incursions of barbarians, a wall that broke the fury of the Huns, the Hungarians, the Mongols, and the Turks. Thus they not only

---

Sämund, Snorro, Resenius, Worm, Torfäus, Stephanius, Bartholin, Keisler, Ihre, Göranson, Thorkelin, Erichsen, the *Magnäi, Anchersen, Eggers,* etc.[6]

**All our riches, except some scattered remnants found here and there, are contained in Schilter's *Thesaurus,*[8] and that is far from considerable.

conquered the largest part of Europe, cultivated it, and shaped its institutions in their fashion, but also sheltered and protected it; otherwise, Europe would not have produced what has appeared in it. Their reputation among other nations, their covenant in war, and their tribal character came to be the foundation walls of the civilization, liberty, and security of Europe; whether they were not also, through their political constitution, a cause of the gradual progress of this civilization will be accounted for by history, an impartial witness.

36

Slavic Peoples

The role played in history by the Slavic nations is greatly disproportionate to the extent of the territory occupied by them; one reason for this, among others, is that they lived at such distance from the Romans. We first notice them on the Don, among the Goths; then on the Danube, amid the Huns and the Bulgarians, with whom they frequently disturbed the Roman Empire, though mainly as associates, auxiliaries, or vassals. Despite their occasional achievements, they were never enterprising warriors or adventurers like the Germans; rather, they followed them quietly, occupying the lands the Germans had evacuated, till at length they were in possession of the vast territory extending from the Don to the Elbe and from the Adriatic Sea to the Baltic. On this side of the Carpathians, their settlements extended from Lüneburg to Mecklenburg, Pomerania, Brandenburg, Saxony, Lusatia, Bohemia, Moravia, Silesia, Poland, and Russia; beyond the Carpathians, where they had settled early in Wallachia and Moldavia, they were continually spreading farther and farther, assisted by various circumstances, until the Emperor Heraclius[1] admitted them also into Dalmatia, and step by step they founded the kingdoms of Slavonia, Bosnia, Serbia, and Dalmatia. They came to be equally numerous in Pannonia[2]; starting from Friuli,[3] they occupied the southeastern corner of Germany, so that their domains included Styria, Carinthia, and Carniola: an immense region, the European part of which is chiefly inhabited by one nation even to this day. Everywhere they settled in lands that others had relinquished, cultivating or using them, as colonists, shepherds, or farmers; after the devastations, transgressions, and migrations that preceded their arrival, their peaceful, diligent presence was thus of great benefit to these countries. They tended toward agriculture, the acquisition of herds and of stores of grain, and various domestic arts; and wherever they dwelt, they began a profitable trade in the produce of their land and their industry. Along the Baltic, starting from Lübeck, they built seaport towns, among which Vineta, on the island of Rügen,[4] was the Amsterdam of the Slavs; thus they interacted with the ancient Prus, Courlanders, and Latvians, as the languages of these peoples show. On the Dnieper they founded Kiev, on the Wolcott, Novogorod, which soon became flourishing commercial centers, connecting the Black Sea with the Baltic and conveying the products of the East to Northern and Western Europe. In Germany they engaged in mining, mastered metal smelting and casting, made salt, wove linen, brewed mead, planted fruit trees, and in their own way led a joyful life enriched by music. They were charitable, hospitable to excess, lovers of pastoral freedom, but submissive and obedient, foes to plunder and rapine. All this did not save them from oppression; rather, it contributed to their being oppressed. For, as they never sought domination of the world, had no warlike hereditary princes among them, and were willing to pay tribute if only they could live in peace on their lands, many other nations, chiefly Germanic in origin, severely violated them.

Wars of suppression were already being waged under Charlemagne. Their motive was clearly commercial advantage, although Christianity was their pretext: it was doubtless convenient for the heroic Franks to treat as vassals an industrious nation devoted to trade and agriculture, instead of mastering and practicing these arts themselves. What the Franks began, the Saxon completed; in whole provinces the Slavs were extirpated or reduced to serfdom, and their lands were divided among bishops and nobles. Northern Germanic peoples destroyed their Baltic trade; the Danes brought their Vineta to a sad end; and their remnants in Germany were reduced to that state to which the Spaniards subjected the Peruvians. Is it to be wondered at that, after this nation had borne the yoke for centuries and cherished the most bitter animosity against its Christian lords and robbers, its gentle character descended to the artful, cruel indolence of the serf? And yet, particularly in lands where they enjoy any degree of freedom, their ancient stamp is still universally perceptible. It was the misfortune of these people that their love of quiet and domestic industry was incompatible with any permanent military establishment, although they were valiant in their passionate defense of their lands; unfortunate that their geographic position brought them so close to the Germans on the one side and on the other left them exposed to the attacks of the Eastern Tatars, from whom, particularly the Mongols, they suffered much and suffered in patient forbearance. The wheel of changing time, however, revolves without ceasing; and since these nations inhabit for the most part the finest regions of Europe, if they were to be fully cultivated and opened to commerce; since politics and legislation are bound in the long run to promote quiet toil and calm discourse among the nations of Europe; so you, once diligent and happy peoples who have sunk so low, will at last awaken from your long and heavy slumber, will be freed from your enslaving chains, will use as your own the beautiful regions from the Adriatic Sea to the Carpathian Mountains, from the Don to the Moldau, and will once again celebrate on them your ancient festivals of peaceful toil and commerce.

As we now have, from various regions, elegant and useful materials for the history of these people,[*] it is to be wished that the existing gaps be filled by reference to others, so that the constantly waning remnants of their customs, songs, and legends may be collected, so that a *comprehensive history of the Slavic peoples* may at last be written, as called for in the panorama of humankind.

---

[*]Frisch, Popowitsch, Müller, Jordan, Stritter, Gerken, Möhsen, Anton, Dobner, Taube, Fortis, Sulzer, Rossignoli, Dobrowski, Voigt, Pelzel, etc.[5]

37

Toward a Culture of Reason
in Europe

In the following chapter, the third-to-last chapter of his monumental *Reflections on the Philosophy of History of Humankind,* Herder gives a survey of the history of theology, philosophy, and jurisprudence until the end of the Middle Ages. It is noteworthy that Herder, living in the Age of Enlightenment, manages to understand the way in which religious movements, mysticism, scholasticism, and law contributed to the ongoing process of enlightenment. Even the most "irrational" developments helped to unfold the human potential for humanizing history, and for Herder it is unquestionable that the course of history tends toward a culture of reason.

In the earliest ages of Christianity, we observed numerous sects that attempted to elucidate, apply, and refine the system of religion by means of a *philosophy of the Morn;* they were oppressed and persecuted as heretics. The *Doctrine of Manes,*[1] which incorporated a system of moral teaching, intended to educate the community, with the ancient Persian philosophy of Zoroaster (Zerduscht), seems to have struck the deepest root. It was persecuted more intensely than merely doctrinal heresies, and thus took refuge in Tibet toward the east, and in the Armenian mountains toward the west, and here and there in European countries, everywhere experiencing the same fate as in Asia. It was long believed to have been suppressed when, in the darkest of ages, and proceeding from a region where it might have been least expected, it burst forth as if by an agreed-upon signal, and suddenly created a frightful uproar in Italy, Spain, France, the Netherlands, Switzerland, and Germany. The country from which it proceeded was *Bulgaria,*[2] a barbarous province for which the Greek and the Roman churches had long contended; there lived its invisible head who, far different from the Roman pope, professed to resemble Christ in poverty. Secret missions went into all parts and attracted not only the common people, especially diligent craftsmen and the suppressed peasantry, but also the wealthy, princes and nobles, especially women, with a power that braved the severest persecutions and even death. Their quiet teachings, which preached pure human virtues, especially diligence, chastity, and withdrawal, and held up a goal of perfection to which the community was to be led with the strictest adherence, turned out to be the loudest outcry against the prevailing abominations of the Church. They especially attacked the immorality of the clergy, their wealth, ambition, and licentiousness; they denied the magic powers of the clergy as immoral, and accepted instead the simple blessing conveyed by the laying on of hands, and the community of the members under their leaders, the ones who had attained perfection. To them, the transubstantiation of the bread, the crucifix, the mass, purgatory, the intercession of the saints, and the inherent privileges of the Roman priesthood were human decrees and inventions. They quite freely passed judgment on the content of Scripture, especially the Old Testament, reducing everything to poverty, purity of conscience and the body, quiet diligence, gentleness, and benevolence; hence in several sects they were called the *bons hommes* (good people). In the most ancient of these sects, the Manicheism of the Morn is unmistakable; they proceeded from the contest between light and darkness, held matter responsible for the origin of sin, and had particularly severe views concerning sensual pleasure; by degrees their system purified itself. Out of Manicheans, who also were called Cathars (heretics), Patarenes, Publicans, *Passagieri*,[3] and other terms appropriate to local conditions, individual teachers, especially Henry and Peter de Bruis,[4] formed less objectionable groups, until at length the Waldensians taught everything that was presented a few centuries later by the Protestants, and insisted upon it with great courage; the earlier sects, on the other hand, appear to be similar to the Anabaptists, the Mennonites,[5] the Bohemian Brethren, and other sects of modern times. All of them spread with such quiet power and such persuasive insistence that the reputation of the established clergy declined in entire provinces, especially since the clergy were inferior to them in disputation. The regions in which the *Provençal language* prevailed were the garden in which they especially flourished; they translated the New Testament[6] (a then unheard-of undertaking) into this language, presented their *Rules of Perfection*[7] in Provençal verse, and thus were the first since the introduction of Roman Christianity who *instructed and shaped the people in their vernacular language.*[*]

---

[*]Among the writings on these sects, of which ecclesiastical history gives a full account, I mention only one book, far less known than it deserves to be, J.C. Füßli, *Neue und unpartheiische Ketzer- und Kirchenhistorie der mittleren Zeit*, 3 vols., 8°, in which very useful documents may be found.[8]

For that reason, they were also persecuted, as far as they were known and could be found. As early as the beginning of the eleventh century, in Orleans, in the heart of France, Manicheans, including the confessor of the Queen, were burned at the stake; they refused to recant, and died for their belief. They were treated no less severely in all the other countries where the clergy could exercise its power, for example in Italy and southern Germany; but in the South of France and in the Netherlands, where the authorities protected them as industrious people, they dwelt unmolested for a long time, until at last, after several disputations and councils, as the anger of the clergy had been raised to a high pitch, the tribunal of the Inquisition was loosed upon them; because their protector, Count Raymond of Toulouse, a genuine martyr for the good of humankind, would not give them up, that dreadful crusade, with its abundance of atrocities, burst forth upon them.[9] The order of friars devoted to preaching against heresies, the Dominicans, founded expressly to oppose them, were their detestable judges; Simon of Montford, the leader of the crusade, was the severest monster the world has known, and from this corner of France, where the poor *bons hommes* had remained concealed for two centuries, the bloody tribunal proceeded against all heretics to Spain, Italy, and most Catholic countries. Hence the confusion regarding the variety of sects of the Middle Ages, because, to this bloody tribunal and the persecuting spirit of the clergy, they were all alike; however, hence also their perseverance and quiet spreading, so that from three to five centuries later the reformation of the Protestants found the same seed in all countries and merely revitalized it. Wycliffe in England roused the Lollards, as Hus did his Bohemians,[10] for Bohemia, akin to the Bulgars in language, had long abounded with sects of this pious kind. Once planted, the germ of truth and of determined hatred against superstition, human servitude, and the insolent and impious clergy of the church could no longer be crushed; the Franciscans and other orders which, as examples of poverty and the imitation of Christ, were set up in opposition to these sects, to overturn and disquiet them, were so far from accomplishing this end, even among the people, that instead they became a renewed irritation to the people. Thus, here too the coming overthrow of the greatest tyrant, the hierarchy, proceeded from the poorest, from their simplicity and goodheartedness; all this did not occur without prejudices and errors, but these simple *bons hommes* spoke more openly in many ways than even some of the later reformers were apt to do.

What plain common sense did on the one hand was promoted, not ineffectually, though more slowly and with greater refinement, on the other by *speculative reason*. In the convent schools, the students were taught to dispute over St. Augustine and the logic of Aristotle, and it became customary to regard this art as a knightly tournament and a joust of learning. The criticism voiced against this freedom of disputation as a rather useless exercise of the Middle Ages is unjust; for this freedom was invaluable particularly for that time. In the course of disputation, doubts could be raised in respect to many issues, and arguments could be sifted for and against, when the times were far from ready for such positive and practical questioning of these matters. Did not the Reformation itself begin with the fact that one hid behind disputations and protected oneself with their freedom? When the monastic schools were then turned into universities, that is, arenas of knightly combat protected by papal and imperial license, a wide field was opened to exercise and sharpen the speaking ability, the presence of mind, the wit and sagacity of the learned disputants. There is not an article of theology, or a subject of metaphysics, that did not occasion the most subtle questions, disputes, and distinctions, being spun out over time to the finest thread. This spider's web, by its nature, possessed less stability than did that rugged structure of positive traditions, which people were bound to believe in blindly; woven by human reason as its own creation, it could also be unraveled and destroyed by human reason. Thanks are due, therefore, to that subtle spirit of disputation of the Middle Ages, and to every sovereign who erected these learned palaces to shelter these webs. If some disputants were persecuted because of envy or because of their own lack of caution, or were even disinterred from consecrated ground after their deaths, still the art continued its progress on the whole and greatly improved the linguistic weapons of reason in Europe.

As the south of France was the first permanent stage of an emerging popular religion, its northern part, especially the celebrated Parisian school, became the *jousting grounds of speculative reason and scholasticism.* Paschasius and Ratramnus[11] once dwelt here; Scotus Eriugena was granted residence and favor in France; Lanfranc and Berengarius, Anselm, Abelard, Peter Lombard, Thomas Aquinas, Bonaventure, Occam, and Duns Scotus,[12] the morning stars and suns of Scholastic philosophy, taught in France, either throughout their lives or during their finest years; from all countries, everyone was drawn to Paris, to obtain the highest wisdom of the age. Whoever gained fame in this school, rose to positions of honor in state and church, for there was so little not accessible to Scholasticism, even in matters of state, that Occam, who defended Philip the Fair and Louis the Bavarian against the popes, could say to the emperor, "Protect me with the sword, and I shall protect you with the pen." The French language shaped itself to philosophical precision before all others because, among other reasons, disputation in France was carried on for so long, so frequently, and with such ease and refinement, and because, owing to the relationship of French to Latin, it is easy to form abstract concepts within it.

That the *translation of the works of Aristotle* contributed more than anything else to the refinement of Scholasticism is made clear by this Greek philosopher's renown in all the schools of Europe for half a millennium; the reason, however, for the ardent inclination of Europeans to these writings—mostly borrowed from the Arabs—is found not in the Crusades, but in the general disposition of the century and its way of thought. The earliest stimulus that came to Europe from the Arabs was found in their excellence in mathematical works, which supposedly contained secrets for the preservation and prolongation of life, for the gaining of immeasurable riches, and for the understanding of the workings of fate itself. The philosopher's stone and the elixir of immortality were sought after; future events were read in the stars, and the tools of mathematics even appeared as magic instruments. Thus men pursued the wonderful like children, so that instead of that goal the truth might some day be found; and to this end the most burdensome journeys were undertaken. Already in the eleventh century, proceeding from Carthage, Constantine the African[13] had crisscrossed the East for thirty-nine years, to collect the secrets of the Arabs in Babylon, India, and Egypt; ultimately, he came to Europe, where as a monk at Monte Cassino he translated many writings from the Arabic, especially those dealing with pharmaceutical knowledge. Poor as the translations may have been, these writings were widely distributed, and owing to the attainments of the Arabs in the healing arts, the first medical school arose impressively at Salerno. From France and England, those in search of knowledge went to Spain, to obtain instruction from the most famous of the Arab teachers themselves; upon their return they were taken for magicians, as they themselves boasted of various secret arts as inspired by magic. In this manner, mathematics, chemistry, and medical arts were introduced into the most celebrated schools of Europe, partly through writings and partly through discoveries and practical experiments. Without the Arabs, there would not have been a Gerbert, an Albertus Magnus, an Arnold of Villanova, a Roger Bacon, a Raymond Lully,[14] and others; they learned either from the Arab teachers themselves in Spain, or from their writings. Even the Emperor Frederick II, who contributed with indefatigable zeal to the translation of the Arab writings and to the revival of this learning, inclined to them not without superstition. The propensity to travel, or the tales of travel to Spain, Africa, and the East, where the most splendid secrets of nature were to be learned from contemplative sages, prevailed for centuries; many secret societies and great guilds of traveling scholars arose from this propensity; and indeed the whole makeup of the philosophical and mathematical sciences betrayed this Arabian origin even beyond the epoch of the Reformation.

No wonder that *mysticism* adhered to such a philosophy, thus molding itself to one of the most refined systems of contemplative perfection. By the era of the earliest Christian church, mysticism had passed from Neoplatonism into several sects; through the translation of the false Dionysius the Areopagite[15] it came to the West and into the monastic communities; some sects of the Manicheans were influenced by it, and at last, with and without the aid of Scholasticism, among monks and nuns it attained a form that soon revealed here the most subtle sophistry of human reason, and there the most delicate tenderness of the loving heart. Mysticism has done its share of good, in that it drew the feeling heart away from mere ceremonial worship, accustomed it to introspection, and supplied it with spiritual nourishment. To lonesome and lonely souls, withdrawn from the world, it provided consolation and relief beyond this world, as it refined the sensibilities by a sort of spiritual romance. It was a precursor of the metaphysics of the heart, just as Scholasticism was a precursor of reason, and the two held one another in balance. Happily for us, the time is almost past when the use of this opiate was a medicine, and an unfortunately necessary one.*

Lastly, *the science of jurisprudence,* that practical philosophy of the sense of justice and sound reason, as it began to brighten the world with new light, has contributed more than mysticism and speculation to the well-being of Europe and the firm establishment of the rights of society. In times of genuine simplicity, not many written laws are needed, and the primitive German peoples rightfully resisted the craftiness of Roman jurists. People in differently governed and partly corrupted countries found indispensable not only written laws of their own, but soon also an excerpt of Roman law. And since an excerpt, in the face of papal legislation that had grown continuously over the centuries, was at length insufficient, it was good that the entire corpus of the Roman law was brought forward, to sharpen the minds and judgment of active commentators. It was not without reason that the emperors recommended this field of study to their universities, especially those in Italy; to them it was a school of arms against the pope, and all the developing free cities had the same interest, to use it against the pope, the emperor, and the lesser tyrants oppressing them. Hence, the numbers of lawyers increased incredibly. As the knights of reason, as the advocates of the freedom and property of the peoples, they enjoyed the highest reputation at the courts, in the cities, and at the universities; and because of them Bologna, a place visited by many, came to be the *learned city.* What France was during the age of Scholasticism, Italy came to be through the promotion of jurisprudence. Ancient Roman law and the

---

*After all that has been written by Poiret, Arnold,[16] and others, we still lack a history of mysticism, particularly of the Middle Ages, composed in a truly philosophical spirit.

canon law competed with one another; several of the popes were men most learned in jurisprudence. It is unfortunate that the renaissance of this science occurred at a time when the sources were still unreliable and the spirit of the ancient Roman law was discernible only through an obstructing fog. It is unfortunate as well that ponderous Scholasticism also laid claim to this practical science, turning the statements of the most reasonable of men into tricky rhetorical delusions. It is unfortunate, finally, that an auxiliary field of study, an exercise of the power of judgment modeled on the greatest sages of antiquity, should have been taken as the positive norm, as a gospel of the law applicable even to the most novel and indeterminate cases. Thus arose that spirit of chicanery, which in time nearly extinguished the character of almost every national code of laws in Europe. Barbarous book learning took the place of living knowledge of things; the legal process became a labyrinth of formalities and quibbles; instead of reflecting a noble sentiment of justice, men's minds were turned to artifice and cunning, which rendered the language of jurisprudence and the law perplexed and unintelligible, and ultimately, in conjunction with the triumphant power of the magistrate, favored a spurious paramount right of the sovereign. The consequences of this have long continued to be felt.

The prospect becomes dismal when the state of the spirit that was reawakening in Europe is compared to that of a few earlier epochs and peoples. Proceeding from primitive and lethargic barbarism, oppressed by spiritual and temporal tyranny, everything that is good emerges fearfully; here, the finest seed is trampled down on a stony path, or it becomes food for the birds of prey; there, it struggles to rise, impeded by a bed of thorns, and it is stifled or withers, because it lacks the benevolent soil of ancient simplicity and goodness. The first popular religion appears amid persecuted and to some degree fanatical heretics; philosophy, in the lecture halls of disputing dialecticians; the most useful sciences, as magic and superstition; the guidance of the human sensibilities, as mysticism; an improved political constitution, as the worn and patched coat of a long-expired and totally inequitable legislation; and through these Europe is to raise itself from a state of the utmost confusion, and to form itself anew. However, what the soil of the civilization lacked in fertile depth, tools and resources of learning, and the general atmosphere in serenity and freedom was compensated for, perhaps, by the extent of the field to be cultivated and the value of the plant to be raised. Not an Athens or a Sparta, but a Europe was here to be formed; not the Kalokagathia[17] of a Greek philosopher or an artist, but a humanity and rationality that in time was to embrace the globe. Let us see what institutions have been framed for this, what discoveries have been scattered in the darkness of ages, to be ripened by the time that followed.

38

Concluding Commentary

Herder's "Concluding Commentary" is indeed the final chapter of his four-volume *Reflections on the Philosophy of History of Humankind*, although he planned an additional volume with another five "books." The *Reflections* remained a colossal fragment. After presenting his huge survey of what was known in the eighteenth century about the ancient history of humankind, including reflections on possible laws of history, Herder gives a clear forecast for Europe. This part of his *Reflections* was published in 1791—that is, two years after the beginning of the French Revolution. When Herder introduces knowledge, dynamism, and competition as the new third force that rises between the Roman Catholic Church on the one hand and secular despotism on the other, and when he calls this third force in 1791 the new "third estate" that was to govern the future, it is obvious that he believed in the enlightened middle classes as the leading cultural, political, and economic power that would shape the future of Europe.

How, therefore, did Europe attain its civilization and the rank due to it above other peoples? Place, time, necessity, the state of affairs, and the course of events impelled it to this; but, above all, *its particular industriousness in the arts,* the result of many *common exertions,* procured this rank for it.

1. Had Europe been as rich as India, as undivided as Tatary, as hot as Africa, as isolated as America, what has appeared in it would never have come to be. Even in a state of the most forlorn barbarism, its location in the world helped it to return to the light; it derived the greatest advantage, however, from its rivers and seas. Take away the Dnieper, the Don, and the Dvina, the Black and the Mediterranean seas, the Atlantic Ocean, the North Sea and the Baltic Sea,[1] with their coasts, islands, and rivers, and the great commercial endeavor to which Europe is indebted for its most fruitful activity would not have existed. But as it was, the two great and wealthy conti-

nents, Asia and Africa, embraced their poorer, smaller sister; they sent their goods and inventions from the extreme borders of the world, from regions with the earliest and most continuous civilizations, thus sharpening Europe's industriousness in the arts and its own inventions. The climate of Europe and the remains of the ancient Greek and Roman worlds were of assistance in all this; and thus the splendor of Europe is founded on *activity and inventiveness,* and on a *common, competitive striving.*

2. The *oppressiveness of the Roman hierarchy* was perhaps a necessary yoke, an indispensable bridle for the primitive peoples of the Middle Ages; without it, Europe would probably have become the prey of despots, a stage of eternal conflict, or even a Mongolian desert. Serving as a counterweight, the Roman hierarchy merits its praise; had it remained the first and continuous wellspring, it would have transformed Europe into a Tibetan Vatican state. As it was, pressure and counterpressure produced an effect not envisioned by either party; want, necessity, and danger drove between the two a third estate,[2] which must be the blood, so to speak, of this great and pulsing body, or the body will decay. This third estate is *science, useful activity, competitive industriousness in the arts;* through this element, knighthood and popery came to the end of their reign of indispensability, though that end came only gradually.

3. The potential nature of the modern civilization of Europe is evident from what has been said; only a civilization of human beings as they were and wanted to be; a civilization driven by industriousness, the sciences, and the arts; whoever did not need or despised or abused these things remained what he was; a universal and thoroughgoing formation of all estates and peoples through education, the laws, and the political constitutions of the individual countries was not then to be thought of, and when will it be? Reason, however, and the intensified, joint endeavors of humankind keep on their unwearied course, and it may even be deemed a good sign when the best fruits do not ripen prematurely.

Notes

Notes to the Introduction

1. For the following, compare especially R. [Rudolf] Haym, *Herder nach seinem Leben und seinen Werken,* 2 vols. (Berlin: Weidmannsche Buchhandlung, 1880, 1885). Also see Robert T. Clark, Jr., *Herder: His Life and Thought* (Berkeley and Los Angeles: University of California Press, 1969).

2. Arnold Gehlen, *Der Mensch. Seine Natur und seine Stellung in der Welt,* 7th ed. (Frankfurt am Main: Athenäum, 1962), p. 84.

3. (Riga: 1796, Frankfurt edition, vol. 9/1, Frankfurt am Main: Deutscher Klassiker Verlag, 1994), pp. 609–724.

4. Ibid., p. 1101.

5. Ibid., p. 621.

6. Ibid., pp. 668–69.

7. Ibid., p. 611.

8. See page 32 in this volume.

9. See Jacob Grimm and Wilhelm Grimm, *Deutsches Wörterbuch,* vol. 4.1, eds. Rudolf Hildebrand and Hermann Wunderlich (Leipzig: S. Hirzel, 1897; reprinted, Munich: 1984), cols. 3763–64.

10. Reinhart Koselleck, "Historia Magistra Vitae. Über die Auflösung des Topos im Horizont neuzeitlich bewegter Geschichte [1967]." In Reinhart Koselleck, *Vergangene Zukunft. Zur Semantik geschichtlicher Zeiten* (Frankfurt am Main: Suhrkamp, 1989), p. 47.

11. Ibid., p. 48.

12. Reinhart Koselleck, "Geschichte, Geschichten und formale Zeitstrukturen [1973]." In Koselleck (see note 10), p. 130.

13. *La philosophie de l'histoire.* Par feu l'Abbé Bazin (Amsterdam: Chez Changuion, 1765). *The Complete Works of Voltaire/Les oeuvres complètes de Voltaire,* eds. Theodore Bestermann et al.; vol. 59, ed. J.H. Brumfitt; 2d ed., rev. (Geneva: Institut et Musée Voltaire; Toronto, Buffalo: University of Toronto Press, 1969), pp. 83–275.

14. "That which compilers of history are usually lacking is philosophical spirit." Voltaire, "Remarques sur l'histoire," in Voltaire, *Oeuvres complètes,* ed. Louis Moland, vol. 16 (Paris: Garnier Frères, 1878), p. 135.

15. See Ulrich Dierse and Gunter Scholz, "Geschichtsphilosophie," in *Historisches Wörterbuch der Philosophie,* ed. Joachim Ritter, vol. 3 (Darmstadt: Wissenschaftliche Buchgesellschaft, 1974), cols. 416–39, esp. 416–20.

16. Christian Wolff, *Philosophia rationalis sive Logica,* part 1, ed. Jean Ecole, reprinted (Hildesheim: Olms, 1983), sec. 3.

17. Ibid., sec. 6. For the context, see Hans Adler, *Die Prägnanz des Dunklen. Gnoseologie—Ästhetik—Geschichtsphilosophie bei Johann Gottfried Herder* (Hamburg: Felix Meiner, 1990), pp. 11–15.

18. Viscount Bryce, *World History.* British Academy, Annual Raleigh Lecture, 1919 (London: Oxford University Press, n.d.), p. 6.

19. Karl Löwith, *Weltgeschichte und Heilsgeschehen. Die theologischen Voraussetzungen der Geschichtsphilosophie* [1949–1953]. Karl Löwith, *Sämtliche Schriften,* vol. 2 (Stuttgart: Metzler, 1983), pp. 7–239.

20. See Ernst Breisach, *Historiography: Ancient, Medieval, and Modern,* 2d ed. (Chicago and London: University of Chicago Press, 1994), pp. 220–21.

21. Ernst Schaumkell, *Geschichte der deutschen Kulturgeschichtsschreibung. Von der Mitte des 18. Jahrhunderts bis zur Romantik im Zusammenhang mit der allgemeinen geistigen Entwicklung* (Leipzig: B.G. Teubner, 1905), p. 50.

22. J.Chr. Gatterer, *Handbuch der Universalhistorie nach ihrem gesamten Umfange* [1761], p. 61. Quoted after ibid., p. 53.

23. See Justus Möser, *Osnabrückische Geschichte,* 2 vols. (Osnabrück: 1768).

24. J.Chr. Gatterer, *Einleitung in die synchronistische Universalhistorie* (Göttingen: 1771), pp. 1–2. Quoted after Reinhart Koselleck, "Geschichte, Historie," in *Geschichtliche Grundbegriffe. Historisches Lexikon zur politisch-sozialen Sprache in Deutschland,* eds. Otto Brunner, Werner Conze, and Reinhart Koselleck, vol. 2 (Stuttgart: Ernst Klett, 1975), pp. 593–717, 688.

25. See Schaumkell, op. cit., pp. 61–67.

26. Ibid., p. 68.

27. Koselleck, op. cit., p. 689.

28. Friedrich Meinecke, *Die Entstehung des Historismus,* ed. Carl Hinrichs (Munich: R. Oldenbourg, 1959), p. 371.

29. Rudolf Stadelmann, *Der historische Sinn bei Herder* (Halle: Niemeyer, 1928).

30. Johann Gottfried Herder, *Ideen zur Philosophie der Geschichte der Menschheit.* In Johann Gottfried Herder, *Sämmtliche Werke,* ed. Bernhard Suphan, vol. 14 (Berlin: Weidmannsche Buchhandlung, 1909), pp. 203, 204–52.

31. Ibid., pp. 204–7.

32. Ibid., pp. 225–34.

33. Ibid., pp. 145–46 (see page 289 in this volume).

34. Ibid., p. 34 (see page 245 in this volume).

35. Ibid., p. 88 (see page 273 in this volume).

36. Ibid., p. 6 (see page 231 in this volume).

37. Ibid., p. 7 (see page 231 in this volume).

38. Ibid., pp. 10–11 (see pages 233–34 in this volume).

39. Ibid., pp. 11–13 (see pages 234–35 in this volume).

40. Ibid., pp. 14–15 (see pages 236–37 in this volume).

41. Ibid., pp. 28–29 (see page 241 in this volume).

42. Ibid., pp. 30–31 (see pages 242–43 in this volume).

43. Ibid., p. 32 (see page 244 in this volume).

44. Ibid., p. 39 (see page 249 in this volume).

45. Johann Gottfried Herder, *Ideen zur Philosophie der Geschichte der Menschheit.* In Johann Gottfried Herder, *Sämmtliche Werke,* ed. Bernhard Suphan, vol. 13 (Berlin: Weidmannsche Buchhandlung, 1887), p. 228 (see page 178 in this volume).

46. Ibid., pp. 231–36 (see pages 180–84 in this volume).

47. Ibid., p. 232 (see page 180 in this volume).
48. Ibid., p. 236 (see pages 183–84 in this volume).
49. Ibid., p. 242 (see page 189 in this volume).
50. Ibid., p. 245 (see page 191 in this volume).
51. Ibid., p. 250 (see page 194 in this volume).
52. Ibid., vol. 14 (see note 30), p. 42.
53. Ibid., p. 58 (see page 257 in this volume).
54. Ibid., p. 52.
55. Ibid., pp. 71–72.
56. Ibid., p. 63 (see page 261 in this volume).
57. Ibid., p. 120.
58. Ibid., p. 177.
59. Ibid., pp. 150–52.
60. Ibid., p. 190.
61. Ibid., p. 89 (see page 274 in this volume).
62. Milan Kundera, *Testaments Betrayed,* trans. Linda Asher (New York: HarperCollins, 1995), p. 110.

Notes to Chapter 1, Early Leaves of *Critical Groves*

1. See the editors' introductory remarks, above.
2. J.J. Winckelmann, *History of Ancient Art,* trans. G. Henry Lodge, vol. 1 (Boston: 1873), p. 149.
3. Allusion to the principle of mechanics, the idea that human history is essentially governed by the same kind of laws as physical nature.
4. The term "pragmatic history" stems from Polybius; Thucydides is considered the first of the "pragmatic" historians. Herder's term aims at integrating the description of historical events into an explanatory system in order to make "history" a part of the instruction of posterity. It should be noted, however, that Herder is skeptical toward this function of historians, as can be seen from the latter part of this text.
5. The type of historian who merely records events.
6. The type of historian who concentrates on selected events, considered to be particularly significant, but does not explicitly integrate them into an overview of history.
7. Latin *acumen,* meaning "the mental power of recognizing differences."
8. Latin *ingenium,* and French *esprit,* meaning "the mental power of recognizing similarities."
9. The Königliches Institut der historischen Wissenschaften zu Göttingen (Royal Institute for Historical Sciences in Göttingen). The historian and geographer Johann Christoph Gatterer (see note 11, below) was the founder and director of this institute (1766). From 1767 on, the institute edited the *Allgemeine Historische Bibliothek.*
10. Herder may be referring to Aristotle (*Poetics,* 9, 1451b): "The true difference [i.e., between a poet and a historian] is that one relates what has happened, the other what may happen. Poetry, therefore, is more philosophical and a higher thing than history: for poetry tends to express the universal, history the particular" (trans. S.H. Butcher). But Herder may also be referring simply to the first letter of the alphabet, which is the initial of the German word for origin *(Anfang).*
11. Lucian of Samosata (ca. A.D. 120–85), Greek sophist and satirist, was the author of a treatise on *How to Write History.* Thomas Abbt (1738–66) was a German critic and philosopher. Johann Christoph Gatterer (1727–99) was a German historian and geographer, and the author of *Outline of Universal History . . .* (1785).

12. Herodotus of Halikarnassos in Asia Minor (ca. 484–25 B.C.). Cicero called him the "father of history"; author of *Histories.*

13. J.Chr. Gatterer, "Vom historischen Plan und der darauf sich gründenden Zusammenfügung der Erzählungen" (1767).

14. The Latin *carmen,* meaning "song," is used here in the sense of "Homeric epic."

15. Not in Herodotus. Herder alludes with this fictitious quotation to the opening verses of Homeric and Virgilian epics.

16. Johannes Hübner (1668–1731) was an author of popular historical and biblical writings.

17. Greek historian (ca. 460–400 B.C.), author of a monograph on the Peloponnesian war (431–4).

18. Thucydides served in 425–24 as an elected strategist. He was exiled after the defeat of the Athenian army at Amphipolis.

19. Thucydides's principle of organizing the history of the war according to these two seasons.

20. The work does not cover the last five years of the war (409–4 B.C.).

21. Xenophon of Athens (ca. 430–354 B.C.) was a Greek historian and a philosophical writer. In the following lines, Herder refers to Xenophon's essays on Socrates (*Memorabilia*), horsemanship (*Peri Hippikes*), the task of the leader of the cavalry (*Hipparchikos*), hunting (*Kynegetikos*), economics (*Oikonomikos*), and the education of princes (*Kyrupaidia*).

22. Xenophon's *Hellenika,* a history of Greece from 411 to 362 B.C.

23. Publius Cornelius Scipio Africanus maior (ca. 235–183 B.C.) was the Roman commander-in-chief who defeated Hannibal. Lucius Licinius Lucullus (117–56 B.C.) was a Roman consul, a politician, and a military leader. Herder assumes an influence of Xenophon's writings on both Scipio and Lucullus.

24. Polybius of Megalopolis (ca. 200–ca. 120 B.C.) was a Greek historian and the author of *Historiai,* in which he describes the rise of Rome (220–146 B.C.). He coined the term "pragmatic history" *(pragmatiké historia).*

25. James Hampton (1721–78) was the translator of books 1–6 of Polybius's *Histories* (London: 1741, 1756–61).

26. Herder deals generously with Hampton's text ("Preface").

27. Publius Cornelius Scipio Aemilianus Africanus Numantinus (ca. 185–29 B.C.) was a Roman politician and military leader. He destroyed Carthage. Polybius, who was a hostage of Rome, was freed by this Scipio.

28. Jean Charles Chevalier de Folard (1669–1752) was a French officer and the author of *Histoire de Polybe. Avec un commentaire . . . par M. de Folard,* 6 vols. (Paris: 1727–30).

29. Sallust, Tacitus, and Cicero.

30. David Hume (1711–76) was a Scottish diplomat, a historian, and a philosopher.

31. See note 9, above.

32. The "famous literary superstition" (S.H. Butcher) of the dramatic unities of time, place, and action. Aristotle's *Poetics* deals only with the unity of action (5, 1451a) and a certain aspect of the unity of time (5, 1449b).

33. Karl Renatus Hausen, *Pragmatische Geschichte der Protestanten in Deutschland* (1767).

Notes to Chapter 2, From *Journal of my Travels*

1. A Latin term meaning "lap of humankind"; here it signifies "origin of humankind."

2. Joseph de Guignes (1721–1800) was a professor of Chinese culture at the

Collège de France. Herder refers to de Guignes's *Mémoire dans lequel on prouve que les chinois sont une colonie égyptienne* of 1759.

3. Hiob Ludolf (1624–1704) was the founder of Ethiopian philology.

4. Johann David Michaelis (1717–91) was professor of Protestant theology and Oriental culture at the University of Göttingen, Germany. He is renowned as the founder of the historical-philological analysis of the Old Testament. Heinrich Benedikt Starke (1672–1727) was a German orientalist.

Notes to Chapter 3, From *This, too, a Philosophy of History*

1. This is Herder's most concise and generic way of defining his concept of criticism in the etymological sense of the word (from Greek: κρινειν, meaning "to differentiate"). Thus a persistent criticism will differentiate everything from every other thing else until the particularity of each phenomenon is laid bare. This side of the critical operation is founded in the human faculty of *acumen* (see note 7 to Chapter 1 in this volume). Later in this text, Herder gives an idea of the counterpart of this analytical process.

2. The iron animal is one of four animals in Daniel's dream in the Old Testament— "frightening and very powerful. It had large iron teeth; it crushed and devoured its victims and trampled underfoot whatever was left" (Daniel 7:7). The four beasts are associated with four kingdoms to come, and the iron animal traditionally represents the Roman Empire.

3. Herder refers to Aristotle's *Poetics* (9, 1451b). See note 10 to Chapter 1 in this volume.

4. Michel de Montaigne (1533–92) was a famous French writer who published his *Essays* between 1580 and 1592.

5. Pierre Bayle (1647–1706) was a French skeptic philosopher. His *Dictionnaire historique et critique* first appeared in 1696–97.

6. Jean-Pierre de Crousaz (1663–1750) was a Swiss theologian and philosopher. His *Examen du Pyrrhonisme ancien et moderne* appeared in 1733.

Notes to Chapter 4, Whether We Need to Know the End of History in Order to Write History

1. Edinburgh: 1779–99, especially vol. 3 (London: 1784).

2. Herder refers to the sixteenth-century persecutions of Christians in these countries.

3. François Levaillant, *Second voyage dans l'interieur de l'Afrique, dans les années 1783–85* (Paris: 1795). Herder had already mentioned and quoted from Levaillant in his 114th and 116th letters.

Notes to Chapter 5, The Nemesis of History

1. Herder just enumerates the most well-known historians of antiquity because he could be certain that his contemporary readers were familiar with their works.

2. Ate was cast out of Olympus by Zeus, and she brings evil and mischief to those who live on earth.

3. The Italian phrase may be translated as "the little bit more and the little bit less."

4. Hugo Grotius (Huigh de Groot; 1583–1645) was a Dutch jurist, statesman, and scholar. Herder mentions his most famous work, *De jure belli ac pacis* (1625), which was groundbreaking for the formulation of international law.

5. Jacques Bénigne Bossuet (1627–1704) was a French bishop, historian, and orator. His *Discours sur l'histoire universelle* appeared in 1681.
6. Samuel Pufendorf (1632–94) was a German jurist. His *Introduction into the History of the most Important Empires and States* appeared in 1682 in German.
7. Johann Jakob Mascou (Mascov; 1689–1761) was a German jurist and historian. He published his *History of the Germans* in 1726 and 1737. For Johann Christoph Gatterer, see note 11 to Chapter 1 in this volume. *Kurzer Begriff der Weltgeschichte* (1785). Heinrich Friedrich Otto (1692–1730) was a German jurist and historian. Georg Christian Gebauer, a German jurist and historian, was cofounder of the University of Göttingen. He published his *Grundriß zu einer umständlichen Historie der vornehmsten europäischen Reiche und Staaten* in 1733. Gottfried Achenwall was the founder of scientific statistics. The first edition of his successful *Staatsverfassung der Europäischen Reiche im Grundrisse* appeared in 1709. Matthias Sprengel, *Geschichte der wichtigsten geographischen Entdeckungen bis zur Ankunft der Portugiesen in Japan 1542*, 2d ed. (Halle: 1792). Ludwig Timotheus Spittler, *Grundriß der Geschichte der christlichen Kirche*, 2d ed. (Göttingen: 1785).

Notes to Chapter 7, History

1. Nicolas Boileau-Despréaux (1636–1711) was a French poet and literary critic. In his *Art poétique* (1674) he formulated the "doctrine classique" of French literature. Boileau was one of the leading figures in support of the *anciens* (see Chapter 6).
2. Jean Racine (1639–99) was a French dramatist who, together with Pierre Corneille, represented French literary classicism.
3. Paul Scarron (1610–60) was a French writer of burlesque prose and drama. For the last eight years of his life, Scarron was married to Françoise d'Aubigné, who later became Marquise de Maintenon and the second wife of Louis XIV.
4. Gabriel Daniel (1649–1728), French Jesuit historian, was appointed historiographer of France by Louis XIV. His *Histoire de France depuis l'établissement de la monarchie française* first appeared in 1713. It is not clear to which of Daniel's works Herder refers.
5. Louis XIV attacked the Netherlands in 1672.
6. Roger de Rabutin, Comte de Bussy (1618–93), was a French soldier and writer. It is not clear to which anecdote Herder refers. Bussy-Rabutin wrote *Maximes d'amours* which were approved by Louis XIV in 1664. He was sent to the Bastille a few weeks later for his *Histoire amoureuse des Gaules*, which was published without the king's consent.
7. François de Salignac de La Mothe-Fénelon (1651–1715), French clergyman and writer, was preceptor of the oldest grandson of Louis XIV, the Duke of Burgundy. Fénelon published his *Télémaque* in 1699. It was suppressed by Louis XIV because of its criticism of absolutism.
8. The references here are to: Louis XIV; William III (1650–1702), Prince of Orange, after 1689 King William III of England; Eugene of Savoy (1663–1736); and John Churchill, first Duke of Marlborough (1650–1722).
9. Swift wrote his *History of the Four Last Years of the Queeen* in 1712–13. It was not published until 1758.
10. Herder quotes from Johann Michael Heinz, *Kleine deutsche Schriften vermischten Inhalts*, vol. 2 (Göttingen: 1789), p. 228.
11. The Duke of Burgundy ordered a report from all the provinces of France. He received, according to Herder's source, forty-two volumes of highly critical material about the devastating social and political situation in France under Louis XIV. The Duke

of Boulainvilliers (1658–1722), who was in charge of the edition, did not dare to present it to the Prince (who read it nonetheless). Herder's source is: *Vie du Dauphin, Père de Louis XV, écrite sur les mémoires de la Cour, enrichie des écrits du même Prince, par l'Abbé Proyart* (Lyon: 1782).

12. Mnemosyne is known as the muse of memory, Clio as the muse of history.

Notes to Chapter 8, Expectations for the Coming Century

1. Herder alludes to the cult of the genius in the last quarter of the eighteenth century in Germany (called "Storm and Stress," or "Sturm und Drang," a literary movement in early German romanticism).

2. Franz Mercurius van Helmont (1618–99) was a Belgian alchemist and theosophist. He published, among other works, *Cabbalah denudata* (1677), *De revolutione animarum humanarum* . . . (1684).

Notes to Chapter 9, On Monuments of the Distant Past

1. James Bruce, *Travels to Discover the Source of the Nile in the Years 1768 . . . and 1763*, 5 vols. (London: 1790–91; German translation, 1791). "Cushites" is a name for inhabitants of the Horn of Africa. "Cushitic" is the name for an Afro-Asiatic language family.

2. The name "Cainites" is mentioned by the Father of the Church Irenaeus and others as a name of a gnostic sect of the second century. The Kabyles are a Berber people of Algeria.

3. Philip Johan Strahlenberg, *Das nord- und östliche Theil von Europa und Asia . . . nebst einer . . . Tabula Polyglotta* (Stockholm: 1730; English translation, London: 1736).

4. Christoph Meiner, *Beschreibung alter Denkmäler in allen Theilen der Erde. . . .* (Nürnberg: 1786).

5. Carsten Niebuhr, *Reisebeschreibung nach Arabien und anderen umliegenden Ländern*, 3 vols. (Copenhagen: 1774–78).

6. Friedrich Christoph Jonathan Fischer, *Geschichte des teutschen Handels*, 4 vols. (Hanover: 1792–97). For Sprengel, see note 7 to Chapter 5 in this volume. George Anderson, *A General View of the Variations which have been made in the Affairs of the East India Company. . . .* (London: 1792).

7. Johann Christoph Gatterer, *Kurzer Begriff der Weltgeschichte. . . .* (Göttingen: 1785).

8. August Ludwig Schlözer, *Weltgeschichte nach ihren Haupttheilen im Auszug und Zusammenhang*, 2 vols. (Göttingen: 1785, 1789).

9. *Magazin für die neue Historie und Geographie, angelegt von A. [Anton] F. [Friedrich] Büsching*, 22 vols. (Hamburg, Halle: 1767–93 [vols. 7–22 in Halle]).

10. Herder probably refers to [Quentin Craufurd,] *Sketches chiefly relating to the history, religion, learning, and manners of the Hindoos with a concise account of the present state of the native powers of Hindostan* (London: 1790).

11. Joseph Tieffenthaler, *Description géographique de l'Indostan* (Berlin: 1786, 1791). German translation in Johann Bernoulli (the Younger), *Description historique et géographique de l'Inde*, vol. 1 (Berlin: 1785, 1786).

12. Richard Gough, *A comparative view of the ancient monuments of India, particularly those in the Island of Salset near Bombay, as described by different writers* (London: 1785).

13. Wilhelm Hodge(s) [i.e., William Hodge], *Monumente indischer Geschichte und Kunst,* translated from the English, ed. A. Riem (Berlin: 1789).

14. Jean Baptiste Tavernier; among his travel reports are: *Recueils de plusieurs Relations et traitez* . . . (Paris: 1679); and *Les six voyages de J.B. Tavernier* . . . 2 vols. (Paris: 1676). John Grose, *A Voyage to the East-Indies* . . . (London: 1757; 2d enlarged ed., 1766). Abraham Hyacinthe Anquetil Du Perron published translations from Sanskrit and travel reports. Herder refers perhaps to his *Recherches historiques et chronologiques sur l'Inde* . . . (1786); in Johann Bernoulli (the Younger), *Description historique et géographique de l'Inde* . . . , 3 vols. (Berlin: 1786–89; German translation, Berlin: 1785–88).

15. Sir William Chambers, *An Account of the Sculptures and Ruins of Mavalipuram;* in *Asiatic Researches. Transactions of the Society instituted in Bengal, for inquiring into the history and antiquities, the arts, sciences and literature of Asia,* 20 vols. (Calcutta: 1788–1839), vol. 1.

16. Philippus Baldaeus, *A True and Exact Description of the most celebrated East-India Coasts of Malabar and Coromandel* . . . (Amsterdam: 1732; translated from the Dutch; German translation, Amsterdam: 1672). Pierre Sonnerat, *Voyages aux Indes Orientales et à la Chine . . . depuis 1774 jusqu'en 1781* . . . , 2 vols. (Paris: 1782).

17. Georg Forster; his annotated Sakuntala edition appeared in Mainz and Leipzig in 1791.

18. Pierre Marie François, Vicomte de Pagès, *Voyages autour du monde et vers les deux pôles* . . . (Paris: 1782). William Mackintosh's *Travels* from 1782 appeared in a German translation in 1785.

19. John Holwell, *Interesting historical events, relative to the Provinces of Bengal* . . . (German translation, 1778). William Jones, *Poeseos Asiaticae commentatorium libri sex, cum appendice* (London: 1772; German translation, 1777).

20. Olfert Dapper; Herder perhaps refers to his *Asia, of Naukeurige beschryving van het rijk des grooten Mogols, en een groot gedeelte van Indien* . . . (Amsterdam: 1672).

21. The *linga* or *lingam* (from Sanskrit "sign") is the ancient symbol of Shiva's creativity and fertility. Usually this symbol was presented in a phallic form together with *yoni,* its counterpart, symbolizing Shakti, Shiva's wife. Herder apparently refers to this ensemble which consists in a stone pillar placed in a sort of stone bowl.

Notes to Chapter 10, On the Earliest Documents of Humankind

1. Herder refers to David Hume's explanation of the origin of religion in *The Natural History of Religion* (1757).

2. The German orientalist Johann David Michaelis followed Hume in explaining the origin of religion out of fear. But, contrary to Hume, Michaelis legitimates divine revelation. Cf. J.D. Michaelis, *Compendium theologiae dogmaticae* (Göttingen: 1760).

3. It should be noted that Herder is quite conscious of the Latin etymology of the word "tradition" (derived from *tradere,* meaning "transmit, hand down, pass on"), which is basically a process of transferring knowledge in different forms from one generation to another. It is important to point out that this procedure of tradition is based on an uncritical reception of the legacy of unquestioned authorities. Thus, tradition is knowledge from the fathers (elsewhere, Herder calls this knowledge "patriotism"—which is derived from the Latin *pater,* meaning "father"), and insofar as it is unquestioned knowledge, it is accepted without any rational judgment—pre-judice in the literal sense of the word.

4. Iroquois is the name of a confederacy of Native American nations (five, later six nations), including Mohawk, Oneida, Onondoga, Cayuga, Seneca, and Tuscarora.

5. Greek *stichois*, meaning "lines of verse."

6. Greek *nomoi*, meaning "laws."

7. [Isaak Iselin,] *Ueber die Geschichte der Menschheit*, 2 vols. (Frankfurt, Leipzig: 1764); published anonymously.

8. *Origines* stands in the German text as a foreign word for the Latin *origins*, and Herder uses it as an equivalent for *Urkunden* ("documents") which is etymologically the very first (arch-)information.

9. Herder alludes to [Jean Astruc,] *Conjectures sur les Memoires Originaux dont il paroit que Moyse s'est servi pour composer le Livre de la Genese* (Brussels: 1753); published anonymously.

10. Perhaps [Johann Friedrich Wilhelm Jerusalem,] *Briefe über die Mosaischen Schriften und Philosophie* (Braunschweig: 1762); published anonymously.

11. Jean Hardouin (1646–1729) was a French theologian. Herder chastises him repeatedly for his speculations.

12. A Greek word for divine inspiration.

Notes to Chapter 11, On the Character of Humankind

1. It should be remembered that "art" (Latin *ars*) has a twofold meaning: (a) "fine arts" and (b) "skills" (Greek *techne*).

2. With the terms "asymptote," "ellipse," and "cycloid," Herder rejects the mathematical quantification or geometrical representation of the "nature" of human history.

3. Herder uses the word "conflict" here in the sense of competition.

4. This is another formulation of Herder's idea that the goal of history (and evolution) is the greatest possible variety.

5. This assumption is the foundation of Herder's optimism.

6. Latin, meaning "Let's hope and act!"

Notes to Chapter 12, On the Term and the Concept "Humanity"

1. Herder refers to remarks of an interlocutor in the previous letter.

2. Johann Christoph Adelung, *Versuch eines vollständigen grammatisch-kritischen Wörterbuchs der hochdeutschen Mundart*, 5 vols. (Leipzig: 1774–86).

3. *Iliad*, Book 21, ll. 446 ff.

4. *Iliad*, Book 17, ll. 442 ff.

5. Christian Gottlob Heyne (1729–1812), German classicist. *Opuscula Academica*, 4 vols. (Göttingen: 1785–96).

6. The German classicist Johann August Ernesti gave his inaugural lecture at the University of Leipzig in 1749.

7. The following etymological speculations are incorrect. Old High German *mennisco* is not a diminutive form.

Note to Chapter 13, Preface to the *Reflections on the Philosophy of the History of Humankind*

1. See, in the Old Testament, Habakkuk 1:14.

Notes to Chapter 14, The Human Being Is Predisposed to the Power of Reason

1. Edward Tyson, *Orang-Outang, sive Homo Sylvestris or: The Anatomy of a Pygmie.* . . .

2. Jacobus Bontius (Jakob or James de Bondt), Dutch physician of the seventeenth century. Herder may be referring to Bontius's *Historiae naturalis & medicae Indiae orientalis libri sex* . . . (Lugduni Batavorum et Amstelodami [Leiden and Amsterdam]: 1658).

3. Andrew Battel was an English naturalist and traveler in the sixteenth century. *The Strange Adventures of Andrew Battell of Leigh in Essex, sent by the Portugals prisoner to Angola* . . . (Part 2 of *Purchas his Pilgrims. In five bookes* . . .) (London: 1625).

4. Gui de la Brosse (d. 1641) was the physician in ordinary of Louis XIII. It is unclear to which of his publications Herder refers.

5. Herder refers to Georges Louis Leclerc, Comte de Buffon, *Histoire naturelle, générale et particulière*, vol. 16 (Paris: 1766).

6. The famous Dutch anatomist Pieter, or Petrus, Camper read this footnote and then published his article *On the Organs of Speech* . . . in his *Kleinere Schriften*, vol. 2 (1785), which he dedicated to Herder.

7. Louis Jean Marie Daubenton (1716–1800) contributed to Buffon's *Histoire naturelle* details of the dissection of 182 species of quadrupeds.

8. Albrecht von Haller, *Elementa physiologiae corporis humani*, 8 vols. (Lausanne: 1757–66).

9. Albrecht von Haller, *Primae lineae physiologiae* (Göttingen: 1747). Heinrich August Wrisberg (1739–1808) was a German anatomist.

10. Thomas Willis (1621–75) was a British physician and professor of natural philosophy in Oxford. Tyson mentions him in his work on the orangutan.

Notes to Chapter 15, Specifically Human Predispositions Besides Reason

1. See Claude Adrien Helvétius, *De l'esprit* (1758).

2. Except for the report of the violent act, Herder seems to draw this information from James Burnet [sic], *Of the Origin and Progress of Language*, 6 vols., vol. 1 (1773; reprinted Menston: Scolar Press, 1967), pp. 180, 190, 223 ff. Burnett (i.e., Monboddo) mentions in a footnote to page 180 of his first volume "an account of this strange phaenomenon published in France by a lady, under the title, *Histoire d'une Fille Savage* [sic], and revised by *Mons. de Condamine*. It was translated into English, and published in Edinburgh in 1767. . . ." Monboddo's spelling of the village in Champagne, France, where the girl was found, is "Songè" (p. 224, footnote). The modern spelling is "Songy".

3. George Berkeley, *An Essay Towards a New Theory of Vision* (1709), sec. 147.

4. This refers to the Leibnizian idea of a mathematical order of the universe; see Gottfried Wilhelm Leibniz, *Principes de la Nature et de la Grace, fondée en raison* (1714), sec. 17.

5. August Friedrich Wilhelm Sack, *Vertheidigter Glaube der Christen* (Berlin: 1748–53).

6. *Des Lord Monboddo Werk von dem Ursprunge und Fortgange der Sprache, übersetzt von E.A. Schmidt* . . . [with a preface by Herder], 2 vols. (Riga: 1784–85). For the English original, see note 2, above.

7. The Fuegians were remnants of an indigenous people in the extreme southern part of South America (Tierra del Fuego). They had the reputation of possessing an extremely primitive culture.

8. Pliny the Elder, *Naturalis historiae libri XXXVII,* book 7, chap. 1.

9. In Burma.

10. This is the title of a speech given by Pietro Moscati, the Italian physician and anatomist, at Pavia. Pietro Moscati, *Von dem körperlichen wesentlichen Unterscheide zwischen der Struktur der Tiere und des Menschen* (translated from the Italian).

11. According to Cicero, Socrates brought philosophy back from heaven to earth.

12. Charles Bonnet, *La Palingénésie philosophique ou Idées sur l'état passé et sur l'état futur des êtres vivants* (Geneva and Lyons: 1770). Bonnet expounded the theory of preformation in the germ.

Note to Chapter 16, The Nature of Humankind Manifests Itself in a System of Spiritual Powers

1. In analogy to medicine, Herder coins the term "semiotics of the soul" for a new discipline of psychology. Instead of "semiotics" we would call it today "symptomatology."

Notes to Chapter 17, The Present State of Humankind Is Probably the Connecting Link between Two Worlds

1. See, e.g., Gottfried Wilhelm Leibniz, *Principes de la Nature et de la Grâce, fondés en raison* (1714), secs. 3, 12, 14.

2. These two stanzas are modified quotations from Anna Louisa Karsch's poem "Von Gott, als sie bei hellem Mondschein erwachte" (1764).

Notes to Chapter 18, The Nature of Peoples in the Vicinity of the North Pole

1. Samuel Engel, *Mémoires géographiques sur l'Asie et l'Amérique* 1766 (German translation 1772). For Pagès, see note 18 to Chapter 9 in this volume.

2. [Constantine John] Phipps, *Journal of a Voyage ... toward the North Pole* (German translation by Samuel Engel) (Bern: 1777). David Cranz, *Historie von Grönland ...* (Barby and Leipzig: 1765).

3. William Ellis, *Voyage to the Hudson Bay by the Dobbs Gallay and California in the Years 1746–1747.* Hans Egede, *Ausführliche und wahrhafte Nachricht vom Anfange und Fortgange der Grönländischen Mission* (Hamburg: 1740). Roger Curtis, *Umständliche Nachricht von der Küste Labrador* (1744); German translation in *Beiträge zur Völker- und Länderkunde,* vol. 1, eds. J.R. Forster and M.C. Sprengel (Leipzig: 1781).

4. The popular chemical theory of the German physician Georg Ernst Stahl (1600–1734) proposed that combustible matter was composed of substances called "phlogiston" (from the Greek *phlegein,* meaning "burn") and "calx." This theory lost its influence from 1774 on, owing to the discovery of oxygen.

5. Per Hoegström, *Beschreibung des schwedischen Lappland,* translated from the Swedish (Stockholm and Leipzig: 1748). Knud Leem, *Beschreibung der Lappen in Finnmark ...* (Copenhagen: 1746); translated into German, 1774. Timotheus Klingstedt, *Mémoire sur les Samojedes et les Lappons* (Königsberg: 1762).

6. Peter Simon Pallas, *Reise durch verschiedene Provinzen des russischen Reiches,* 3 vols. (St. Petersburg: 1771–76). Johann Georg Gmelin, *Reise durch Sibirien* . . . , 4 vols. (Göttingen: 1751–52). *Merkwürdigkeiten der Morduanen, Kosaken . . . Ein Auszug aus Pallas Reisen* (Frankfurt and Leipzig: 1773). *Merkwürdigkeiten der obischen Ostjaken, Samojeden, daurischen Tungusen* . . . (Frankfurt and Leipzig: 1777). *Merkwürdigkeiten verschiedener unbekannter Völker des russischen Reichs. Aus Georgis Bemerkungen* (Frankfurt and Leipzig: 1777).

Notes to Chapter 19, The Nature of Peoples Along the Asian Spine of the Earth

1. Peter Simon Pallas, *Sammlungen historischer Nachrichten über die mongolischen Völkerschaften,* vol. 1 (St. Petersburg: 1776). Johann Gottlieb Georgi, *Beschreibung aller Nationen des Rußischen Reichs* . . . (St. Petersburg: 1776). Johann Christian Schnitscher, *Nachricht von den Ajuckischen Calmücken,* translated from the Swedish, in Gerhard Friedrich Müller (ed.), *Sammlung Rußischer Geschichte,* vol. 4, part 4 (St. Petersburg: 1760), pp. 275–364. August Ludwig Schlözer, *Auszug aus D. Gottlob Schobers bisher noch ungedrucktem Werke: Memorabilia Russico-Asiatica,* in G.F. Müller, ed., *Sammlung Rußischer Geschichte,* vol. 7, parts 1 and 2 (St. Petersburg: 1762).
2. An appearance indicating an unhealthy state of the fluids of the body.
3. *Allgemeine Historie der Reisen zu Wasser und zu Lande oder Sammlung aller Reisebeschreibungen* . . . , translated from the English and the French, 21 vols. (Leipzig: 1748–74). Herder usually quotes this collection as *Allgemeine Reisen.* The Jesuit missionary Pierre François Xavier de Charlevoix contributed to this collection of travel accounts, as did the Swedish clergyman and explorer Olof Toree.
4. Peter Simon Pallas, *Neue nordische Beiträge zur physikalischen und geographischen Erd- und Völkerbeschreibung, Naturgeschichte und Oekonomie,* 7 vols. (St. Petersburg: 1781–96), vol. 4, p. 280.
5. The French author Jean Baptiste Tavernier contributed to vol. 10 of *Allgemeine Reisen* (see note 3, above).
6. The English court chaplain and explorer John Ovington contributed to vol. 10 of *Allgemeine Reisen* (see note 3, above).
7. William Marsden, *Natürliche und bürgerliche Beschreibung der Insel Sumatra in Ostindien,* translated from the English (Leipzig: 1785).
8. The scientist and explorer Georg Wilhelm Steller contributed to vol. 20 of *Allgemeine Reisen* (see note 3, above).
9. See note 2, above.
10. William Ellis, *Zuverlässige Nachricht von der dritten und letzten Reise der Capitaines Cook und Clerke* . . . , translated from the English (Frankfurt and Leipzig: 1783). Johann Reinhold Forster, *Tagebuch einer Entdeckungsreise nach der Südsee in den Jahren 1776–1780* (Berlin: 1781).
11. Latin phrase meaning "anthropological gleanings."

Notes to Chapter 20, The Nature of Peoples Favored by the Temperate Zone

1. François Bernier (1620–88) was a French physician and explorer.
2. Members of tribes inhabiting the region lying east of the Caspian Sea and about the Sea of Aral, formerly known as Turkestan or Turkmenistan.

Notes to Chapter 21, The Nature of the African Peoples

1. The biblical progenitor of the Hamites; see Genesis, 10:6–20.

2. Herder contracts passages from pages 494 and 495 of Buffon's *Histoire naturelle, générale et particulière. Servant de suite à l'Histoire Naturelle de l'Homme,* supplément, vol. 4 (Paris: Imprimerie Royale, 1777), where Buffon publishes notes which he had received from Bruce. That is why Herder talks about Bruce's "preliminary communications." Bruce's travel account appeared in 1790–91; see note 1 to Chapter 9 in this volume. Jerome Lobo, *Voyage historique en Abissinie, traduit du Portugais . . .* (Paris, The Hague: 1728), p. 85.

3. Jobus Ludolf, *Historia Aethiopica sive descriptio regni Habessiniorum* (Frankfurt: 1681).

4. Georg Hoest, *Nachrichten von Maroko und Fes . . . ,* translated from the Danish (Copenhagen: 1781).

5. *Dr. Schotts Nachrichten über den Zustand vom Senega,* in eds. J.R. Forster and M.C. Sprengel, *Beiträge zur Völker- und Länderkunde,* vol. 1 (1781).

6. African people in Senegal and the Gambia.

7. Sudanese people of partly non-Negro extraction.

8. A large group of peoples living along the upper Niger River.

9. Schott [i.e., Johann Peter Schotte], *Nachrichten vom Senega, Allgemeine Reisen,* vols. 3–5.

10. Andreas Sparrmann, *Reisen in Afrika . . . ,* translated from the Swedish (Berlin: 1783).

11. Peoples numbering together about 30,000 in the fifteenth century, living on the lower part of the Congo River; see *Allgemeine Reisen,* vol. 5, pp. 51–52.

12. According to Ptolemy (a map of c. 140), there existed a mountain chain (*Lunae Montes*) across the eastern part of Ethiopia, the snowcaps of which provided the water for the two main headstreams of the Nile River. This assumption could be corrected only in the second half of the nineteenth century.

13. Georg Andreas Oldendorp, *Geschichte der Mission der evangelischen Brüder auf den karaibischen Inseln . . .* (Barby: 1777).

14. Liévain-Bonaventure Proyart, *Histoire de Loango, Kakongo . . .* (1776); German translation (Leipzig: 1777). The account mentioned here is given in an appendix to the book.

15. Peter Camper, *Kleinere Schriften . . .* (Leipzig: 1782).

16. Schott's (see note 9, above) report on the *Synochus atrabiliosa* (black bile fever) appeared in vol. 3, part 6, in 1783.

Notes to Chapter 22, The Nature of the Peoples on the Islands of the Tropical Zone

1. Matthias Sprengel, *Geschichte der Philippinen,* and Johann Reinhold Forster's account, in J.G. Forster and M.C. Sprengel, eds., *Beiträge zur Völker- und Länderkunde,* vol. 2, and *Allgemeine Reisen* (see note 3 to Chapter 19 in this volume), vol. 11. Christoph Daniel Ebeling, ed., *Neue Sammlung von Reisebeschreibungen,* 10 vols. (Hamburg: 1780–90). Le Gentil's account *(Guillaume Hyancinthe Legentil de la Galaisière)* is published in the same collection *(Le Gentils Reisen in den indischen Meeren,* vols. 2 and 4).

2. A collection of English travel accounts translated into German, *Historischer Bericht von den sämtlichen durch Engländer geschehenen Reisen um die Welt . . . ,* 6 vols. (Leipzig: 1775–80).

3. A people inhabiting Northern Luzon.
4. The former name of Australia.
5. William Dampier (1652–1715) was one of the most famous English corsairs and explorers.
6. Johann Reinhold Forster, *Bemerkungen über Gegenstände der physischen Erdbeschreibung, Naturbeschreibung und sittlichen Philosophie, auf seiner Reise gesammelt* . . . (Berlin: 1783).

Notes to Chapter 23, The Nature of the Americans

1. See note 10 to Chapter 19 in this volume.
2. A Siouan people of northern Montana and adjacent parts of Canada.
3. According to Herder's source, the Cristinaux lived in the Hudson Bay region.
4. James Adair, *Geschichte der amerikanischen Indianer* (Breslau: 1782).
5. Cadwallader Colden, *History of the Five Indian Nations* (1747). Woodes Rogers, *Beschreibung von Nordamerika* (1762–63). Henry Timberlake, *The Memoirs* (1765; German translation, 1767). For the "Five Nations," see note 4 to Chapter 10 in this volume.
6. The Choctaws were part of the Mushkogees who lived in southern Mississippi.
7. The southern part of what is now Venezuela.
8. Ethnic groups in the region of what is now Surinam, Guyana, French Guiana, and Venezuela.
9. Christoph d'Acunja, *Allgemeine Historie der Reisen zu Wasser und zu Lande,* vol. 16, pp. 8–24. Joseph Gumilla, *El Orinoco Ilustrado, Historia natural, civil, y geográfica* . . . (Madrid: 1741). Jean de Léry, *Histoire d'un voyage fait en terre du Brésil* (La Rochelle: 1578). Georg Markgraf, *Historia rerum naturalium Brasiliae* (Amsterdam: 1648). Charles-Marie de la Condamine, *Relation abrégée d'un voyage fait dans l'intérieur de l'Amérique méridionale* (1745).
10. Martin Dobrizhofer, *Geschichte der Abiponer,* translated from the Latin by A. Kreil (Vienna: 1783).
11. The Mapuche living in Chile and Argentina were called "Araucanians" ("brave warriors") by the conquistadores. Two of the dialects spoken by this large ethnic group are Moluche and Puelche. Concerning the "Telhuelhets," it is unclear whether Herder refers to the Tehuelche, who lived in Chile and Argentina, or whether he uses "Tehuelche" as a generic term equivalent to "Patagonians."
12. It is not Commerson but Bougainville who is quoted here, from the *Supplément au voyage de M. de Bougainville* (Paris: 1772). Eberhard August Wilhelm Zimmermann, *Geographische Geschichte des Menschen und der allgemein verbreiteten vierfüssigen Tiere* (Leipzig: 1778–83). William Robertson, *Geschichte von Amerika,* translated from the English, 2 vols. (Leipzig: 1777).
13. Thomas Falkner, *Beschreibung von Patagonien und angrenzenden Theilen von Südamerika,* translated from the English (Gotha: 1775). A translation of Felipe Gomez Vidaurre's *Geographical, Natural, and Civil History of the Kingdom of Chile* appeared in part 4 of Ebeling's *Reisebeschreibungen.*
14. Robertson quotes from Antonio de Ulloa, *Physikalische und historische Nachrichten vom südlichen und nordöstlichen Amerika.* 2 vols. (Leipzig: 1781), where Ulloa says that when you have seen one American, you know them all.
15. With "Cessares," Herder may be referring to the Kauescar, which is another name for the former Chilean Aksana.

Notes to Chapter 24, The Search for the Origin of Humankind and the Beginning of History on the Basis of Written Sources

1. The author of this *Essay on the Origin of the Knowledge of Truth and the Sciences* is Karl Franz Irwing (1728–1801), a member of the High Consistory and school superintendent in Berlin.

2. See note 12 to Chapter 21 in this volume.

3. Genesis 1:27, 2:2.

4. In this speech, Karl Linné (latinized *Linnaeus*) describes the primeval world as a mountain in the middle of the sea.

5. *Herrn P.S. Pallas Beobachtungen über die Berge, und die Veränderungen der Erdkugel* . . . , in *Vermischte Beyträge zur physikalischen Erdbeschreibung,* vol. 3 (Halle: 1780), pp. 250 f.

6. Christian Wilhelm Büttner (1716–1801) was a professor of philosophy at Göttingen until 1783, then comparative linguist in Weimar.

7. Pegu, Ava, and Arracan are regions in what is now Burma.

8. The two parts of this work by Büttner appeared in 1771 and 1779.

9. Herder consulted the German translation of Antoine-Yves Goguet, *De l'origine des lois, des arts et des sciences, et de leurs progrès chez les anciens peuples* (Paris: 1758).

10. See note 19 to Chapter 9 in this volume.

11. This German translation of the French work appeared in two volumes.

12. See note 1 to Chapter 22 in this volume.

13. Herder refers to the mythic mountain nymph who pined away for love of Narcissus until only her voice remained.

14. The "Ox Tamer," Chinese emperor from 2852 B.C.

15. The "Yellow Emperor," from 2697 B.C.

16. Herder refers to a French edition of the I Ching, the Book of Changes.

17. A legendary ruler who reigned from 2357 to 2256 B.C.

18. P'an-ku, the first human being, according to Chinese mythology; the three Hoangs are legendary rulers of early China.

19. See note 16 to Chapter 9 in this volume.

20. For Baldaeus, see note 16 to Chapter 9 in this volume; for Holwell, see note 19 to Chapter 9. Alexander Dow's *History of Hindostan* appeared in a German translation, *Die Geschichte von Hindostan* . . . , 3 vols. (Leipzig: 1772–74).

21. Sanchoniathon (ca. ninth century B.C.) was a Phoenician author of cosmogonic and zoogonic texts.

22. "Those who regard the skies," primeval beings in the Syrian myth of creation.

23. An ancient country in what is now northwestern Iran.

24. An ancient country in central and northwest Asia Minor.

25. An ancient region in the eastern part of the Balkan Peninsula (part of what is now Bulgaria, Turkey, and Greece).

26. Hebrew, meaning "God, Gods."

27. Herder refers to his own interpretation of the Mosaic account of creation in the Old Testament in his *Most Ancient Document of Humankind* (1774).

28. This is one of the passages in Herder's work which clearly demonstrate that he, despite all seemingly evolutionist ideas, is not an incipient Darwinian.

29. See Wisdom of Solomon 11:20.

30. Herder refers to Buffon's late *Epoques de la nature* (1778).
31. The Greek *paradeisos* means "garden."
32. Herder apparently tries to show how the explanation of ancient translations of the name "Ganges" (the Sanskrit *ganga* means "holy water," "river") may contribute to the understanding of geographical absurdities. The Greek word *pisos* means "humid low ground." It is unknown to which source Herder refers.
33. Johannes Otter, *Reisen in die Türkey und nach Persien . . .*, translated from the French, 2 vols. (Nürnberg and Halle: 1781, 1789).
34. Hindu-Kush.
35. Himalaya.
36. An Asian people living in modern Georgia.
37. A chimera of Persian legend: a very old and monstrous bird, endowed with reason and speech.
38. Demons of Hinduism.
39. Land of the jinns.
40. The Hebrew *Chavvâh* means "life giver."
41. The descendants of Seth and Cain, sons of Adam and Eve.
42. The Arab *qabā'il* means "tribes."
43. Herder refers to the etymology of the names mentioned in Genesis 4:16–22.
44. Ziusudra of Shuruppak is the hero of the Sumerian epic account of the Great Flood.
45. The Hebrew *yephet* means "expansion"; *shêm* means "name"; *châm* means "hot."
46. "Cave dwellers."

Notes to Chapter 25, China

1. Alexej Leontiew, *Auszug aus der Sinesischen Reichsgeographie*, in Büsching's *Magazin* (see note 9 to Chapter 9 in this volume). Benedict Franz Johann von Herrmann, *Beiträge zur Physik, Oekonomie, Mineralogie . . . besonders der russischen Länder*, 3 vols. (Berlin: 1786–88).
2. Confucius (ca. 551–ca. 478 B.C.), Chinese philosopher and teacher; the founder of the Chinese state religion. Lao-tzu (sixth century B.C.), the reputed founder of Taoism; supposedly wrote the Tao Te Ching.
3. The accounts were compiled by the missionaries of Beijing and appeared in Paris beginning in 1776.
4. Franciscus Noel, *Sinensis imperii libri classici VI . . . (Six Classical Books of the Chinese Empire)* (Prague: 1711). Philippe Couplet, *Catalogus Patrum Societatis Jesu . . .* (catalog of the Jesuits who worked as missionaries in China since 1581, including a bibliography) (Paris: 1686). Joseph-Anne-Marie de Moyriac de Mailla, *Histoire générale de la Chine ou annales de cet empire*, translated from the Chinese, 13 vols. (Paris: 1777–85). The author of the *Nouveaux mémoires* was the Jesuit Louis Daniel Le Comte.
5. Genghis Khan (1162–1227), the famous Mongol conqueror. The Manchu conquered China in the seventeenth century and established a dynasty there (Manchu dynasty or Ch'ing, 1644–1912).
6. The Torguts were a migratory Mongol people.
7. Here, Herder alludes to Joseph de Guignes's notion of China as an Egyptian colony. See note 2 to Chapter 2 in this volume.
8. An ancient country between Hindu-Kush and Oxus.
9. Herder refers to the I Ching and the Tao Te Ching.

Notes to Chapter 26, India

1. See note 20 to Chapter 24 in this volume.
2. A talapoin is a Buddhist monk.
3. An idol of Krishna at Puri in Oressa, India (also, a Juggernaut).
4. *Zend-Avesta, ouvrage de Zoroastre.* . . . Traduit en François par M. Anquetil du Perron, vol. 1 (Paris: 1771). For Niebuhr, see note 5 to Chapter 9 in this volume.
5. Alexander Ross, *Pansebia, or a View of all Religions of the World* (London: 1658). *Neuere Geschichte der Evangelischen Mission-Anstalten* . . . , vol. 1 (Halle: 1776). *Lettres édifiantes et curieuses écrites des missions étrangères par quelques missionaires de la Compagnie de Jésus,* 18 vols. (Paris: 1711–43). For Holwell, Sonnerat, and Mackintosh, see note 19 to Chapter 9, note 16 to Chapter 9, and note 18 to Chapter 9, respectively, all in this volume.
6. Nathaniel Brassey Halhed, *A Code of Gentoo Laws, or Ordinations of the Pundits* . . . (London: 1776). For Le Gentil, see note 1 to Chapter 22 in this volume.

Notes to Chapter 27, General Reflections on the History of the Asian States

1. A Russian town on the Selinga River, which leads into Lake Baikal.
2. Cornelius de Pauw, *Réflexions philosophiques sur les Egyptiens et les Chinois* (Berlin: 1773). Jean-Isouard Delisle de Sales, *Histoire philosophique du monde primitif,* 3 vols. (Paris: 1779).
3. Herder seems to coin a hyperbolic name. Gaea is the goddess of earth, "Mother Earth." *Protogaea* would thus mean a goddess before Gaea.

Notes to Chapter 28, Babylonia, Assyria, and Chaldea

1. Anton Friedrich Büsching, *Neue Erdbeschreibung,* part 5, section 1 (Hamburg: 1768).
2. See Genesis 10:8–10.
3. King of Assyria and husband of Semiramis.
4. A.L. Schlözer, *Von den Chaldäern,* in *Repertorium für biblische und morgenländische Literatur,* ed. J.G. Eichhorn, 18 vols. (Leipzig: 1777–86), vol. 8, pp. 113 f.
5. A variant of the name Baal.
6. A town and a mountain in ancient Media.
7. Pietro della Valle, *Viaggi descritti in lettere familiari* . . . *(Travels Described in Private Letters)* (Rome: 1650–53; German translation, Geneva: 1674).
8. Johann Gottfried Eichhorn, *Geschichte des ostindischen Handels vor Mahomet* (Gotha: 1775). Johann Christoph Gatterer, *Einleitung in die synchronistische Universalhistorie* . . . (Göttingen: 1771).

Notes to Chapter 29, The Hebrews

1. Herder dealt with the Persians in his previous chapter, which is not included in this volume.
2. The Egyptian priest Manetho wrote in Greek (ca. 300 B.C.) a history of Egypt. Only fragments of it have been preserved in the works of other authors.
3. Herder characterizes Moses in accordance with Johann David Michaelis, *Mosaisches Recht,* 6 vols. (Frankfurt am Main: 1770–75).

4. Herder refers to his own work, *The Spirit of Hebrew Poetry* (1782–83).

5. The Sadder is a Persian canonical book concerning religious duties and customs.

6. Daniel 2:31–44.

7. Joshua 10:12–13.

8. There has been fierce criticism of this passage, resulting in the condemnation of Herder as an anti-Semite. In a purely ideological reading, Paul Lawrence Rose "discovers" a straight line from Herder to Houston Stewart Chamberlain (P.L. Rose, *German Question/Jewish Question. Revolutionary Antisemitism from Kant to Wagner* [Princeton, NJ: 1992], pp. 97–109). Rose mentions, however, several scholars who see Herder as a philo-Semite (p. 97, note 13), and we might add two titles that are dedicated to this problem: Emil Adler, "Johann Gottfried Herder und das Judentum," in *Herder Today,* ed. Kurt Mueller-Vollmer (Berlin, New York: 1990), pp. 382–401; and Ernest A. Menze, "Herder's 'German Kind of *Humanity*' and the Jewish Question: Historical Context and Contemporary Criticism," in Martin Bollacher (ed.), *Johann Gottfried Herder: Geschichte und Kultur* (Würzburg: Königshausen and Neumann, 1994), pp. 213–28. Conclusions like Rose's are totally unfounded, and fail to take into account the historical and systematical context of the term "parasitical." Most of the criticism proceeds from a context of awareness of National Socialist ideology, in which metaphors of this nature were prominently employed. But Herder did not provide arguments to the National Socialists, although no author is immune to a selective ideological reception. (As Bernhard Becker has shown conclusively on a solid empirical basis, Herder was not a preferred author of the National Socialists. See Bernhard Becker, *Herder-Rezeption in Deutschland. Eine ideologiekritische Untersuchung* [St. Ingbert: 1987], pp. 133 ff.) It would be historically incorrect to read Herder as if he were aware of, and writing for an audience shaped by his own awareness of, events that occurred between 1933 and 1945. Undoubtedly, the metaphor of the "parasites" hints at a weakness of Herder's organological model, which demonstrates a limited capacity to incorporate historical phenomena; in any event, one should attempt to screen out the modern value-loaded connotations of the word "parasitic," and instead strive to apply the term, in accordance with Herder's organological metaphor, in its original biological context.

Notes to Chapter 30, Egypt

1. The ancient region in upper Egypt surrounding Thebes.

2. A people inhabiting a region bordering the Black Sea.

3. Cave dwellers.

4. Diodorus Siculus, the Greek historian who wrote a universal history (*Bibliotheke*) in forty volumes.

5. Osiris is the king and judge of the dead, the husband and brother of Isis, and father of Horus. Isis is the goddess of fertility and mother of Horus. Horus is a solar deity in Egyptian religion.

6. Cambyses II was the Persian king who made Egypt a Persian province.

Notes to Chapter 32, The Language, Mythology, and Poetry of Greece

1. A mythic poet and bard.

2. A member of the middle rank of the Persian Parsee caste.

3. Christian Gottlob Heyne, *De fontibus . . . (About the sources and reasons for the mistakes in the history of myth)* (1763); *De caussis . . . (About the natural causes of*

legends) (1785); *De origine* . . . *(About the origin and causes of the Homeric legends)* (1778); *De Theogonia* . . . *(About Hesiod's* Theogony) (1783). For Heyne, see note 5 to Chapter 12 in this volume.

4. This is a part of Georgi's description of all the nations of the Russian Empire; see note 1 to Chapter 19 in this volume.

5. According to Cicero (*De oratore,* III), the Athenian tyrant Pisistratus (560–27 B.C.) initiated the collection of Homer's texts.

6. Thomas Blackwell, *Enquiry into the Life and Writings of Homer* (London: 1735). Robert Wood, *Essay on the Genius of Homer* (London: 1769). These publications began the historically oriented investigation of the works of Homer.

7. A legendary Gaelic poet and hero; Herder at this point still believed in his historical existence.

Notes to Chapter 33, Greek Arts

1. Pausanias the "Periheget," author of a guide to Greece (*Perihegesis tes Hellathos*). For Pliny, see note 8 to Chapter 15 in this volume.

2. The forefather and patron of Athenian craftsmen. The Greek "daidalos" means "skillful."

3. Johann Joachim Winckelmann, *Geschichte der Kunst des Altertums* (Dresden: 1764); see, in this volume, p. 23. Heyne's corrections and additions appeared in vol. 1 (1771) of the *Deutsche Schriften* of the Academy of Göttingen.

4. Phidias was a famous Greek sculptor (ca. 500–432 B.C.).

5. Christian Gottlob Heyne, *Über den Kasten des Kypselus* . . . (Göttingen: 1770).

6. Both Phryne and Lais were famous hetaerae who are supposed to have served as models to the painter Apelles and the sculptor Praxiteles.

7. The smith Hephaestos (Latin *Vulcanus*) decked out Apollo's shield as described in Homer's *Iliad,* Book 18, ll. 647 ff.

8. In the pseudo-Hesiodian poem *Aspis* (*The Shield*), Hercules's shield is described (ll. 139 ff.).

9. Herder refers to Pindar's Olympic, Pythic, Nemeic, and Isthmic odes, which were written to praise the winners of the games. What Herder says here about the "economy"—i.e., the simplicity—of the odes is due to his misunderstanding of the complex metric structure of these poems.

10. The Odeum was the music and theater hall; the Prytaneum was the building where the members of the Greek city councils met; the Pnyx was the top of a hill in Athens where meetings were held.

11. See, in this volume, p. 23.

12. The Greek colonies and settlements in southern Italy.

13. The bronze statue of Apollo, one of the Seven Wonders of the World, which was destroyed by an earthquake.

Notes to Chapter 34, General Reflections on the History of Greece

1. The time of Pericles (ca. 490–29 B.C.), when Athens was culturally and materially preeminent.

2. Ancient name for the mountains forming the Strait of Gibraltar.

3. According to Herodotus (*Histories,* Book 6, 119) the inhabitants of the Greek town Eretria were deported to Asia as prisoners of war.

4. An allusion to Homer's *Odyssey,* Book 5, l. 13, and Books 6–8 passim.

5. Sir William (Friedrich Wilhelm) Herschel (1738–1822) was a German-British astronomer.

6. Henry Saint John, First Viscount of Bolingbroke (1678–1751) was a British statesman, writer, and orator.

7. Another name for Sparta.

8. An Athenian politician and general (ca. 450–4 B.C.), who led a life of adventurous political and military activities.

Notes to Chapter 35, Germanic Peoples

1. Ariovistus was the leader of the Suevi. Marbutus, or Maroboduus, was the leader of the Marcomans. Arminius defeated the Romans in 9 A.D.

2. Justus Möser's *Osnabrückische Geschichte* appeared in two volumes (Osnabrück: 1768). His *Patriotische Phantasien* came out in four parts (Berlin: 1774–86).

3. All four belong to Germanic mythology. Tuisto (also called Theut or Tuisko) is the earth-born god who created Mannus out of himself. Hertha, or Nerthus, is the goddess of fertility and death. Odin (also called Wotan or Wodan) is the highest god in Germanic mythology.

4. Herder refers to the Elder *Edda* or Song-*Edda,* a collection of Old Norse songs of gods and heroes, the manuscript of which (dating from the thirteenth century) was discovered in 1643 in Iceland.

5. Old Nordic court poets and singers.

6. Here, Herder simply lists the names of those who have contributed to the knowledge of his time concerning either the *Edda* or old Nordic culture in general.

7. Peter Friedrich von Suhm (1728–98) was a Danish historian.

8. Johann Schilter, *Thesaurus antiquitatum Teutonicarum,* 3 vols. (Ulm: 1726–28). This is a thesaurus of ancient German texts.

Notes to Chapter 36, Slavic Peoples

1. The Croats and Serbs immigrated to Bosnia and Dalmatia during the reign of the East Roman emperor Herakleios (575–641).

2. A region north of what is now Croatia.

3. A region west-northwest of what is now Croatia.

4. Vineta was actually situated on one of the islands east of Rügen (Usedom, Wollin). According to the legend, this wealthy town was destroyed in an earthquake and since that time has lain at the bottom of the Baltic Sea. Herder refers to the report according to which Vineta was destroyed by the Danes in 1184.

5. Herder simply enumerates a series of names of linguists and historians who dealt with Slavic languages and history.

Notes to Chapter 37, Toward a Culture of Reason in Europe

1. The religious movement of Manichaeism was founded by the Persian Manes (ca. 218–76). The doctrine is based on a strictly dualistic (Zarathustran) principle (light

versus darkness) and eclectically incorporates gnostic, Jewish, Christian, and other elements. The rigorous ethics of Manichaeism made it particularly attractive to the lower and pauperized classes in parts of Europe and Asia.

2. Herder refers to the Bogomils, who propagated their gnostic and Manichaean ideas throughout the Balkans during the twelfth century.

3. The formation and the temporary success of these different religious groups were an expression of a violent criticism of the secularized church in the eleventh through the thirteenth centuries. The Cathars were influenced by the Bogomils. The Patarenes (Italian "pates" means "rags"), the Publicans, and the Passagieri were religious movements in northern Italy.

4. Pierre de Bruys was an Anabaptist preacher in the Languedoc at the beginning of the twelfth century. After he was burned at the stake, Henry of Lausanne succeeded him.

5. The Mennonites, founded by Menno Simons (1492–1559), formed their Anabaptist movement in the Netherlands and northern Germany.

6. These early translations of 1170 (Etienne d'Anse), 1277, and 1380 are almost entirely lost.

7. Herder alludes to the "small Bible," containing seven poems in the Provençal language (fourteenth or fifteenth century). One of them, a versification of the Sermon on the Mount, bears the title La Nóbla leiçon (The Perfect Instruction).

8. The author of this three-volume work was the Swiss historian and theologian Johann Conrad Füssli (1707–75). Füssli stands in the tradition of Gottfried Arnold's apology of all those Christians who did not adhere to the institutionalized Roman Catholic church. Arnold's work of 1699–1700 covers the time from the beginning of the New Testament until 1688; Füssli's work covers the Middle Ages.

9. In 1208, Pope Innocent III called for a crusade against the Albigenses, who formed a part of the heretic movements mentioned above (note 3). They were exterminated by the crusade and the Inquisition.

10. John Wycliffe's (ca. 1320–84) criticism of the papacy and his teaching were propagated by the Lollards from the fourteenth century to the sixteenth century. The Lollards were dedicated to nursing and to burying the dead. John Hus (ca. 1370–1415), Czech religious reformer and nationalist, was burned at the stake.

11. Paschasius Radbertus (ca. 790–ca. 856), who was Abbot of Corbie in France, and the monk Ratramnus had a dispute about transubstantiation in the 840s.

12. In this passage Herder simply lists the most important representatives of Scholasticism.

13. Constantinus Africanus (d. 1087) translated medical texts from the Arabic and Greek. He established the reputation of the School of Medicine at Salerno, Italy.

14. Gerbert (b. 947), Archbishop of Reims, was later (999–1003) Pope Sylvester II. Albertus Magnus (1193–1280), was a Dominican who taught philosophy and natural sciences in Paris and Cologne. Arnold of Villa Nova (Arnoldo Bachuone, 1238–1311) was one of the most important physicians of the European Middle Ages. Roger Bacon (ca. 1214–94) was an English philosopher and scientist. He made a clear distinction between theology and the sciences by emphasizing empirical experiments and mathematics. Ramón Lull (Raimundus Lullus, ca. 1235–1315) was a Spanish scholastic who taught in Paris and in Montpellier, France.

15. Dionysius the Areopagite (member of the council [Areopag] in Athens) was converted to Christianity by the apostle Paul. Several writings were falsely attributed to him (Pseudo-Dionysius).

16. Pierre Poiret (1646–1719), French pietist, published *Bibliotheca mysticorum selecta* (*Selected Mystical Writings*) (Amsterdam: 1708). Gottfried Arnold, *Historie und Beschreibung der mystischen Theologie* (Frankfurt: 1703).

17. A Greek term meaning "beautiful and good." Kalokagathia was Plato's ethical (not aesthetic) ideal of education.

Notes to Chapter 38, Concluding Commentary

1. It is clear from this passage that Herder's concept of Europe is not geographically identical to the modern idea of it.

2. See the introductory remarks to this chapter.

Selected Bibliography

This bibliography gives the reader the information necessary to start further research on Herder. The bibliography does not intend to list all the texts mentioned in this volume. Instead, it attempts to point out relevant literature about Herder as a historian and philosopher of history.

A. Bibliographies

Günther, Gottfried, Albina A. Volgina, and Siegfried Seifert. *Herder-Bibliographie*. Ed. Nationale Forschungs- und Gedenkstätten der klassischen deutschen Literatur und der Staatlichen Allunionsbibliothek für ausländische Literatur in Moskau. Berlin, Weimar: Aufbau-Verlag, 1978.

Kuhles, Doris. *Herder-Bibliographie 1977–1992. Personalbibliographien zur neueren deutschen Literatur*. Vol. 1, ed. Michael Knoche and Reinhard Tgahrt. Stuttgart, Weimar: Metzler Verlag, 1994.

Markworth, Tino. *Johann Gottfried Herder. A Bibliographical Survey 1977–1987*. Hürth-Efferen: Gabel Verlag, 1990.

B. Periodicals

Herder Yearbook, vol. 1. Ed. Karl Menges, Wulf Koepke, and Wilfried Malsch. Columbia, SC: Camden House, 1992.

Herder Jahrbuch/Herder Yearbook 1994 [vol. 2]. Ed. Wilfried Malsch and Wulf Koepke. Stuttgart, Weimar: Metzler Verlag, 1994.

HerderJahrbuch/Herder Yearbook 1996 [vol. 3]. Ed. Hans Adler, Wulf Koepke, and Wilfried Malsch. Stuttgart, Weimar: Metzler Verlag, 1996. From this volume on, the *Herder Yearbook* includes an updated current bibliography.

C. Editions

Johann Gottfried Herder. *Sämmtliche Werke*. 33 vols. Ed. Bernhard Suphan et al. Berlin: Weidmannsche Buchhandlung, 1877 ff.; 3d reprint edition, 1994–95. Still the most comprehensive edition. Very few annotations.

———. *Ideen zur Philosophie der Geschichte der Menschheit*. 2 vols. Ed. Heinz Stolpe. Berlin, Weimar: Aufbau-Verlag, 1965. Valuable because of its extensive annotations.

————. *Briefe zu Beförderung der Humanität.* 2 vols. Ed. Heinz Stolpe, Hans-Joachim Kruse, and Dietrich Simon. Berlin, Weimar: Aufbau-Verlag, 1971. Valuable because of its extensive annotations.
————. *Werke in zehn Bänden.* Ed. Gottfried Arnold et al. Frankfurt am Main: Deutscher Klassiker Verlag, 1993 ff. Valuable because of its extensive annotations.

D. Translations

Johann Gottfried v. Herder. *Outlines of a Philosophy of the History of Man.* Translated from the German *Ideen zur Philosophie der Geschichte der Menschheit* by T. Churchill. London: 1800; reprint, New York: Bergman Publishers, n.d.
Johann Gottfried Herder. *Reflections on the Philosophy of the History of Mankind.* Abridged and with an introduction by Frank E. Manuel. Chicago, London: University of Chicago Press, 1968. Reproduces parts from the 1800 Churchill edition.
J.G. Herder on Social and Political Culture. Translated, edited, and with an introduction by F[rederick] M. Barnard. Cambridge, U.K.: University Press, 1969.
Johann Gottfried Herder. *Selected Early Works, 1764–1767.* Ed. Ernest A. Menze and Karl Menges. Translated by Ernest A. Menze with Michael Palma. University Park: Pennsylvania University Press, 1992.

E. Biographies

Clark, Robert T., Jr. *Herder: His Life and Thought.* 1955; Berkeley and Los Angeles: University of California Press, 1969.
Gillies, Alexander. *Herder.* Oxford, U.K: Basil Blackwell, 1945.
Haym, R[udolf]. *Herder nach seinem Leben und seinen Werken.* 2 vols. Berlin: Rudolph Gaertner, 1877–85; reprinted, Berlin: Aufbau-Verlag, 1954 and 1958.
Pénisson, Pierre. *J.G. Herder. La raison dans les peuples.* Paris: Les Éditions du Cerf, 1992.

F. Secondary Literature on Herder as a Historian and as a Philosopher of History

Adler, Hans. *Die Prägnanz des Dunklen. Gnoseologie—Ästhetik—Geschichtsphilosophie bei Johann Gottfried Herder.* Hamburg: Felix Meiner, 1990.
Barnard, F[rederick] M. "Culture and Political Development." *American Political Science Review* 63 (1969): 379–97.
————. "Herder's Treatment of Causation and Continuity in History." *Journal of the History of Ideas* 24 (1963): 197–212.
Bollacher, Martin, ed. *Johann Gottfried Herder: Geschichte und Kultur.* Würzburg: Königshausen und Neumann, 1994.
Cassirer, Ernst. *Freiheit und Form. Studien zur Geistesgeschichte.* 1916; Darmstadt: Wissenschaftliche Buchgesellschaft, 1975.
Förster, Wolfgang. "Geschichtsphilosophie und Humanitätsbegriff Herders." *Jahrbuch für Geschichte* 19 (1979): 7–43.
Gillies, Alexander. "Herder's Approach to the Philosophy of History." *Modern Language Review* 35 (1940): 193–206.
Hassinger, Erich. "Zur Genesis von Herders Historismus." *Deutsche Vierteljahrsschrift für Literaturwissenschaft und Geistesgeschichte* 53 (1979): 251–74.
Iggers, Georg G. *The German Conception of History: The National Tradition of the*

Historical Thought from Herder to the Present. Middletown, CT: Wesleyan University Press, 1968; rev. ed., 1983.

Koepke, Wulf. "Nemesis und Geschichtsdialektik." In *Herder Today: Contributions from the International Herder Conference, Nov. 5–8, 1987, Stanford, California,* ed. Kurt Mueller-Vollmer, 85–96. Berlin, New York: Walter de Gruyter, 1990.

Lovejoy, Arthur O. "Herder and the Enlightenment Philosophy of History." In Arthur O. Lovejoy, *Essays in the History of Ideas,* 166–82. Baltimore: Johns Hopkins Press, 1948; several later editions.

Lüttge, Albert. *Herders Auffassung der Weltgeschichte.* Stendal: 1868.

Megill, Allan. "Aesthetic Theory and Historical Consciousness in the Eighteenth Century." *History and Theory* 17, no. 1 (1978): 29–62.

Meinecke, Friedrich. *Die Entstehung des Historismus.* Ed. Carl Hinrichs. Friedrich Meinecke, *Werke,* vol. 3. Munich: R. Oldenbourg, 1959. English translation, *Historism: The Rise of a New Historical Outlook,* trans. E. Anderson; translation revised by H.D. Schmitt; with a foreword by Isaiah Berlin. London: Routledge and K. Paul, 1972.

Neff, Emery. *The Poetry of History: The Contribution of Literature and Literary Scholarship to the Writing of History since Voltaire.* 1947; New York: Octagon Books, 1979.

Rouché, Max. *La philosophie de l'histoire de Herder.* Publications de la faculté des lettres de l'université de Strasbourg, fasc. 93. Paris: 1940.

Schaumkell, Ernst. *Geschichte der deutschen Kulturgeschichtsschreibung. Von der Mitte des 18. Jahrhunderts bis zur Romantik im Zusammenhang mit der allgemeinen geistigen Entwicklung.* Leipzig: B.G. Teubner, 1905.

Spitz, Lewis W. "Natural Law and the Theory of History in Herder." *Journal of the History of Ideas* 16 (1955): 453–75.

Stadelmann, Rudolf. *Der historische Sinn bei Herder.* Halle an der Saale: Niemeyer, 1928.

Stolpe, Heinz. *Die Auffassung des jungen Herder vom Mittelalter. Ein Beitrag zur Geschichte der Aufklärung.* Weimar: Böhlau, 1955.

Wells, G[eorge] A. "Herder's Two Philosophies of History." *Journal of the History of Ideas* 21 (1960): 527–37.

Index

This index includes historical and mythical names with the exception of Johann Gottfried Herder. Not included are names from the Selected Bibliography and the List of Sources. Variants of names are shown in parentheses. The German umlaute/diaereses (*ä, ö, ü*) are treated in alphabetical order as *ae, oe, ue*. The German *ß* is treated as *ss*.

About the Editors and the Translators

Hans Adler received his Dr. phil. degree in 1978 and his habilitation degree in 1987 from the Ruhr-University at Bochum, Germany, where he taught in the German department from 1978 to 1990. He has held visiting professorships in Germany, Canada, and the United States. Since 1990, he has been teaching in the Department of German of the University of Wisconsin at Madison, where he is professor of German. He has published several books and numerous articles on German literature, philosophy, and the history of aesthetics from the eighteenth to the twentieth centuries. At present, he is president of the International Herder Society.

Ernest A. Menze (Ph.D., Columbia University) is Professor Emeritus at Iona College (New Rochelle, New York), where he taught history for thirty-five years. He served as Iona's Dean of Arts and Science from 1987 until 1994 and is currently Adjunct Professor of History at Edison Community College (Fort Myers, Florida). His numerous publications have focused on modern Germany, with particular emphasis on the works of Johann Gottfried Herder. A former Woodrow Wilson Fellow, he has been a visiting professor at the University Erlangen-Nürnberg and has held a senior Fulbright Research Fellowship at the Free University, Berlin. He has also been the recipient of Thyssen Foundation and NEH Awards and is a founding member of the International Herder Society and the World History Association, having served as an officer of the latter.

Michael Palma has published *The Egg Shape* (poems) and translations of Guido Gozzano (*The Man I Pretend to Be,* Princeton, 1981) and Diego

Valeri (*My Name on the Wind,* Princeton, 1989). He coedited *New Italian Poets* (Story Line, 1991) with Dana Gioia. His poems and translations have appeared in *Poetry, Paris Review, Grand Street,* and other journals, as well as in several anthologies, including *Unsettling America* (Viking Penguin).

*

That my body, I , has/have
come to do such and such
rather than chosen to do it
is merely linguistic;
but the cause - to - do
connects one back to cause,
the great cause , God ,
the chosen leads to the
virtual world of endless
possibilities and poetizing.
When language is dominated
by one or the other mode
for too long there can be problems
in the former, strict rule
enforcing, in the latter
immorality in the name of
freedom.
The former is correct though
we must often occasioned by
shoulder the burden on our body -